Old Souls

Old Souls

Written by
Brian McDonald

Art by
Les McClaine

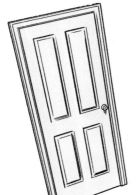

:01
First Second
New York

First Second

Text copyright © 2019 by Brian McDonald
Illustrations copyright © 2019 by Les McClaine

Published by First Second
First Second is an imprint of Roaring Brook Press,
a division of Holtzbrinck Publishing Holdings Limited Partnership
175 Fifth Avenue, New York, NY 10010

Don't miss your next favorite book from First Second!
For the latest updates go to firstsecondnewsletter.com
and sign up for our enewsletter.

Library of Congress Control Number: 2018944910

ISBN: 978-1-62672-732-8

Our books may be purchased in bulk for promotional, educational, or business use.
Please contact your local bookseller or the Macmillan Corporate and Premium Sales Department
at (800) 221-7945 ext. 5442 or by email at MacmillanSpecialMarkets@macmillan.com.

First edition, 2019

Edited by Mark Siegel and Dennis Pacheco
Book design by Dezi Sienty
Chinese translation by Ondi Lingenfelter

Drawn entirely digitally in Clip Studio Paint EX,
using a Wacom Cintiq 20WSX tablet monitor and a Mac Pro.

Printed in China
1 3 5 7 9 10 8 6 4 2

For Thomas and Scott, a father and son whose bond was strong. I miss you both.

—Brian McDonald

For my wife, Crystal

—Les McClaine

They sat in the dark,
reminiscing about their deaths...

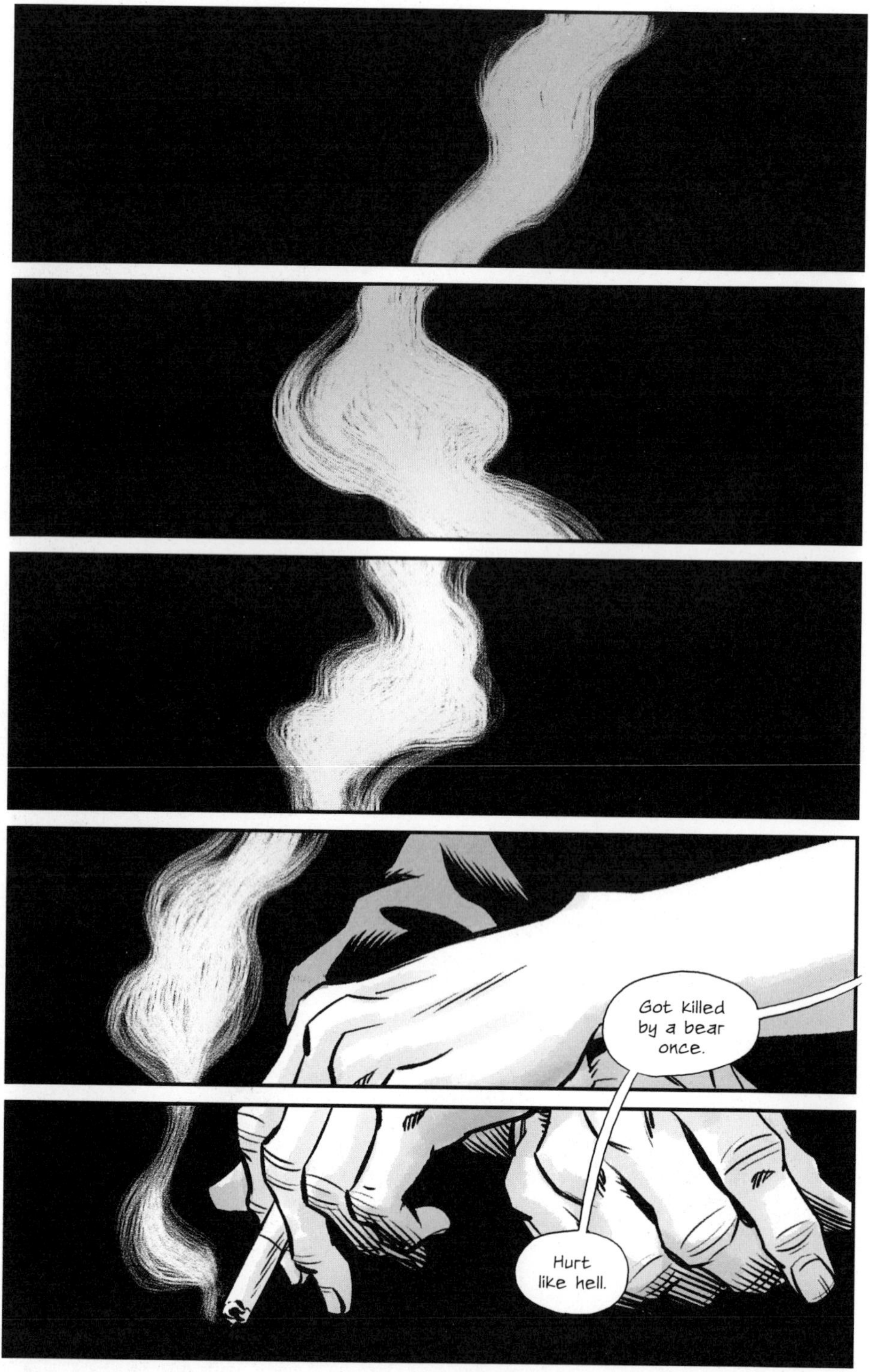
Got killed by a bear once.
Hurt like hell.

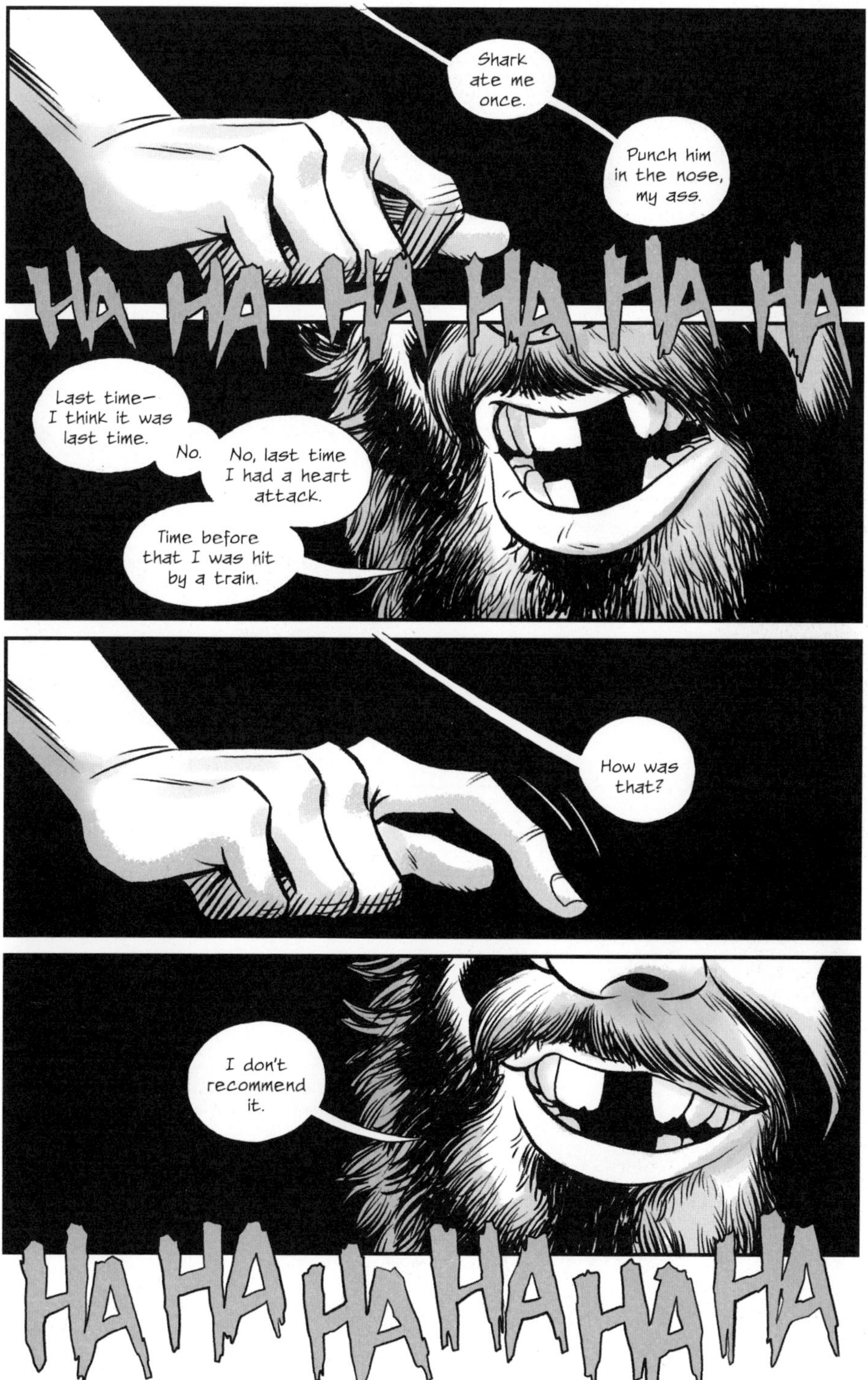

Shark ate me once.
Punch him in the nose, my ass.
HA HA HA HA HA HA
Last time— I think it was last time.
No.
No, last time I had a heart attack.
Time before that I was hit by a train.
How was that?
I don't recommend it.
HA HA HA HA HA HA HA

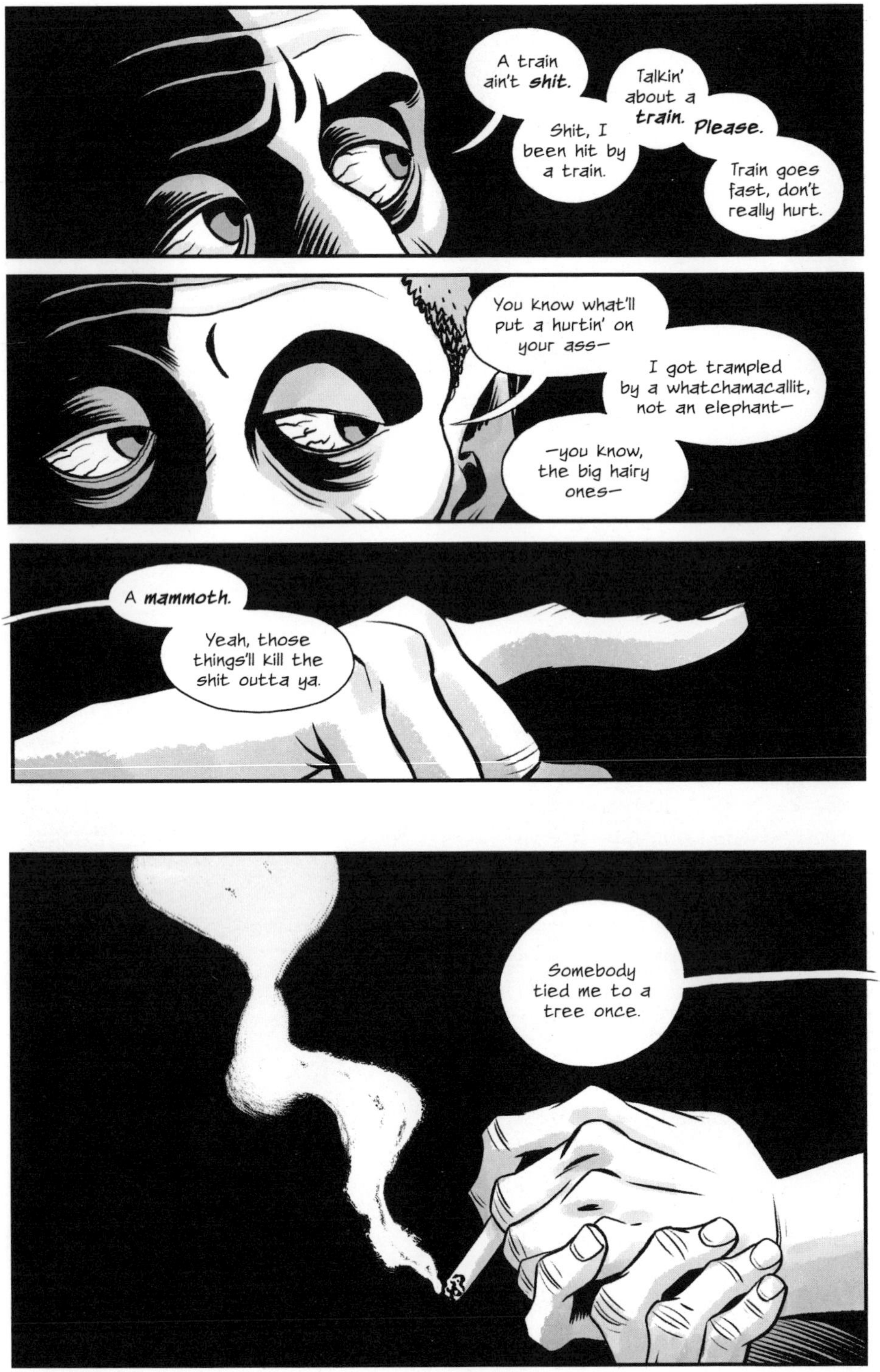
A train ain't **shit.**
Shit, I been hit by a train.
Talkin' about a **train.**
Please.
Train goes fast, don't really hurt.
You know what'll put a hurtin' on your ass—
I got trampled by a whatchamacallit, not an elephant—
—you know, the big hairy ones—
A **mammoth.**
Yeah, those things'll kill the shit outta ya.
Somebody tied me to a tree once.

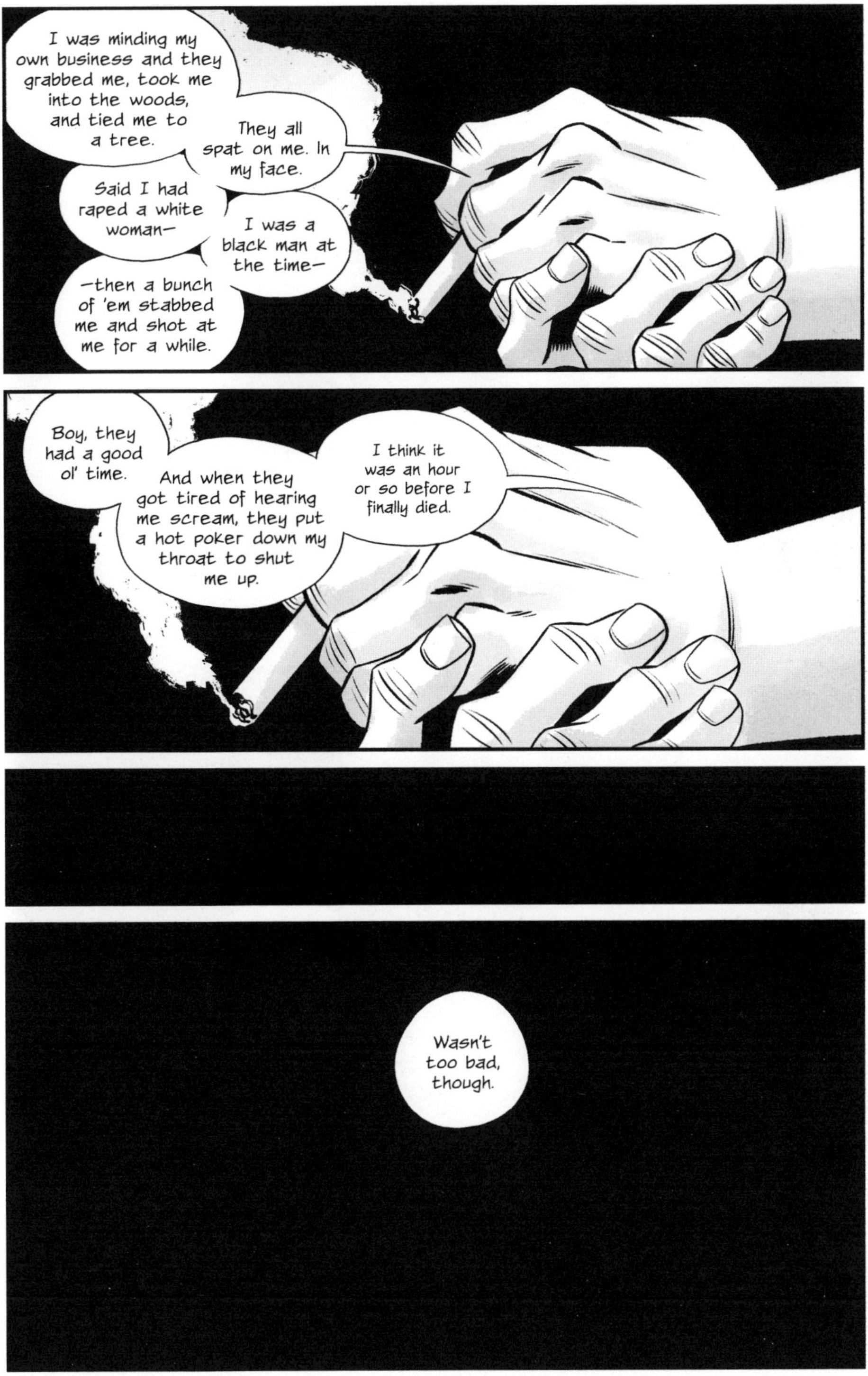
I was minding my own business and they grabbed me, took me into the woods, and tied me to a tree.
They all spat on me. In my face.
Said I had raped a white woman—
I was a black man at the time—
—then a bunch of 'em stabbed me and shot at me for a while.
Boy, they had a good ol' time.
And when they got tired of hearing me scream, they put a hot poker down my throat to shut me up.
I think it was an hour or so before I finally died.
Wasn't too bad, though.

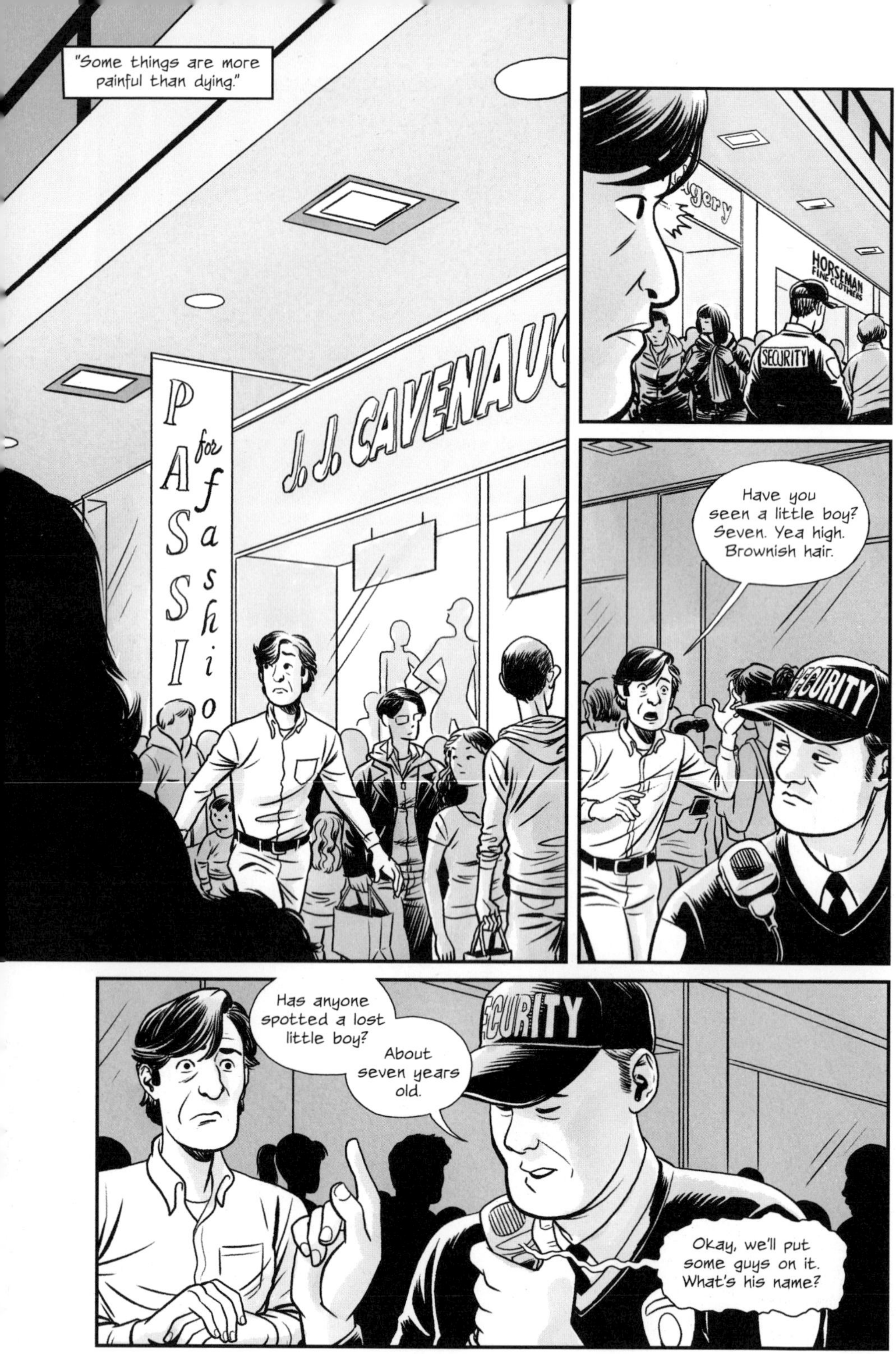
"Some things are more painful than dying."
PASSION for fashion
J.J. CAVENAUG
gery
HORSEMAN FINE CLOTHIERS
SECURITY
Have you seen a little boy? Seven. Yea high. Brownish hair.
SECURITY
Has anyone spotted a lost little boy?
About seven years old.
ECURITY
Okay, we'll put some guys on it. What's his name?

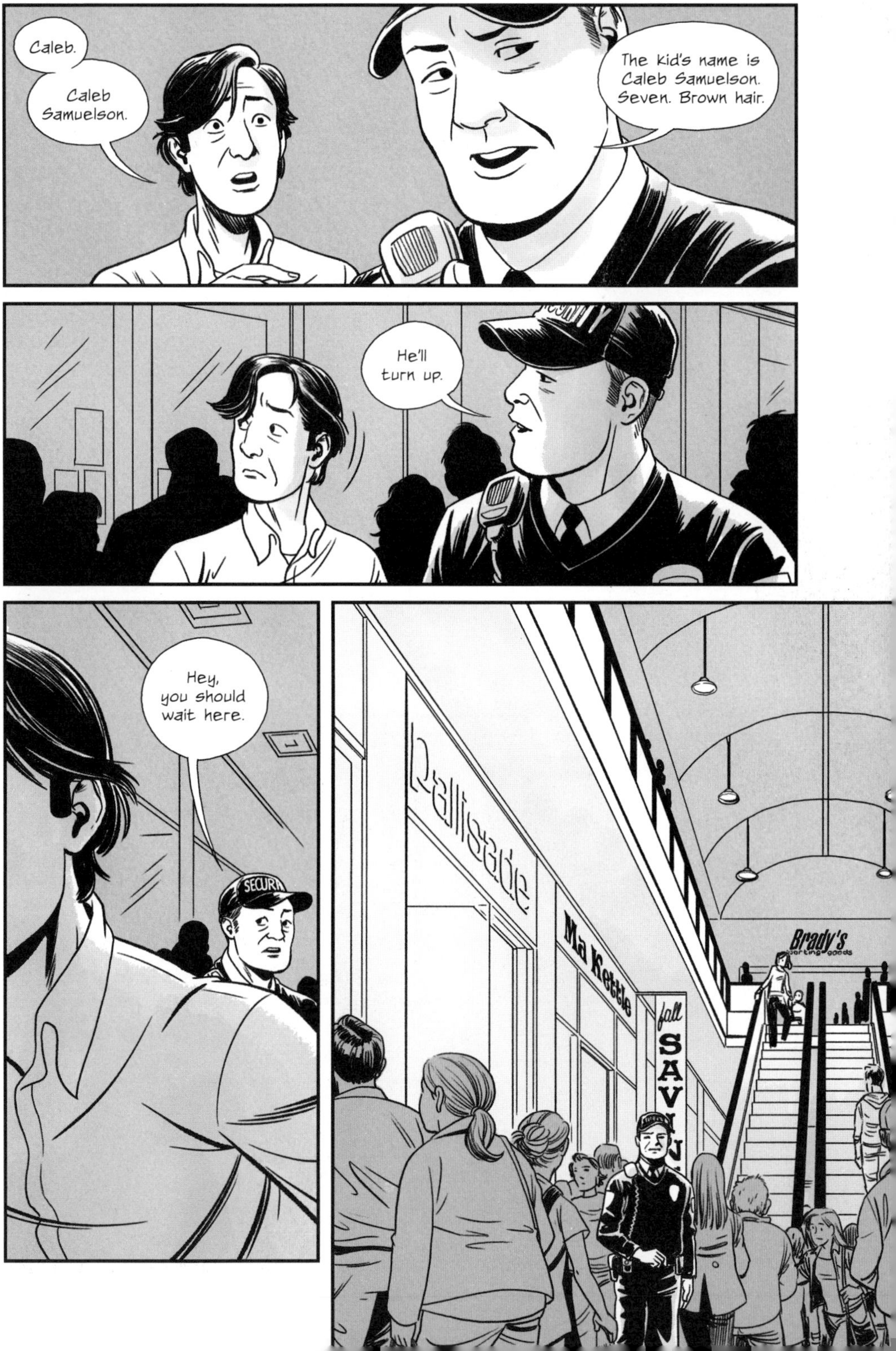
Caleb.
Caleb Samuelson.
The kid's name is Caleb Samuelson. Seven. Brown hair.
He'll turn up.
Hey, you should wait here.
Palisade
Ma Kettle
fall
Brady's

NEW PHONE and 1ST MONTH'S SERVICE only $17.76!

Is this for real? What do you *really* pay?

No, it's real. It's a pretty good phone, too.

C'mon, seriously. There's always some hidden fee.

Here, take a flyer. It tells you about the different plans and everything.

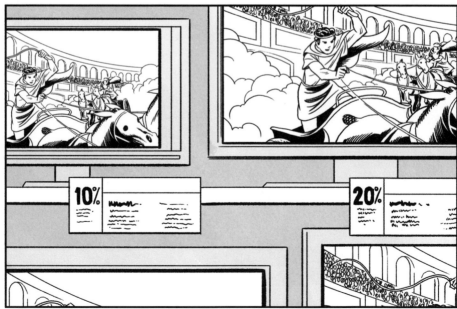

10%

20%

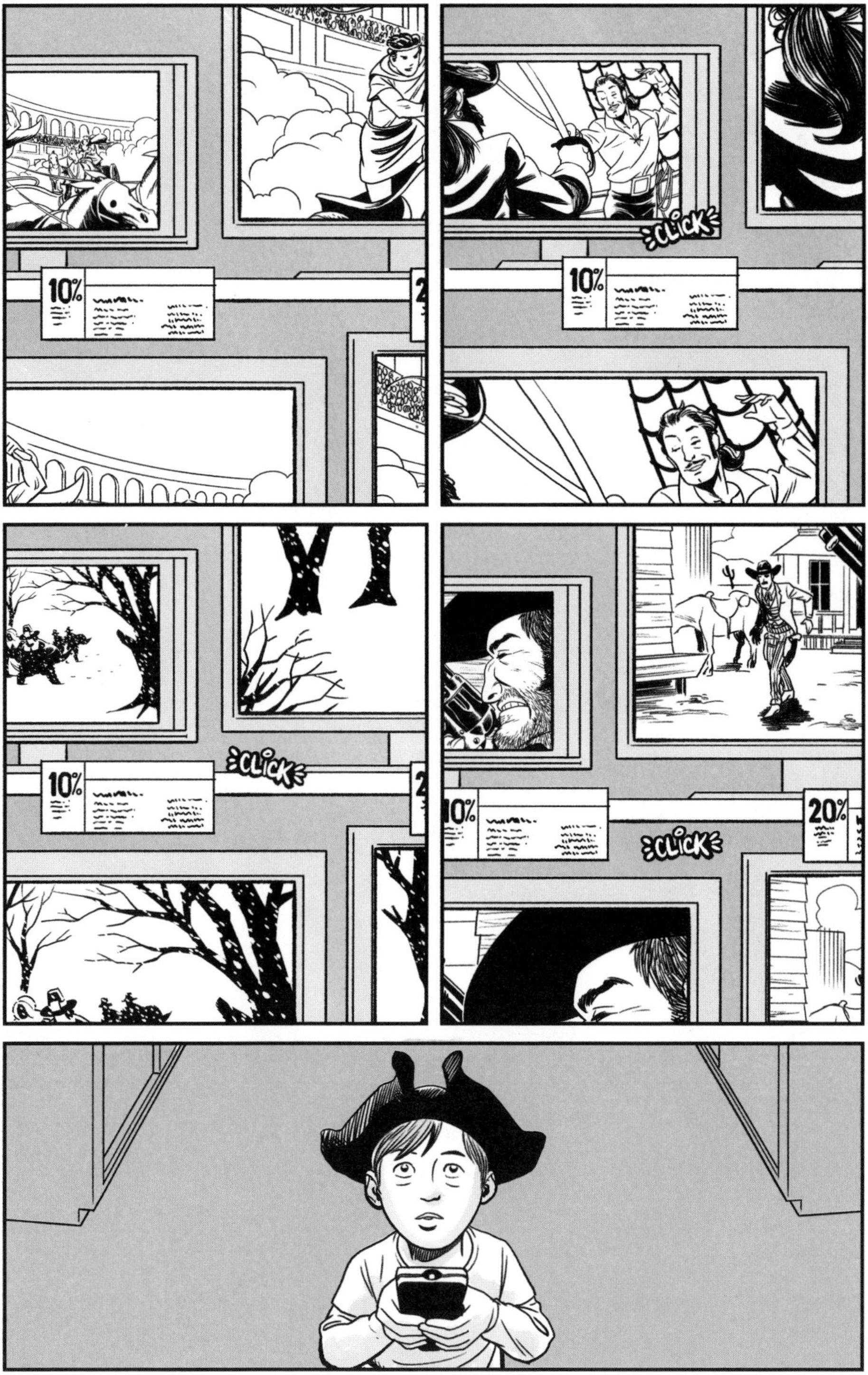
10%
CLICK
10%
10%
CLICK
10%
CLICK
20%

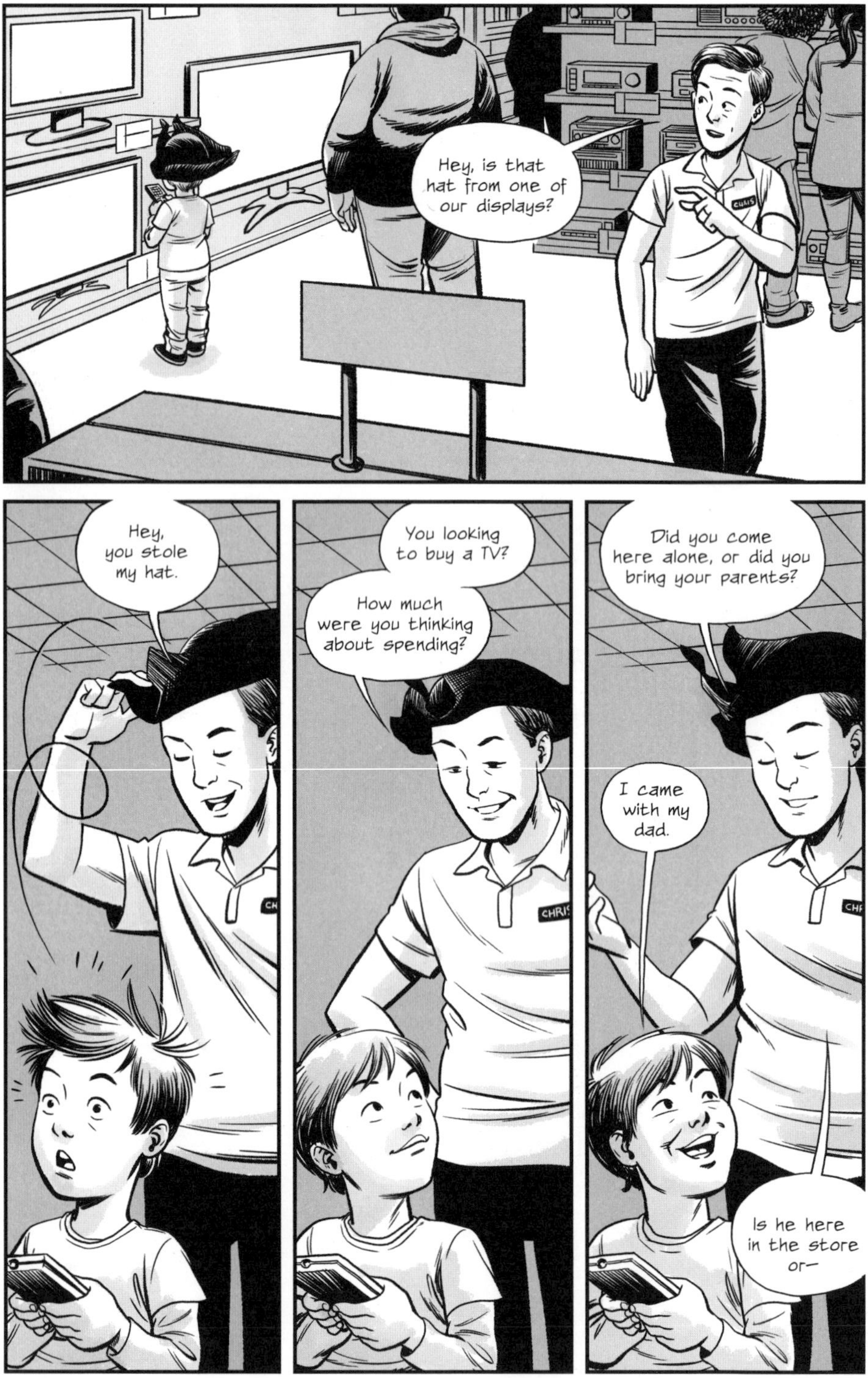
Hey, is that hat from one of our displays?
Hey, you stole my hat.
You looking to buy a TV?
How much were you thinking about spending?
Did you come here alone, or did you bring your parents?
I came with my dad.
Is he here in the store or—

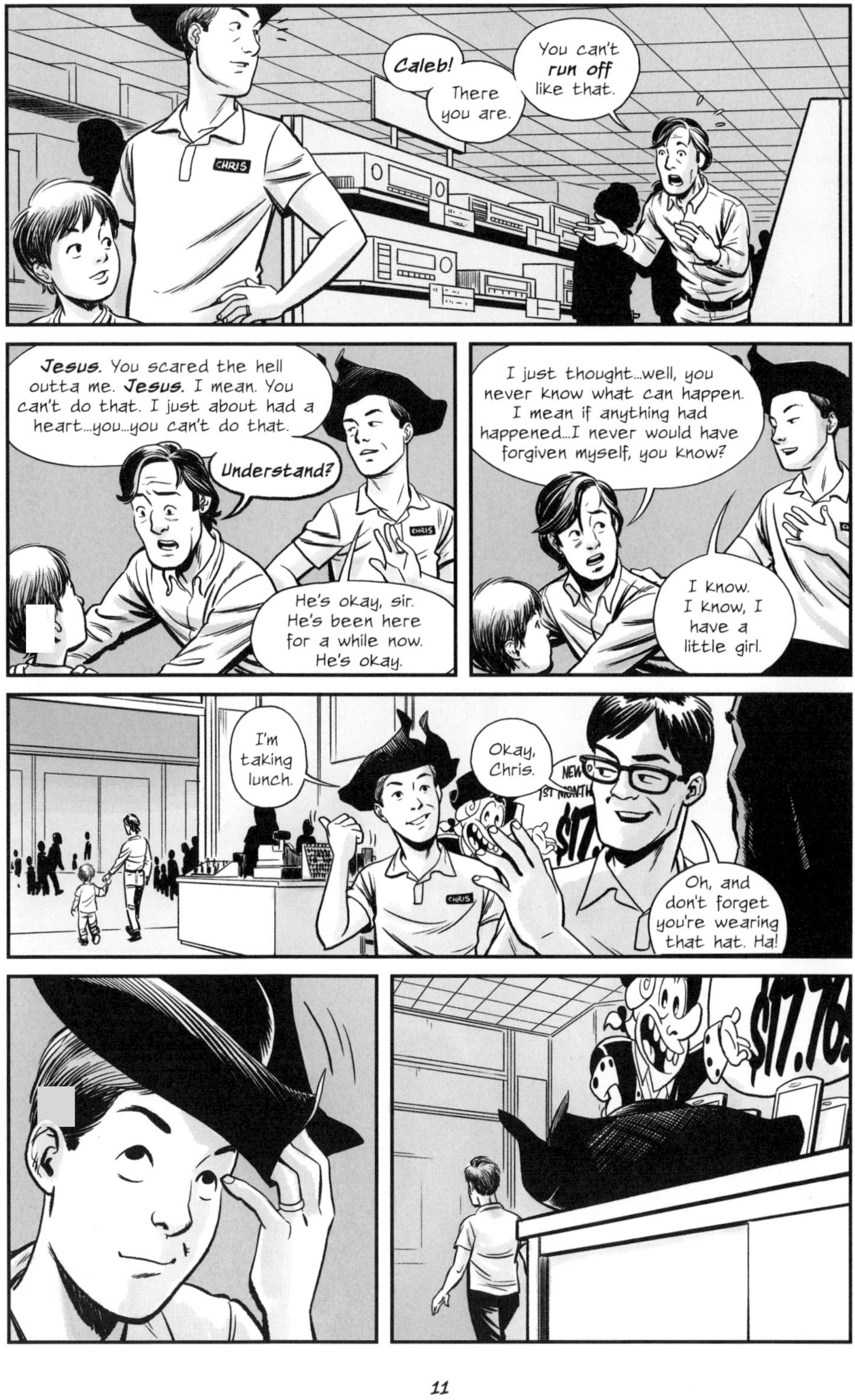

Caleb!
There you are.
You can't run off like that.
Jesus. You scared the hell outta me. Jesus. I mean. You can't do that. I just about had a heart...you...you can't do that.
Understand?
He's okay, sir. He's been here for a while now. He's okay.
I just thought...well, you never know what can happen. I mean if anything had happened...I never would have forgiven myself, you know?
I know. I know, I have a little girl.
CHRIS
I'm taking lunch.
Okay, Chris.
Oh, and don't forget you're wearing that hat. Ha!

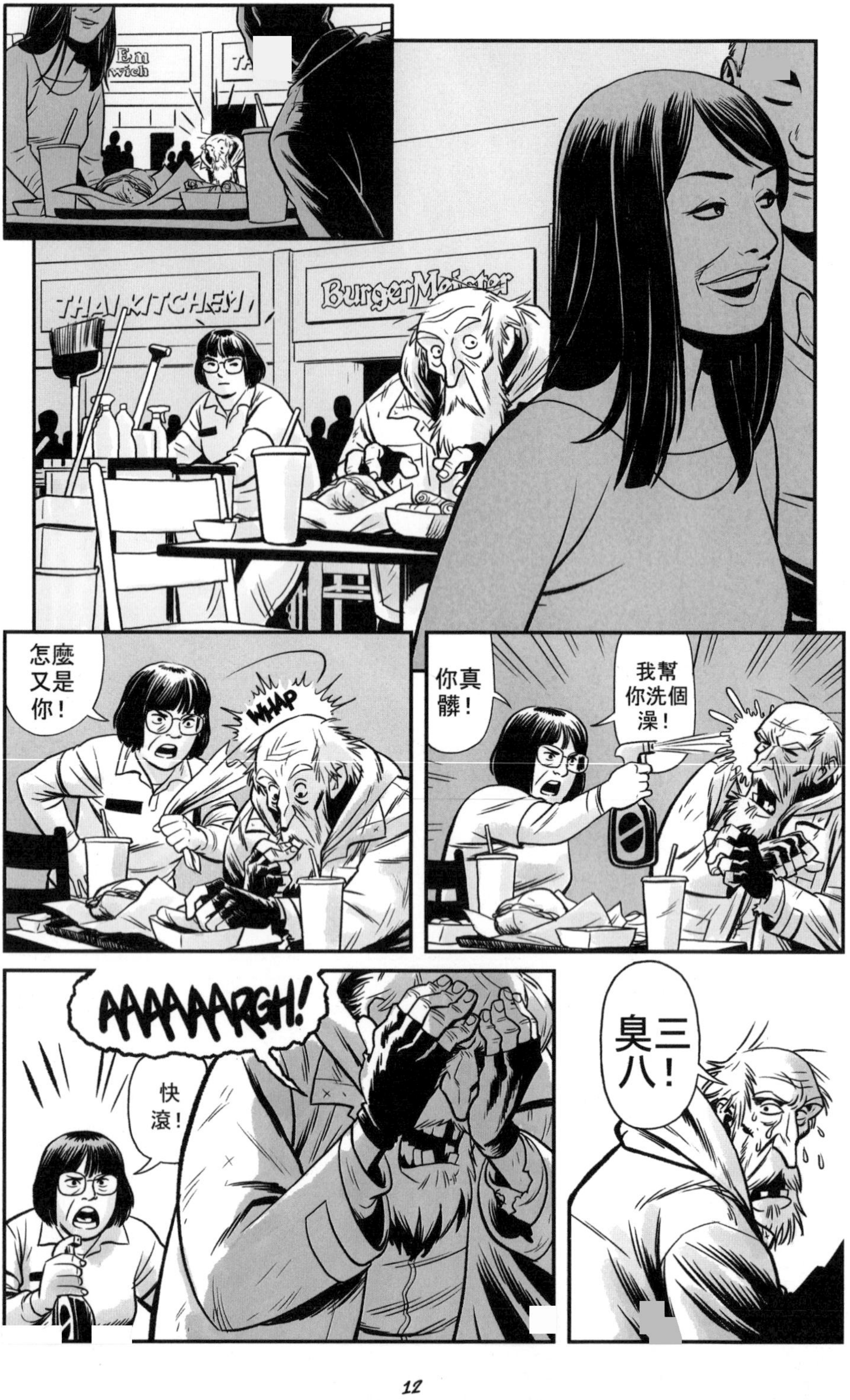
Em
wich
THAI KITCHEN
Burger Meister
怎麼又是你！
WHAP
你真髒！
我幫你洗個澡！
AAAAAARGH!
快滾！
臭三八！

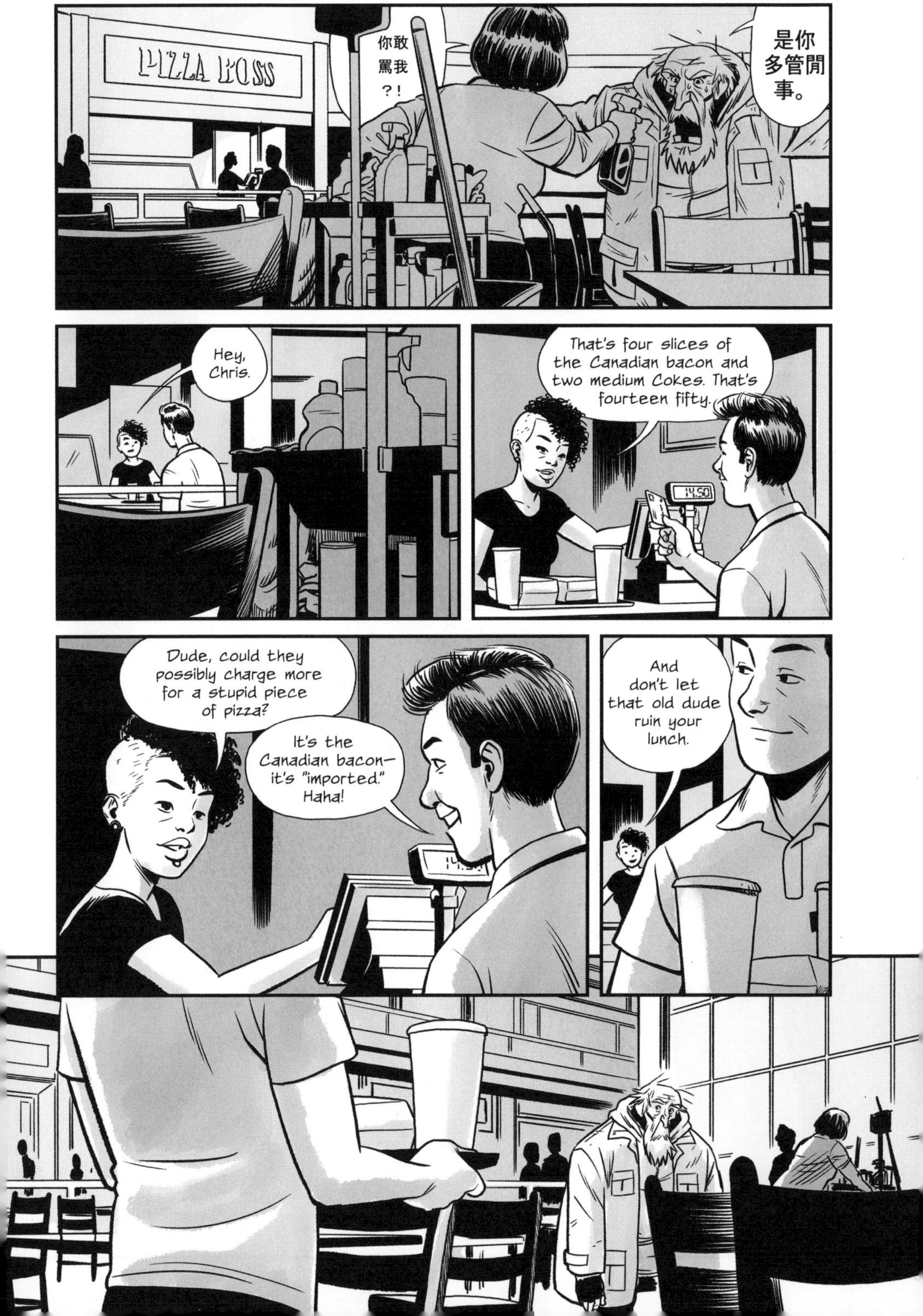
PIZZA BOSS
你敢罵我?!
是你多管閒事。
Hey, Chris.
That's four slices of the Canadian bacon and two medium Cokes. That's fourteen fifty.
14.50
Dude, could they possibly charge more for a stupid piece of pizza?
It's the Canadian bacon— it's "imported." Haha!
And don't let that old dude ruin your lunch.

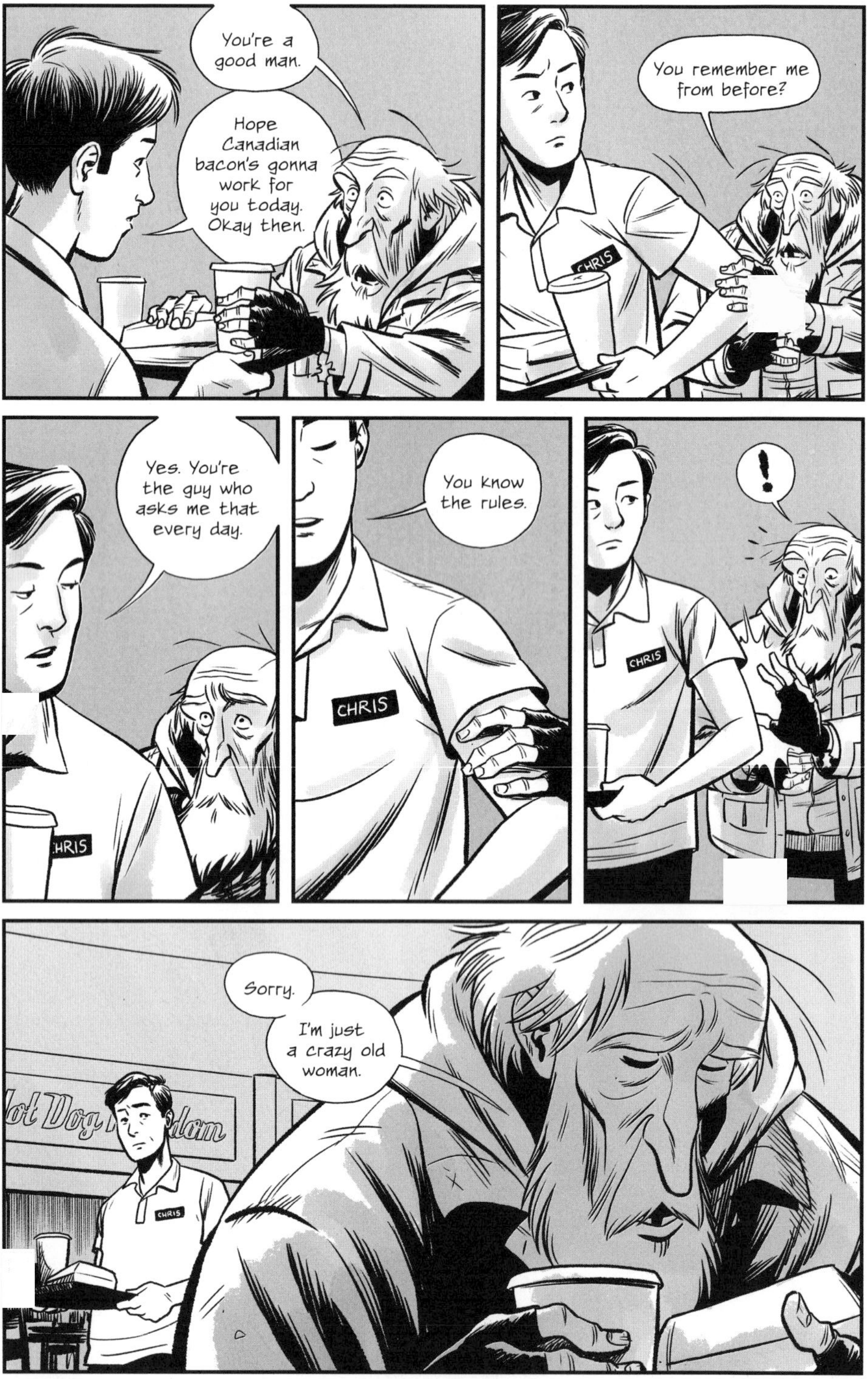
You're a good man.
Hope Canadian bacon's gonna work for you today. Okay then.
CHRIS
You remember me from before?
Yes. You're the guy who asks me that every day.
CHRIS
CHRIS
You know the rules.
!
CHRIS
Sorry.
I'm just a crazy old woman.
CHRIS

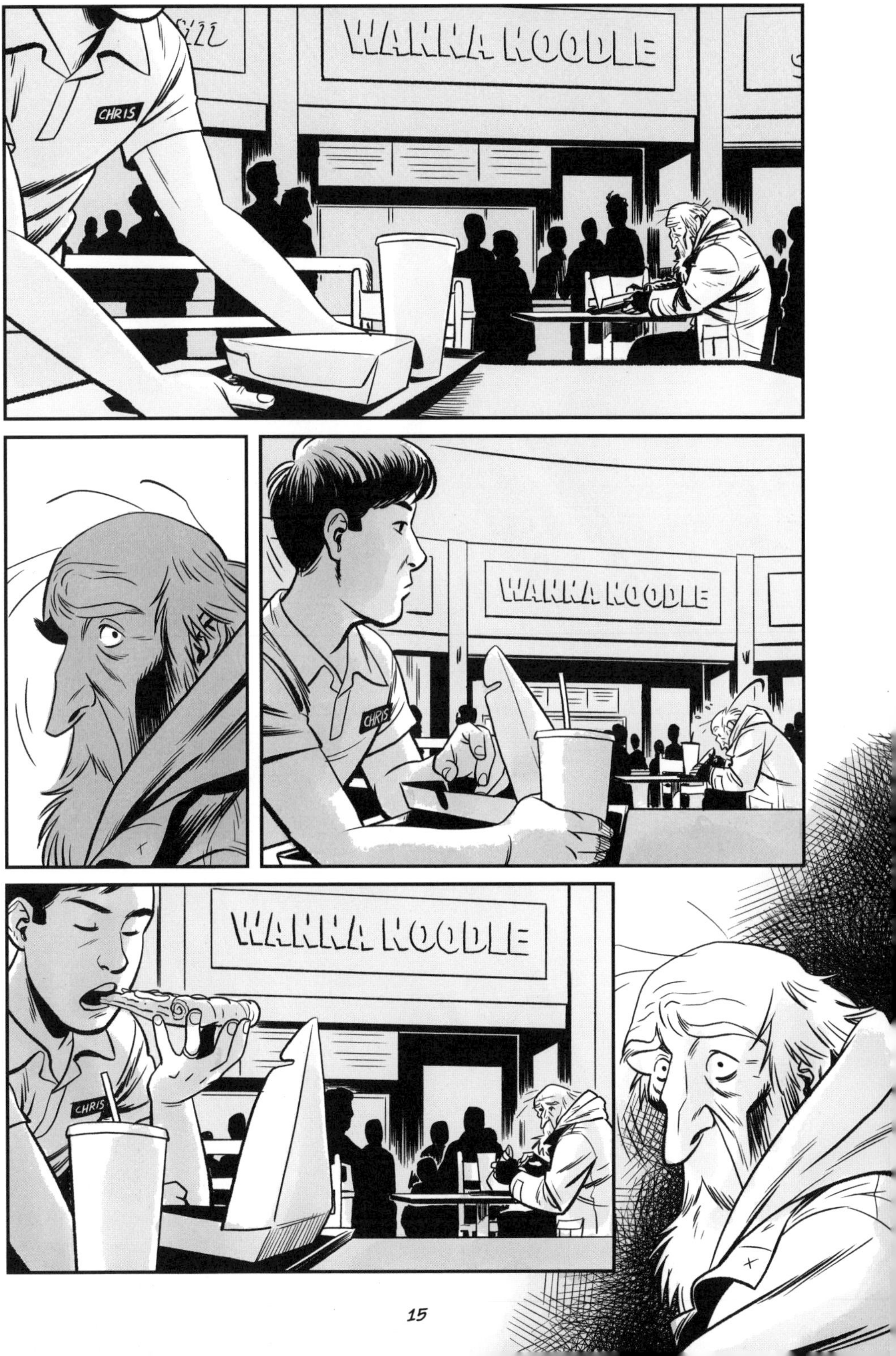
WANNA NOODLE
CHRIS
CHRIS
WANNA NOODLE
WANNA NOODLE
CHRIS

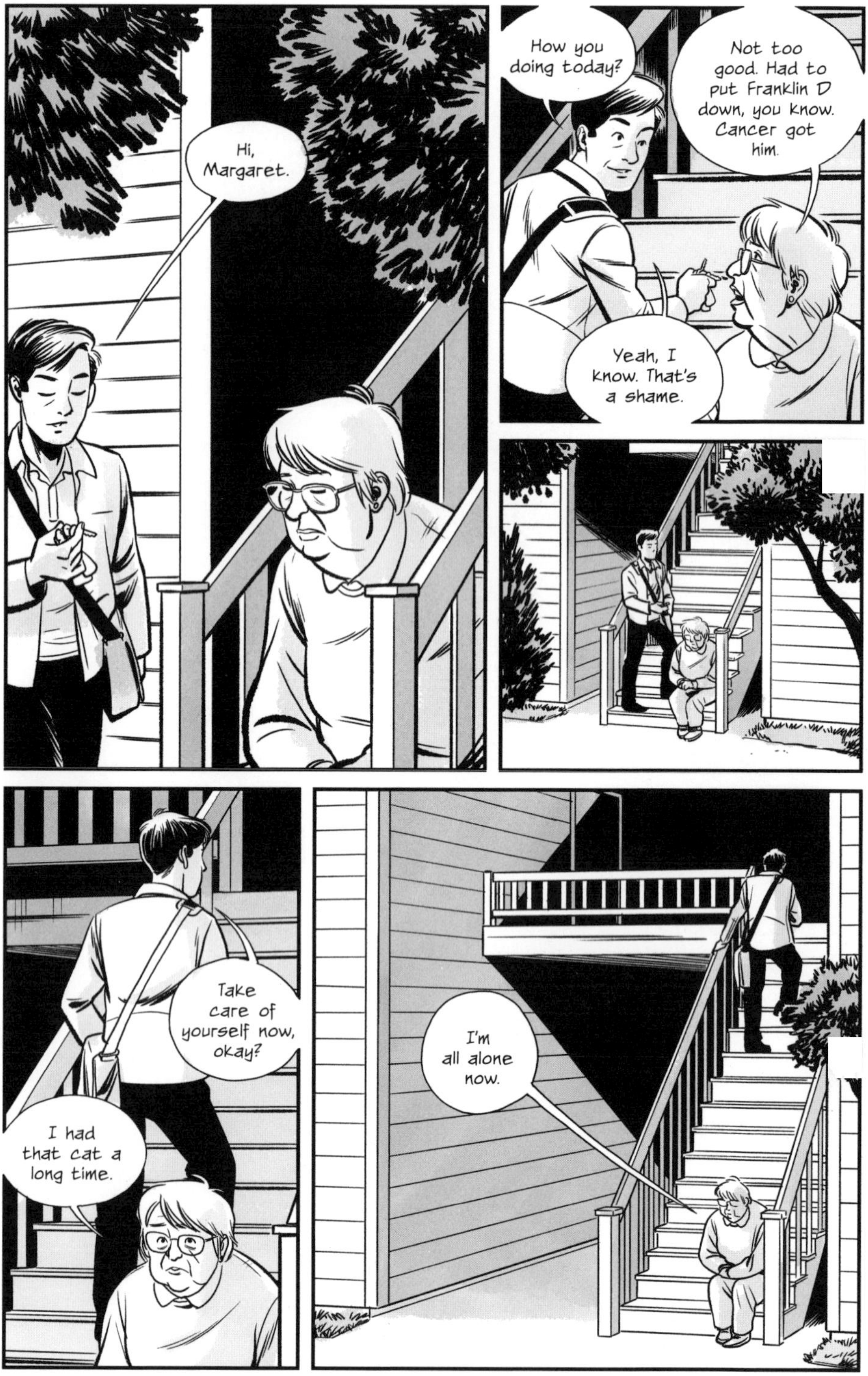
Hi, Margaret.
How you doing today?
Not too good. Had to put Franklin D down, you know. Cancer got him.
Yeah, I know. That's a shame.
Take care of yourself now, okay?
I had that cat a long time.
I'm all alone now.

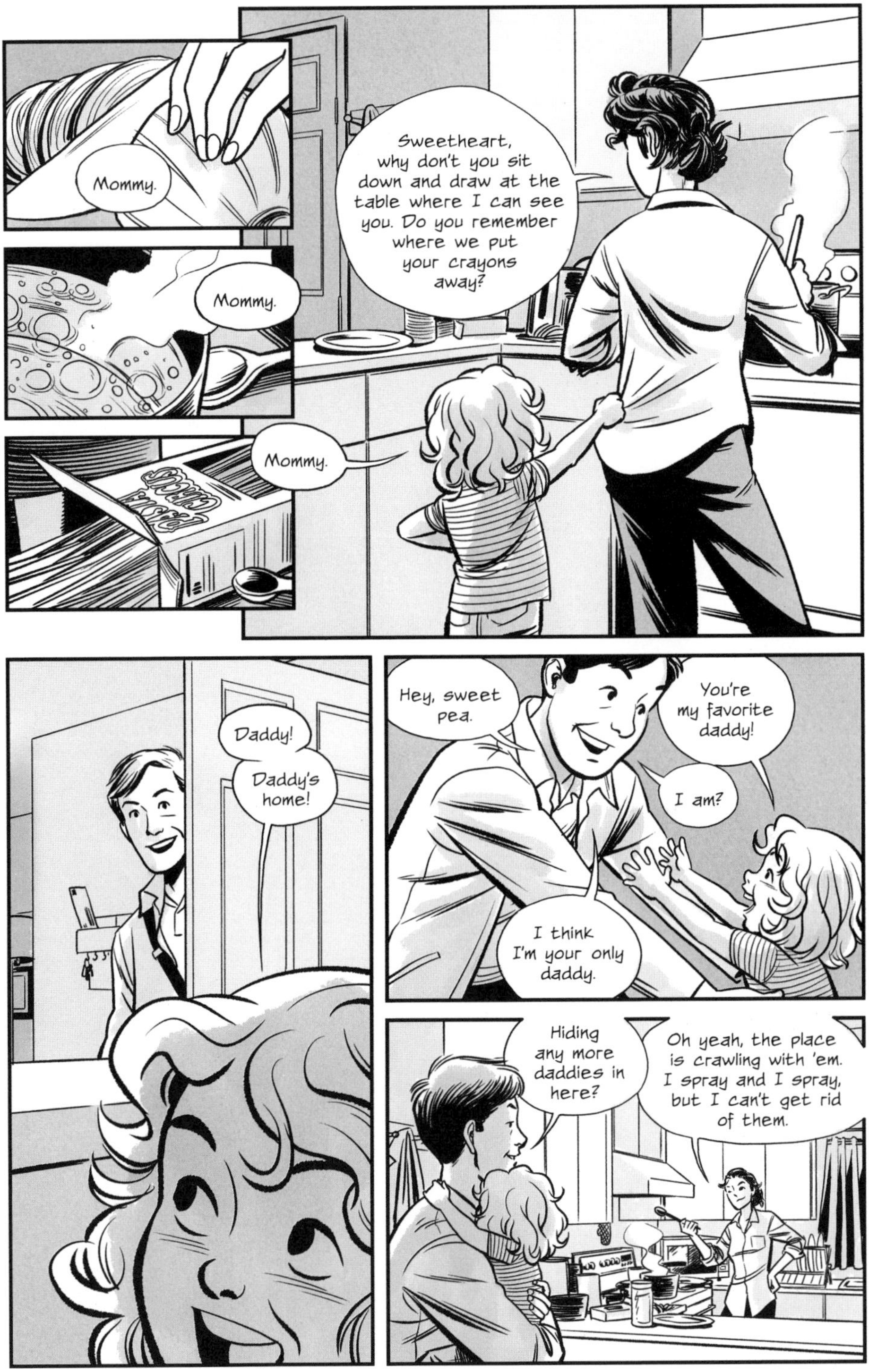
Mommy.
Mommy.
PASTA CIRCUS
Mommy.
Sweetheart, why don't you sit down and draw at the table where I can see you. Do you remember where we put your crayons away?
Daddy!
Daddy's home!
Hey, sweet pea.
You're my favorite daddy!
I am?
I think I'm your only daddy.
Hiding any more daddies in here?
Oh yeah, the place is crawling with 'em. I spray and I spray, but I can't get rid of them.

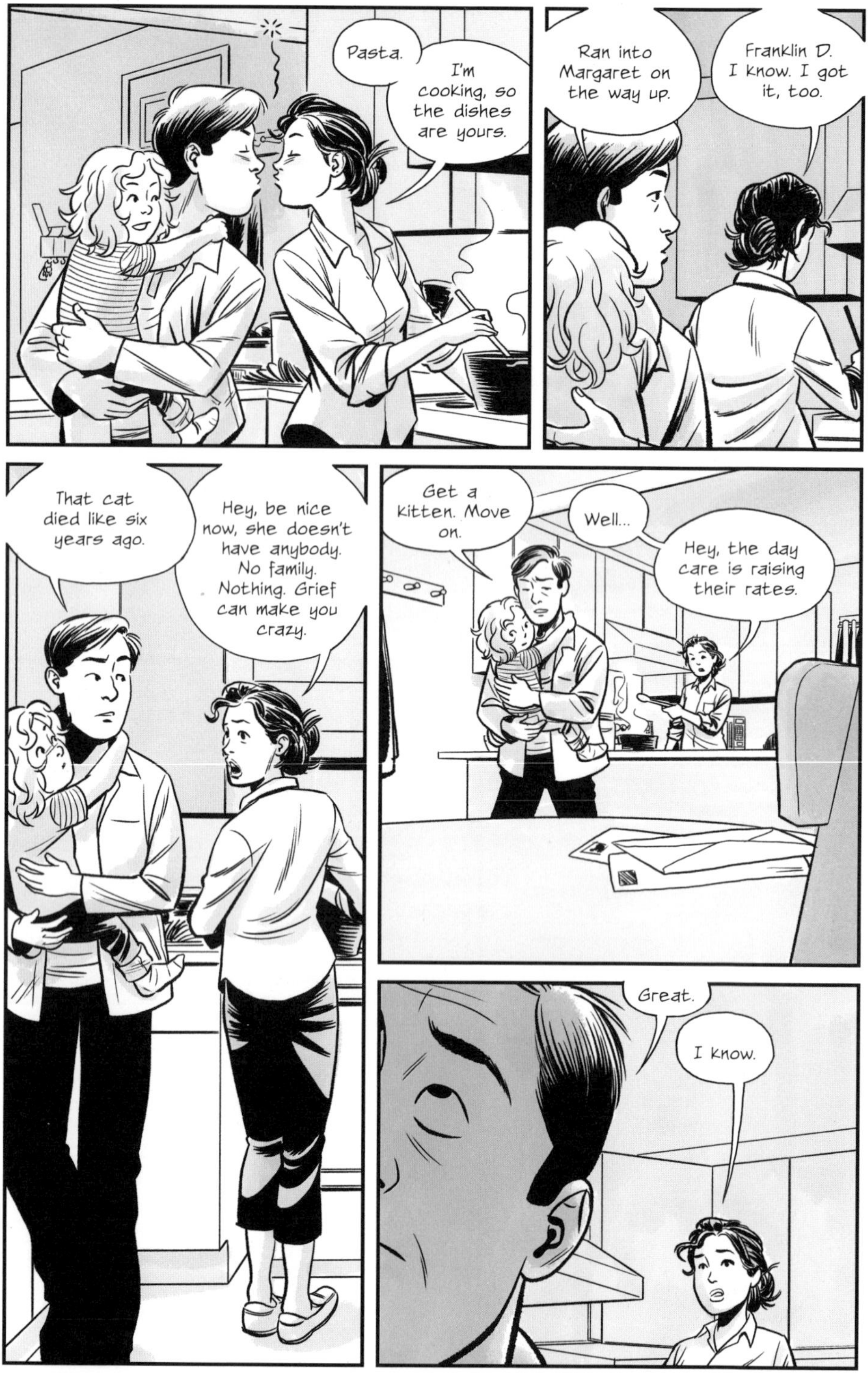
Pasta.
I'm cooking, so the dishes are yours.
Ran into Margaret on the way up.
Franklin D. I know. I got it, too.
That cat died like six years ago.
Hey, be nice now, she doesn't have anybody. No family. Nothing. Grief can make you crazy.
Get a kitten. Move on.
Well...
Hey, the day care is raising their rates.
Great.
I know.

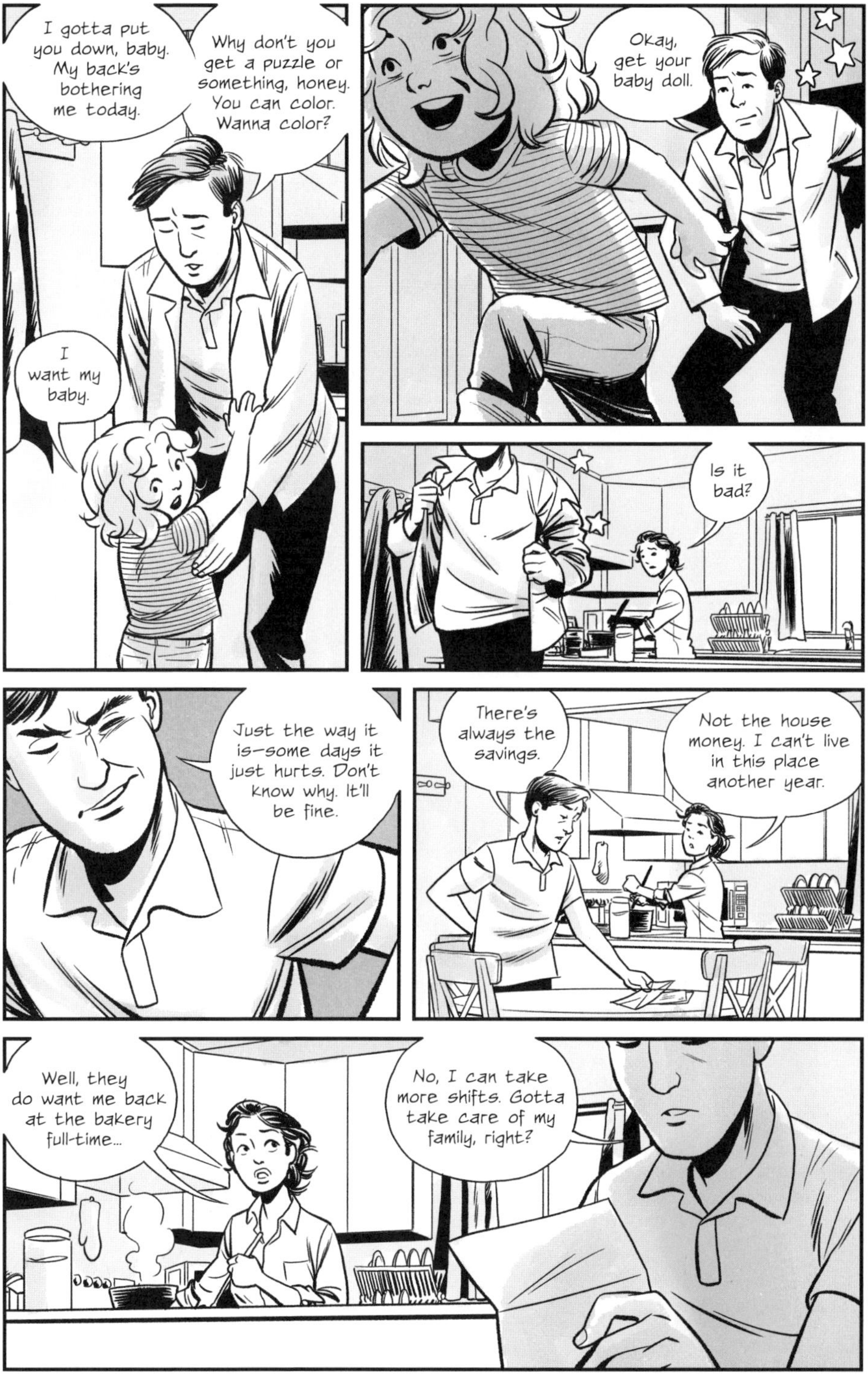
I gotta put you down, baby. My back's bothering me today.
Why don't you get a puzzle or something, honey. You can color. Wanna color?
I want my baby.
Okay, get your baby doll.
Is it bad?
Just the way it is—some days it just hurts. Don't know why. It'll be fine.
There's always the savings.
Not the house money. I can't live in this place another year.
Well, they do want me back at the bakery full-time...
No, I can take more shifts. Gotta take care of my family, right?

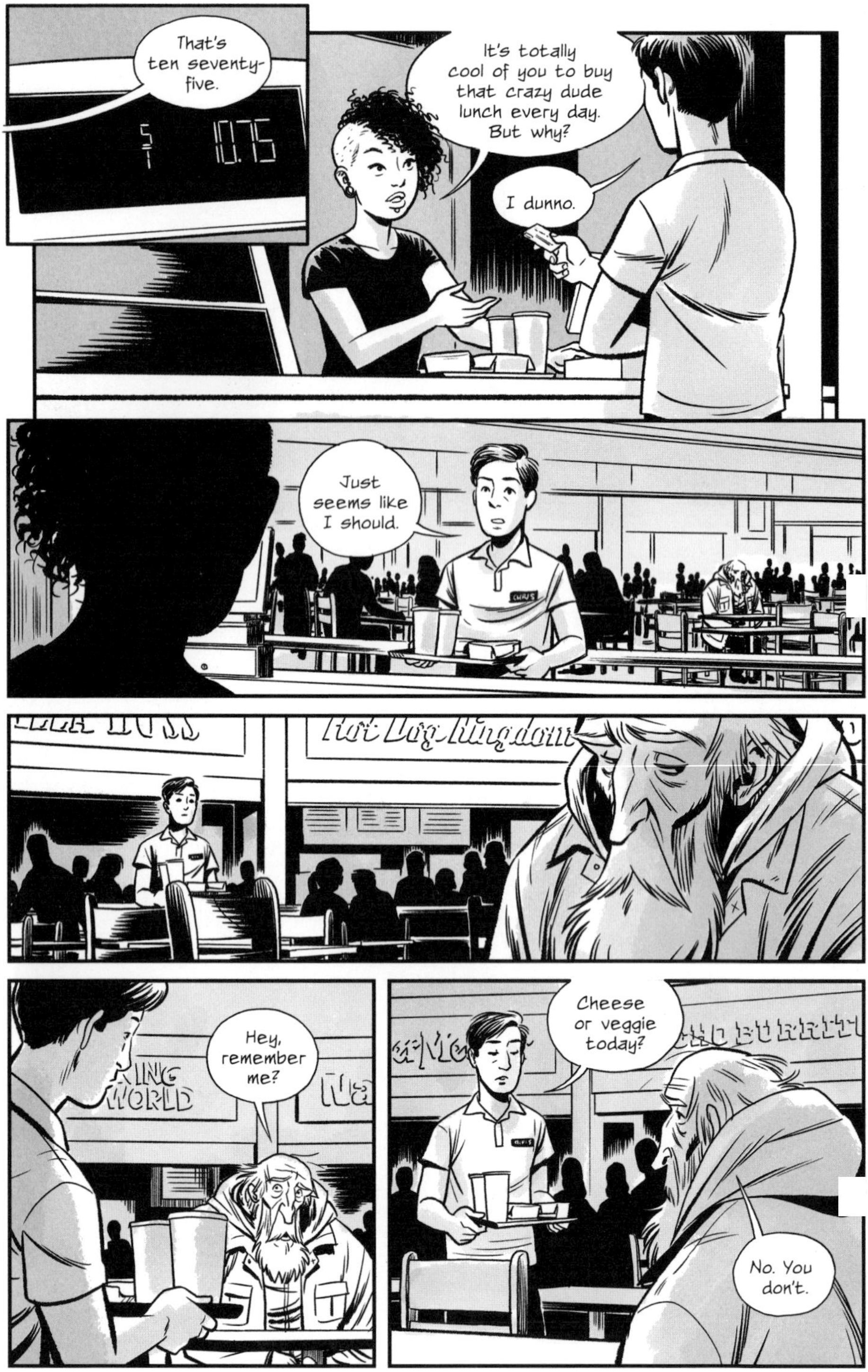
That's ten seventy-five.
$ 10.75
It's totally cool of you to buy that crazy dude lunch every day. But why?
I dunno.
Just seems like I should.
CHRIS
Hot Dog Kingdom
Hey, remember me?
KING WORLD
Cheese or veggie today?
No. You don't.

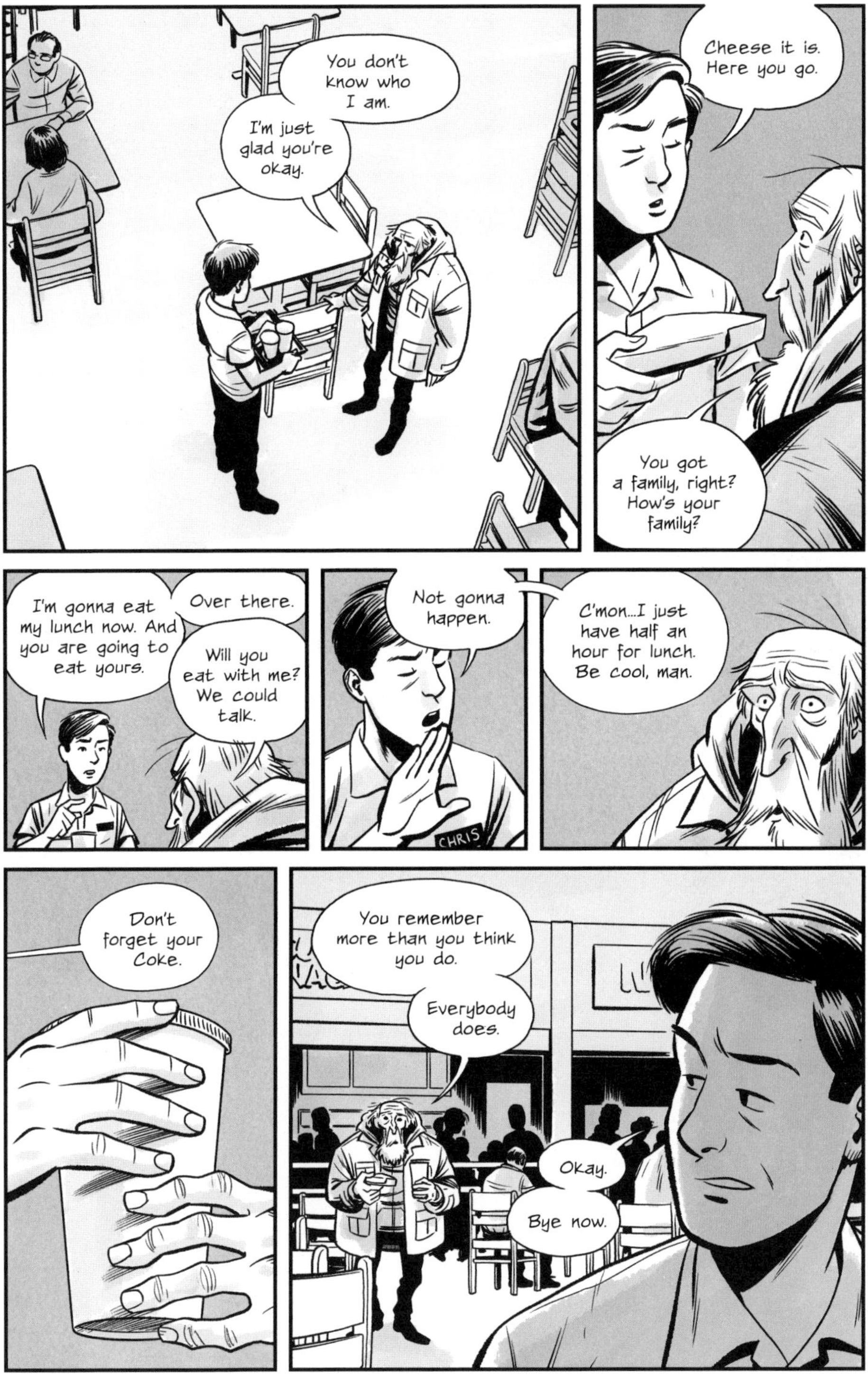
You don't know who I am.
I'm just glad you're okay.
Cheese it is. Here you go.
You got a family, right? How's your family?
I'm gonna eat my lunch now. And you are going to eat yours.
Over there.
Will you eat with me? We could talk.
Not gonna happen.
CHRIS
C'mon...I just have half an hour for lunch. Be cool, man.
Don't forget your Coke.
You remember more than you think you do.
Everybody does.
Okay.
Bye now.

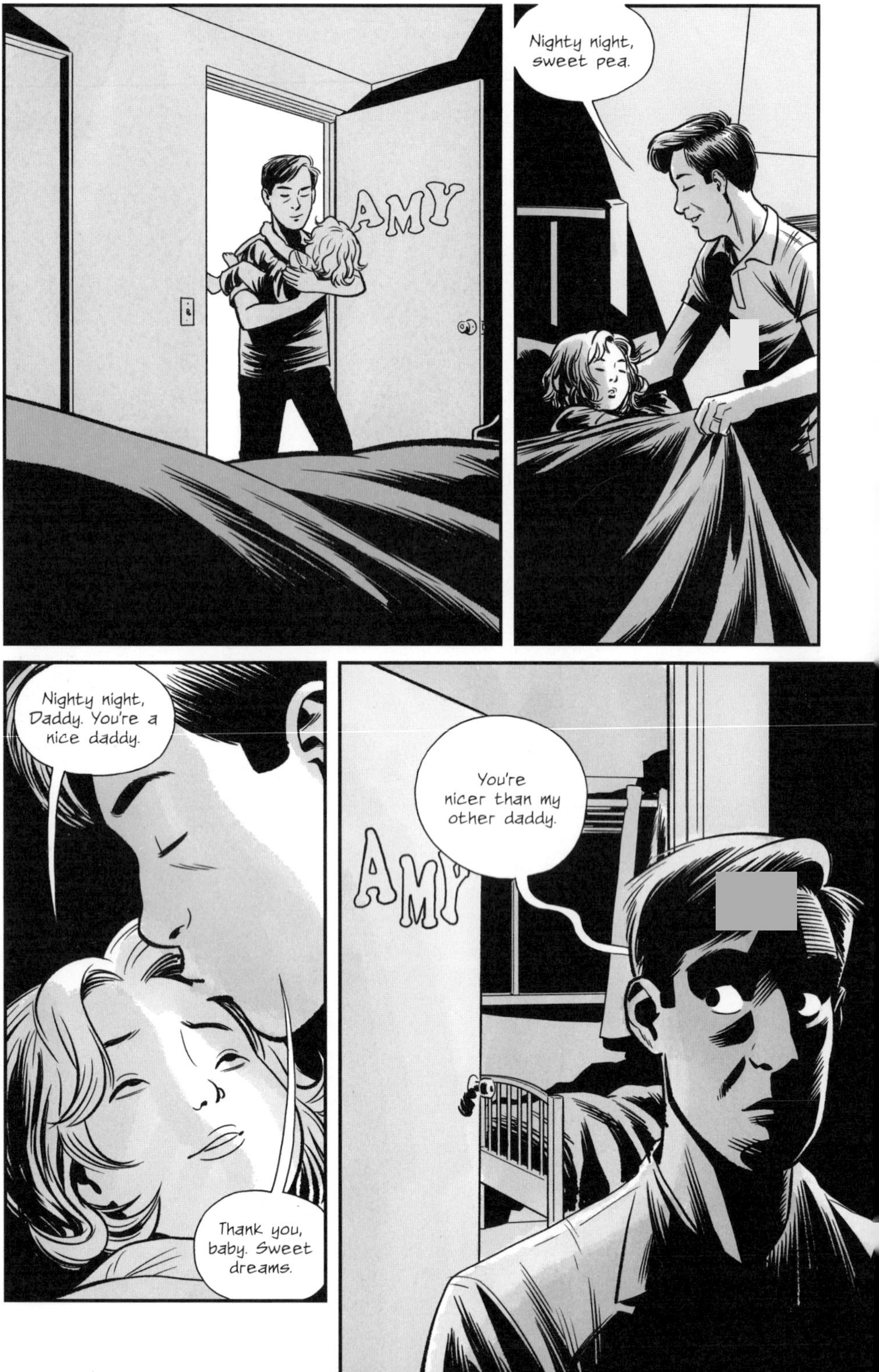
AMY
Nighty night, sweet pea.
Nighty night, Daddy. You're a nice daddy.
Thank you, baby. Sweet dreams.
AMY
You're nicer than my other daddy.

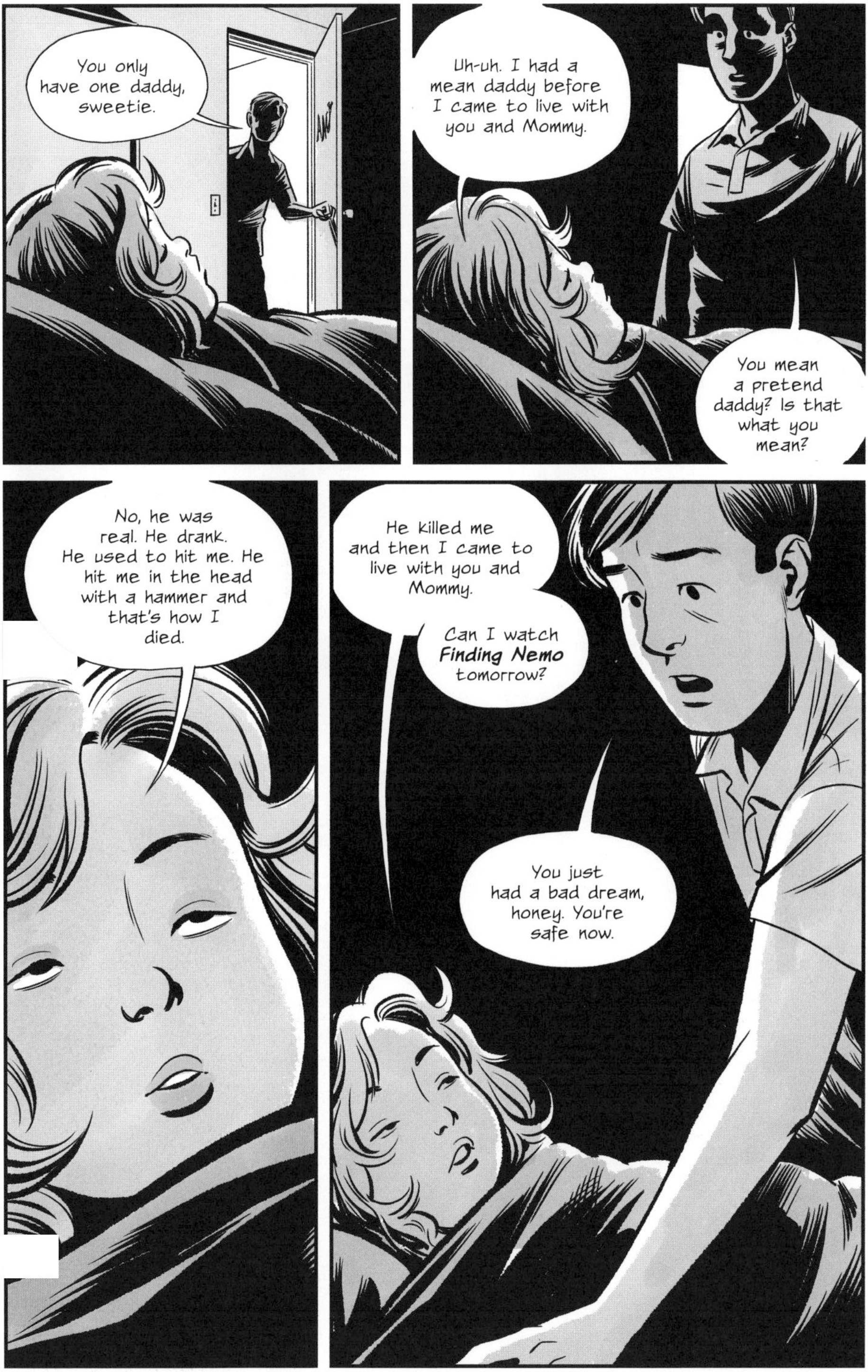
You only have one daddy, sweetie.
Uh-uh. I had a mean daddy before I came to live with you and Mommy.
You mean a pretend daddy? Is that what you mean?
No, he was real. He drank. He used to hit me. He hit me in the head with a hammer and that's how I died.
He killed me and then I came to live with you and Mommy.
Can I watch Finding Nemo tomorrow?
You just had a bad dream, honey. You're safe now.

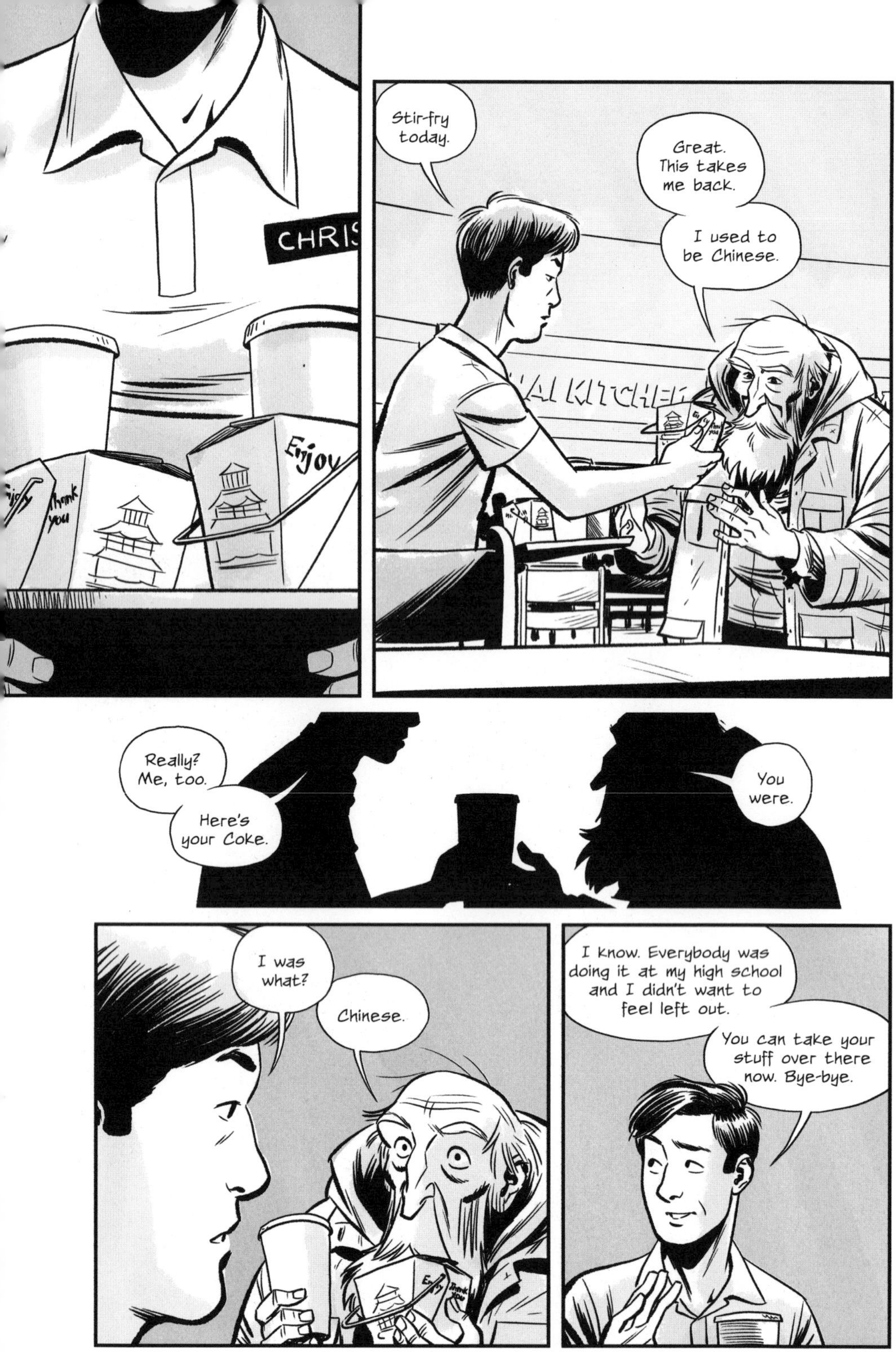
CHRIS
Enjoy
Thank you
Stir-fry today.
Great. This takes me back.
I used to be Chinese.
Really? Me, too.
Here's your Coke.
You were.
I was what?
Chinese.
I know. Everybody was doing it at my high school and I didn't want to feel left out.
You can take your stuff over there now. Bye-bye.

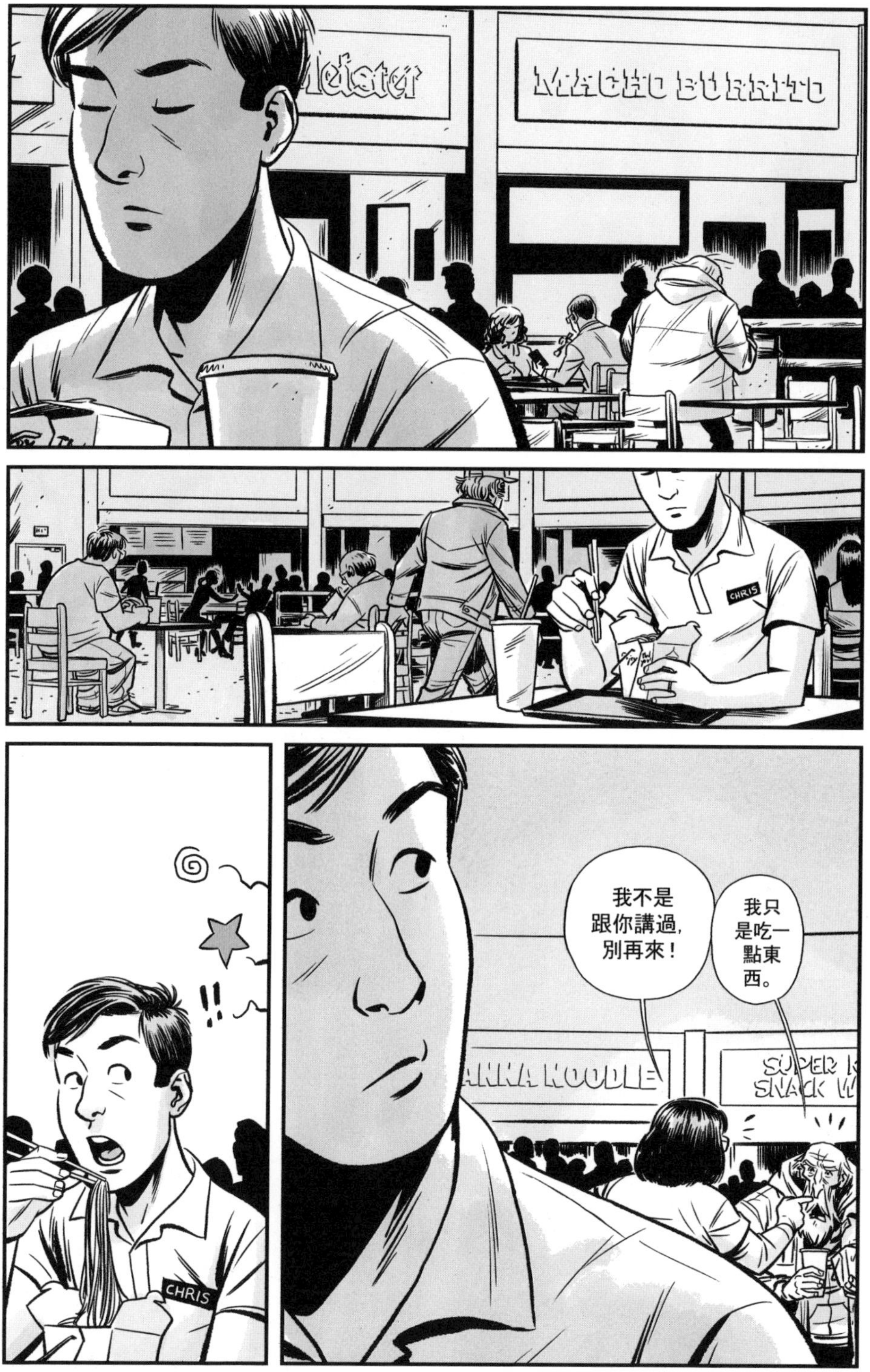
MACHO BURRITO
CHRIS
CHRIS
我不是跟你講過，別再來！
我只是吃一點東西。
ANNA NOODLE

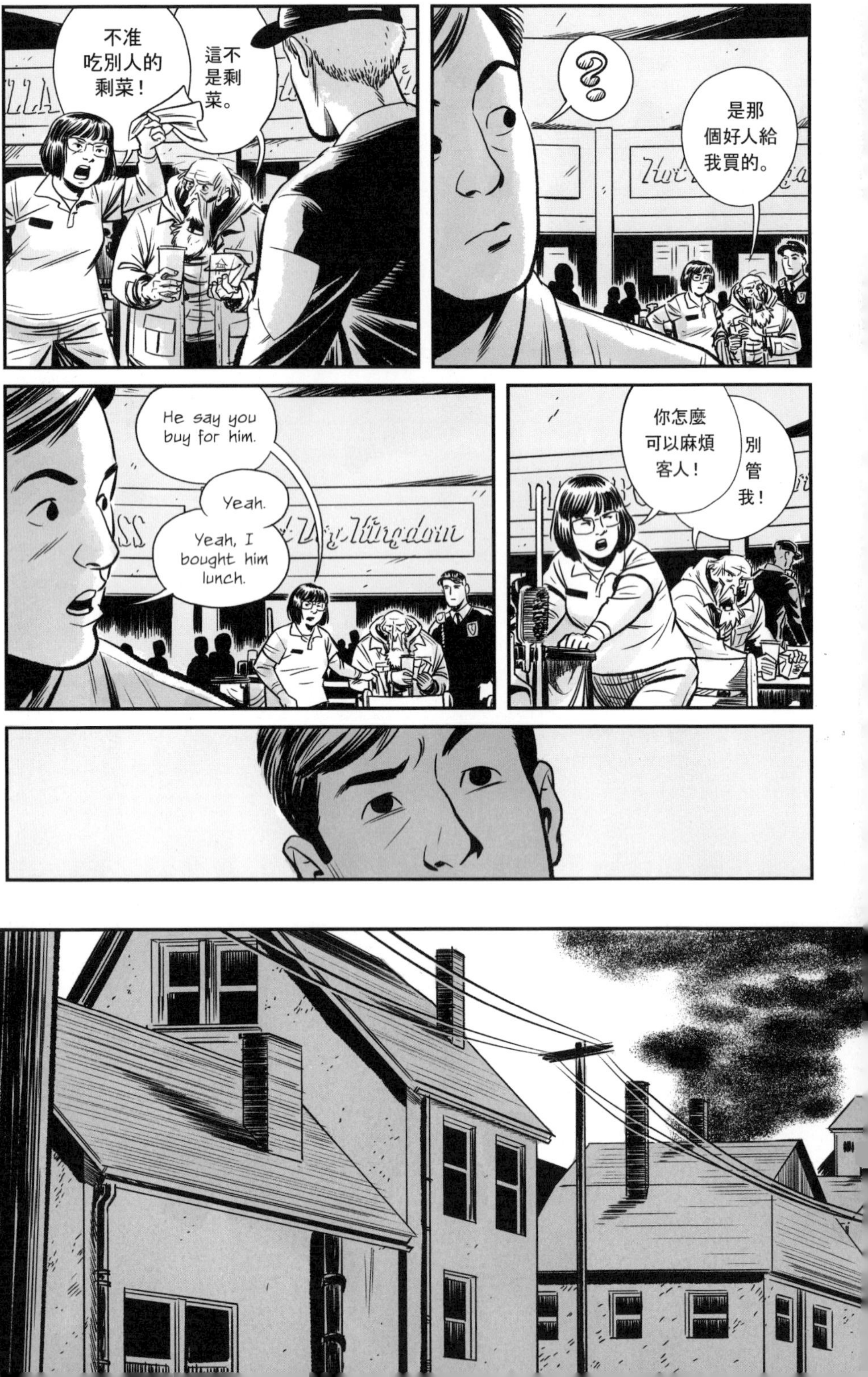

不准吃別人的剩菜！
這不是剩菜。
?
是那個好人給我買的。
He say you buy for him.
Yeah.
Yeah, I bought him lunch.
你怎麼可以麻煩客人！
別管我！

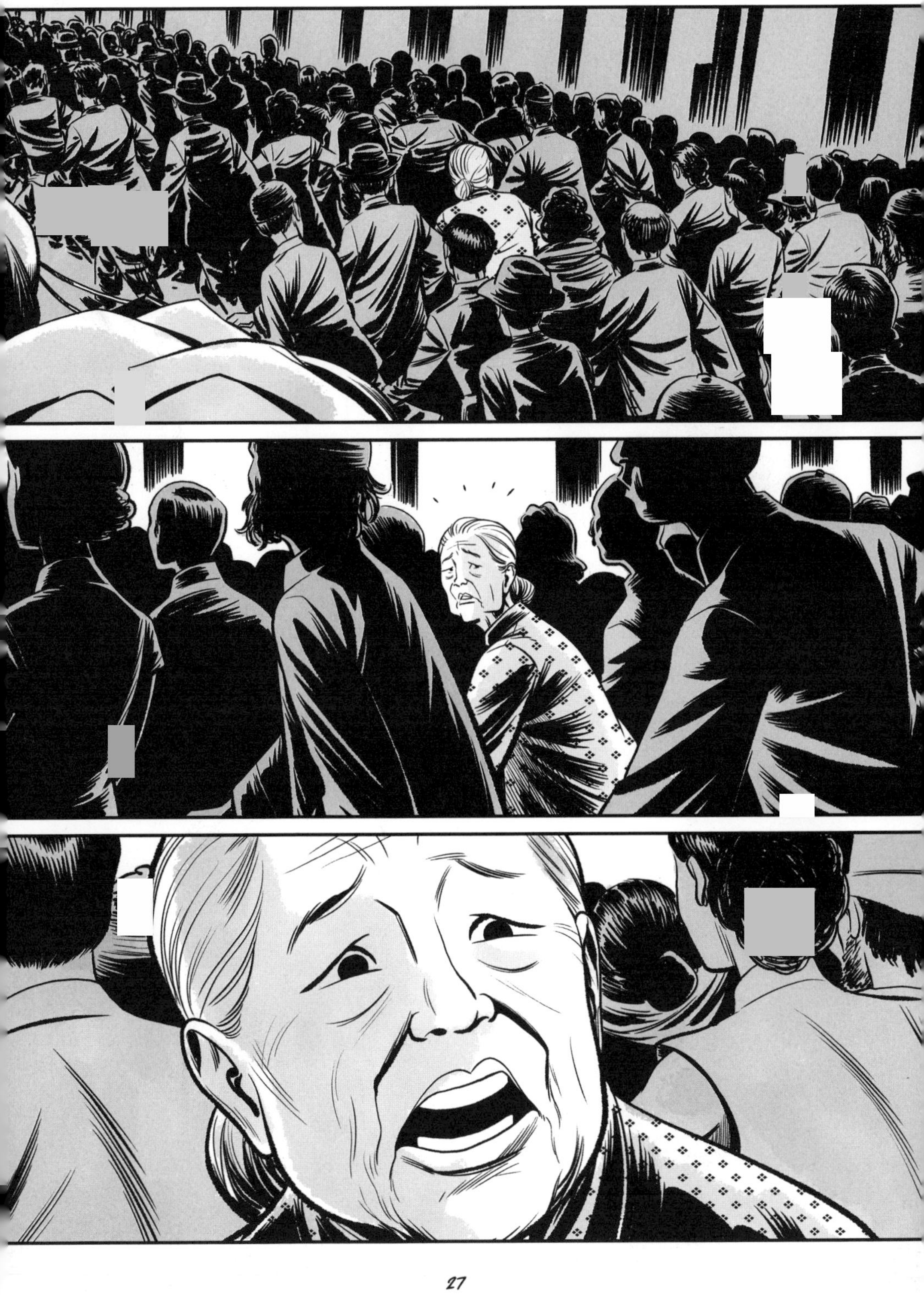

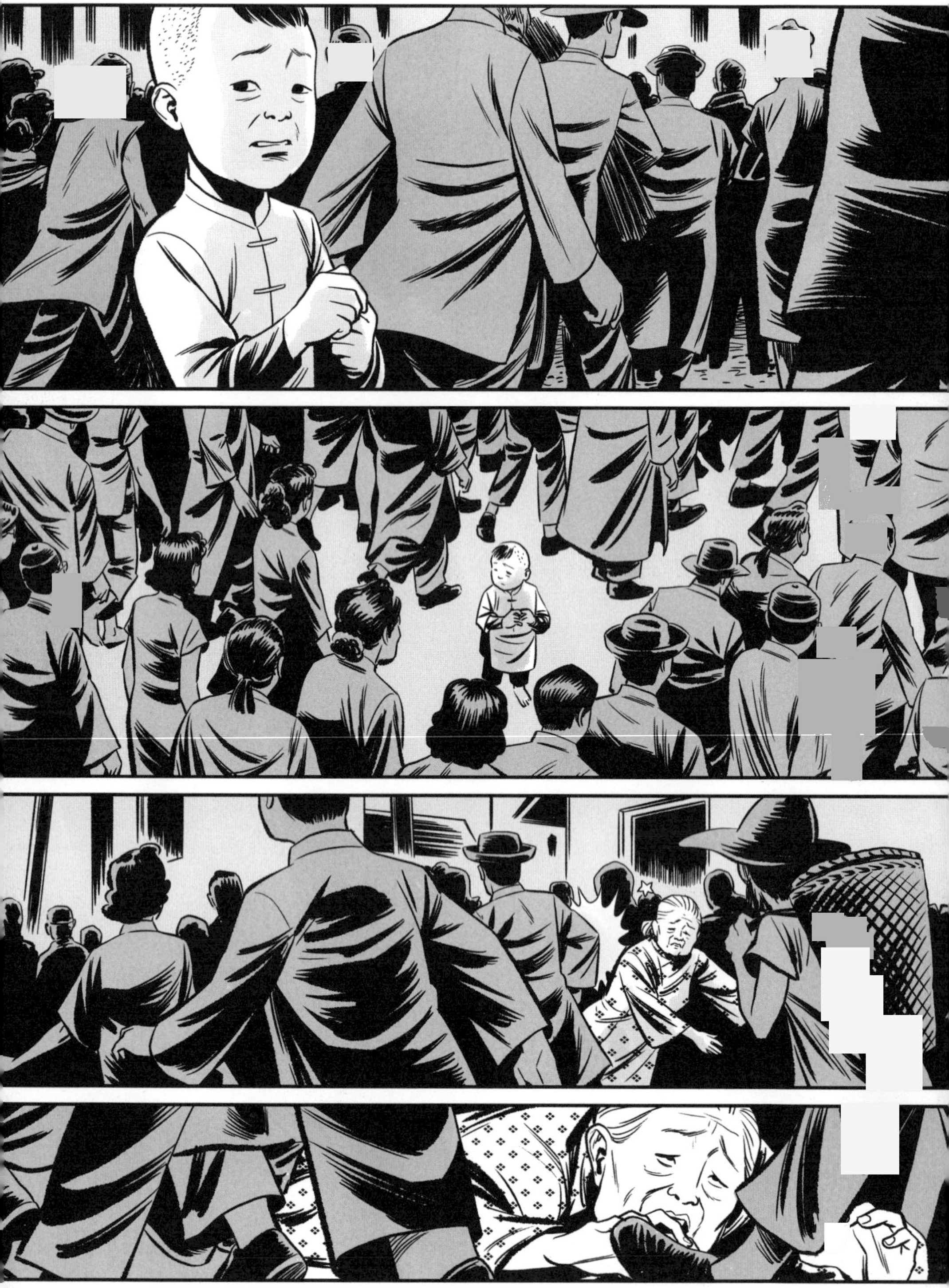

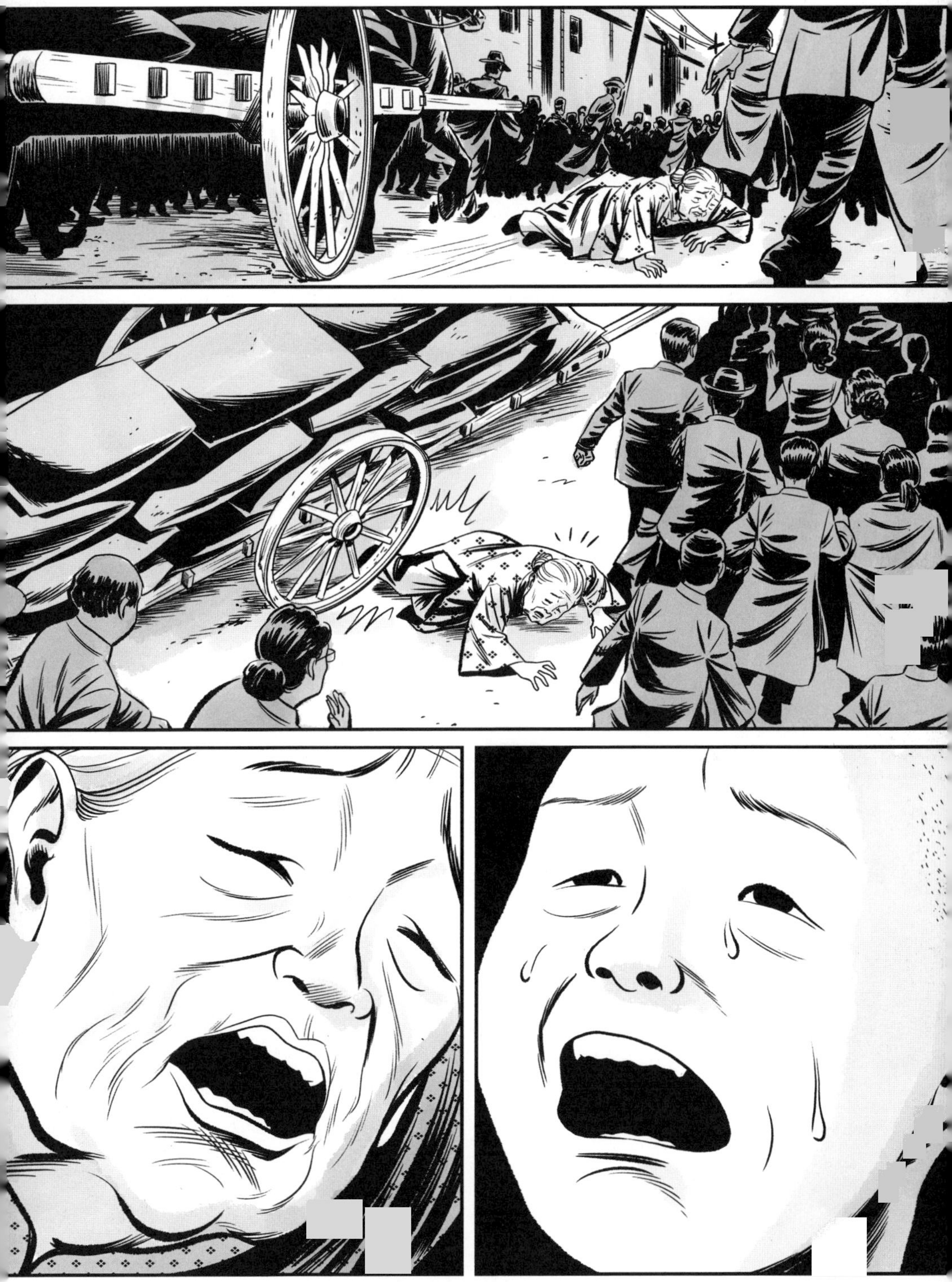

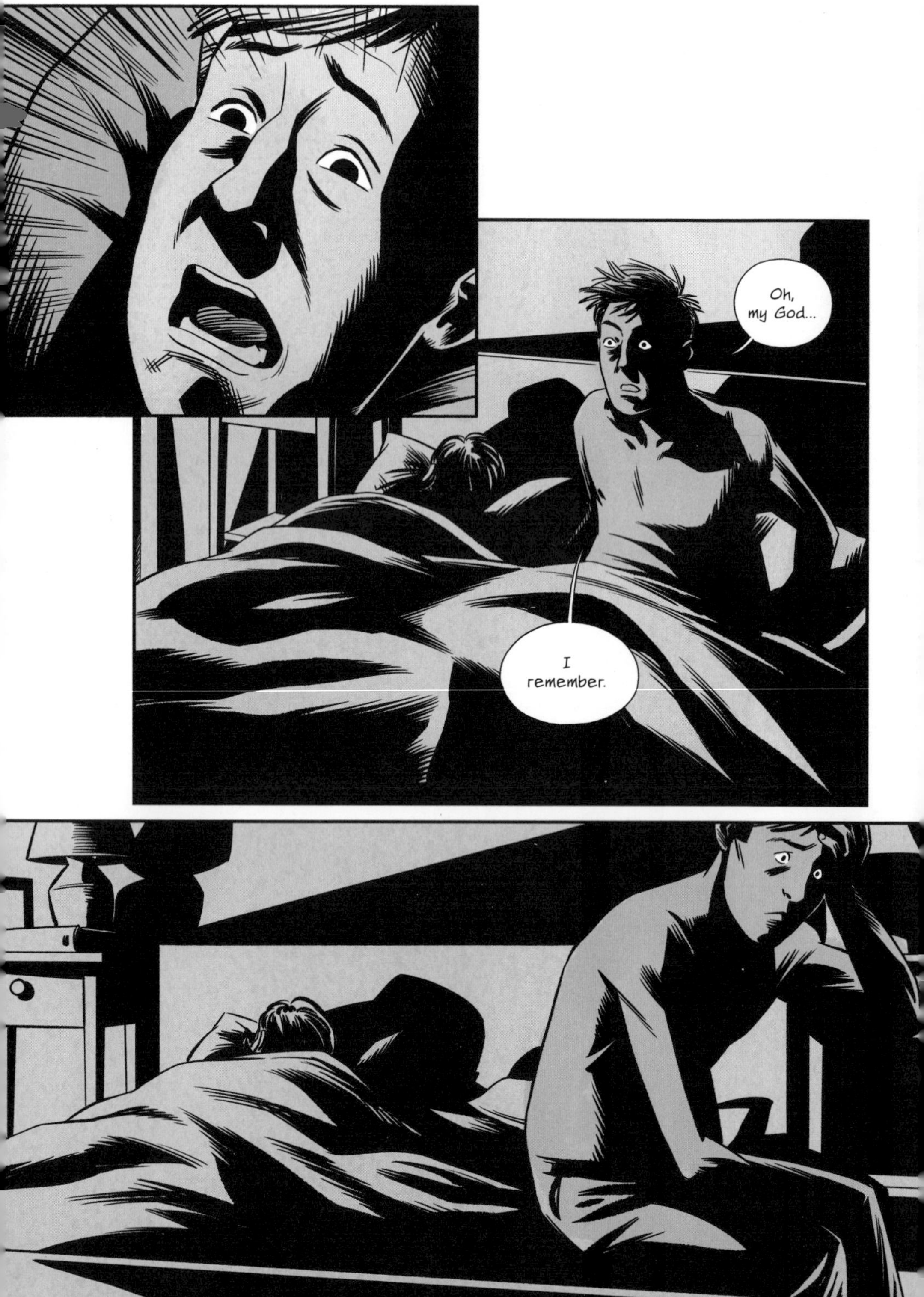
Oh, my God...
I remember.

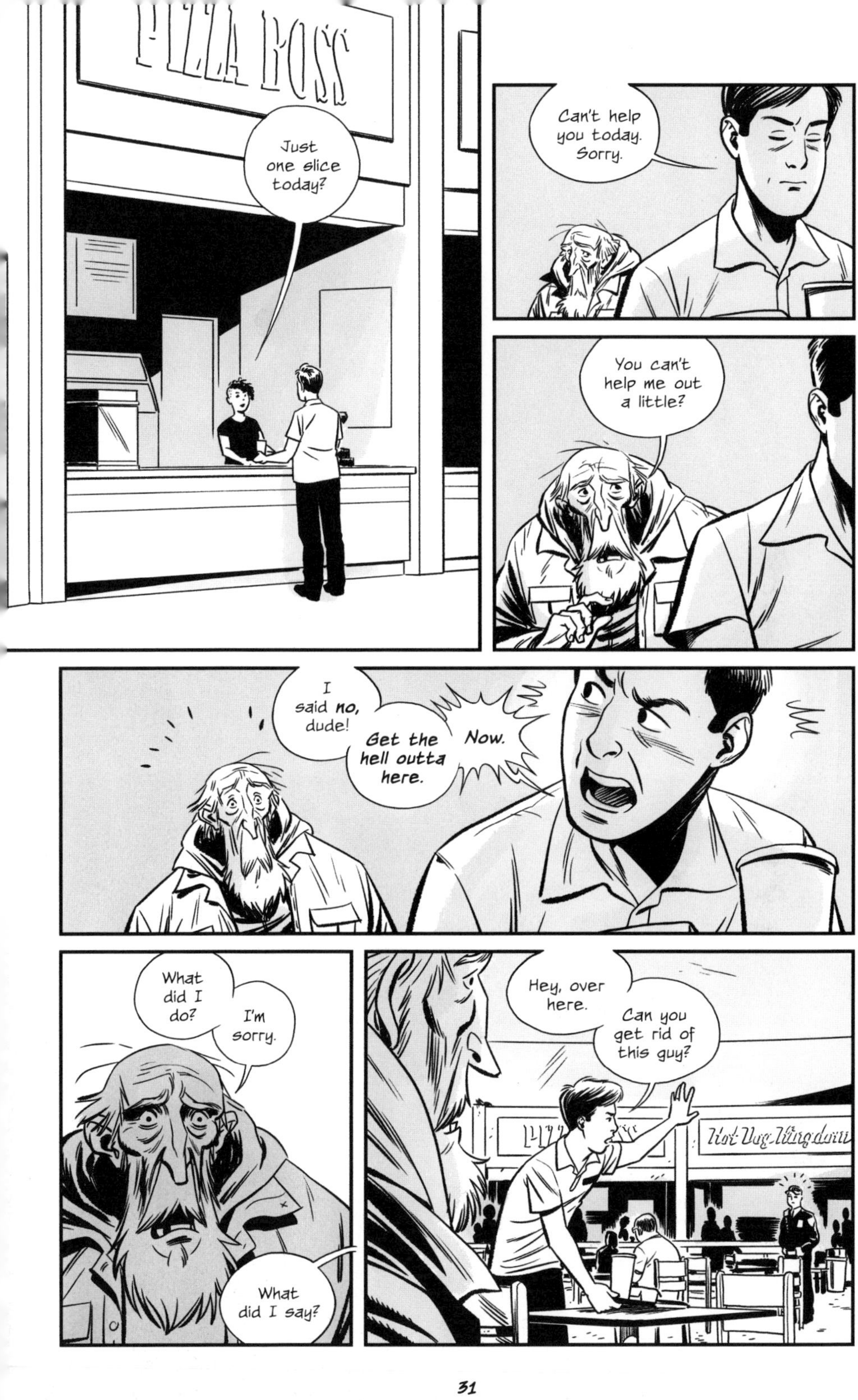
PIZZA BOSS
Just one slice today?
Can't help you today. Sorry.
You can't help me out a little?
I said **no**, dude!
Get the hell outta here.
Now.
What did I do?
I'm sorry.
What did I say?
Hey, over here.
Can you get rid of this guy?
Hot Dog Kingdom

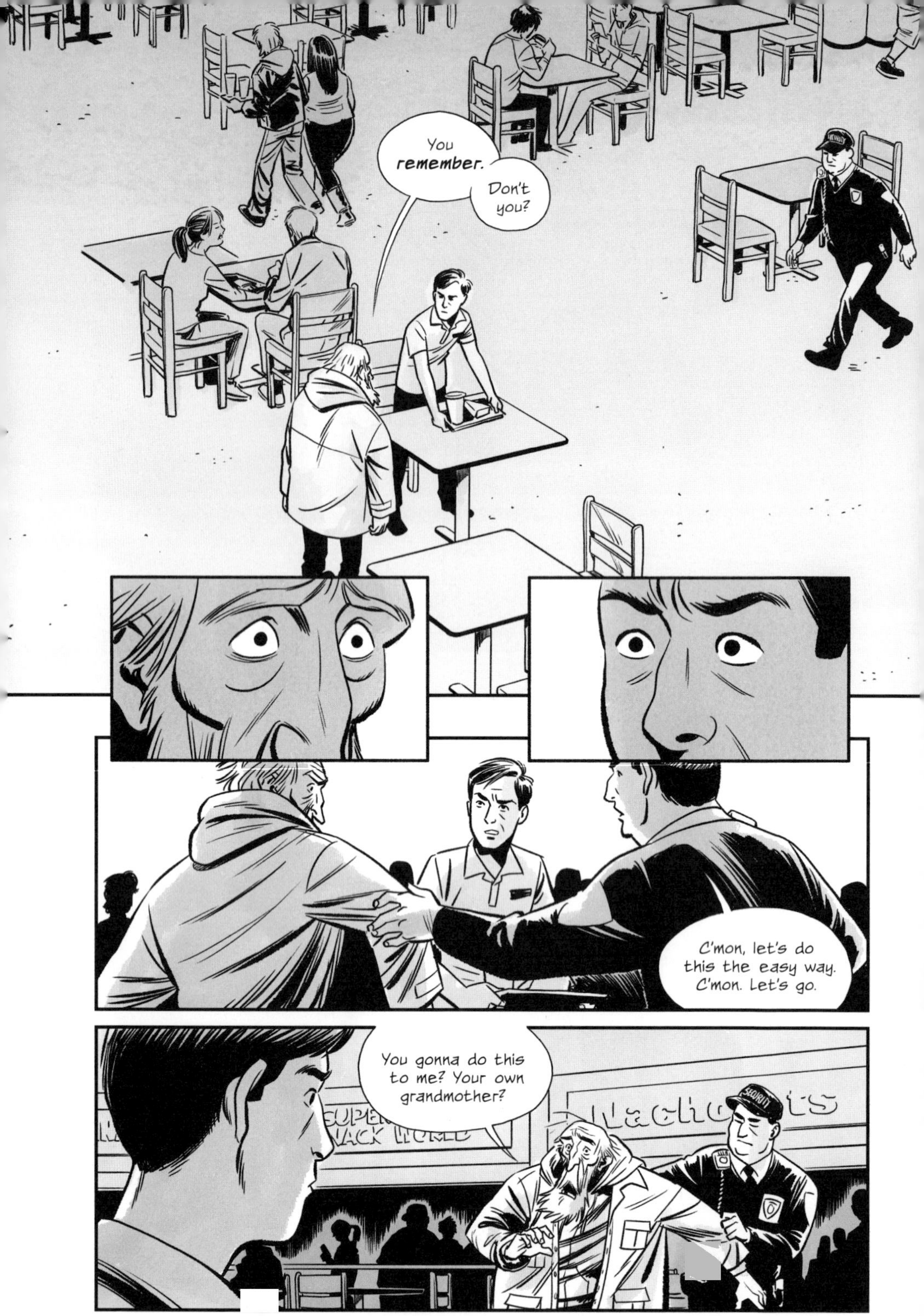
You remember.
Don't you?
C'mon, let's do this the easy way. C'mon. Let's go.
You gonna do this to me? Your own grandmother?
SECURITY

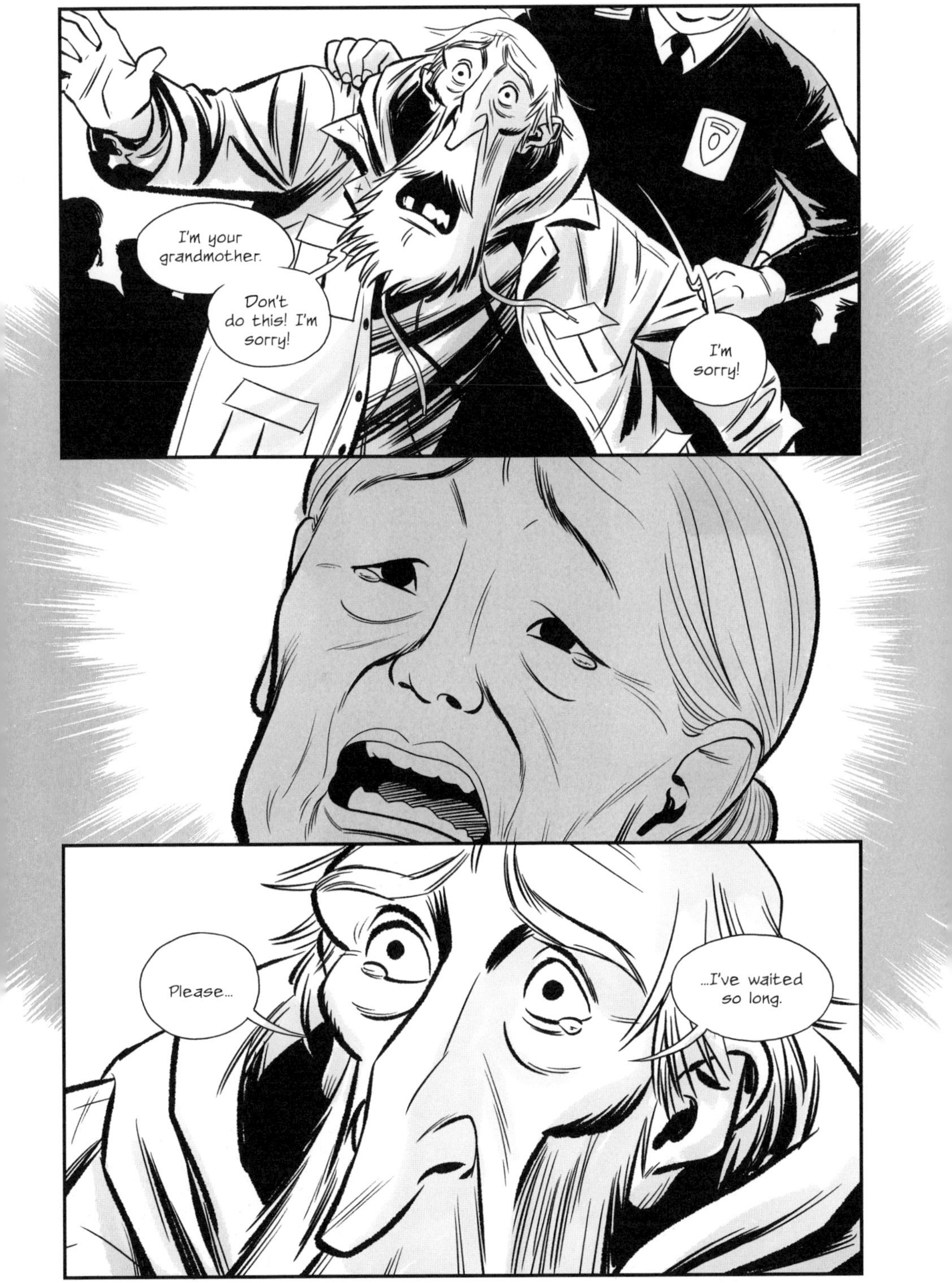
I'm your grandmother.
Don't do this! I'm sorry!
I'm sorry!
Please...
...I've waited so long.

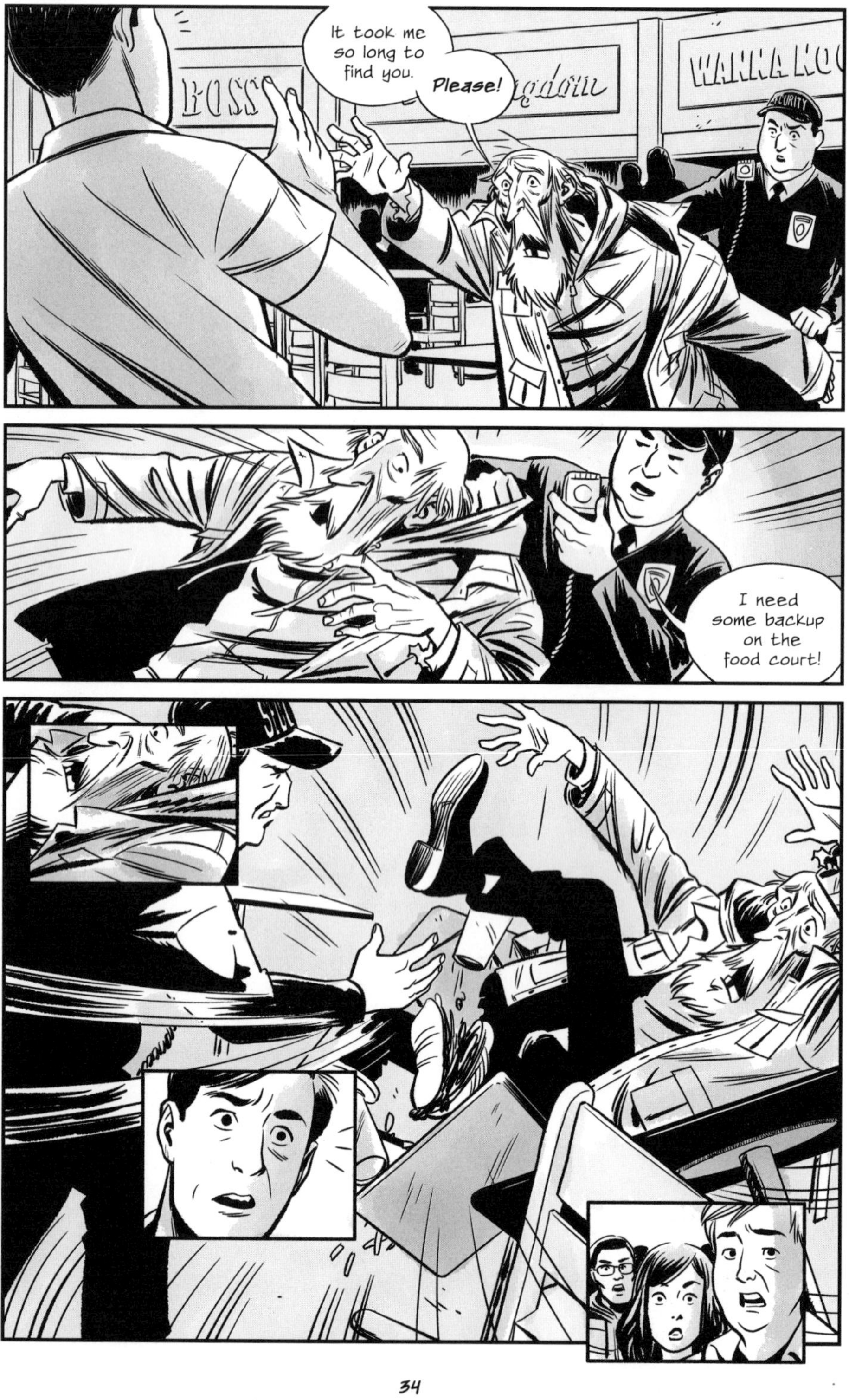
It took me so long to find you.
Please!
I need some backup on the food court!

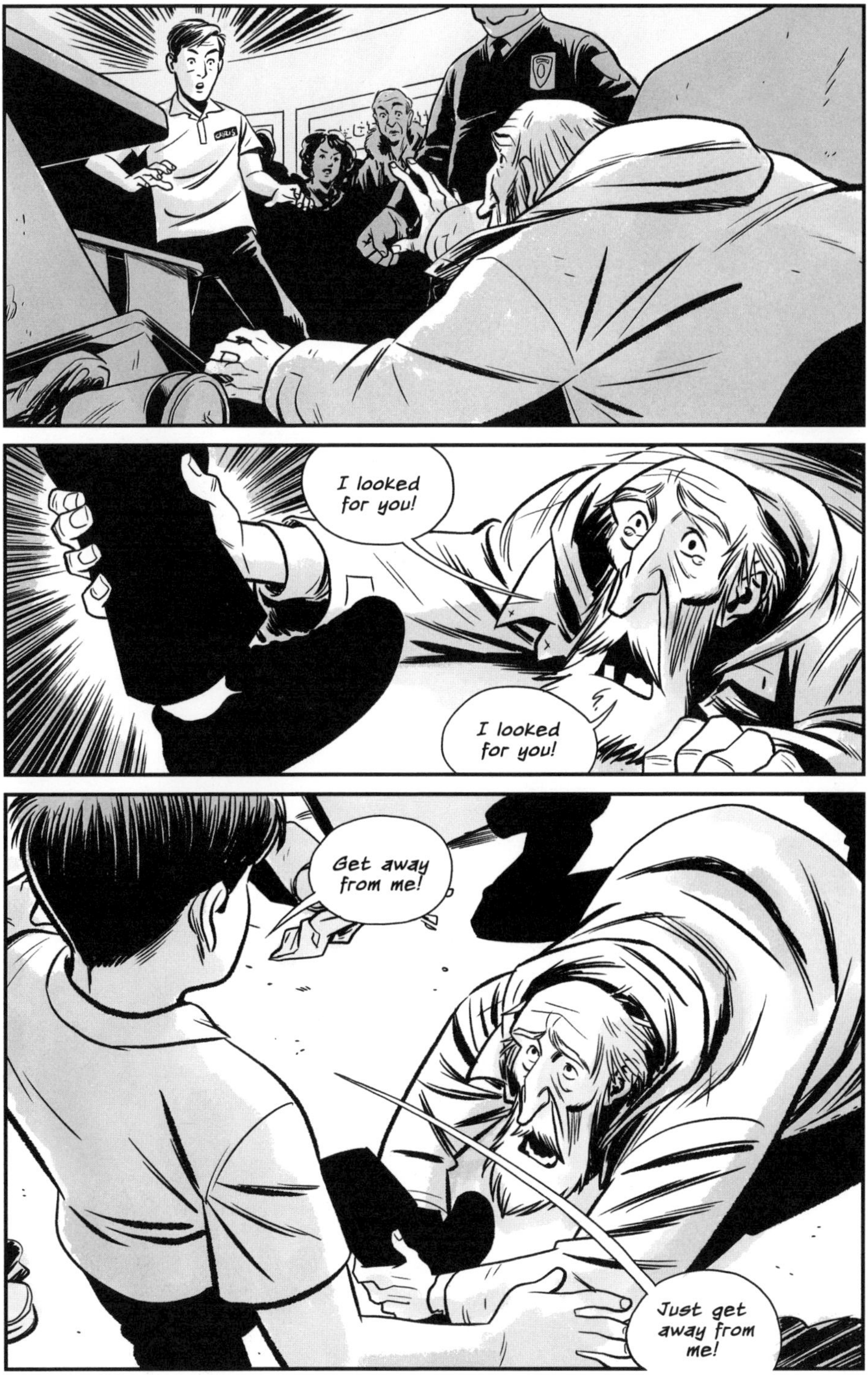
I looked for you!
I looked for you!
Get away from me!
Just get away from me!

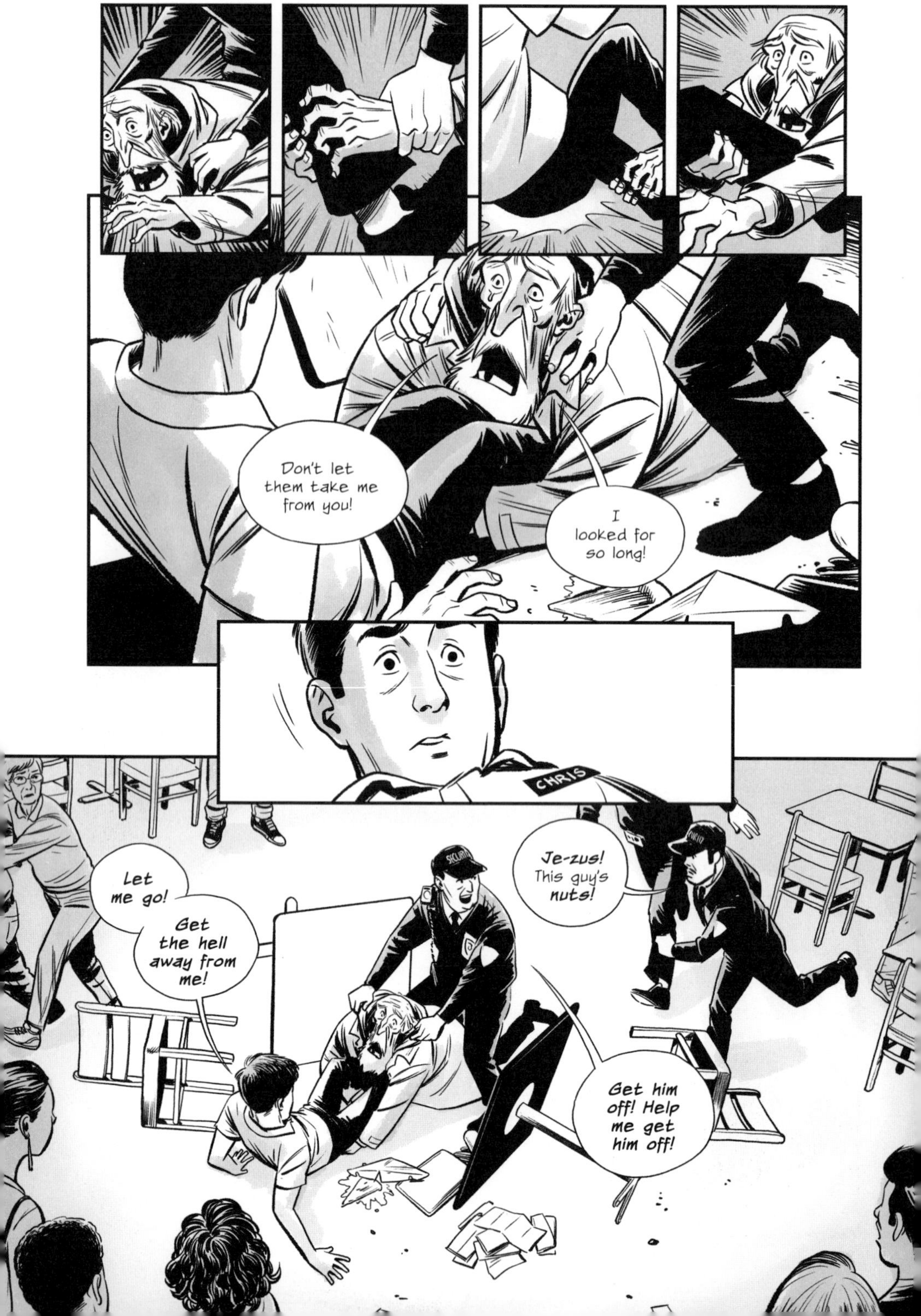
Don't let them take me from you!
I looked for so long!
CHRIS
Let me go!
Get the hell away from me!
Je-zus! This guy's nuts!
Get him off! Help me get him off!

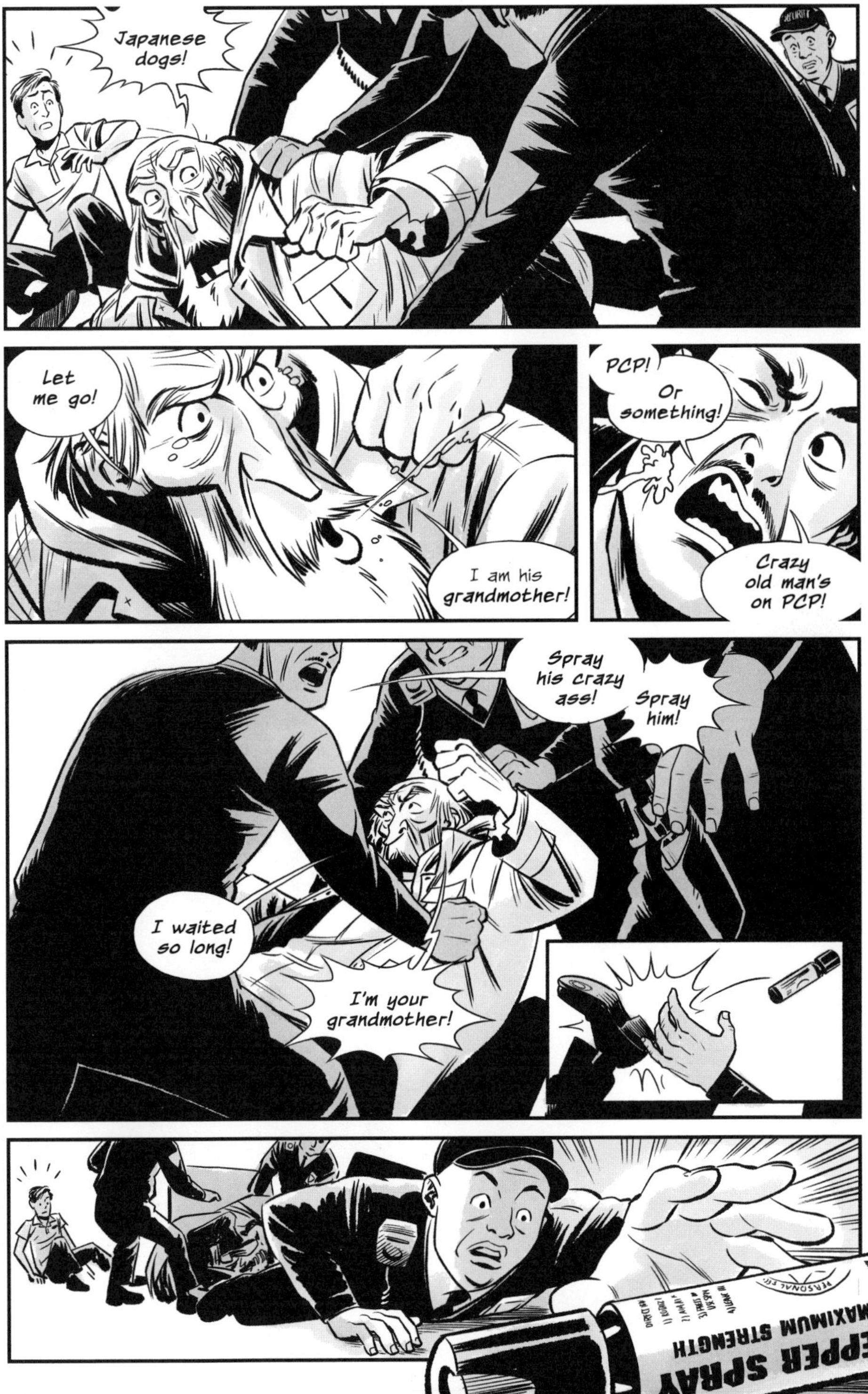
Japanese dogs!
Let me go!
I am his grandmother!
PCP!
Or something!
Crazy old man's on PCP!
Spray his crazy ass!
Spray him!
I waited so long!
I'm your grandmother!
PEPPER SPRAY
MAXIMUM STRENGTH

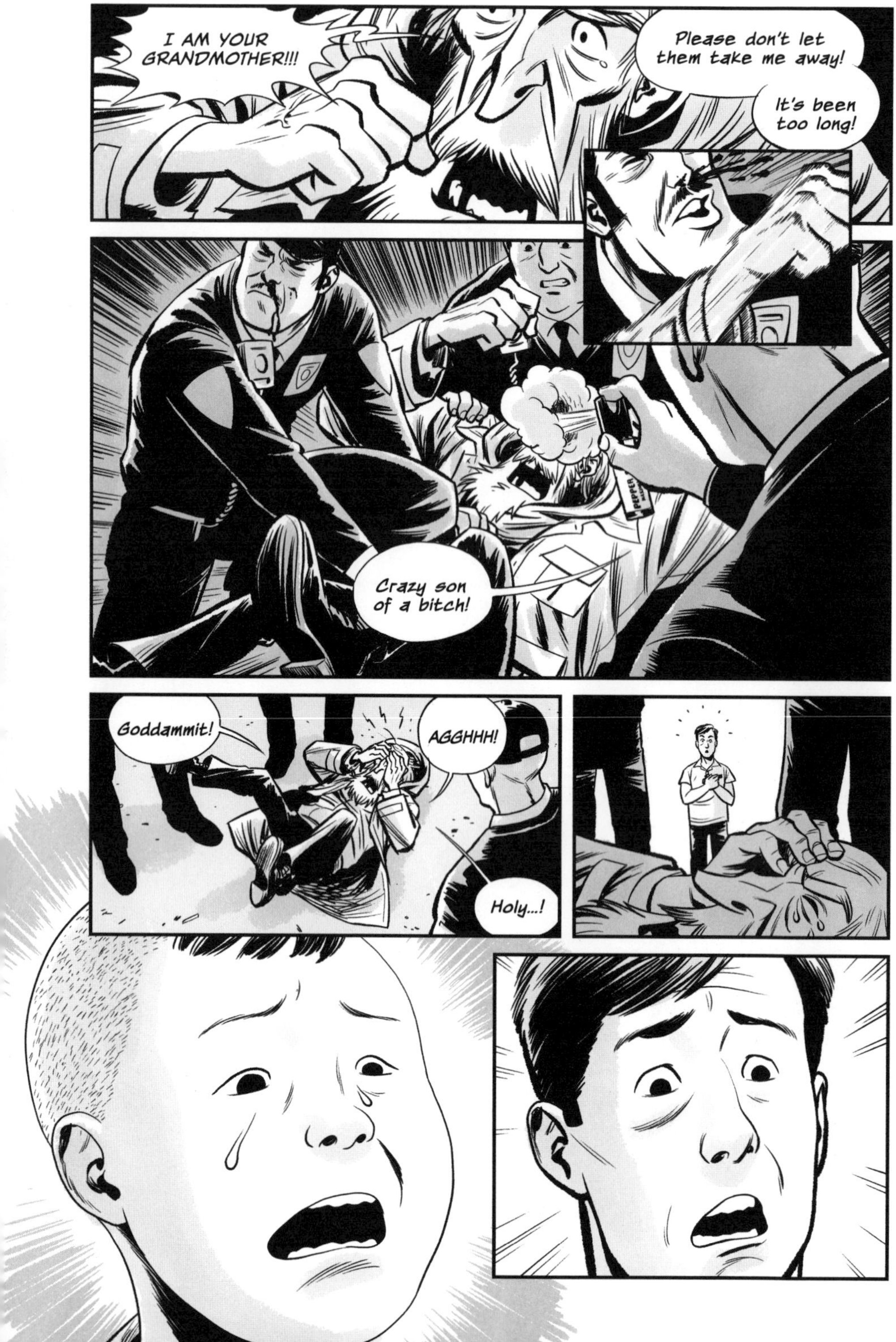
I AM YOUR GRANDMOTHER!!!
Please don't let them take me away!
It's been too long!
Crazy son of a bitch!
Goddammit!
AGGHHH!
Holy...!

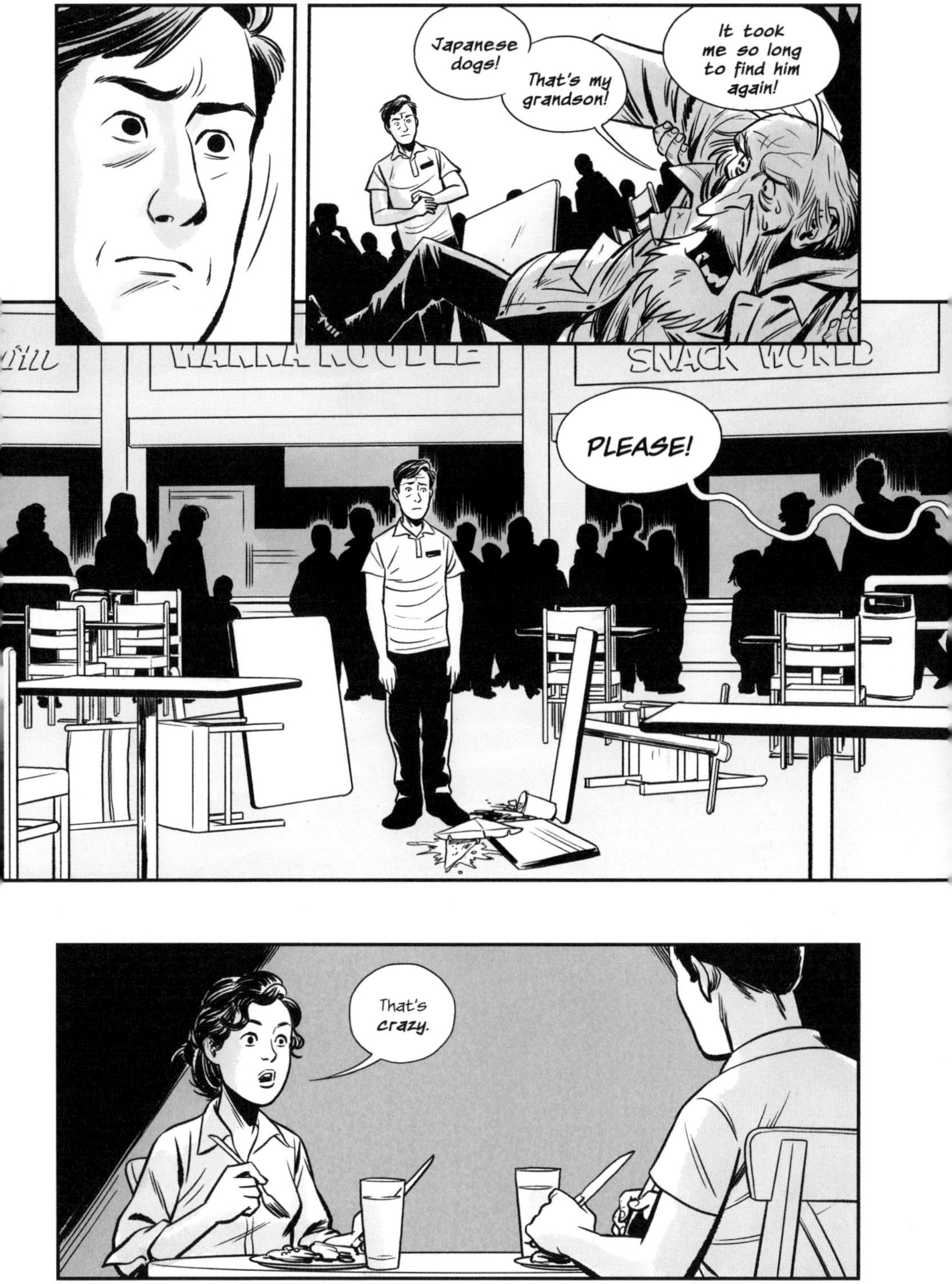
Japanese dogs!
That's my grandson!
It took me so long to find him again!
SNACK WORLD
PLEASE!
That's crazy.

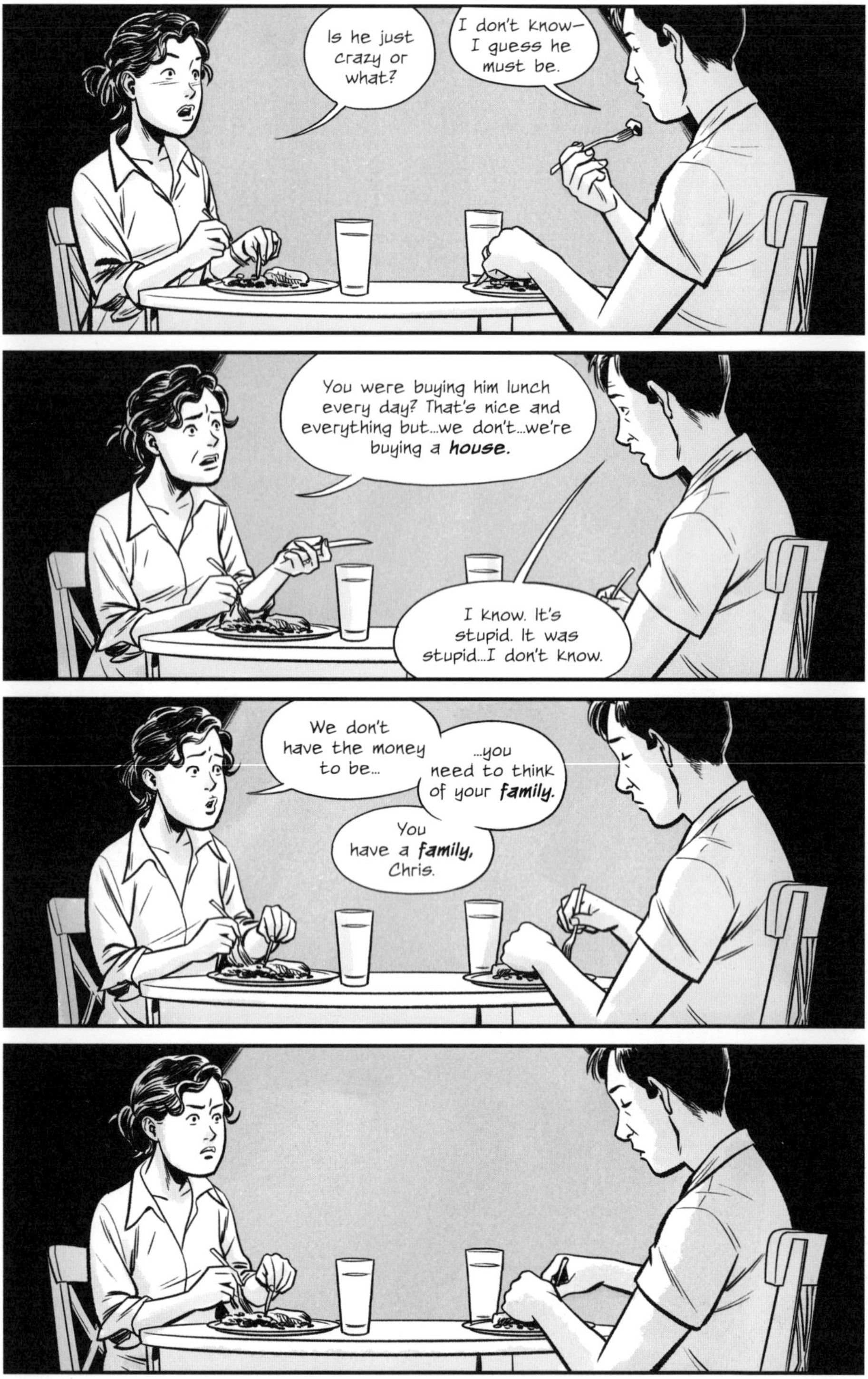
Is he just crazy or what?
I don't know— I guess he must be.
You were buying him lunch every day? That's nice and everything but...we don't...we're buying a **house.**
I know. It's stupid. It was stupid...I don't know.
We don't have the money to be...
...you need to think of your **family.**
You have a **family,** Chris.

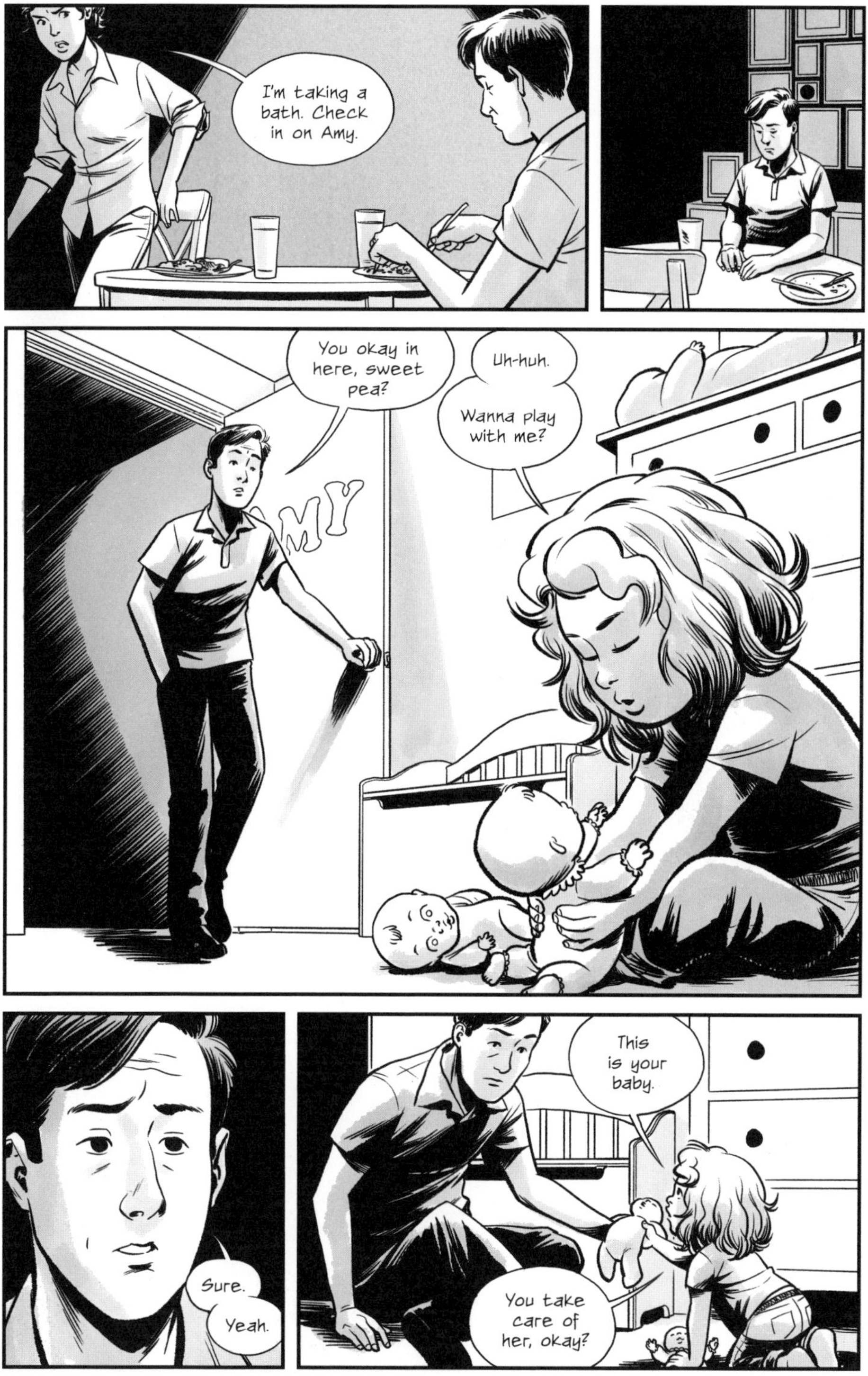
I'm taking a bath. Check in on Amy.
You okay in here, sweet pea?
Uh-huh.
Wanna play with me?
AMY
Sure.
Yeah.
This is your baby.
You take care of her, okay?

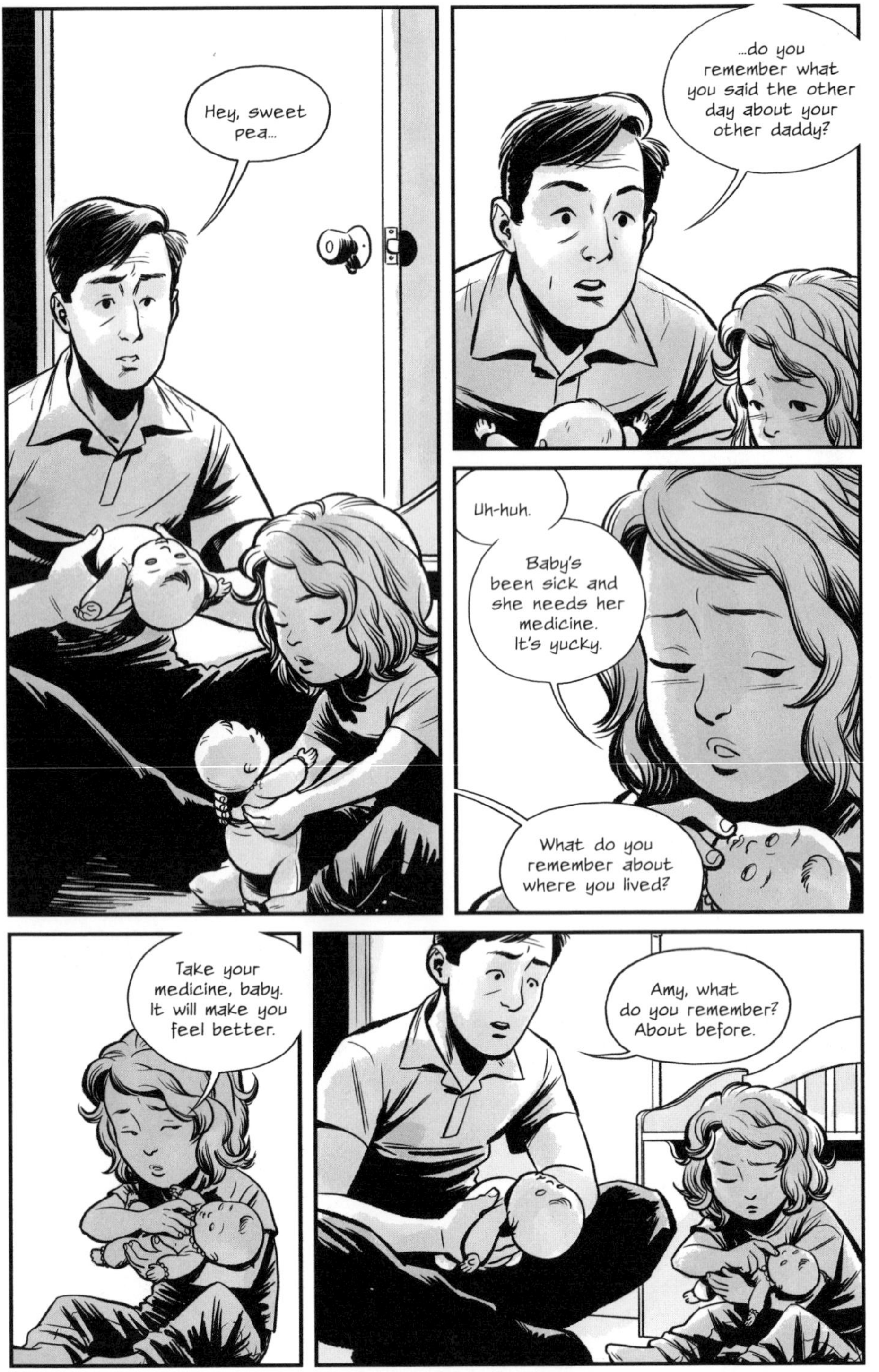
Hey, sweet pea...
...do you remember what you said the other day about your other daddy?
Uh-huh.
Baby's been sick and she needs her medicine. It's yucky.
What do you remember about where you lived?
Take your medicine, baby. It will make you feel better.
Amy, what do you remember? About before.

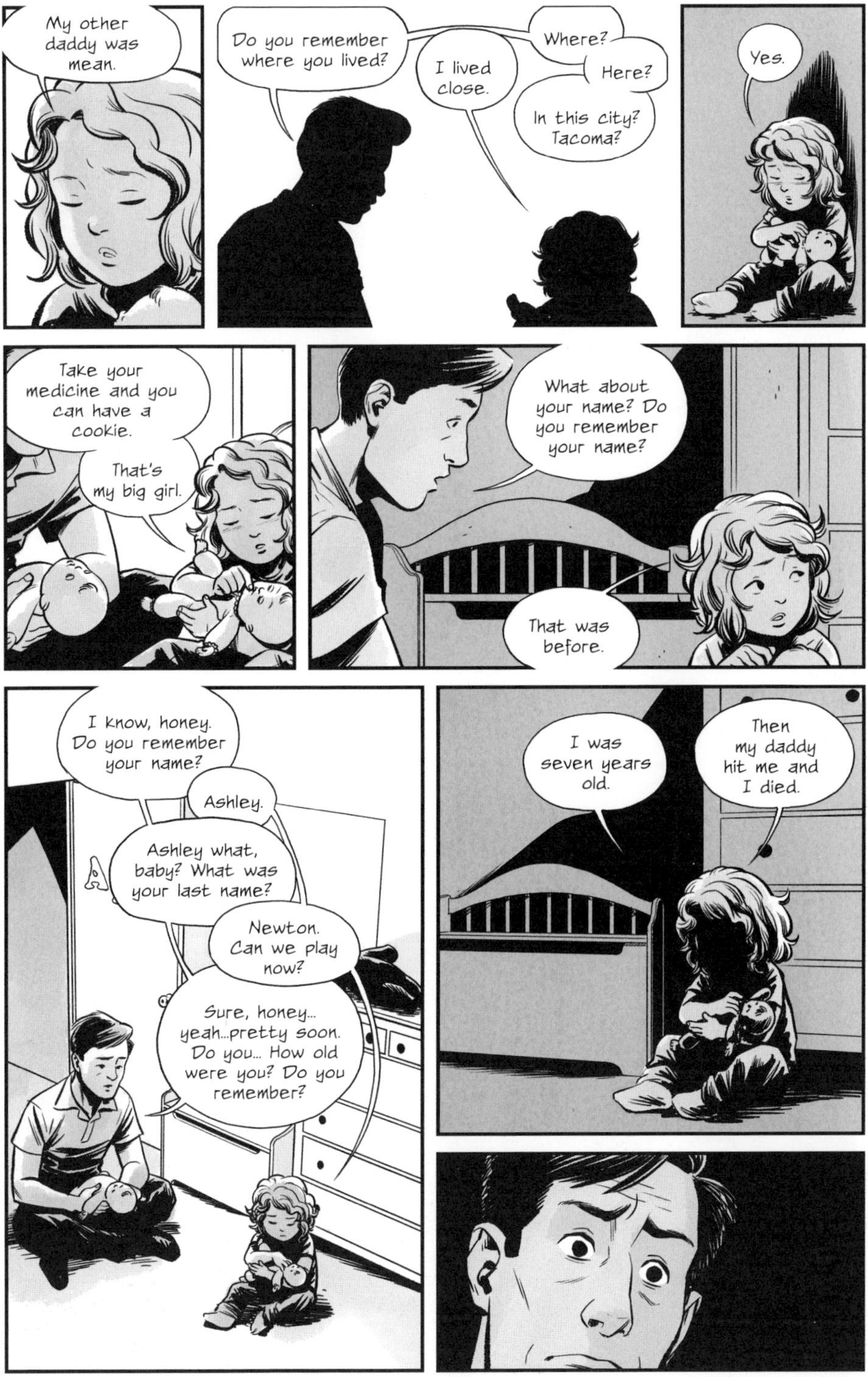
My other daddy was mean.
Do you remember where you lived?
I lived close.
Where?
Here?
In this city? Tacoma?
Yes.
Take your medicine and you can have a cookie.
That's my big girl.
What about your name? Do you remember your name?
That was before.
I know, honey. Do you remember your name?
Ashley.
Ashley what, baby? What was your last name?
Newton. Can we play now?
Sure, honey... yeah...pretty soon. Do you... How old were you? Do you remember?
I was seven years old.
Then my daddy hit me and I died.

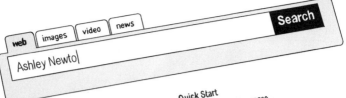

doggle

web | images | video | news | Search

Ashley Newton|

Quick Start
Make Doggle Your Homepage

even-Year-Old Girl Murdered by Father
ttps://frontpage.tacomajournalonline.com/news/518712578/sev…
ACOMA—The trial of Jeffrey Newton concluded today…accused of the murder of hi
aughter, Ashley Newton, 7…police testimony, along with witnesses,led the jury to c

Ashley Newton Murder: New Appeal Moves Forward
https://washingtoncrimereport.org/cs-content/223645
District Court Judge Anneke Bellows today…Ashley Newton, who was just seven
at the time. Judge Bellows allowed Mr. Newton's defense to provide new evidenc

Jeffrey Newton, Convicted of Murdering His Daughter, Found D
https://tacomajournalonline.com/news/63287459/jeffrey-newt…
Convicted of the murder of his daughter, Ashley Newton, 7, Jeffrey Newton h
cy Medical Providers responded quickly, but were not in time to save

Case

You coming to bed, honey?

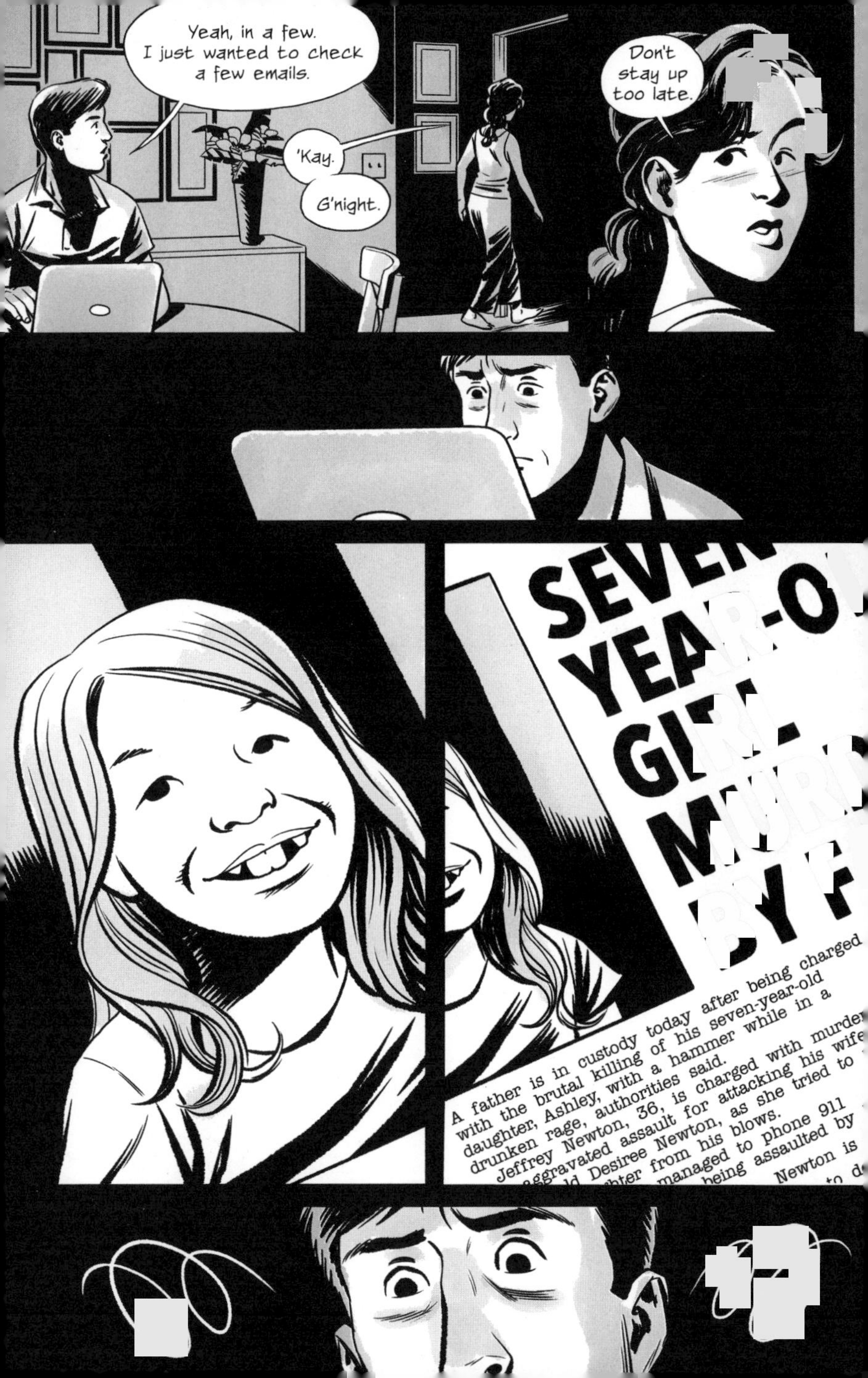

Yeah, in a few. I just wanted to check a few emails.
Don't stay up too late.
'Kay.
G'night.
A father is in custody today after being charged
with the brutal killing of his seven-year-old
daughter, Ashley, with a hammer while in a
drunken rage, authorities said.
Jeffrey Newton, 36, is charged with murder
aggravated assault for attacking his wife
Desiree Newton, as she tried to
from his blows.
managed to phone 911
being assaulted by
Newton is

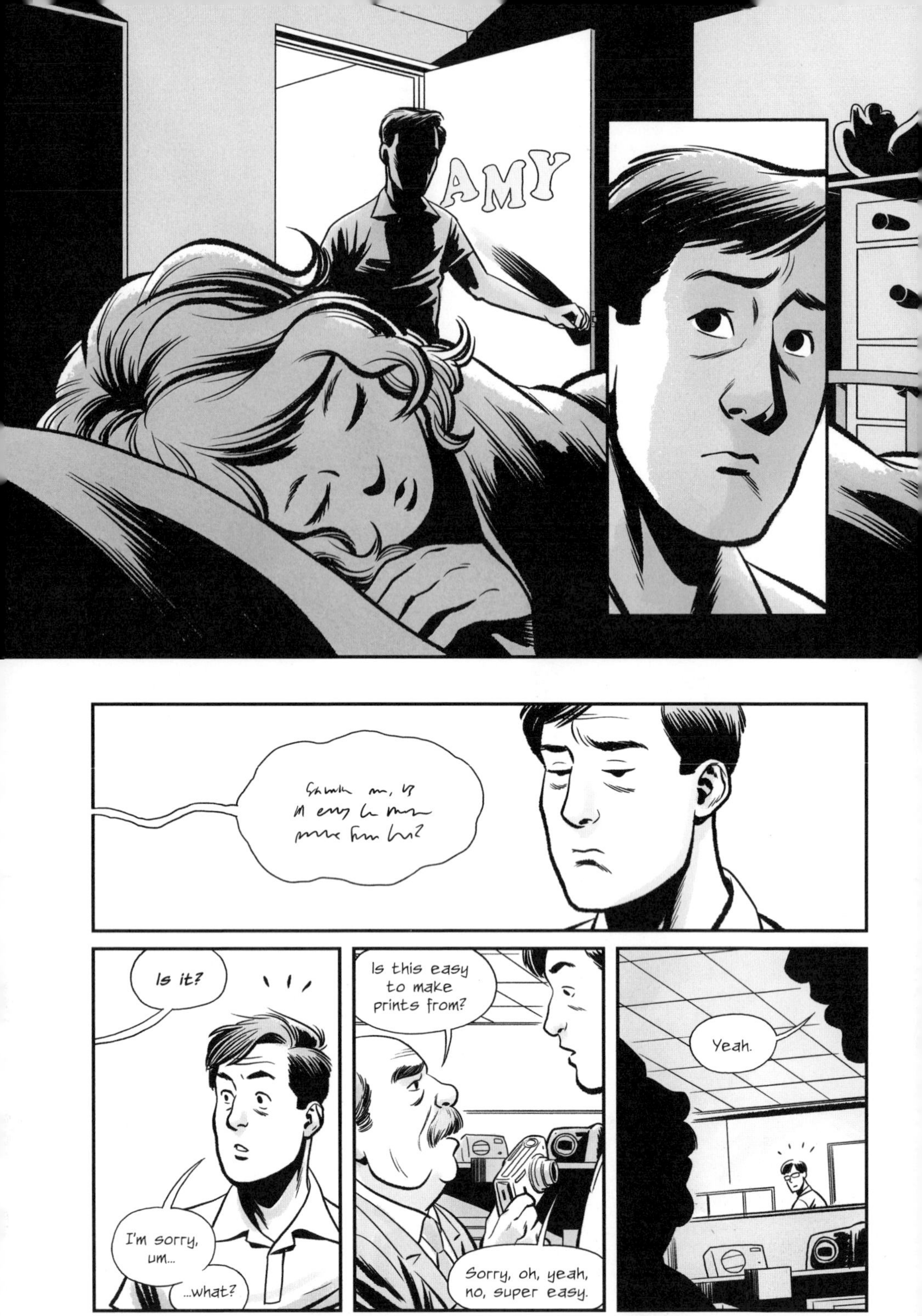
AMY
Is it?
I'm sorry, um...
...what?
Is this easy to make prints from?
Sorry, oh, yeah, no, super easy.
Yeah.

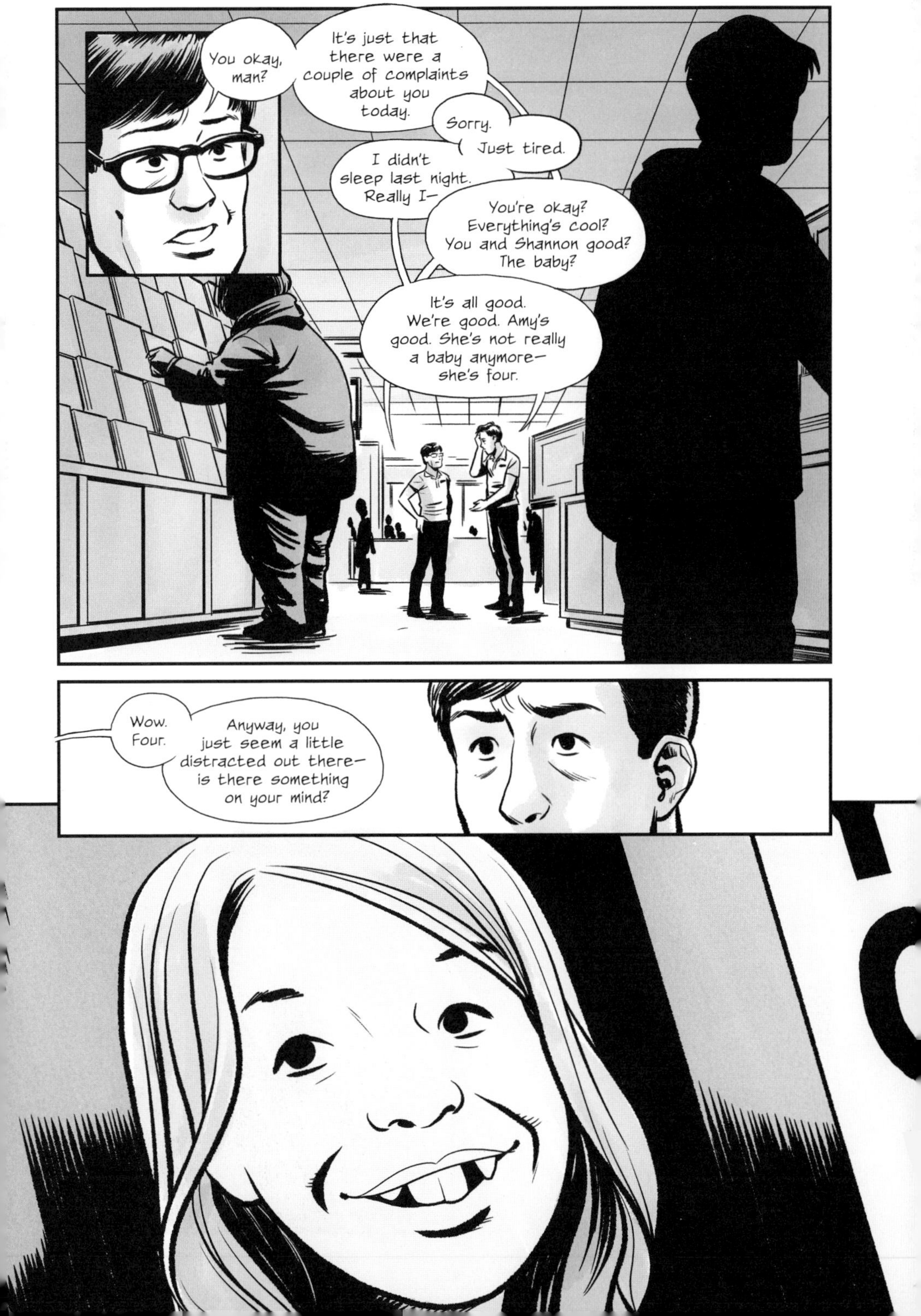
You okay, man?
It's just that there were a couple of complaints about you today.
Sorry.
Just tired.
I didn't sleep last night. Really I—
You're okay? Everything's cool? You and Shannon good? The baby?
It's all good. We're good. Amy's good. She's not really a baby anymore— she's four.
Wow. Four.
Anyway, you just seem a little distracted out there— is there something on your mind?

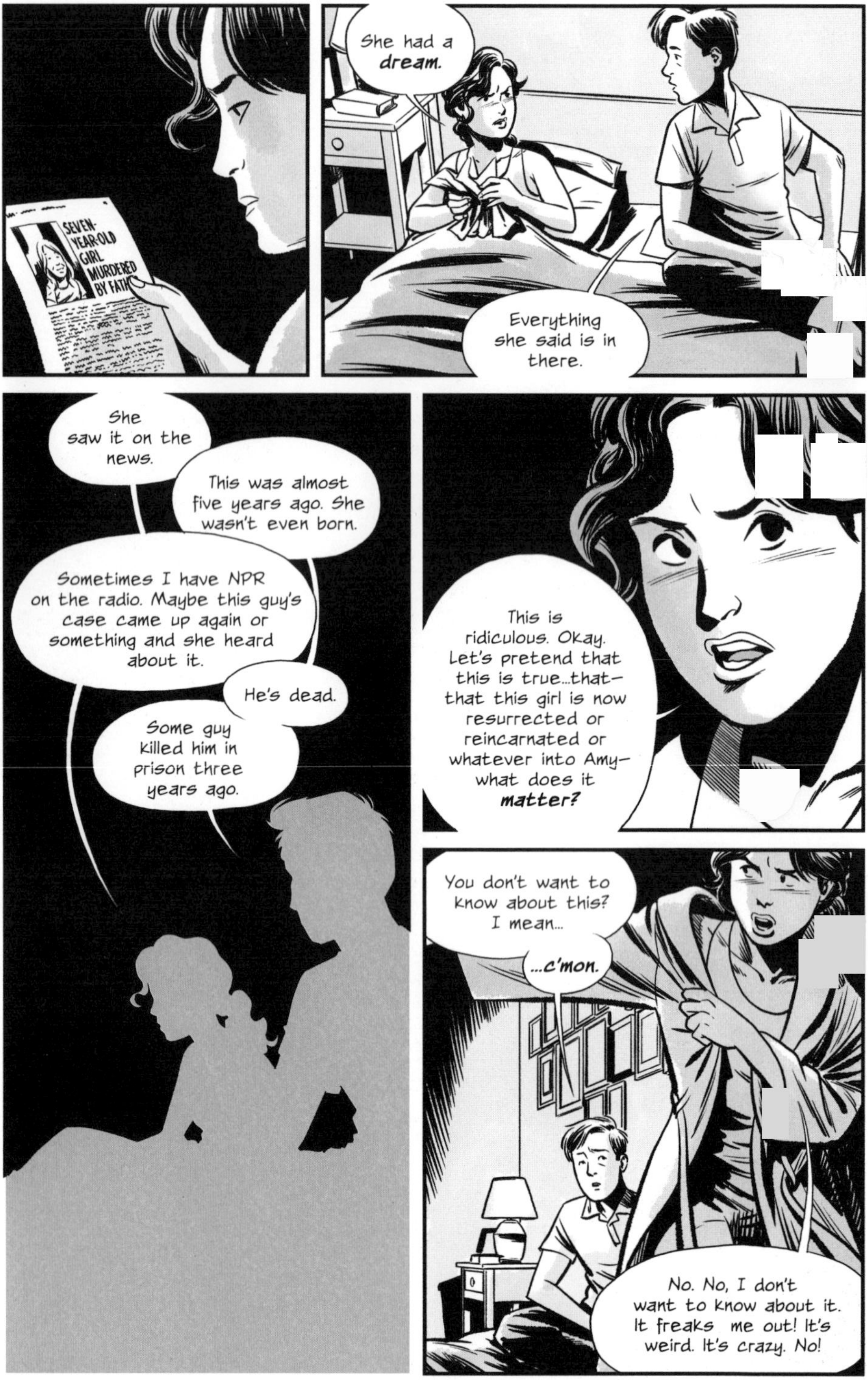
SEVEN-YEAR-OLD GIRL MURDERED BY FATH
She had a **dream.**
Everything she said is in there.
She saw it on the news.
This was almost five years ago. She wasn't even born.
Sometimes I have NPR on the radio. Maybe this guy's case came up again or something and she heard about it.
He's dead.
Some guy killed him in prison three years ago.
This is ridiculous. Okay. Let's pretend that this is true...that—that this girl is now resurrected or reincarnated or whatever into Amy—what does it ***matter?***
You don't want to know about this? I mean...
...c'mon.
No. No, I don't want to know about it. It freaks me out! It's weird. It's crazy. No!

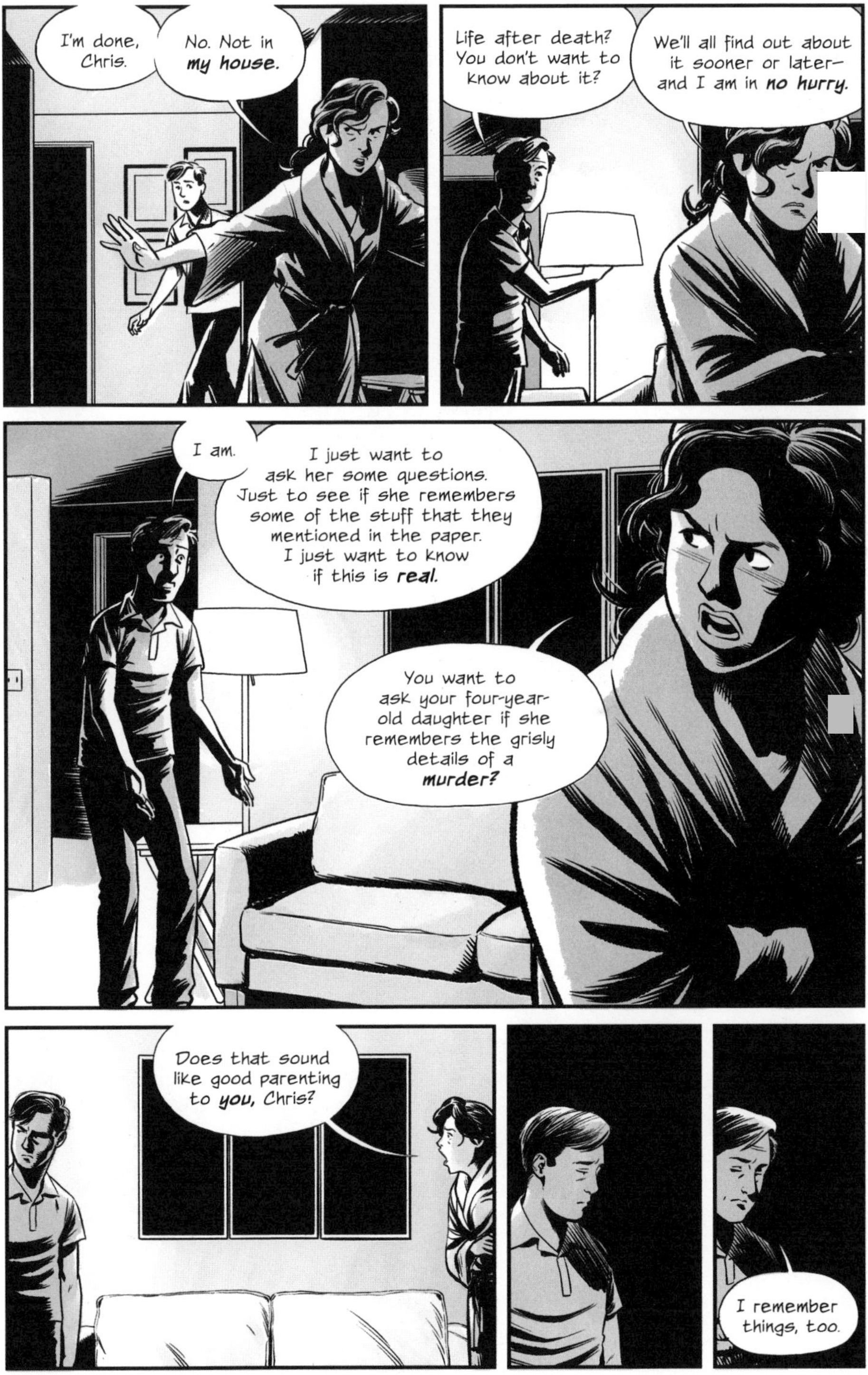
I'm done, Chris.
No. Not in **my house.**
Life after death? You don't want to know about it?
We'll all find out about it sooner or later— and I am in **no hurry.**
I am.
I just want to ask her some questions. Just to see if she remembers some of the stuff that they mentioned in the paper. I just want to know if this is **real.**
You want to ask your four-year-old daughter if she remembers the grisly details of a **murder?**
Does that sound like good parenting to **you,** Chris?
I remember things, too.

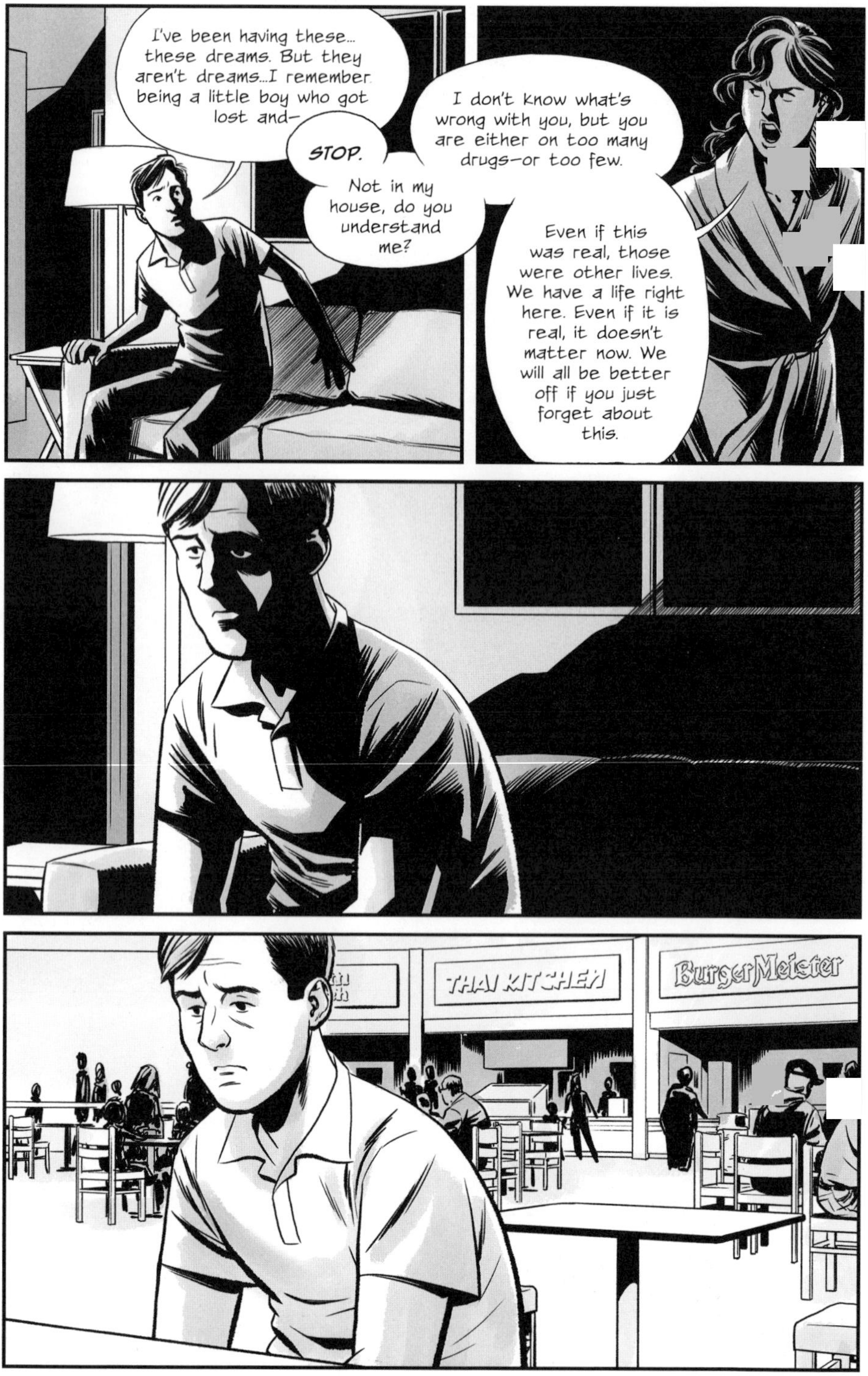
I've been having these... these dreams. But they aren't dreams...I remember being a little boy who got lost and—
STOP.
Not in my house, do you understand me?
I don't know what's wrong with you, but you are either on too many drugs—or too few.
Even if this was real, those were other lives. We have a life right here. Even if it is real, it doesn't matter now. We will all be better off if you just forget about this.
THAI KITCHEN
BurgerMeister

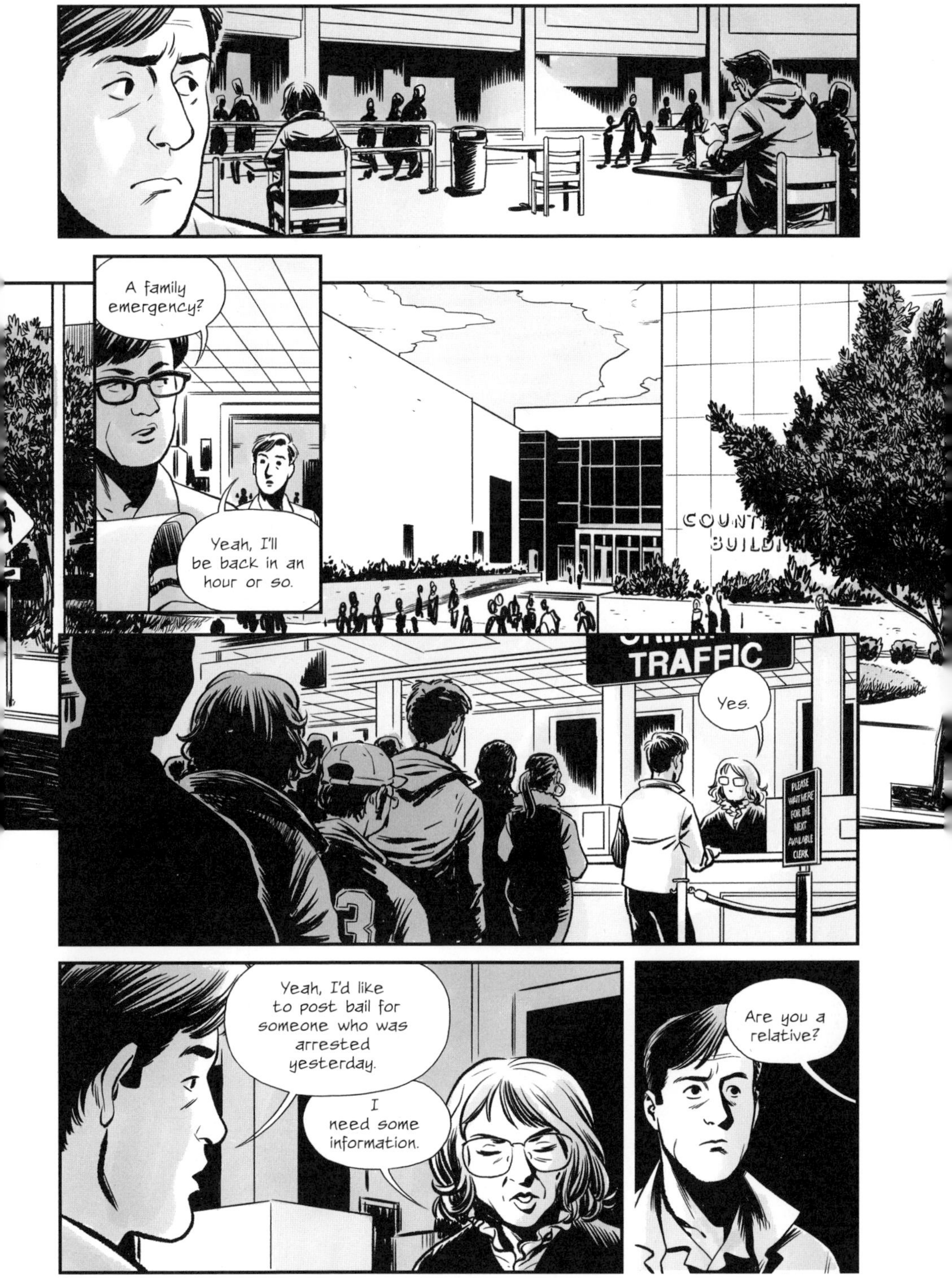
A family emergency?
Yeah, I'll be back in an hour or so.
TRAFFIC
Yes.
PLEASE WAIT HERE FOR THE NEXT AVAILABLE CLERK
Yeah, I'd like to post bail for someone who was arrested yesterday.
I need some information.
Are you a relative?

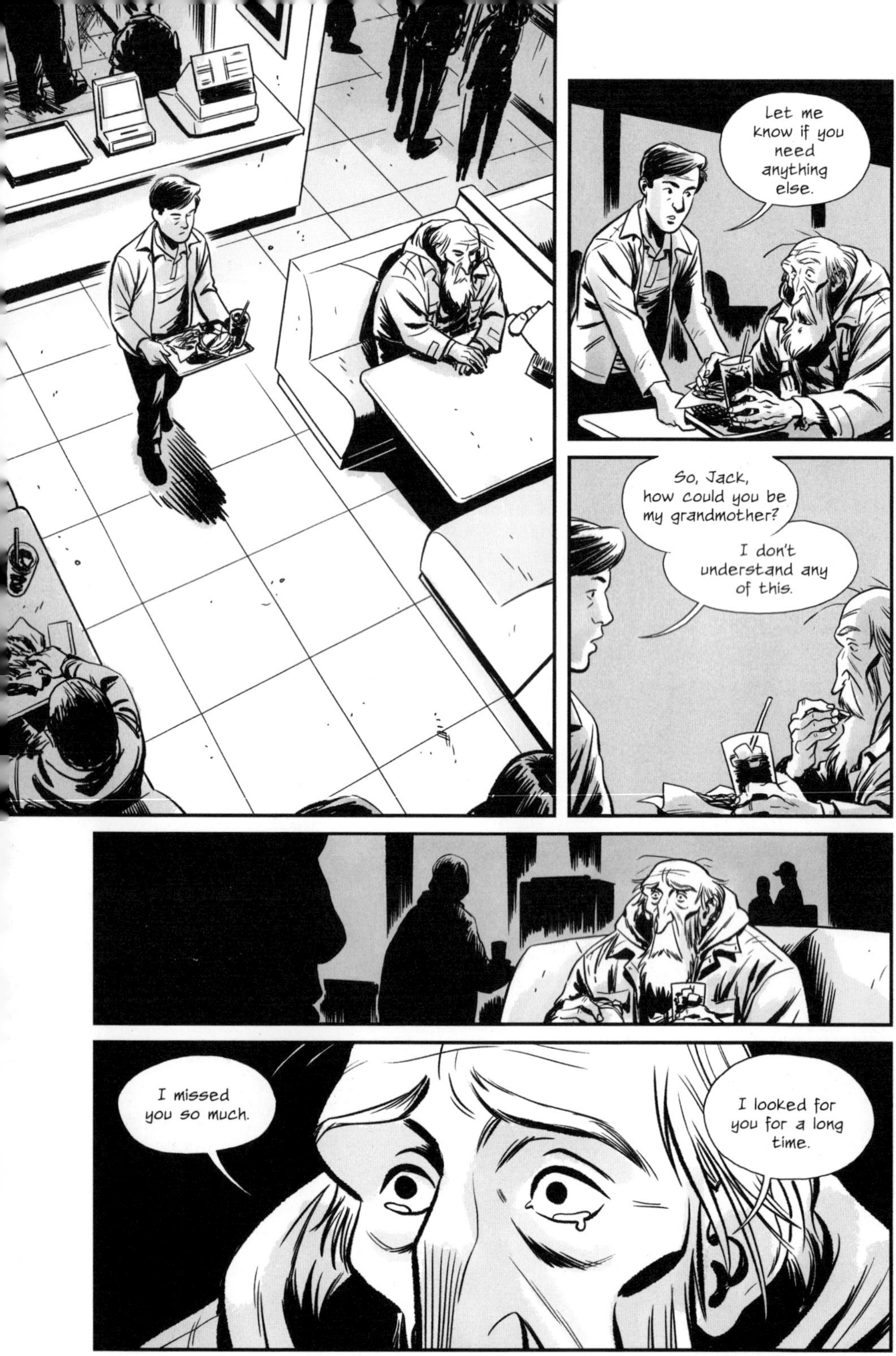
Let me know if you need anything else.
So, Jack, how could you be my grandmother?
I don't understand any of this.
I missed you so much.
I looked for you for a long time.

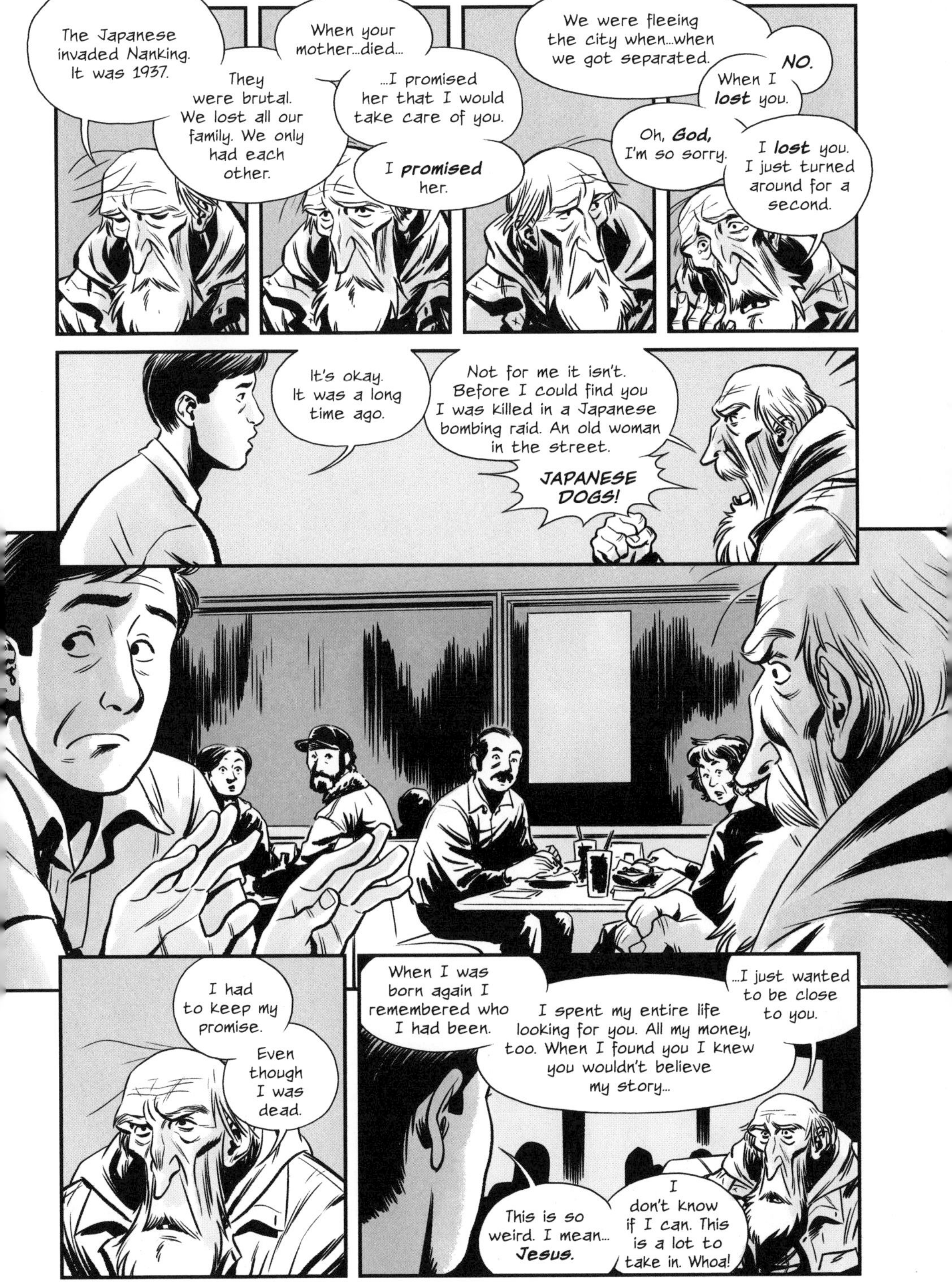
The Japanese invaded Nanking. It was 1937.
They were brutal. We lost all our family. We only had each other.
When your mother...died...
...I promised her that I would take care of you.
I **promised** her.
We were fleeing the city when...when we got separated.
NO.
When I **lost** you.
Oh, **God,** I'm so sorry.
I **lost** you. I just turned around for a second.
It's okay. It was a long time ago.
Not for me it isn't. Before I could find you I was killed in a Japanese bombing raid. An old woman in the street.
JAPANESE DOGS!
I had to keep my promise.
Even though I was dead.
When I was born again I remembered who I had been.
I spent my entire life looking for you. All my money, too. When I found you I knew you wouldn't believe my story...
...I just wanted to be close to you.
This is so weird. I mean... **Jesus.**
I don't know if I can. This is a lot to take in. Whoa!

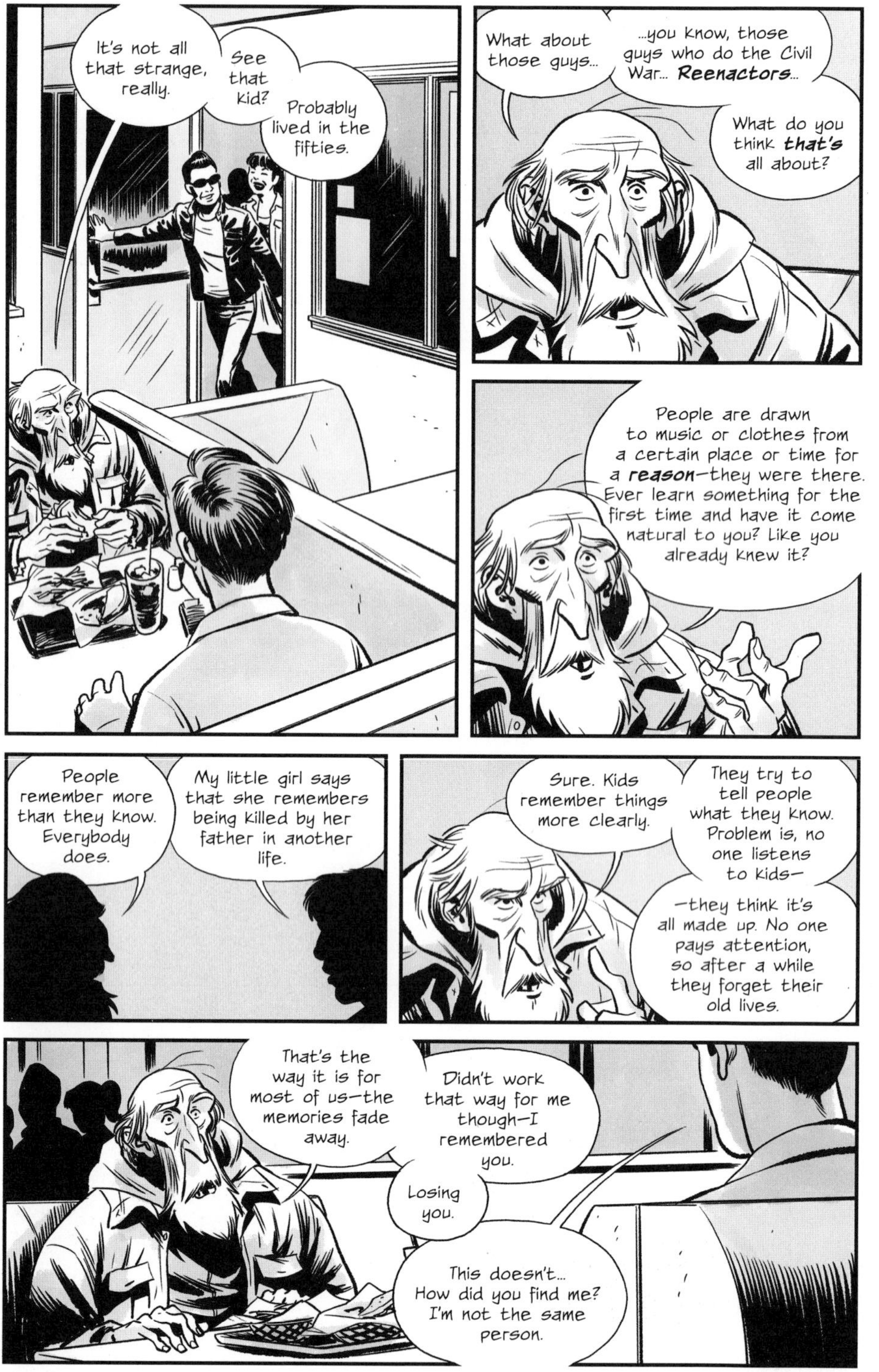
It's not all that strange, really.
See that kid?
Probably lived in the fifties.
What about those guys...
...you know, those guys who do the Civil War... **Reenactors**...
What do you think **that's** all about?
People are drawn to music or clothes from a certain place or time for a **reason**—they were there. Ever learn something for the first time and have it come natural to you? Like you already knew it?
People remember more than they know. Everybody does.
My little girl says that she remembers being killed by her father in another life.
Sure. Kids remember things more clearly.
They try to tell people what they know. Problem is, no one listens to kids—
—they think it's all made up. No one pays attention, so after a while they forget their old lives.
That's the way it is for most of us—the memories fade away.
Didn't work that way for me though—I remembered you.
Losing you.
This doesn't... How did you find me? I'm not the same person.

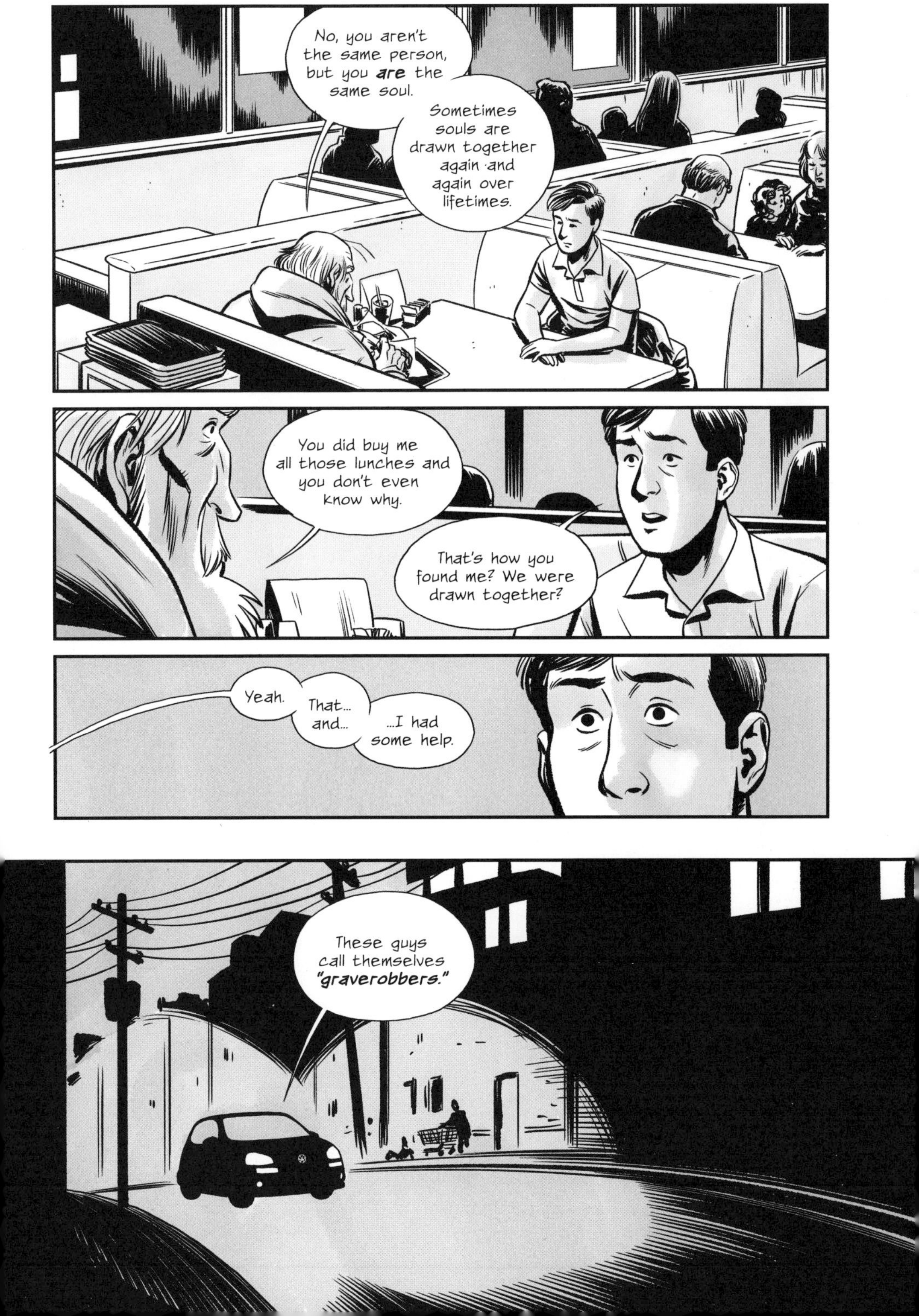
No, you aren't the same person, but you **are** the same soul.
Sometimes souls are drawn together again and again over lifetimes.
You did buy me all those lunches and you don't even know why.
That's how you found me? We were drawn together?
Yeah.
That... and...
...I had some help.
These guys call themselves ***"graverobbers."***

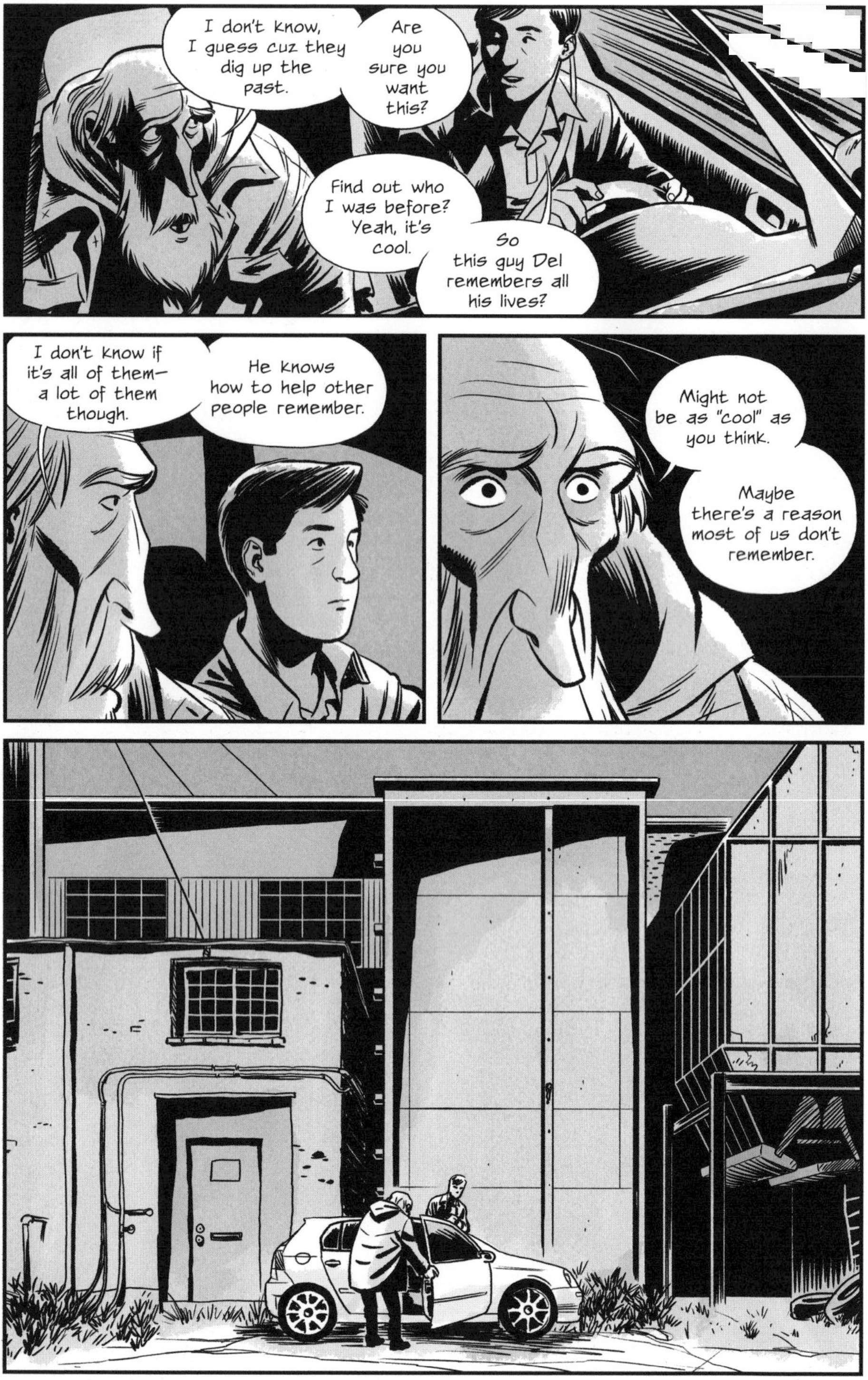
I don't know, I guess cuz they dig up the past.
Are you sure you want this?
Find out who I was before? Yeah, it's cool.
So this guy Del remembers all his lives?
I don't know if it's all of them— a lot of them though.
He knows how to help other people remember.
Might not be as "cool" as you think.
Maybe there's a reason most of us don't remember.

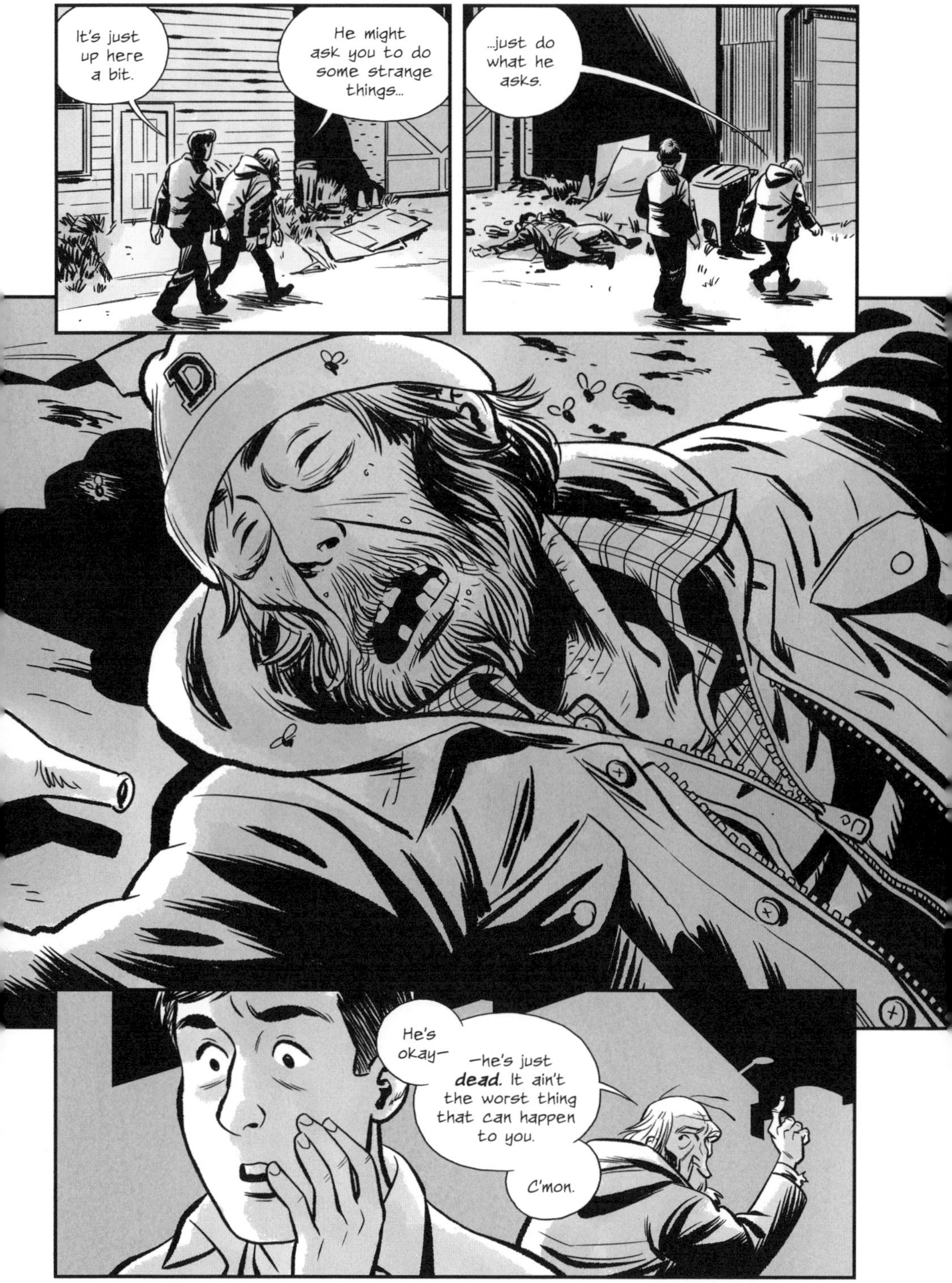
It's just up here a bit.
He might ask you to do some strange things...
...just do what he asks.
He's okay—
—he's just **dead.** It ain't the worst thing that can happen to you.
C'mon.

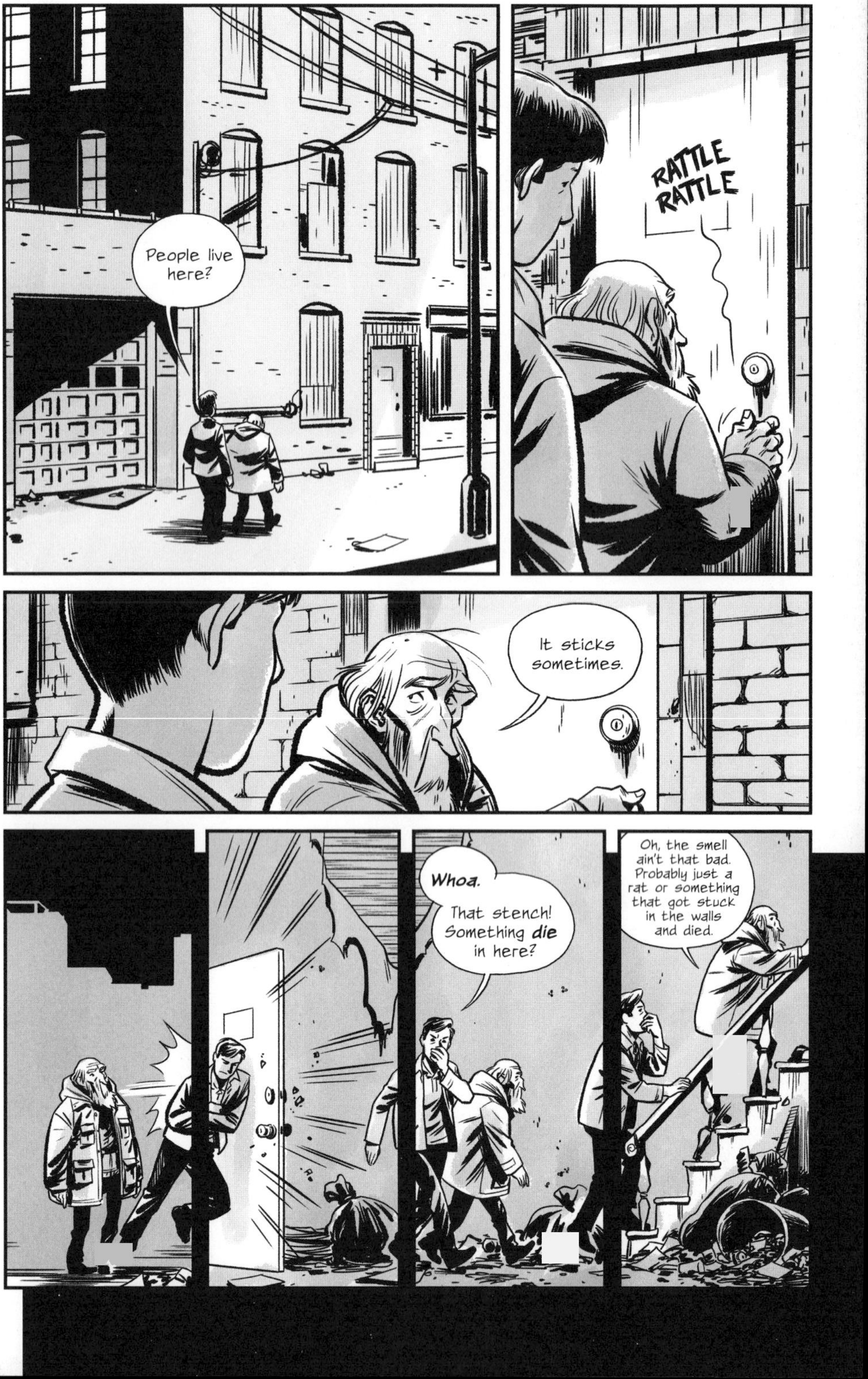

People live here?
RATTLE RATTLE
It sticks sometimes.
Whoa.
That stench! Something *die* in here?
Oh, the smell ain't that bad. Probably just a rat or something that got stuck in the walls and died.

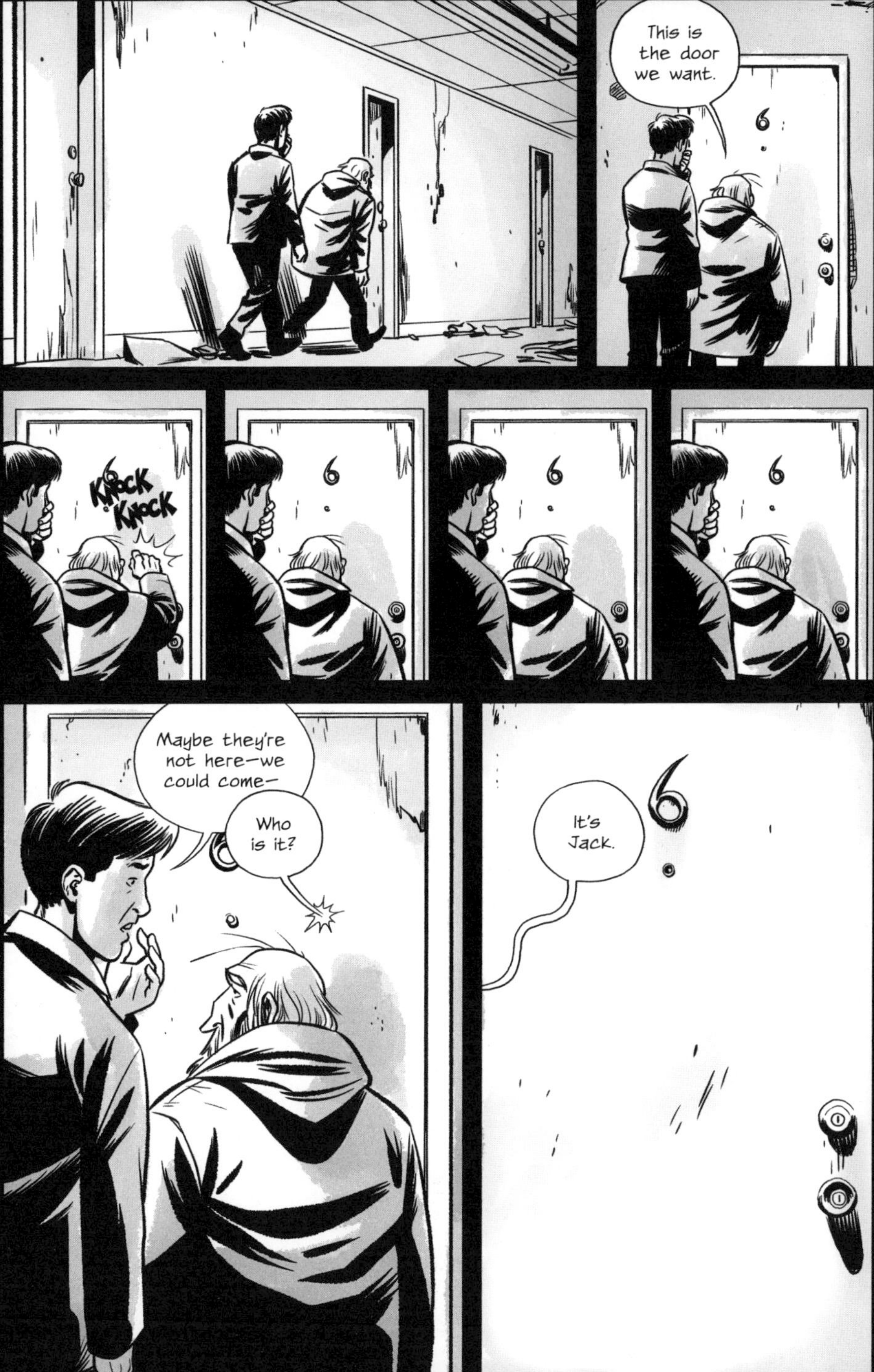
This is the door we want.
KNOCK KNOCK
Maybe they're not here—we could come—
Who is it?
It's Jack.

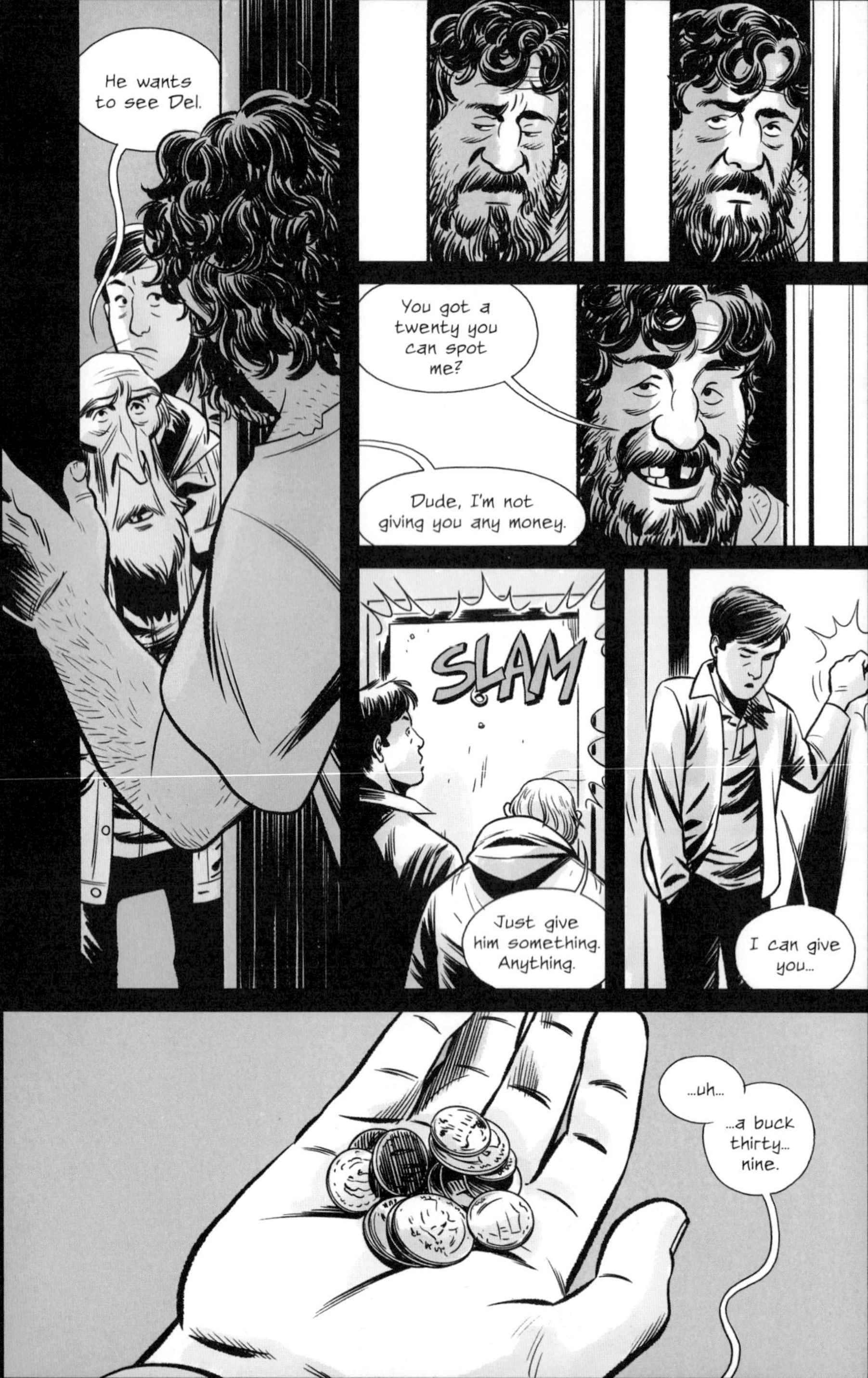
He wants to see Del.
You got a twenty you can spot me?
Dude, I'm not giving you any money.
SLAM
Just give him something. Anything.
I can give you...
...uh...
...a buck thirty... nine.

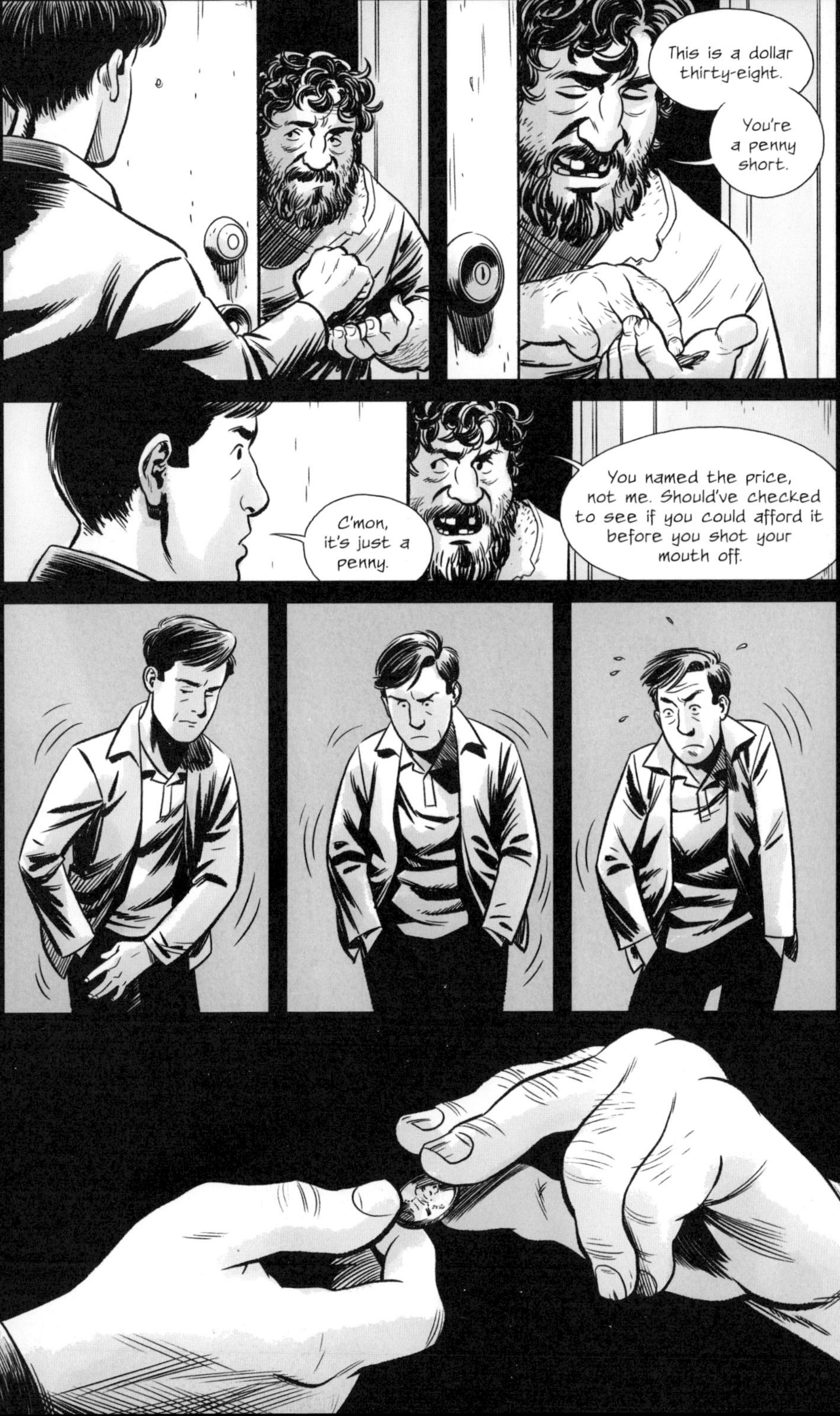
This is a dollar thirty-eight.
You're a penny short.
C'mon, it's just a penny.
You named the price, not me. Should've checked to see if you could afford it before you shot your mouth off.

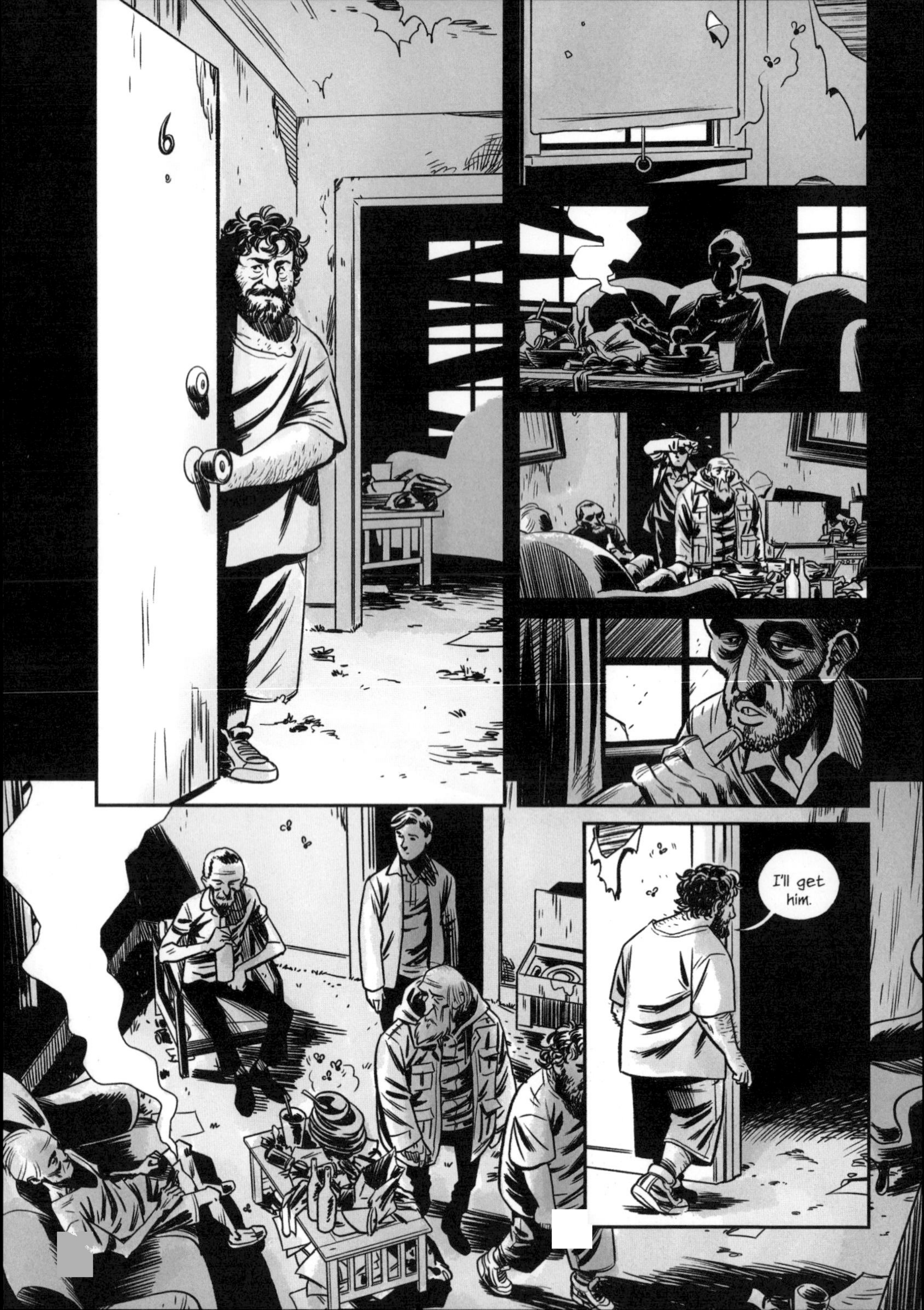
I'll get him.

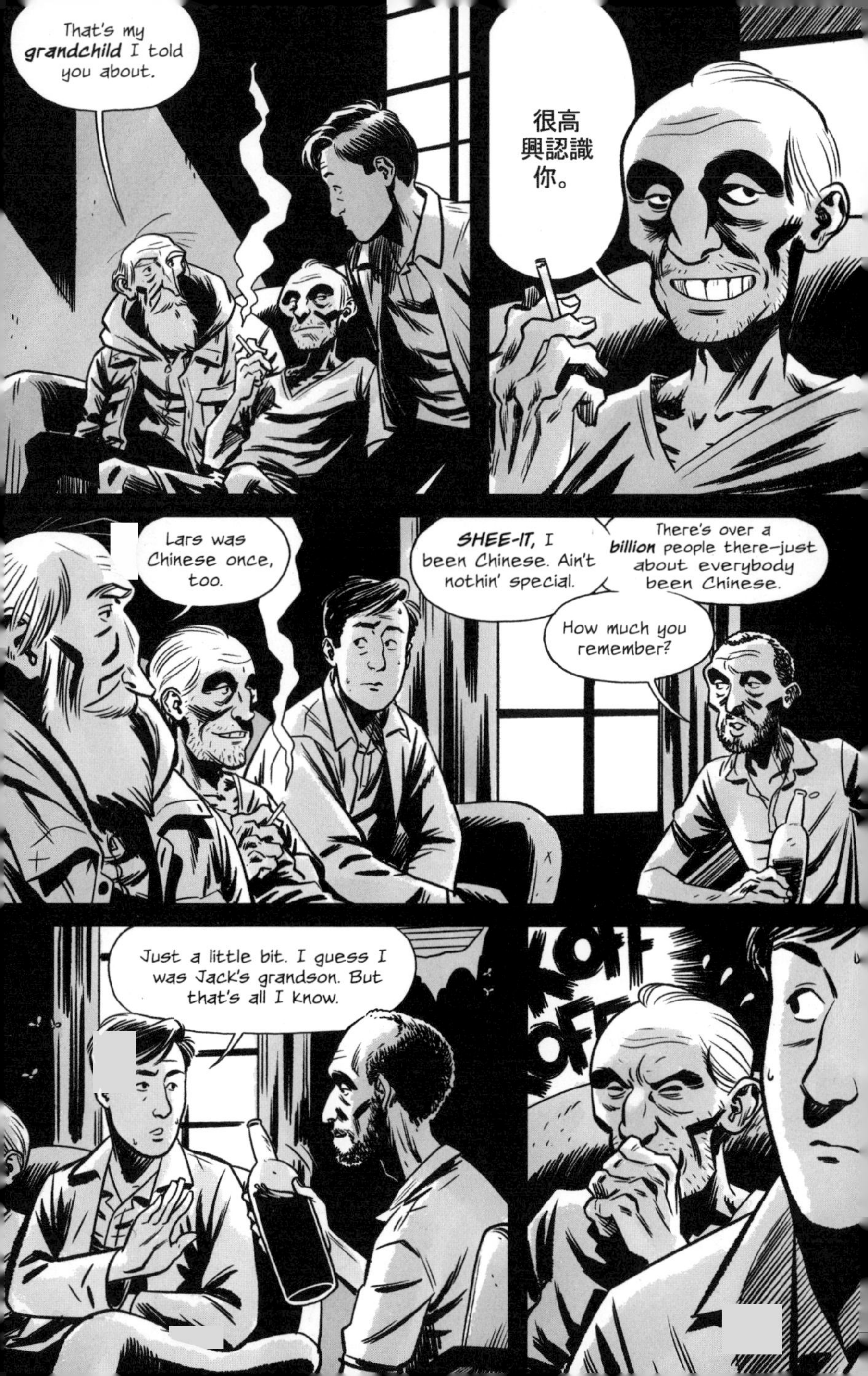
That's my **grandchild** I told you about.
很高興認識你。
Lars was Chinese once, too.
SHEE-IT, I been Chinese. Ain't nothin' special.
There's over a **billion** people there—just about everybody been Chinese.
How much you remember?
Just a little bit. I guess I was Jack's grandson. But that's all I know.
KOFF
KOFF

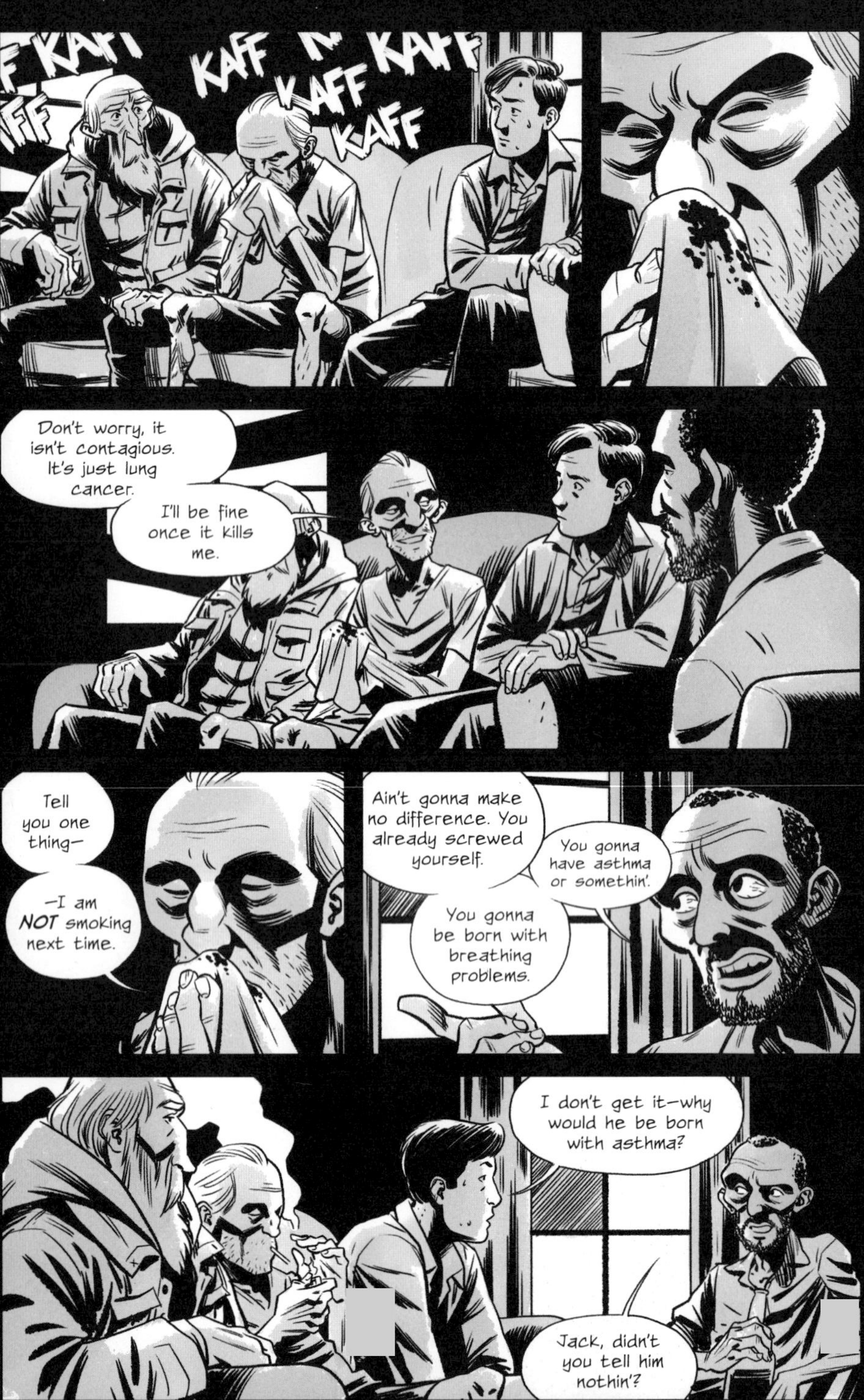

KAFF
KAFF
KAFF
KAFF
Don't worry, it isn't contagious. It's just lung cancer.
I'll be fine once it kills me.
Tell you one thing—
—I am NOT smoking next time.
Ain't gonna make no difference. You already screwed yourself.
You gonna have asthma or somethin'.
You gonna be born with breathing problems.
I don't get it—why would he be born with asthma?
Jack, didn't you tell him nothin'?

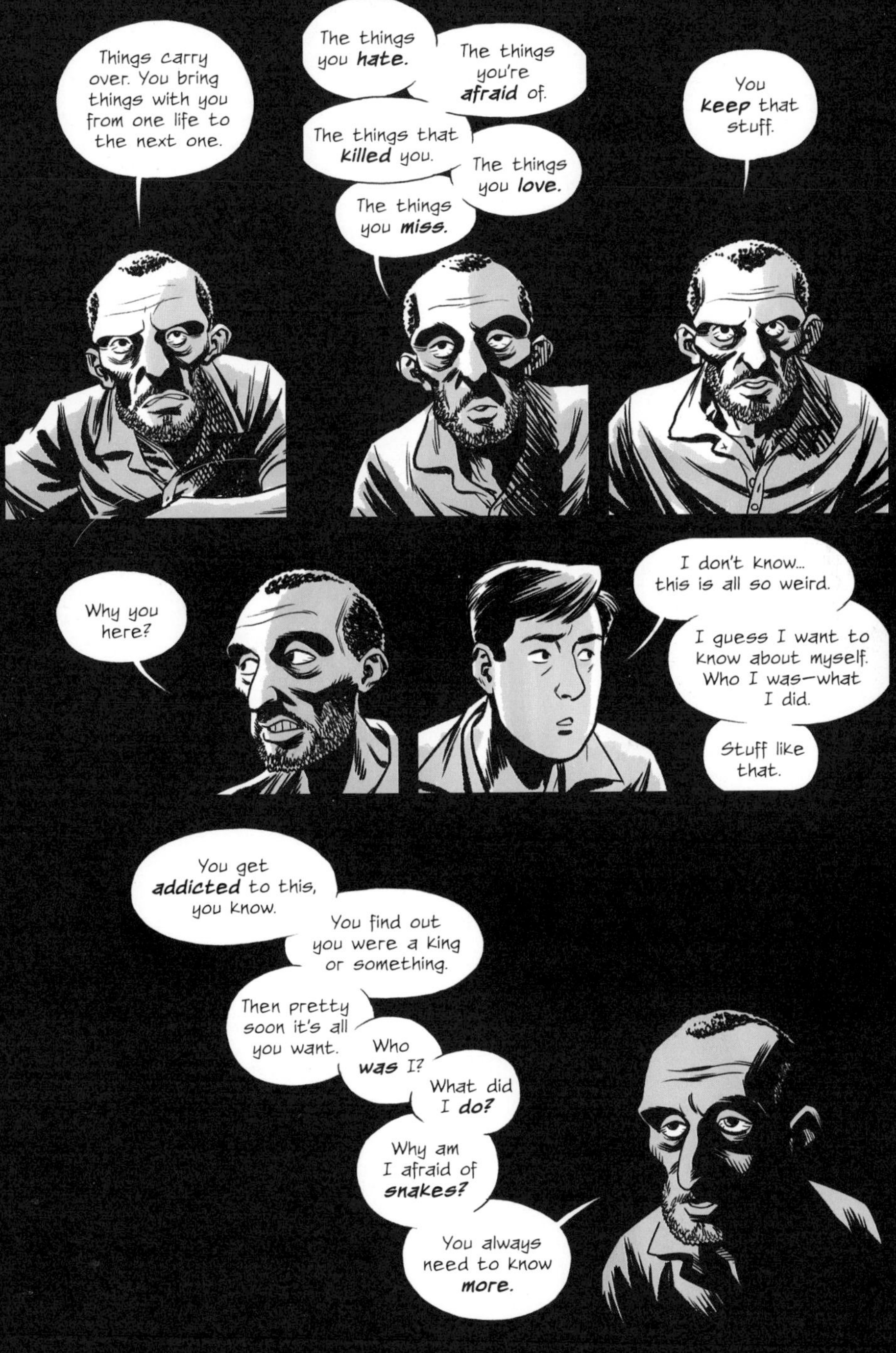
Things carry over. You bring things with you from one life to the next one.
The things you **hate.**
The things you're **afraid** of.
The things that **killed** you.
The things you **love.**
The things you **miss.**
You **keep** that stuff.
Why you here?
I don't know... this is all so weird.
I guess I want to know about myself. Who I was—what I did.
Stuff like that.
You get **addicted** to this, you know.
You find out you were a king or something.
Then pretty soon it's all you want.
Who **was** I?
What did I **do?**
Why am I afraid of **snakes?**
You always need to know **more.**

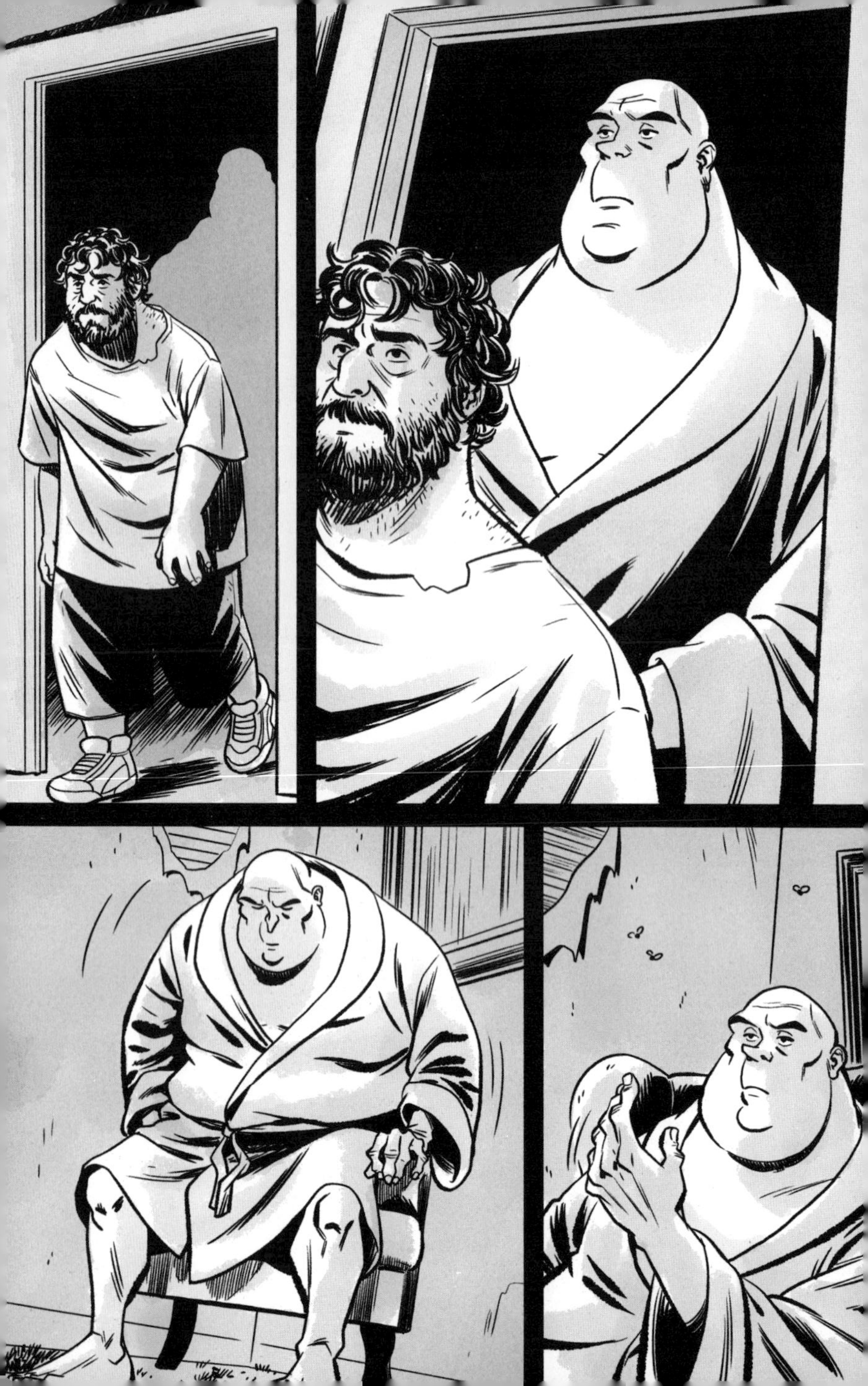

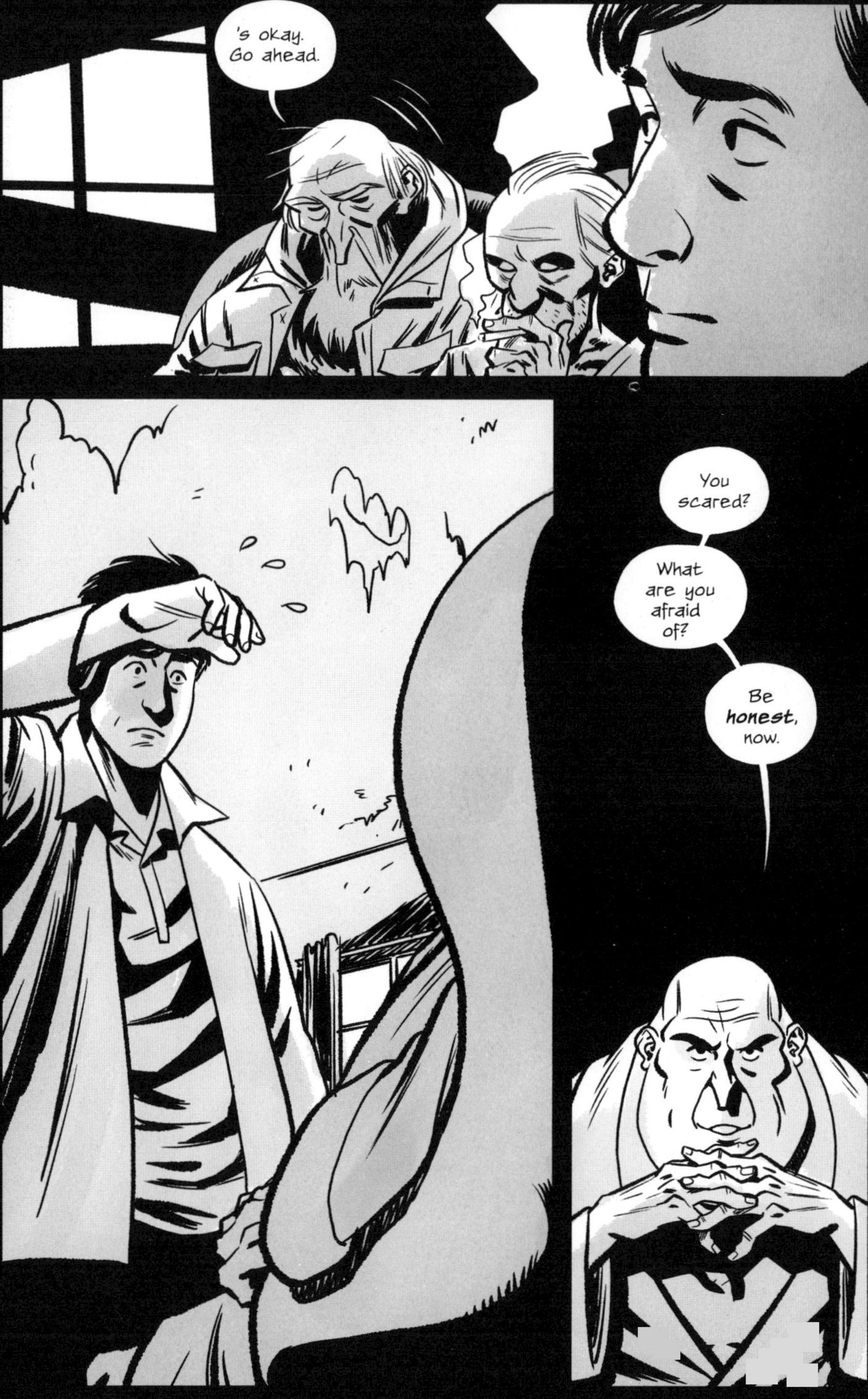
's okay. Go ahead.
You scared?
What are you afraid of?
Be **honest,** now.

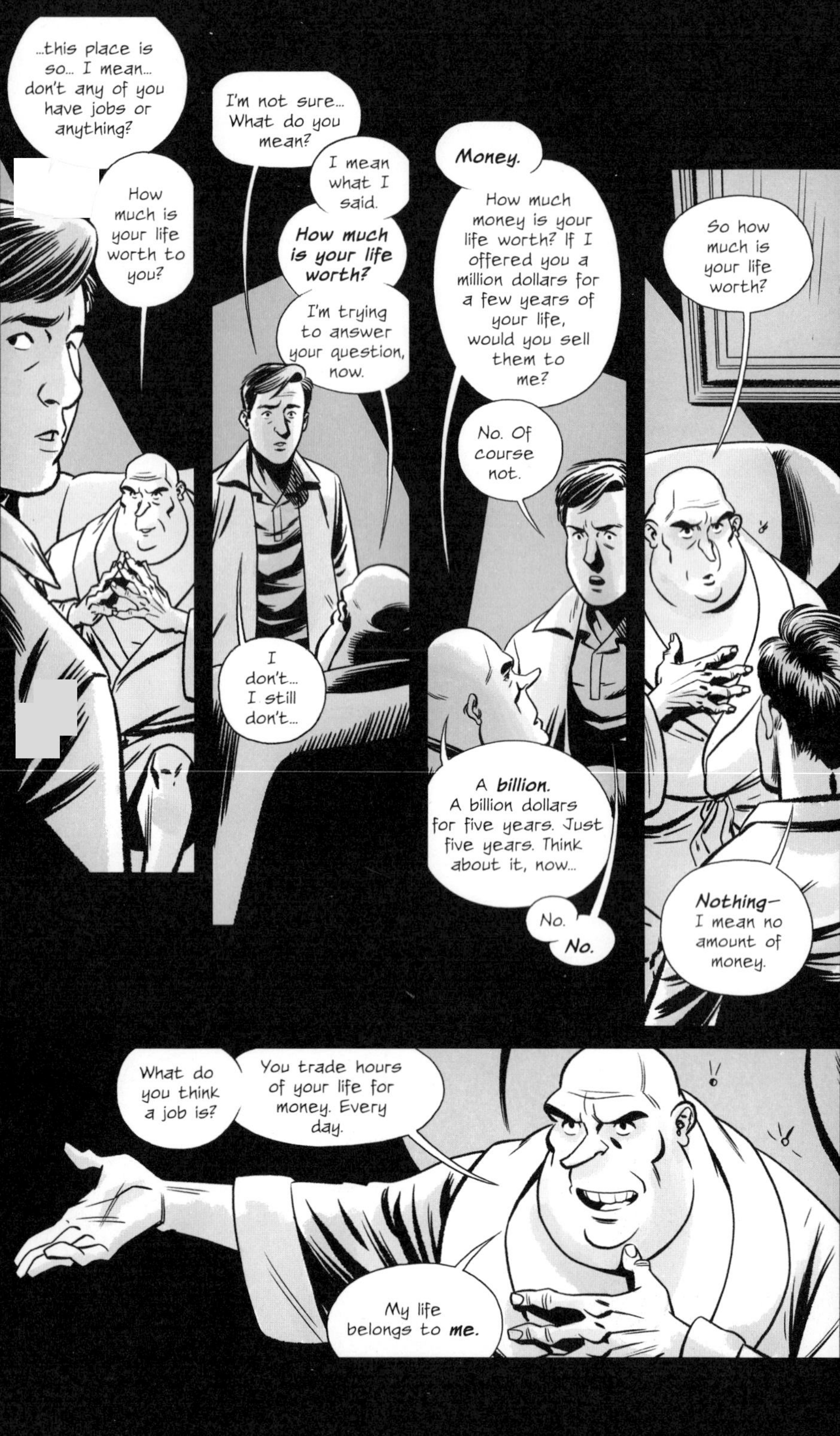
...this place is so... I mean... don't any of you have jobs or anything?
How much is your life worth to you?
I'm not sure... What do you mean?
I mean what I said.
How much is your life worth?
I'm trying to answer your question, now.
I don't... I still don't...
Money.
How much money is your life worth? If I offered you a million dollars for a few years of your life, would you sell them to me?
No. Of course not.
A billion. A billion dollars for five years. Just five years. Think about it, now...
No. No.
So how much is your life worth?
Nothing— I mean no amount of money.
What do you think a job is?
You trade hours of your life for money. Every day.
My life belongs to me.

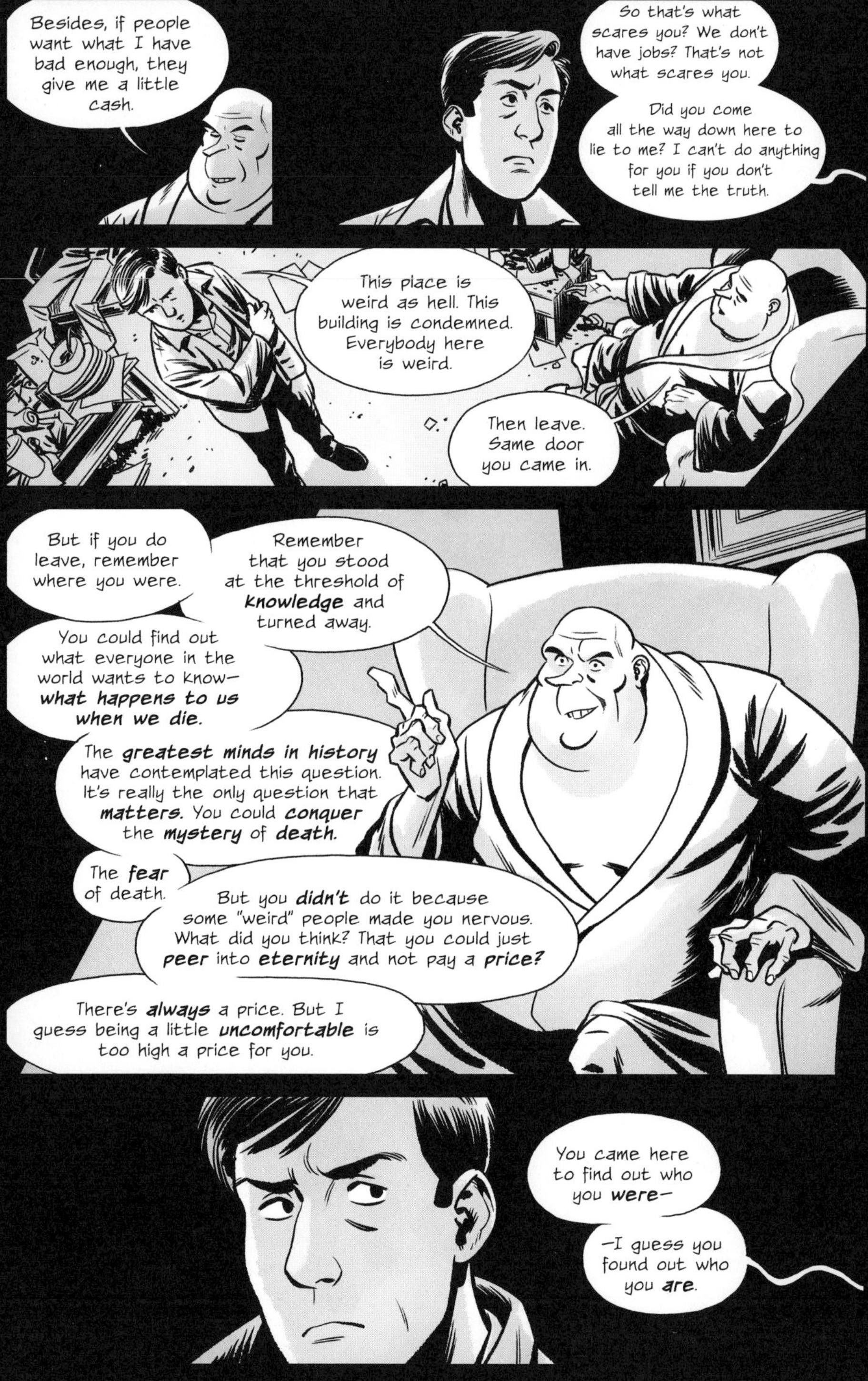
Besides, if people want what I have bad enough, they give me a little cash.
So that's what scares you? We don't have jobs? That's not what scares you.
Did you come all the way down here to lie to me? I can't do anything for you if you don't tell me the truth.
This place is weird as hell. This building is condemned. Everybody here is weird.
Then leave. Same door you came in.
But if you do leave, remember where you were.
Remember that you stood at the threshold of **knowledge** and turned away.
You could find out what everyone in the world wants to know—**what happens to us when we die.**
The **greatest minds in history** have contemplated this question. It's really the only question that **matters.** You could **conquer** the **mystery** of **death.**
The **fear** of death.
But you **didn't** do it because some "weird" people made you nervous. What did you think? That you could just **peer** into **eternity** and not pay a **price?**
There's **always** a price. But I guess being a little **uncomfortable** is too high a price for you.
You came here to find out who you **were**—
—I guess you found out who you **are**.

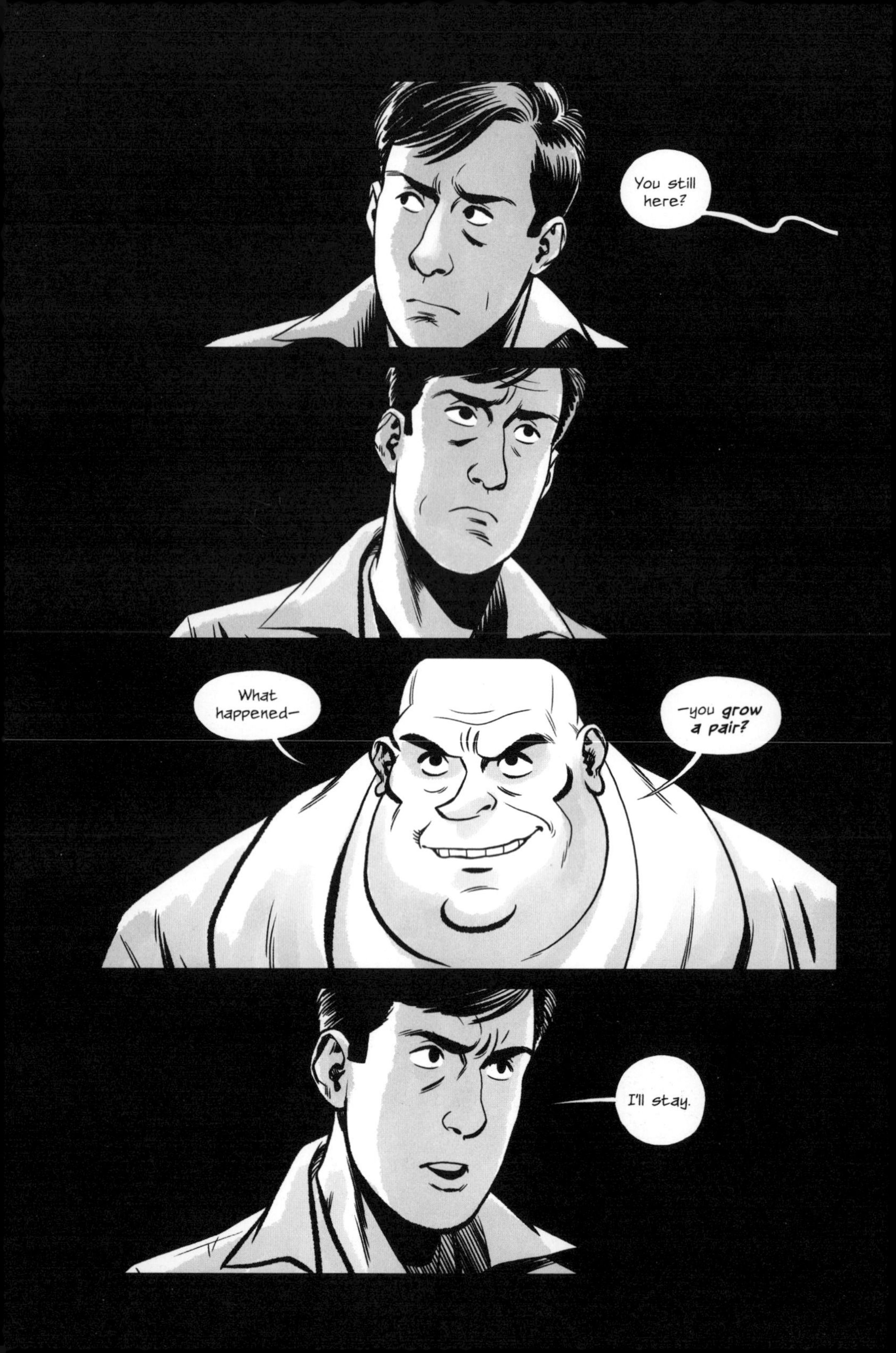
You still here?
What happened—
—you **grow a pair?**
I'll stay.

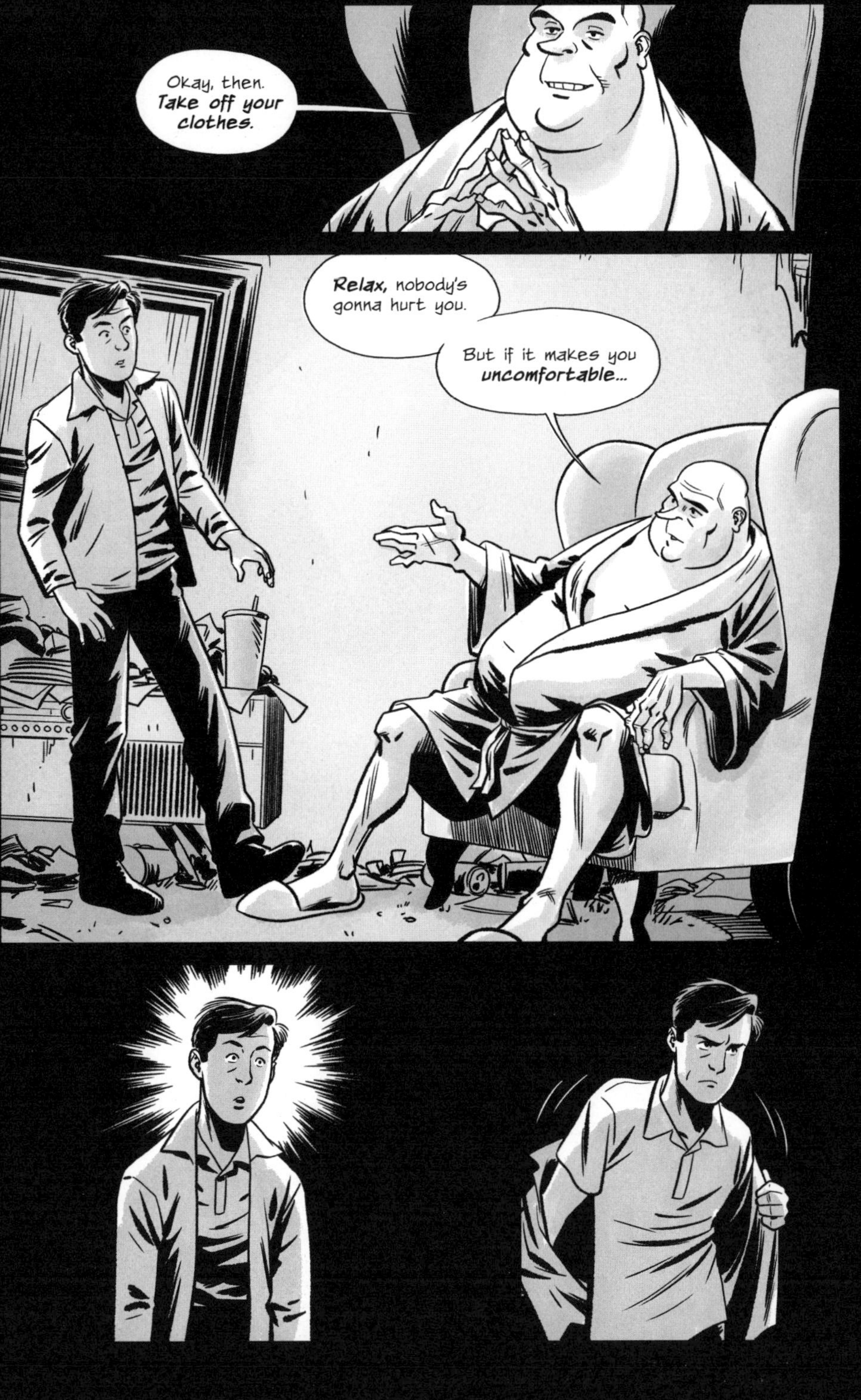
Okay, then. Take off your clothes.
Relax, nobody's gonna hurt you.
But if it makes you uncomfortable...

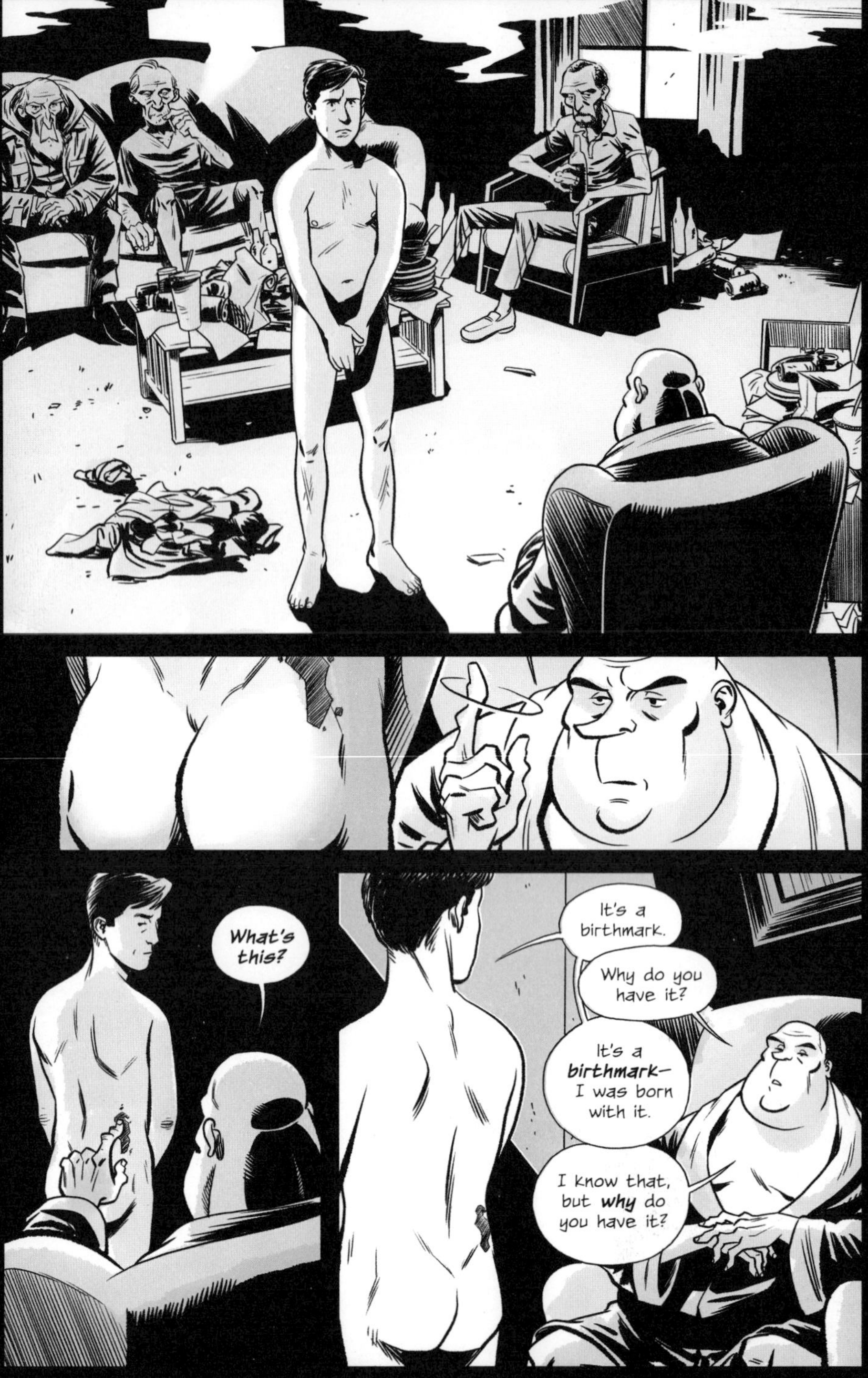
What's this?
It's a birthmark.
Why do you have it?
It's a birthmark— I was born with it.
I know that, but why do you have it?

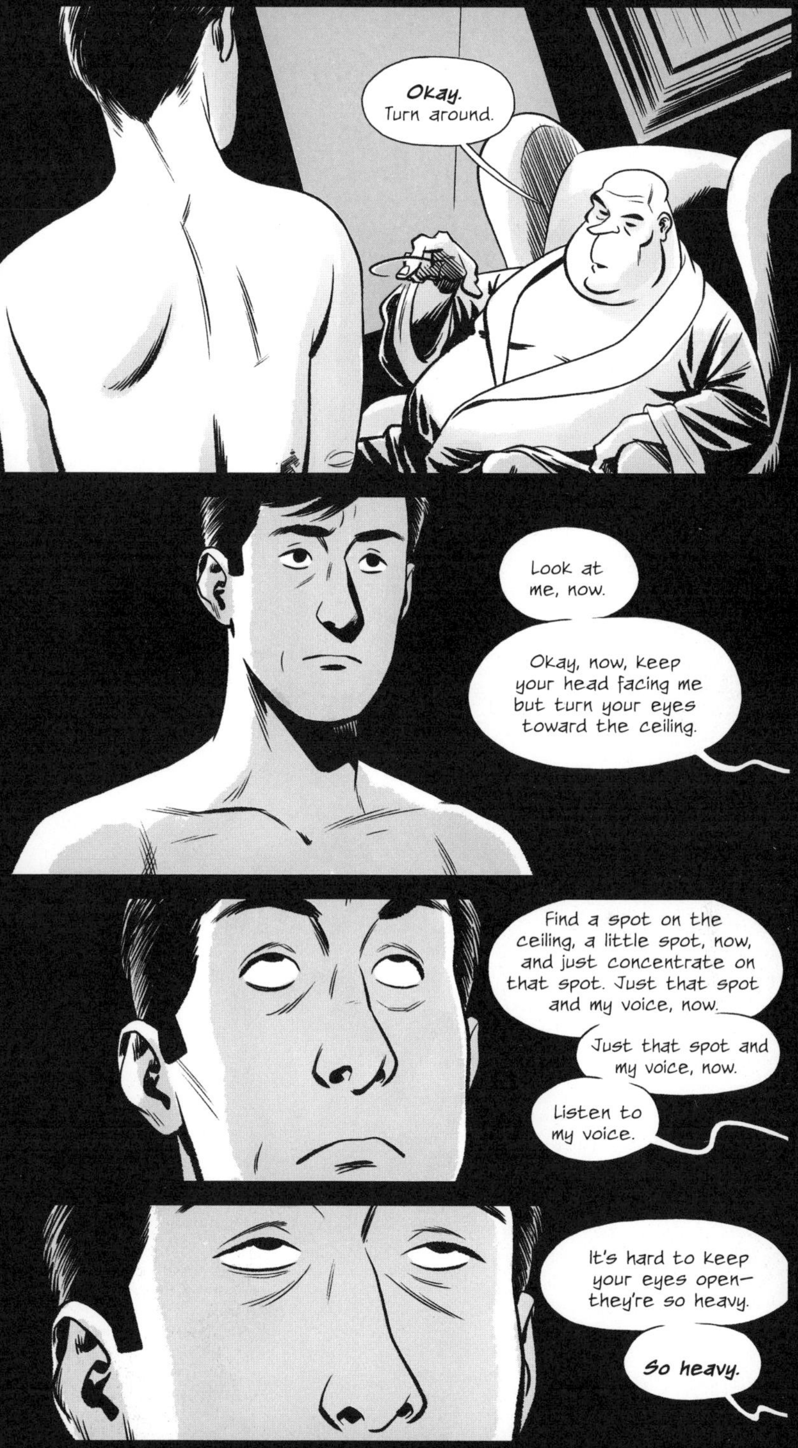
Okay. Turn around.
Look at me, now.
Okay, now, keep your head facing me but turn your eyes toward the ceiling.
Find a spot on the ceiling, a little spot, now, and just concentrate on that spot. Just that spot and my voice, now.
Just that spot and my voice, now.
Listen to my voice.
It's hard to keep your eyes open—they're so heavy.
So heavy.

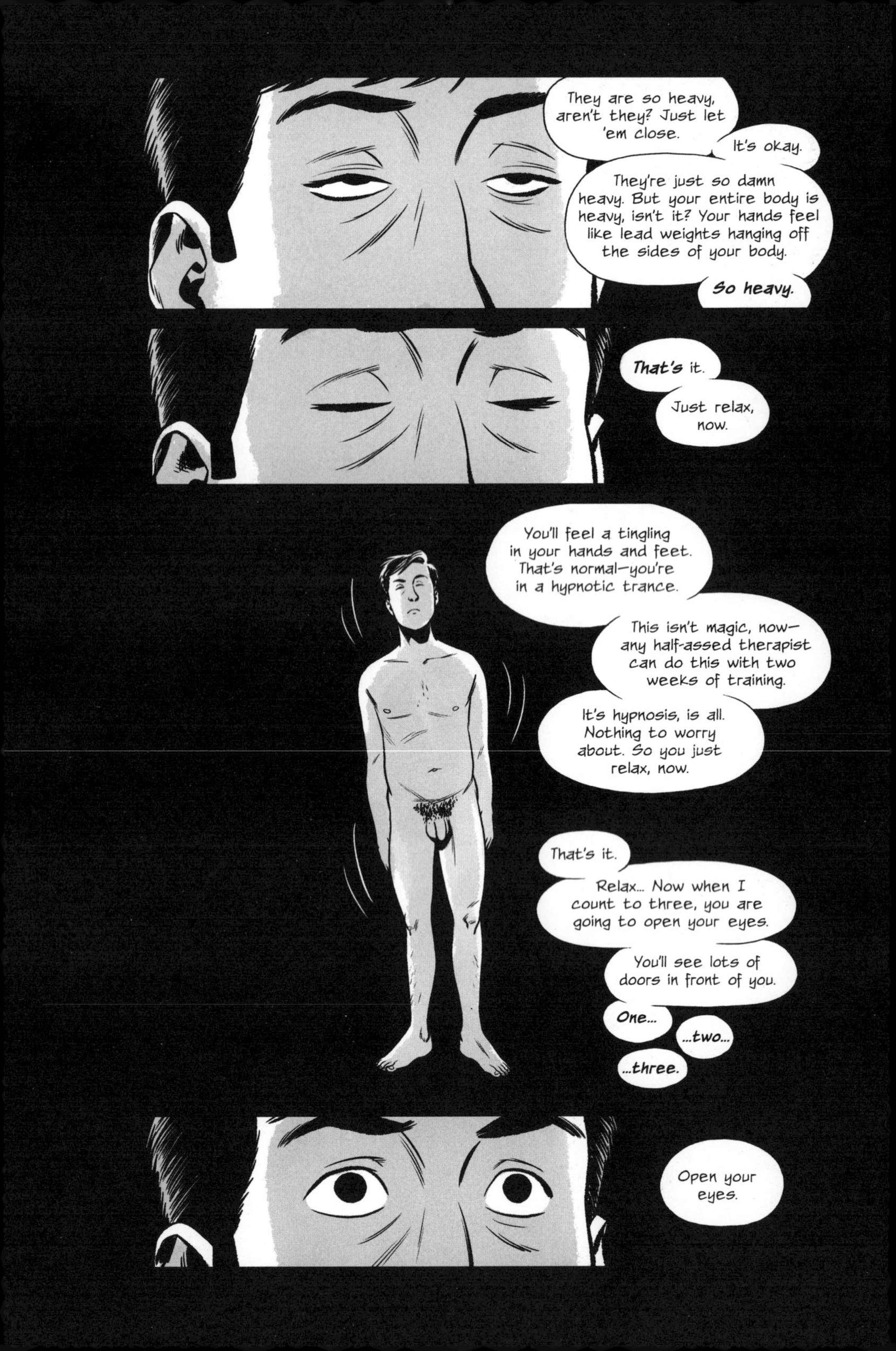
They are so heavy, aren't they? Just let 'em close.
It's okay.
They're just so damn heavy. But your entire body is heavy, isn't it? Your hands feel like lead weights hanging off the sides of your body.
So heavy.
That's it.
Just relax, now.
You'll feel a tingling in your hands and feet. That's normal—you're in a hypnotic trance.
This isn't magic, now—any half-assed therapist can do this with two weeks of training.
It's hypnosis, is all. Nothing to worry about. So you just relax, now.
That's it.
Relax... Now when I count to three, you are going to open your eyes.
You'll see lots of doors in front of you.
One...
...two...
...three.
Open your eyes.

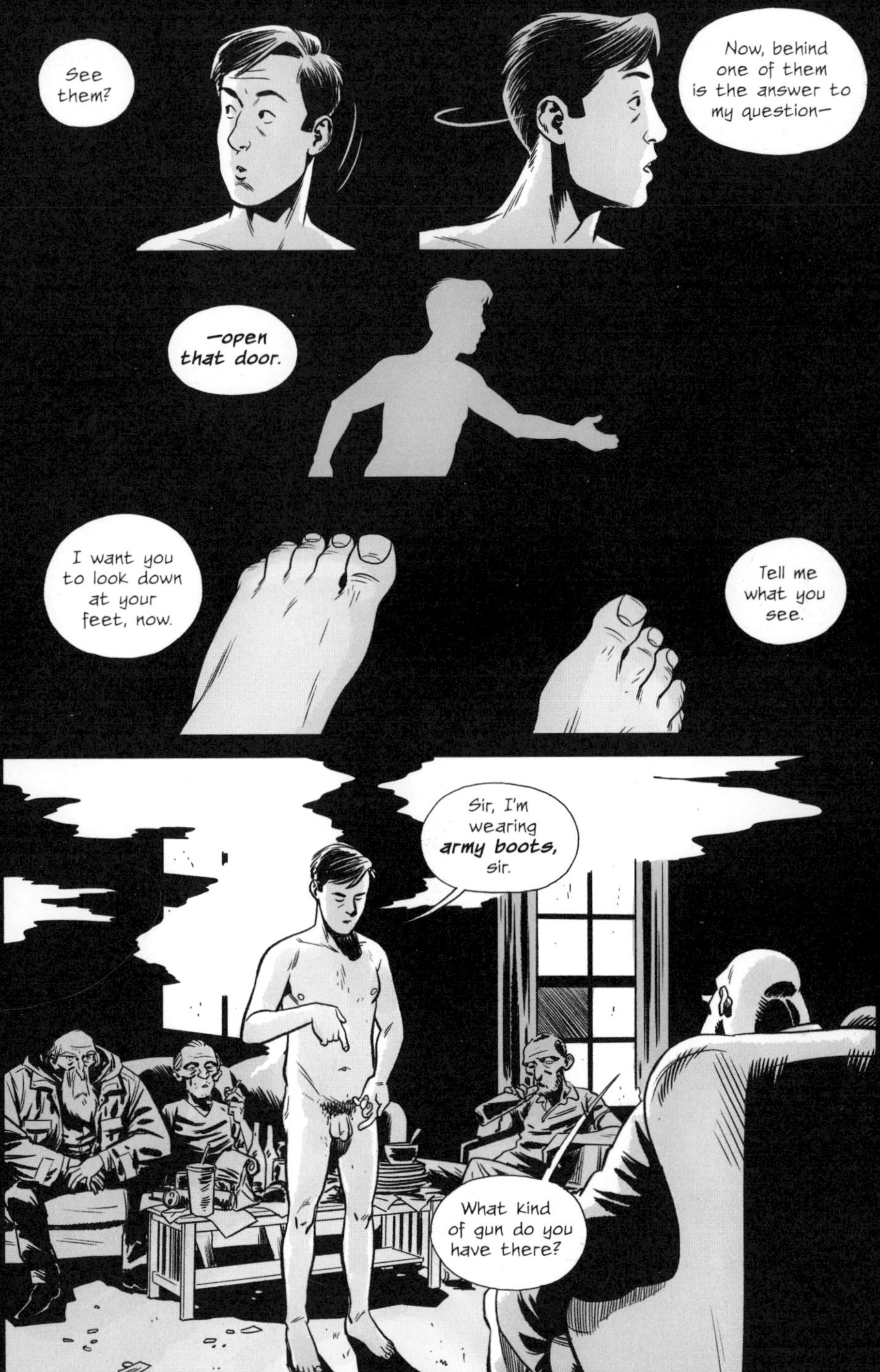
See them?
Now, behind one of them is the answer to my question—
—open that door.
I want you to look down at your feet, now.
Tell me what you see.
Sir, I'm wearing army boots, sir.
What kind of gun do you have there?

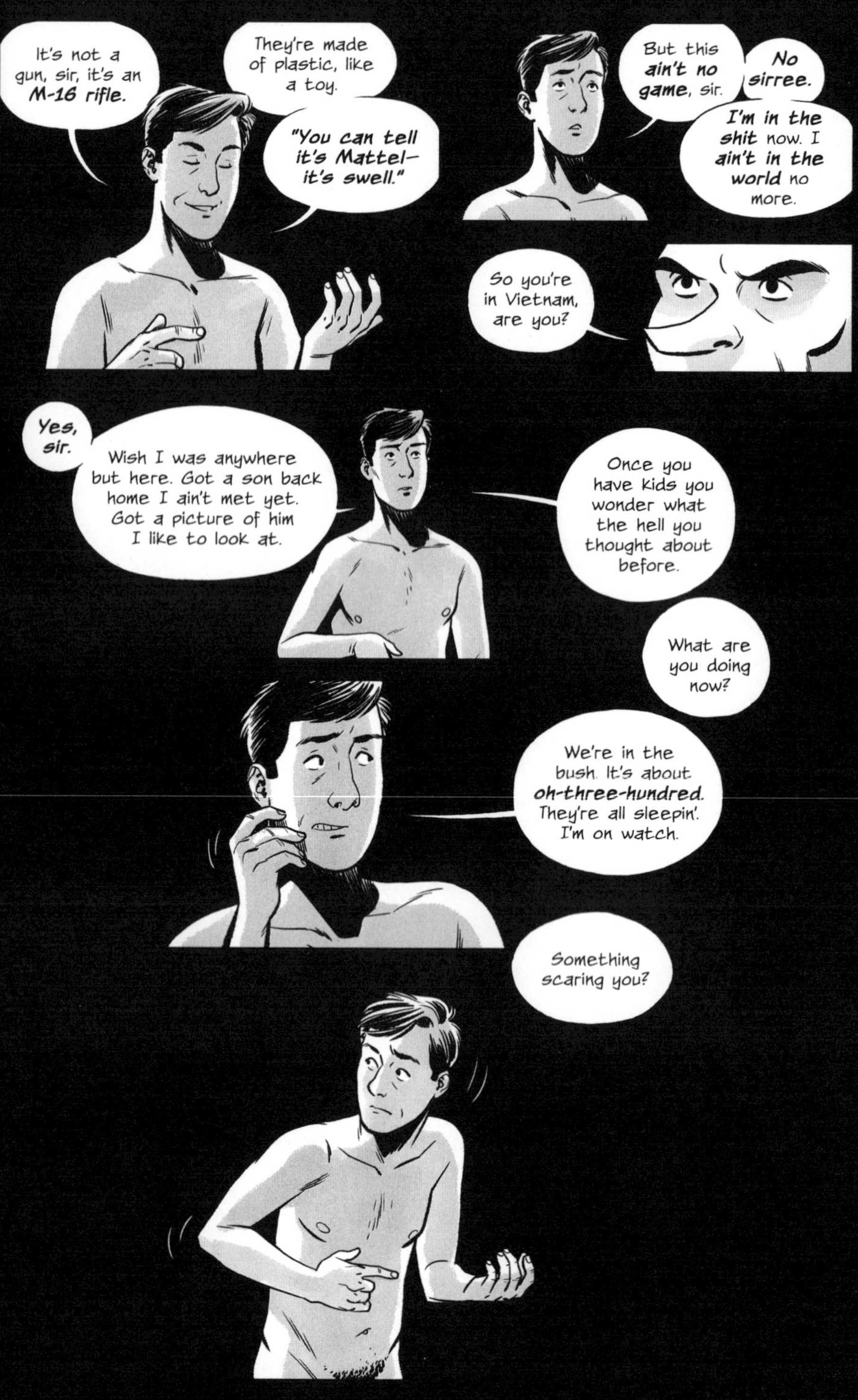
It's not a gun, sir, it's an **M-16 rifle.**
They're made of plastic, like a toy.
"You can tell it's Mattel— it's swell."
But this **ain't no game,** sir.
No sirree.
I'm in the shit now. I **ain't in the world** no more.
So you're in Vietnam, are you?
Yes, sir.
Wish I was anywhere but here. Got a son back home I ain't met yet. Got a picture of him I like to look at.
Once you have kids you wonder what the hell you thought about before.
What are you doing now?
We're in the bush. It's about **oh-three-hundred**. They're all sleepin'. I'm on watch.
Something scaring you?

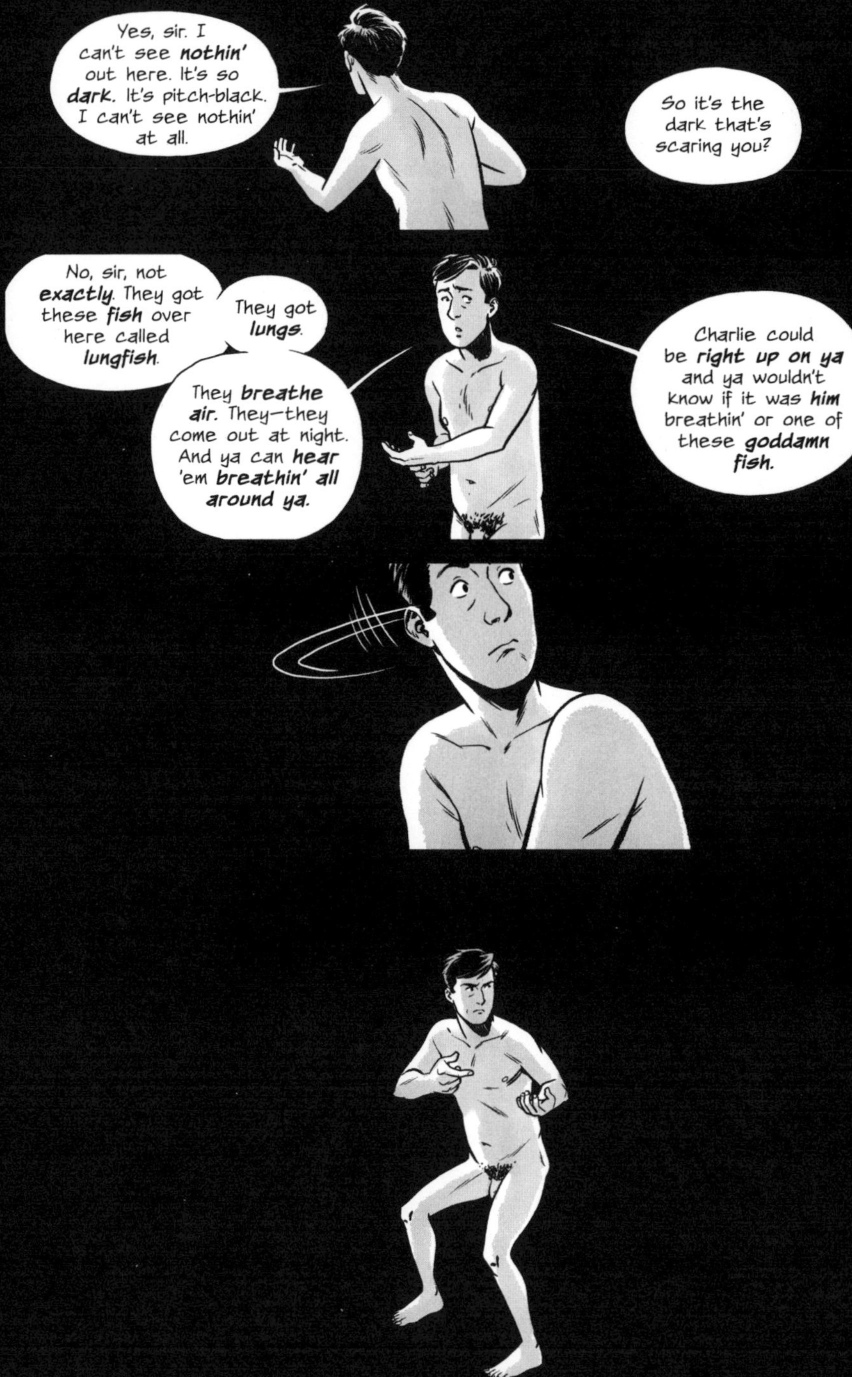
Yes, sir. I can't see nothin' out here. It's so dark. It's pitch-black. I can't see nothin' at all.
So it's the dark that's scaring you?
No, sir, not exactly. They got these fish over here called lungfish.
They got lungs.
They breathe air. They—they come out at night. And ya can hear 'em breathin' all around ya.
Charlie could be right up on ya and ya wouldn't know if it was him breathin' or one of these goddamn fish.

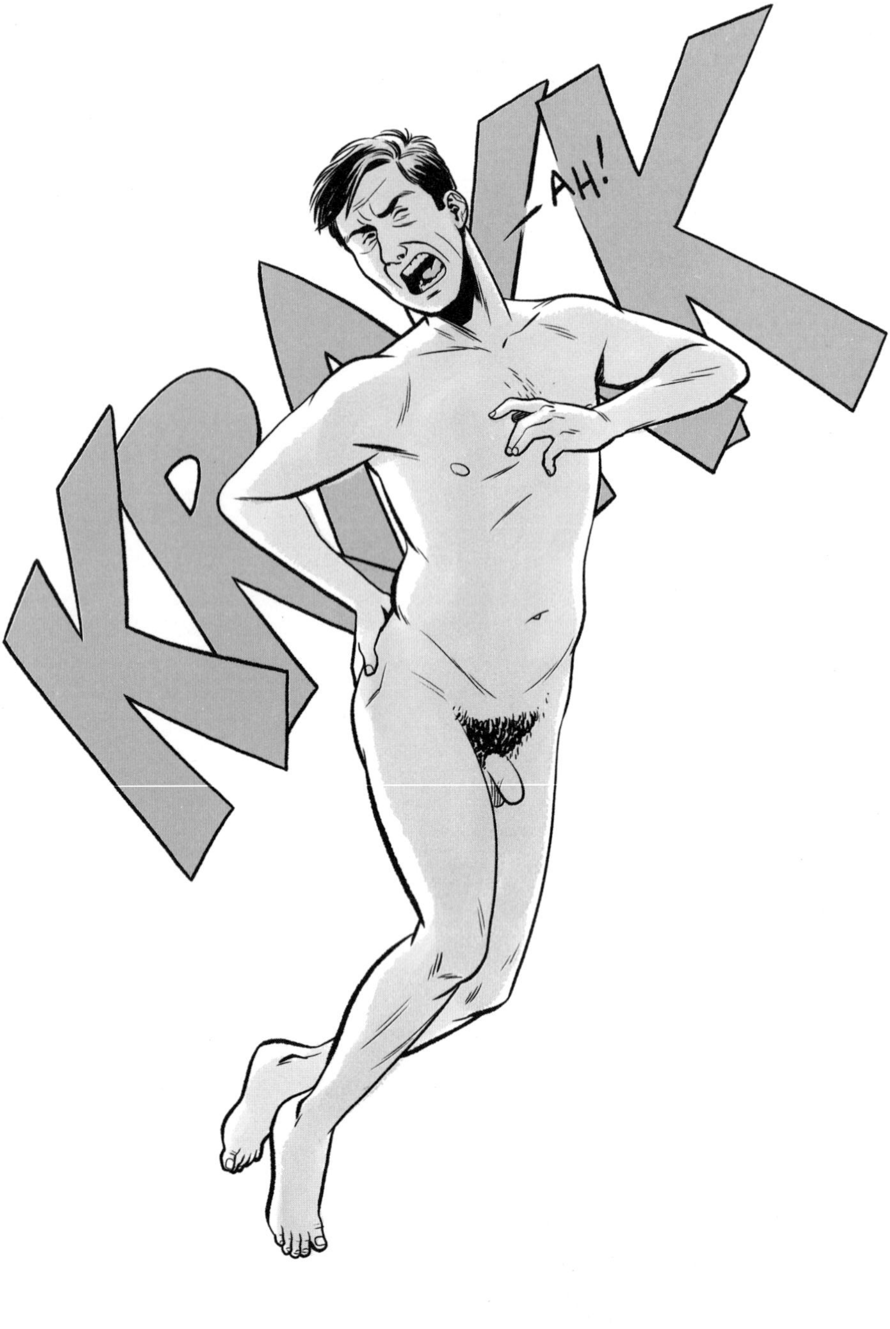
KRAKK
AH!

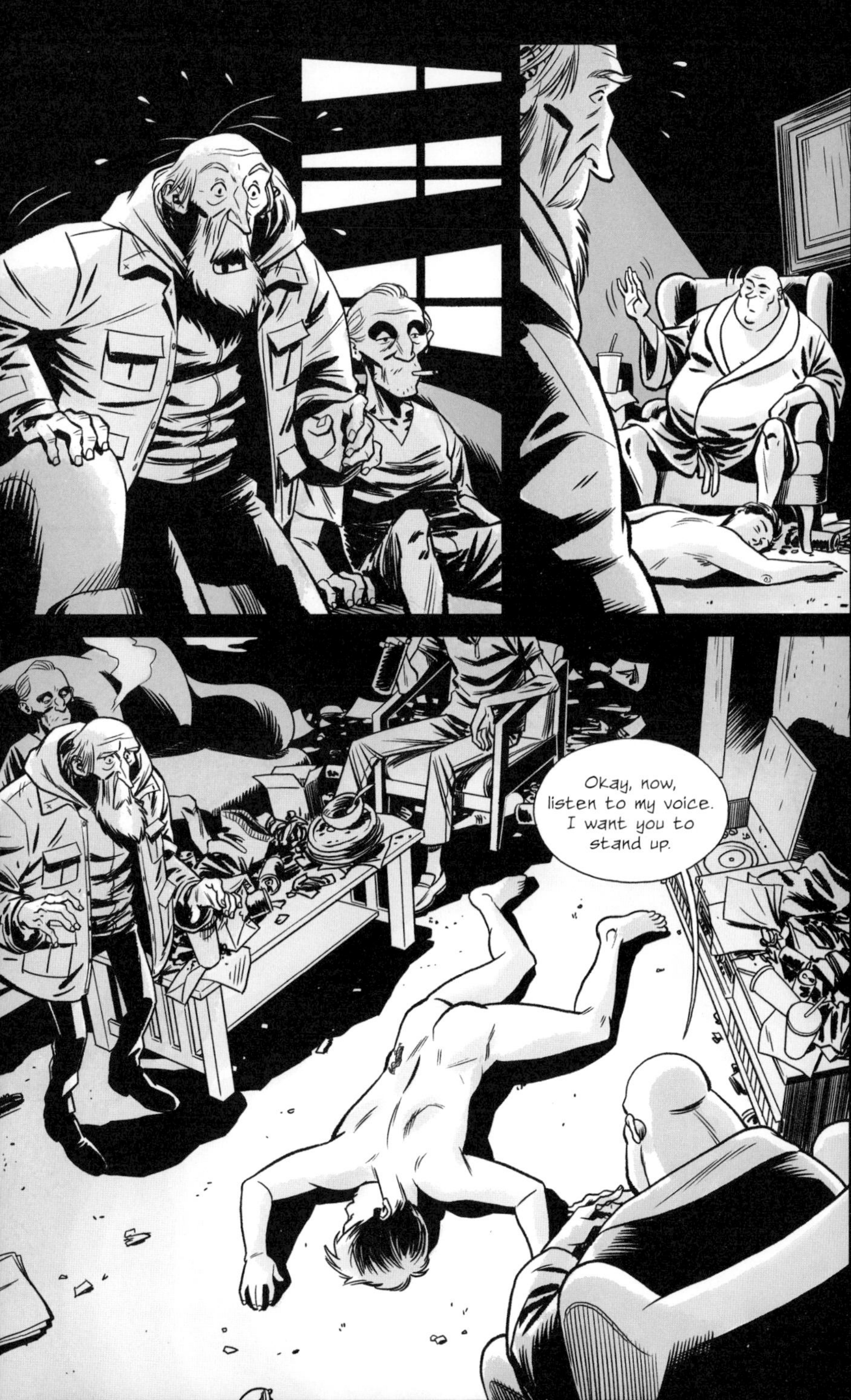
Okay, now, listen to my voice. I want you to stand up.

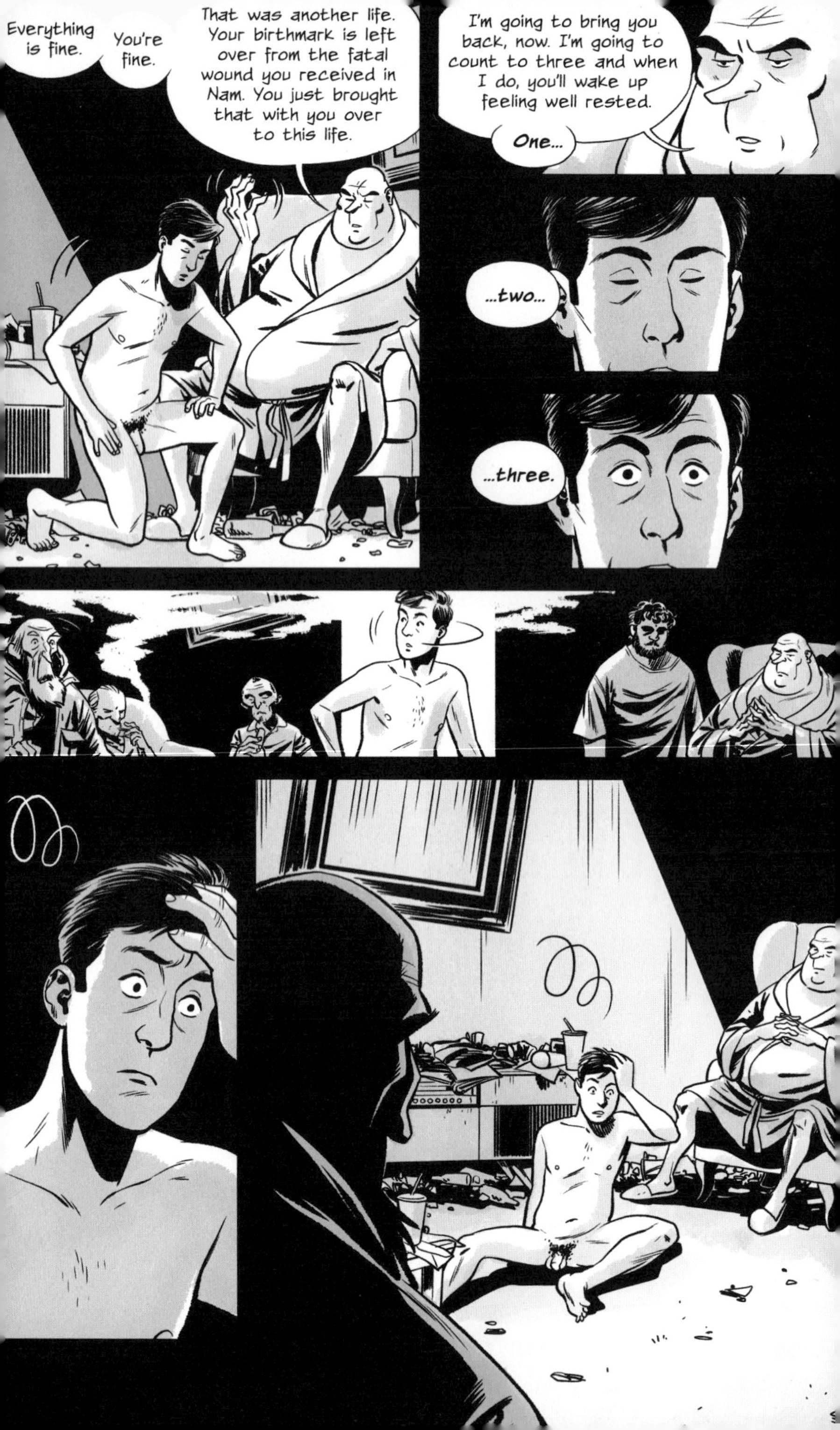
Everything is fine.
You're fine.
That was another life. Your birthmark is left over from the fatal wound you received in Nam. You just brought that with you over to this life.
I'm going to bring you back, now. I'm going to count to three and when I do, you'll wake up feeling well rested.
One...
...two...
...three.

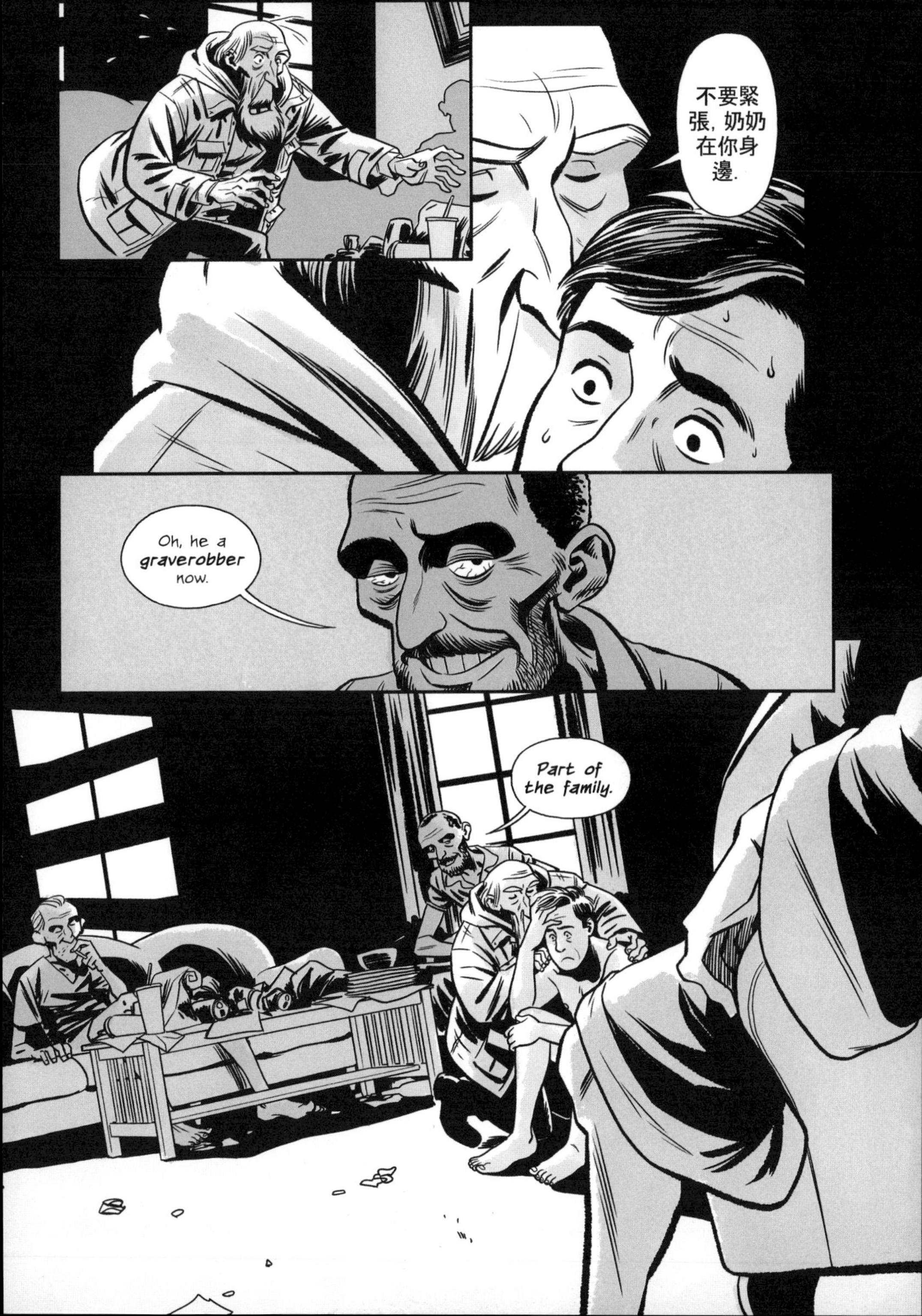

不要緊張, 奶奶在你身邊.
Oh, he a graverobber now.
Part of the family.

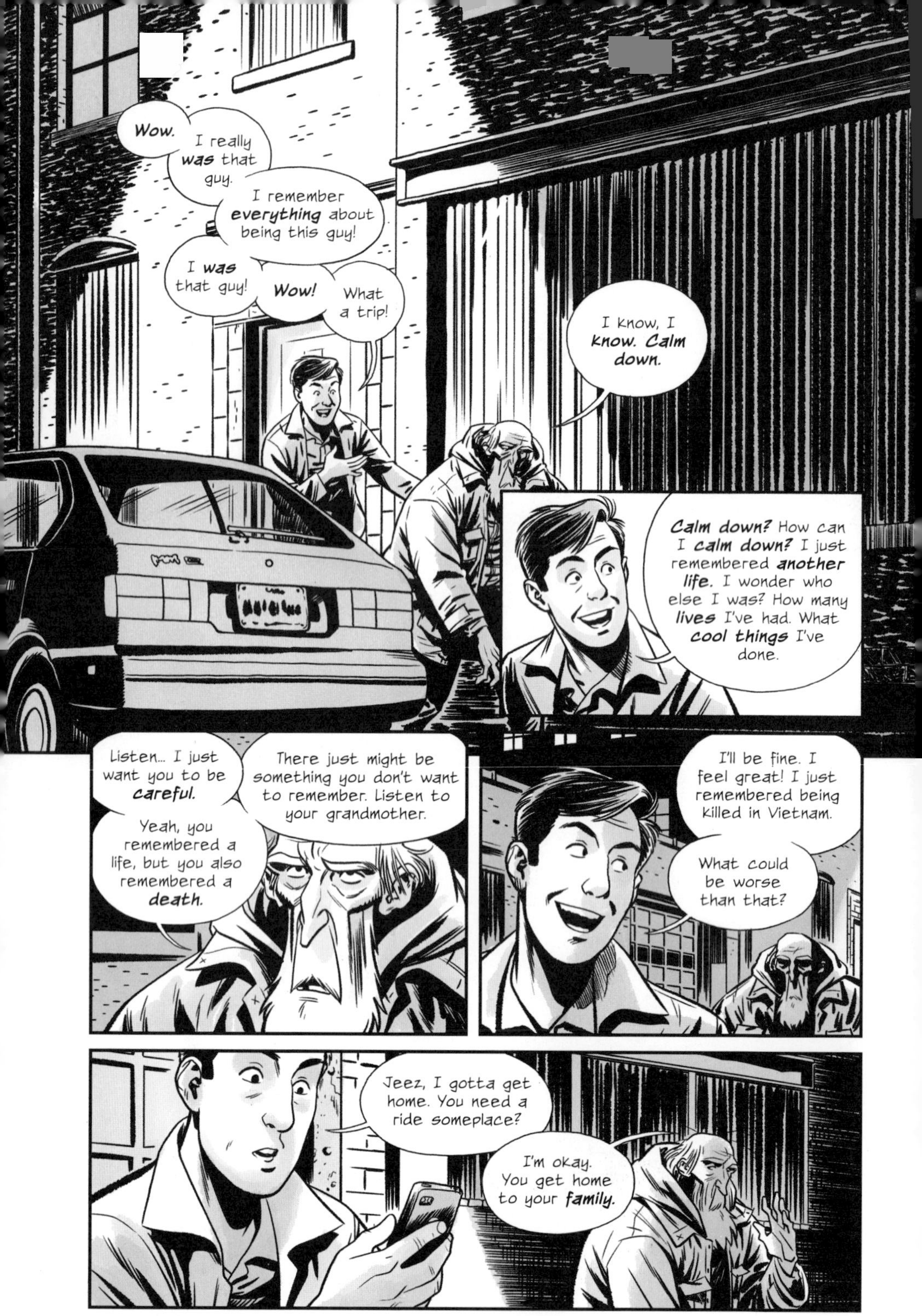
Wow.
I really was that guy.
I remember everything about being this guy!
I was that guy!
Wow!
What a trip!
I know, I know. Calm down.
Calm down? How can I calm down? I just remembered another life. I wonder who else I was? How many lives I've had. What cool things I've done.
Listen... I just want you to be careful.
Yeah, you remembered a life, but you also remembered a death.
There just might be something you don't want to remember. Listen to your grandmother.
I'll be fine. I feel great! I just remembered being killed in Vietnam.
What could be worse than that?
Jeez, I gotta get home. You need a ride someplace?
I'm okay. You get home to your family.

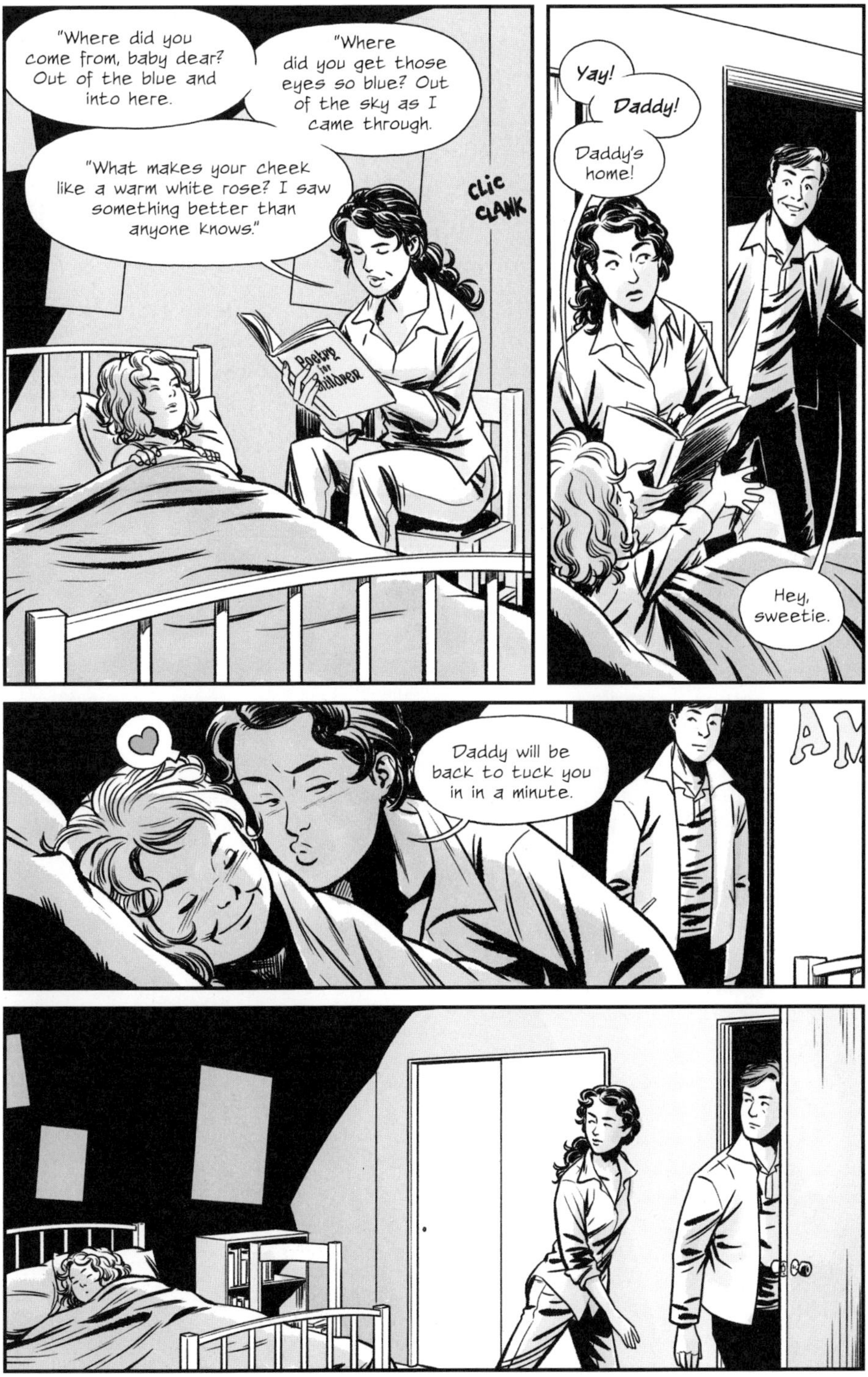
"Where did you come from, baby dear? Out of the blue and into here.
"Where did you get those eyes so blue? Out of the sky as I came through.
"What makes your cheek like a warm white rose? I saw something better than anyone knows."
CLIC CLANK
Poetry for Children
Yay!
Daddy!
Daddy's home!
Hey, sweetie.
Daddy will be back to tuck you in in a minute.

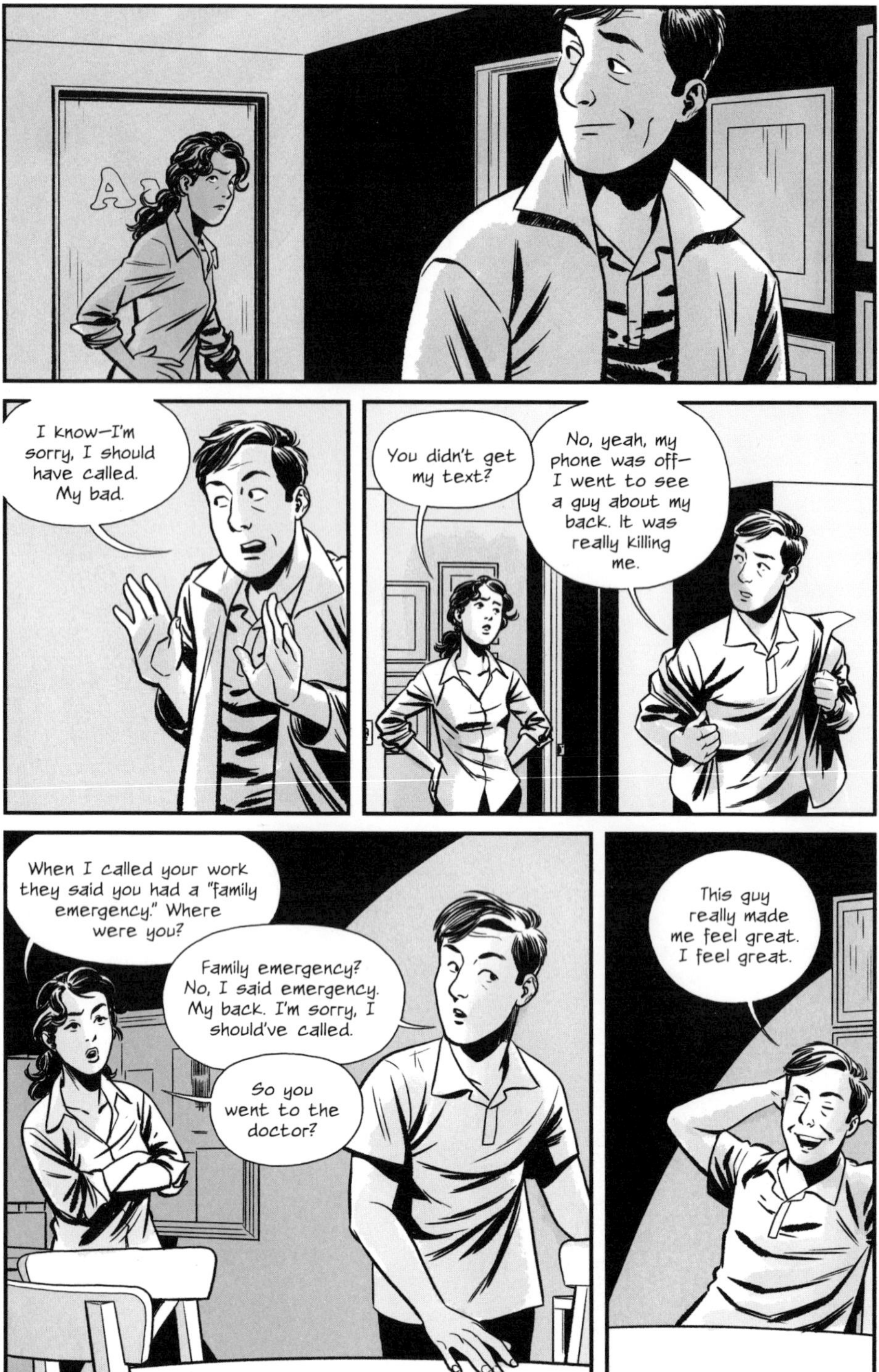
I know—I'm sorry, I should have called. My bad.
You didn't get my text?
No, yeah, my phone was off—I went to see a guy about my back. It was really killing me.
When I called your work they said you had a "family emergency." Where were you?
Family emergency? No, I said emergency. My back. I'm sorry, I should've called.
So you went to the doctor?
This guy really made me feel great. I feel great.

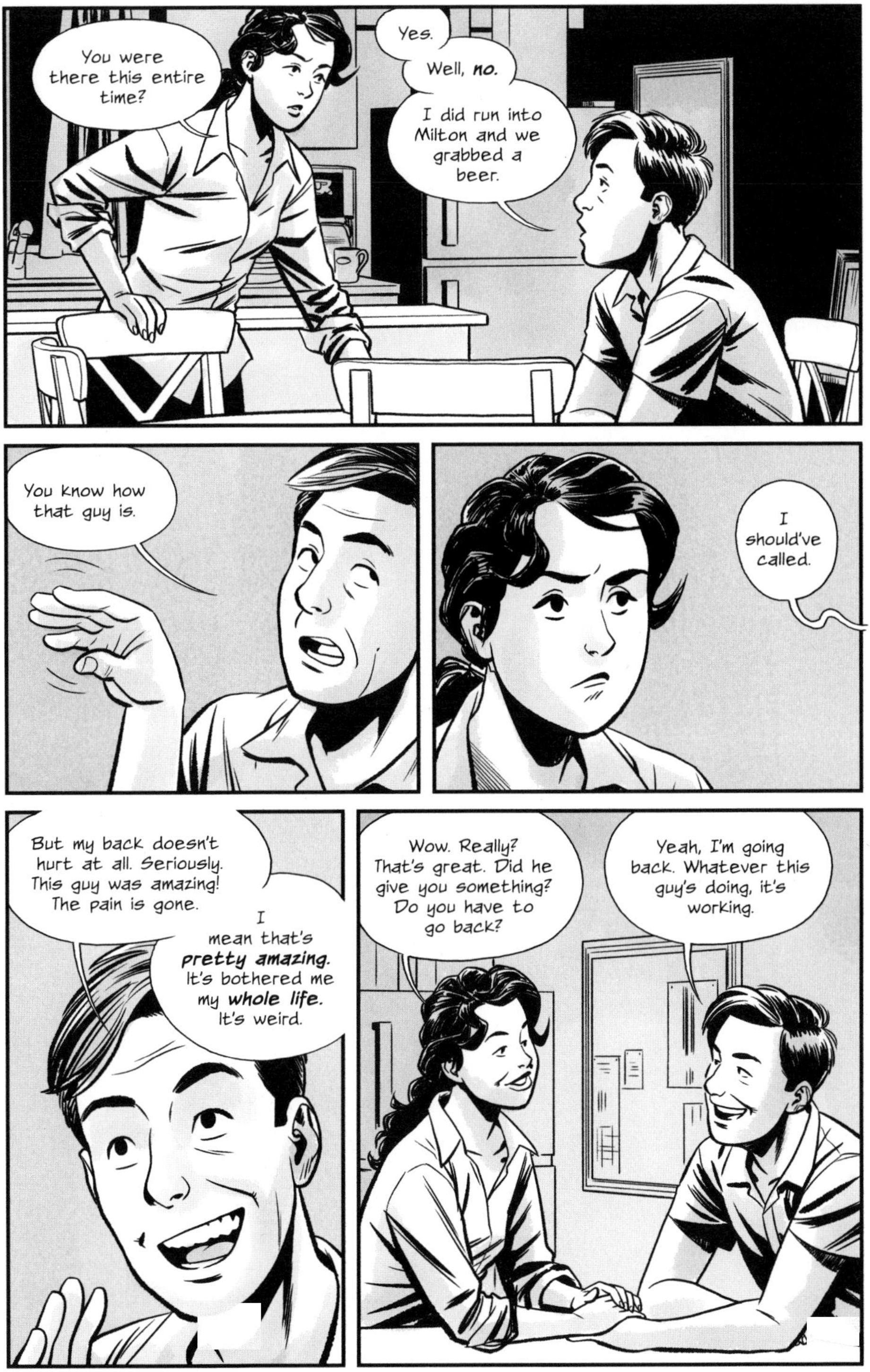
You were there this entire time?
Yes.
Well, **no.**
I did run into Milton and we grabbed a beer.
You know how that guy is.
I should've called.
But my back doesn't hurt at all. Seriously. This guy was amazing! The pain is gone.
I mean that's **pretty amazing.** It's bothered me my **whole life.** It's weird.
Wow. Really? That's great. Did he give you something? Do you have to go back?
Yeah, I'm going back. Whatever this guy's doing, it's working.

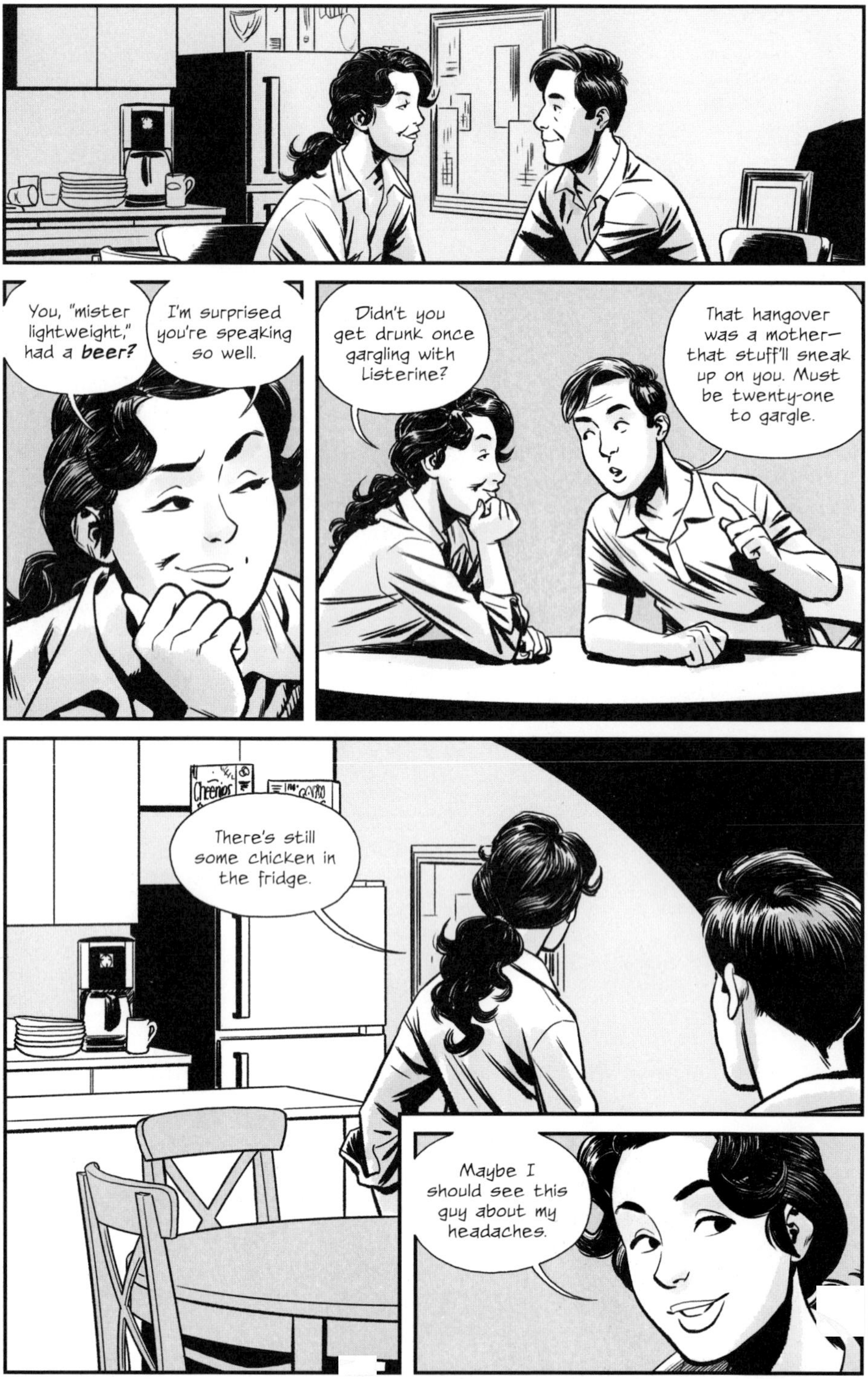
You, "mister lightweight," had a **beer?**
I'm surprised you're speaking so well.
Didn't you get drunk once gargling with Listerine?
That hangover was a mother—that stuff'll sneak up on you. Must be twenty-one to gargle.
There's still some chicken in the fridge.
Maybe I should see this guy about my headaches.

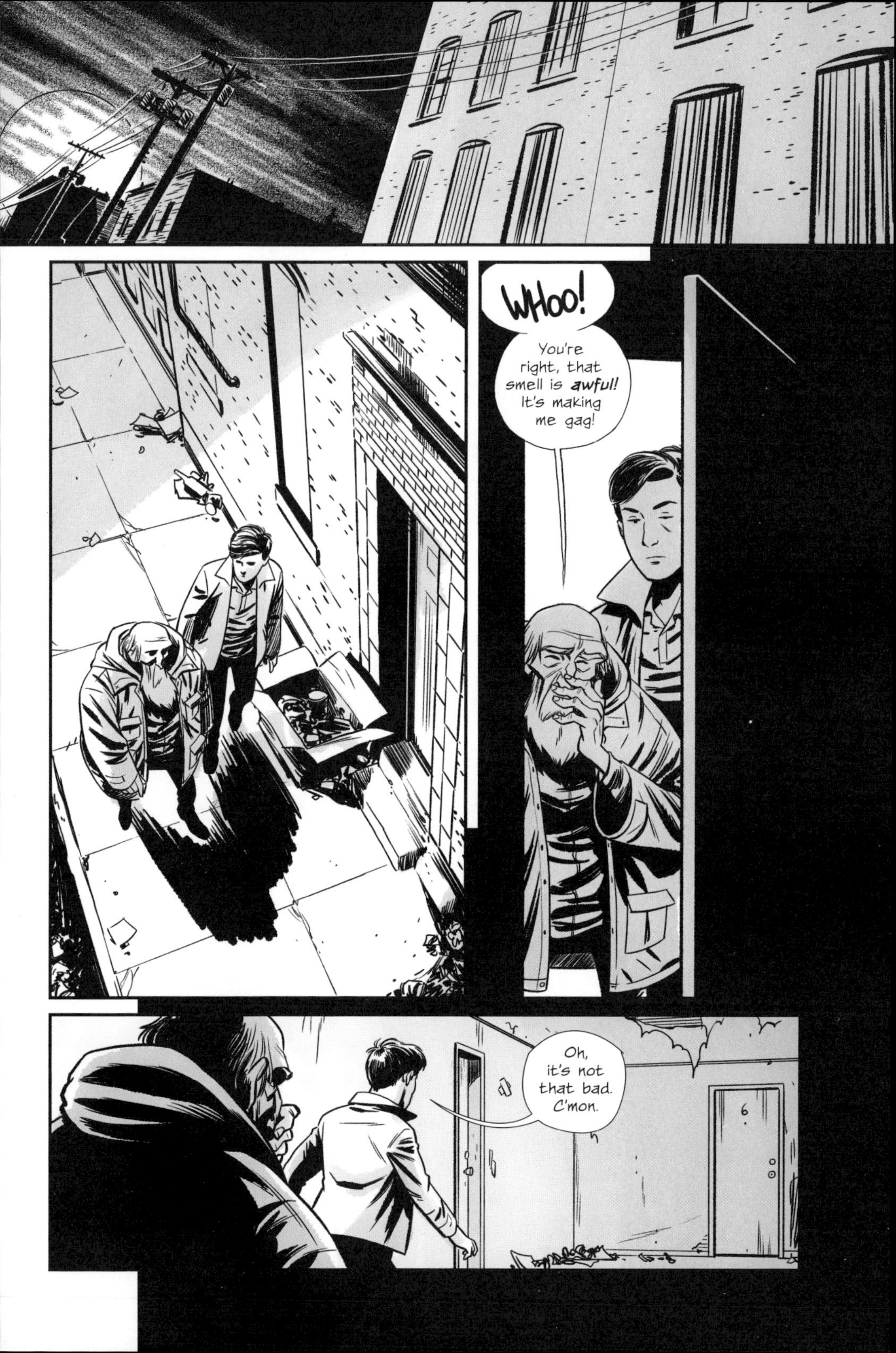
WHOO!
You're right, that smell is awful! It's making me gag!
Oh, it's not that bad. C'mon.
6

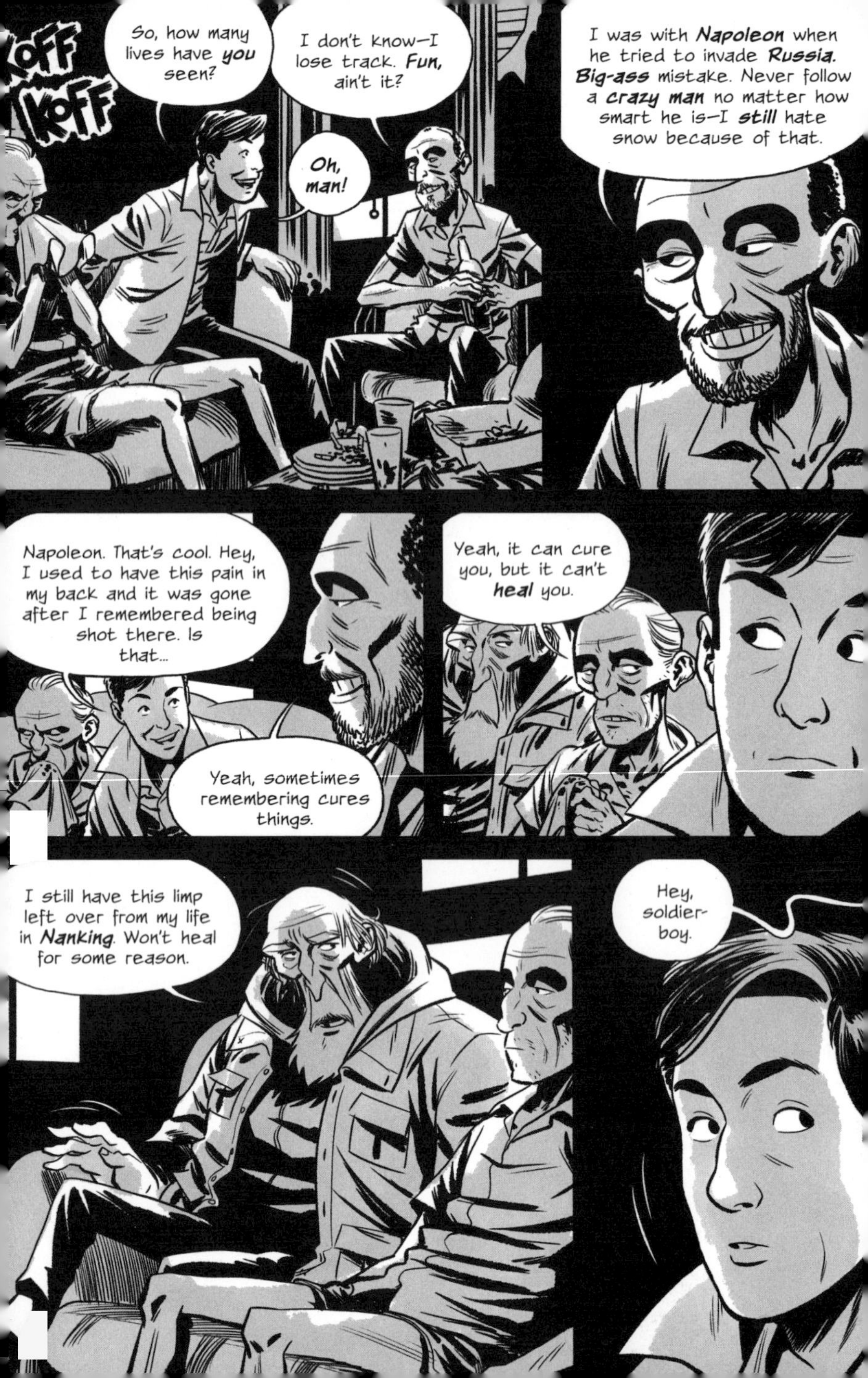
KOFF KOFF
So, how many lives have *you* seen?
I don't know—I lose track. *Fun,* ain't it?
Oh, man!
I was with *Napoleon* when he tried to invade *Russia.* *Big-ass* mistake. Never follow a *crazy man* no matter how smart he is—I *still* hate snow because of that.
Napoleon. That's cool. Hey, I used to have this pain in my back and it was gone after I remembered being shot there. Is that...
Yeah, sometimes remembering cures things.
Yeah, it can cure you, but it can't *heal* you.
I still have this limp left over from my life in *Nanking*. Won't heal for some reason.
Hey, soldier-boy.

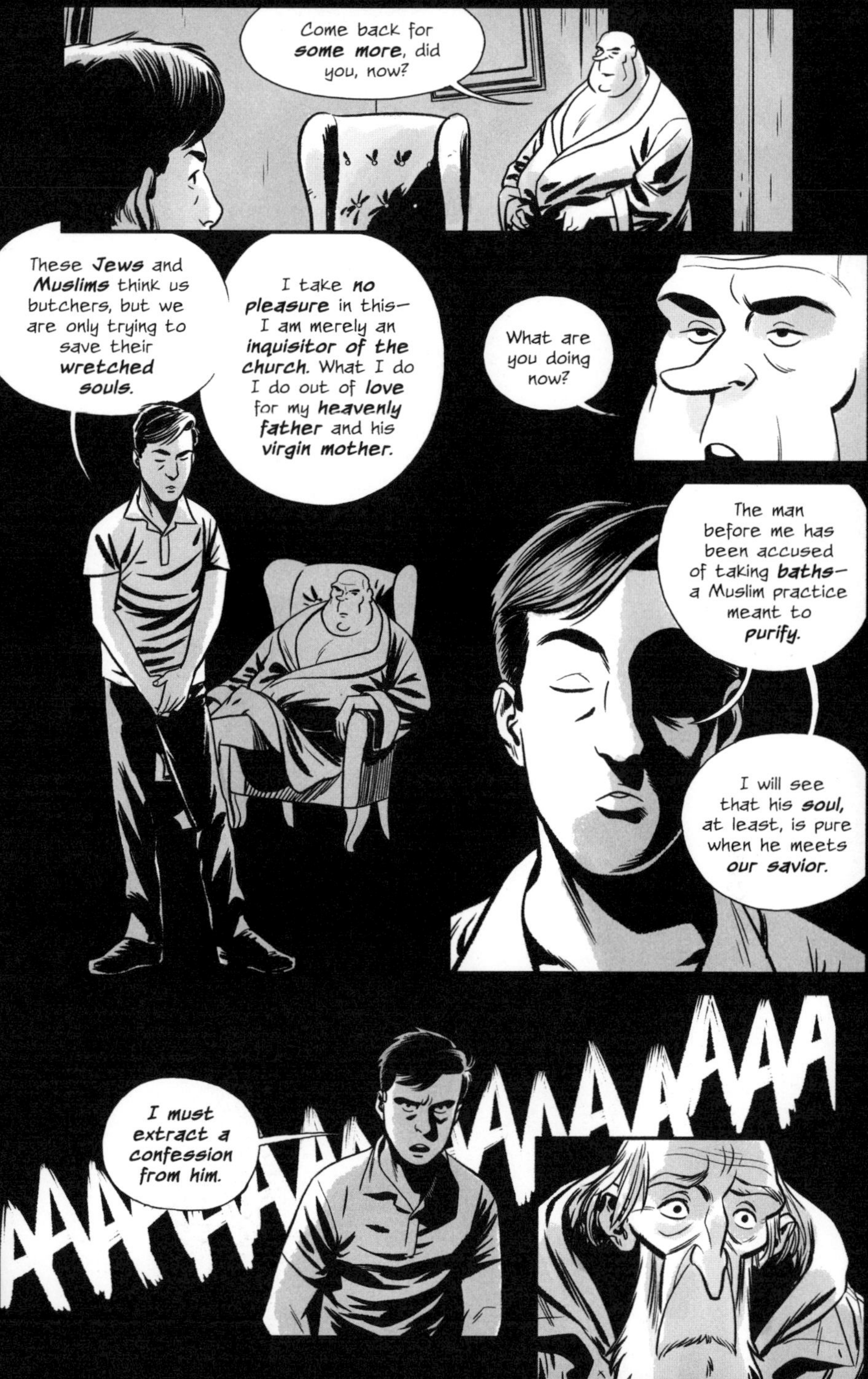
Come back for **some more**, did you, now?
These **Jews** and **Muslims** think us butchers, but we are only trying to save their **wretched souls.**
I take **no pleasure** in this— I am merely an **inquisitor of the church.** What I do I do out of **love** for my **heavenly father** and his **virgin mother.**
What are you doing now?
The man before me has been accused of taking **baths**— a Muslim practice meant to **purify.**
I will see that his **soul,** at least, is pure when he meets **our savior.**
I must extract a confession from him.
AAAAAAAAAAAAAAAAA

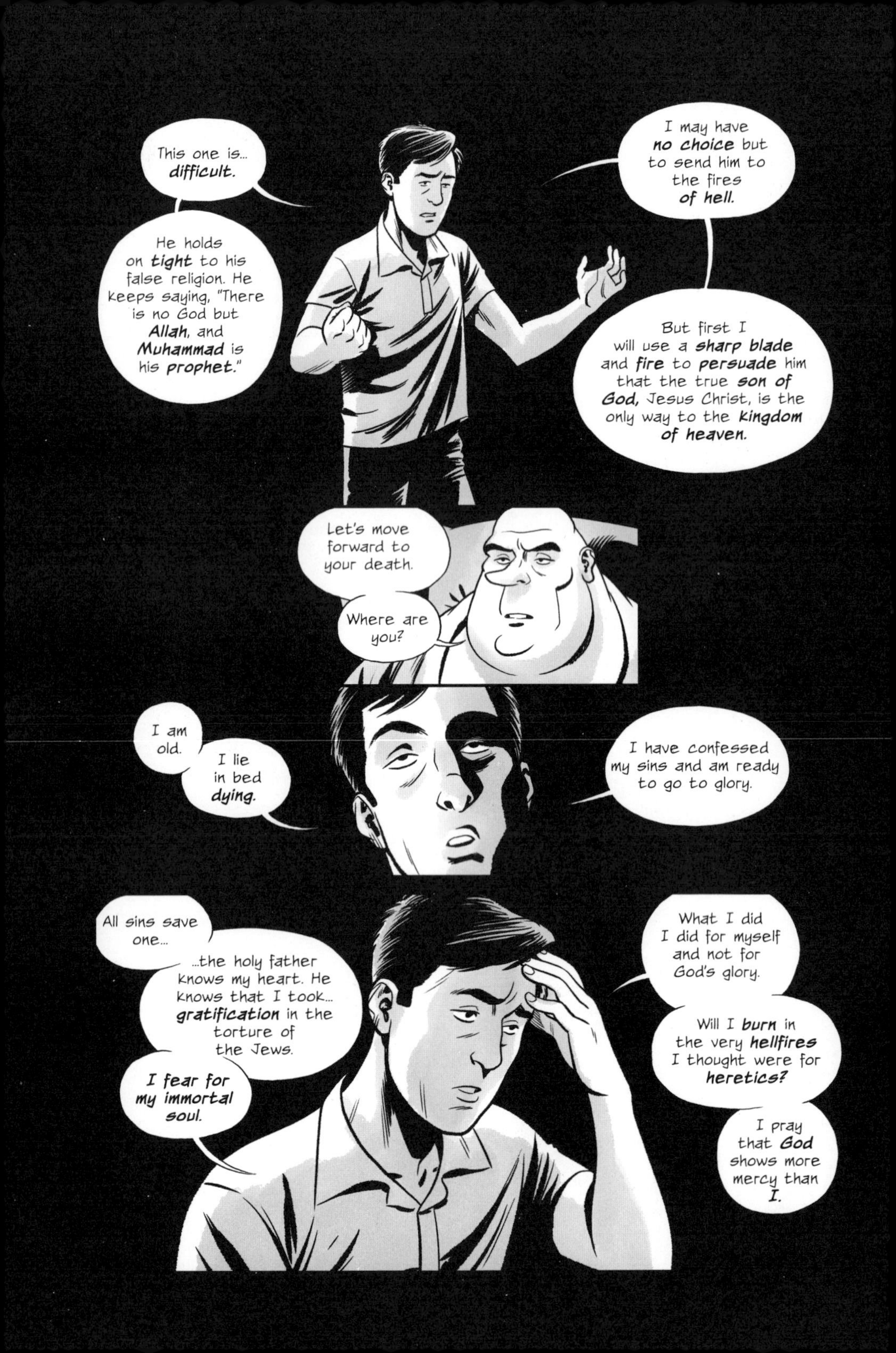
This one is... difficult.
He holds on tight to his false religion. He keeps saying, "There is no God but Allah, and Muhammad is his prophet."
I may have no choice but to send him to the fires of hell.
But first I will use a sharp blade and fire to persuade him that the true son of God, Jesus Christ, is the only way to the kingdom of heaven.
Let's move forward to your death.
Where are you?
I am old.
I lie in bed dying.
I have confessed my sins and am ready to go to glory.
All sins save one...
...the holy father knows my heart. He knows that I took... gratification in the torture of the Jews.
I fear for my immortal soul.
What I did I did for myself and not for God's glory.
Will I burn in the very hellfires I thought were for heretics?
I pray that God shows more mercy than I.

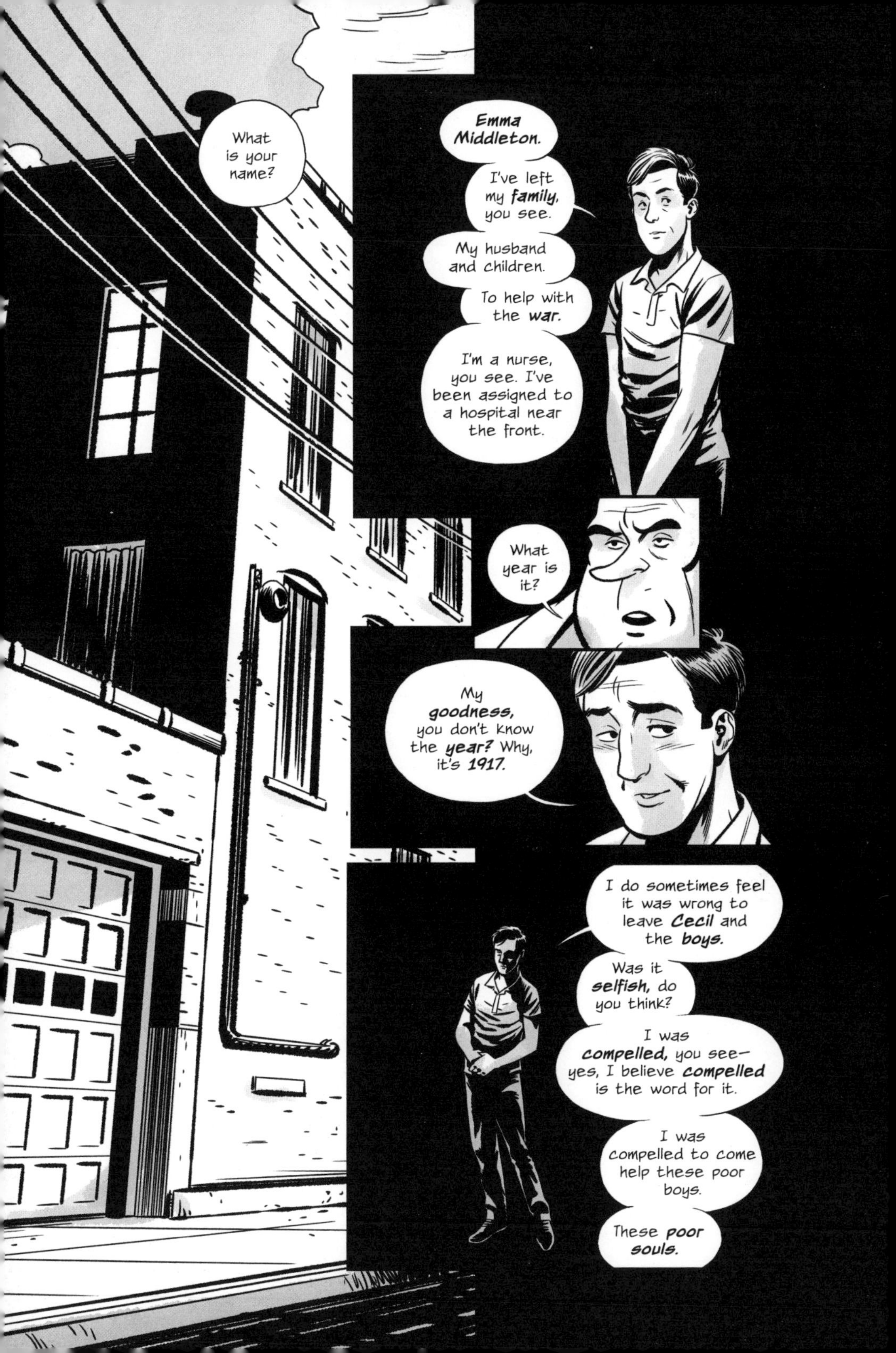
What is your name?
Emma Middleton.
I've left my family, you see.
My husband and children.
To help with the war.
I'm a nurse, you see. I've been assigned to a hospital near the front.
What year is it?
My goodness, you don't know the year? Why, it's 1917.
I do sometimes feel it was wrong to leave Cecil and the boys.
Was it selfish, do you think?
I was compelled, you see— yes, I believe compelled is the word for it.
I was compelled to come help these poor boys.
These poor souls.

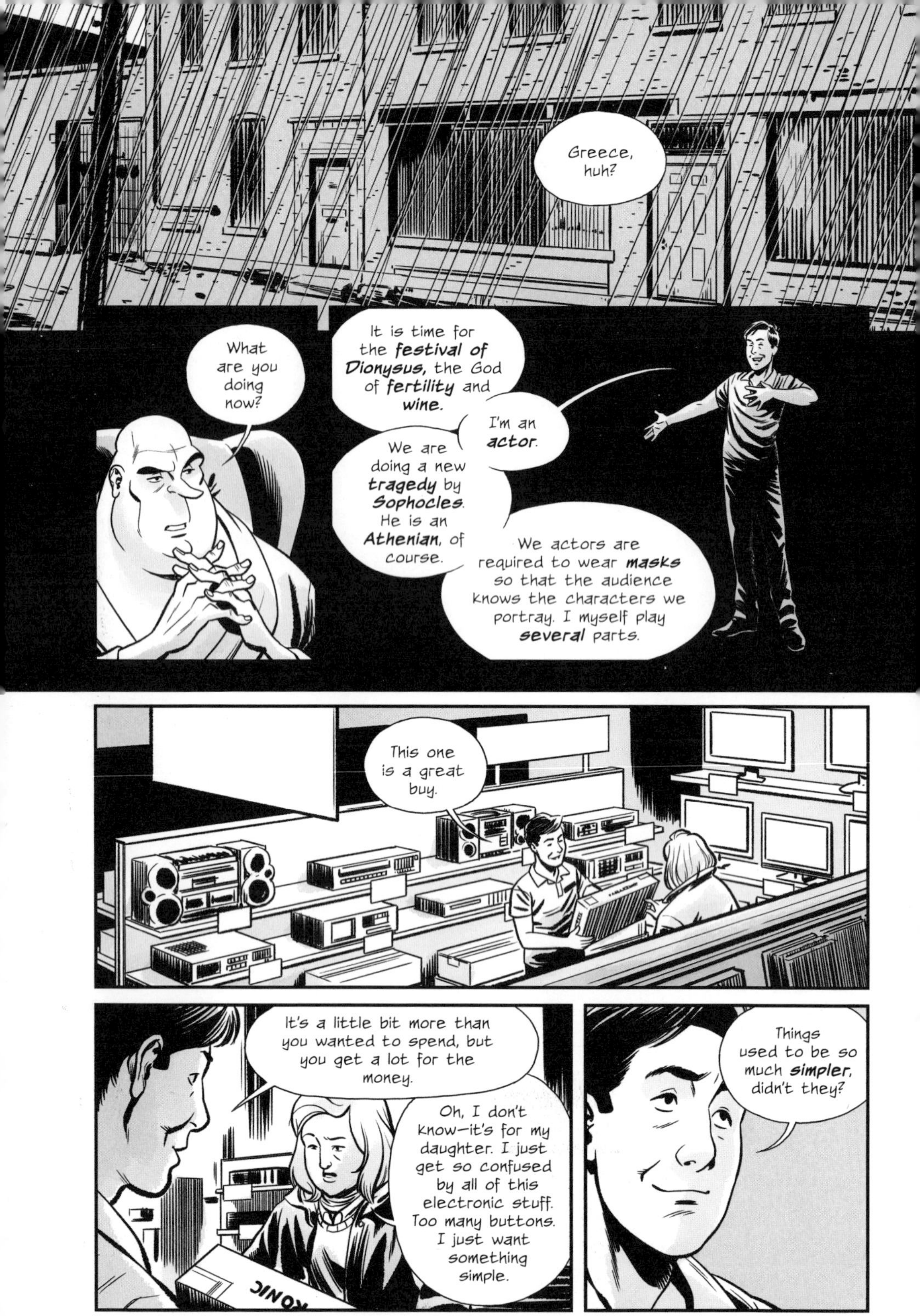
Greece, huh?
What are you doing now?
It is time for the festival of Dionysus, the God of fertility and wine.
I'm an actor.
We are doing a new tragedy by Sophocles. He is an Athenian, of course.
We actors are required to wear masks so that the audience knows the characters we portray. I myself play several parts.
This one is a great buy.
It's a little bit more than you wanted to spend, but you get a lot for the money.
Oh, I don't know—it's for my daughter. I just get so confused by all of this electronic stuff. Too many buttons. I just want something simple.
Things used to be so much simpler, didn't they?

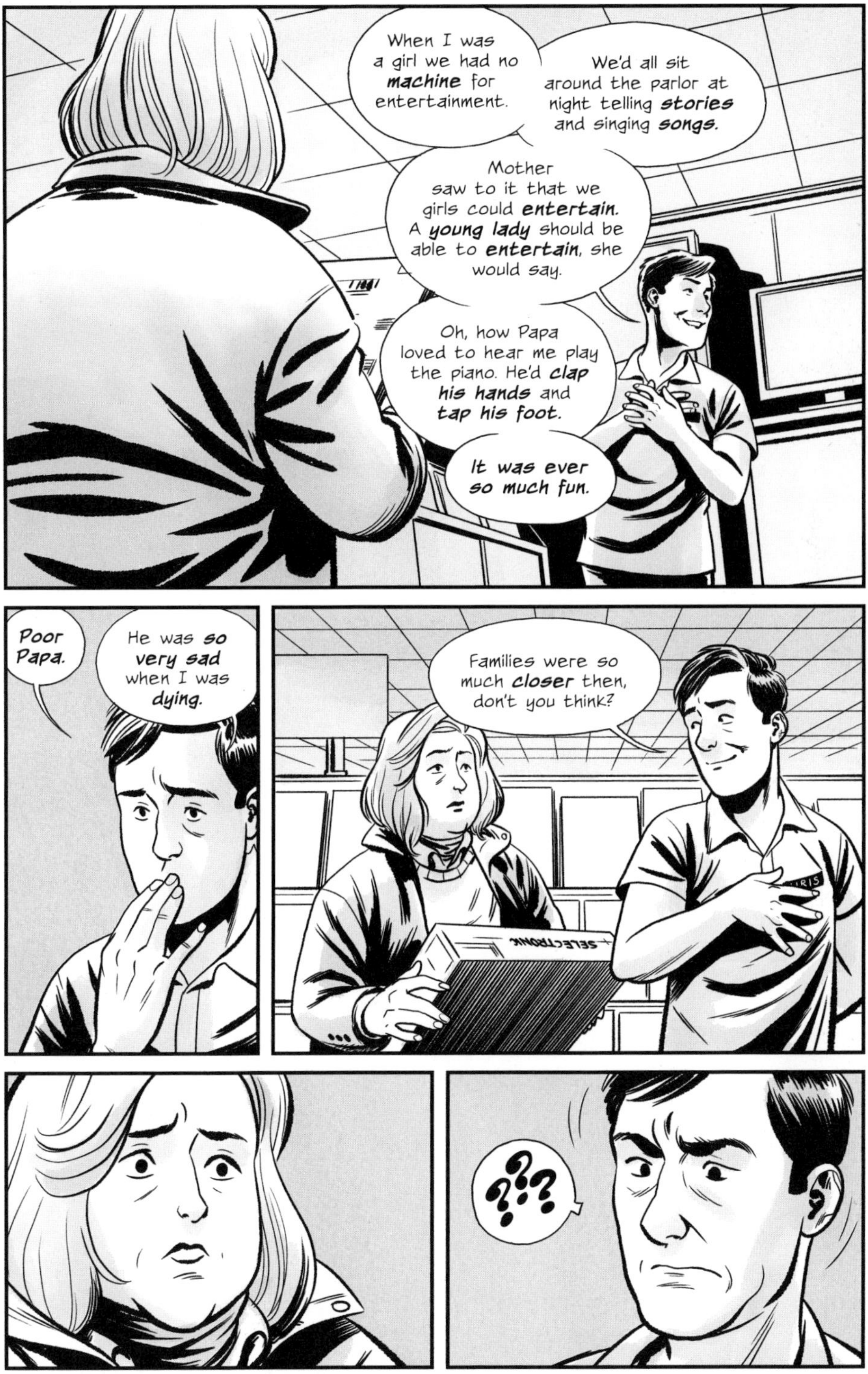

When I was a girl we had no **machine** for entertainment.
We'd all sit around the parlor at night telling **stories** and singing **songs.**
Mother saw to it that we girls could **entertain.** A **young lady** should be able to **entertain**, she would say.
Oh, how Papa loved to hear me play the piano. He'd **clap his hands** and **tap his foot.**
It was ever so much fun.
Poor Papa.
He was **so very sad** when I was **dying.**
Families were so much **closer** then, don't you think?
SELECTRONIC

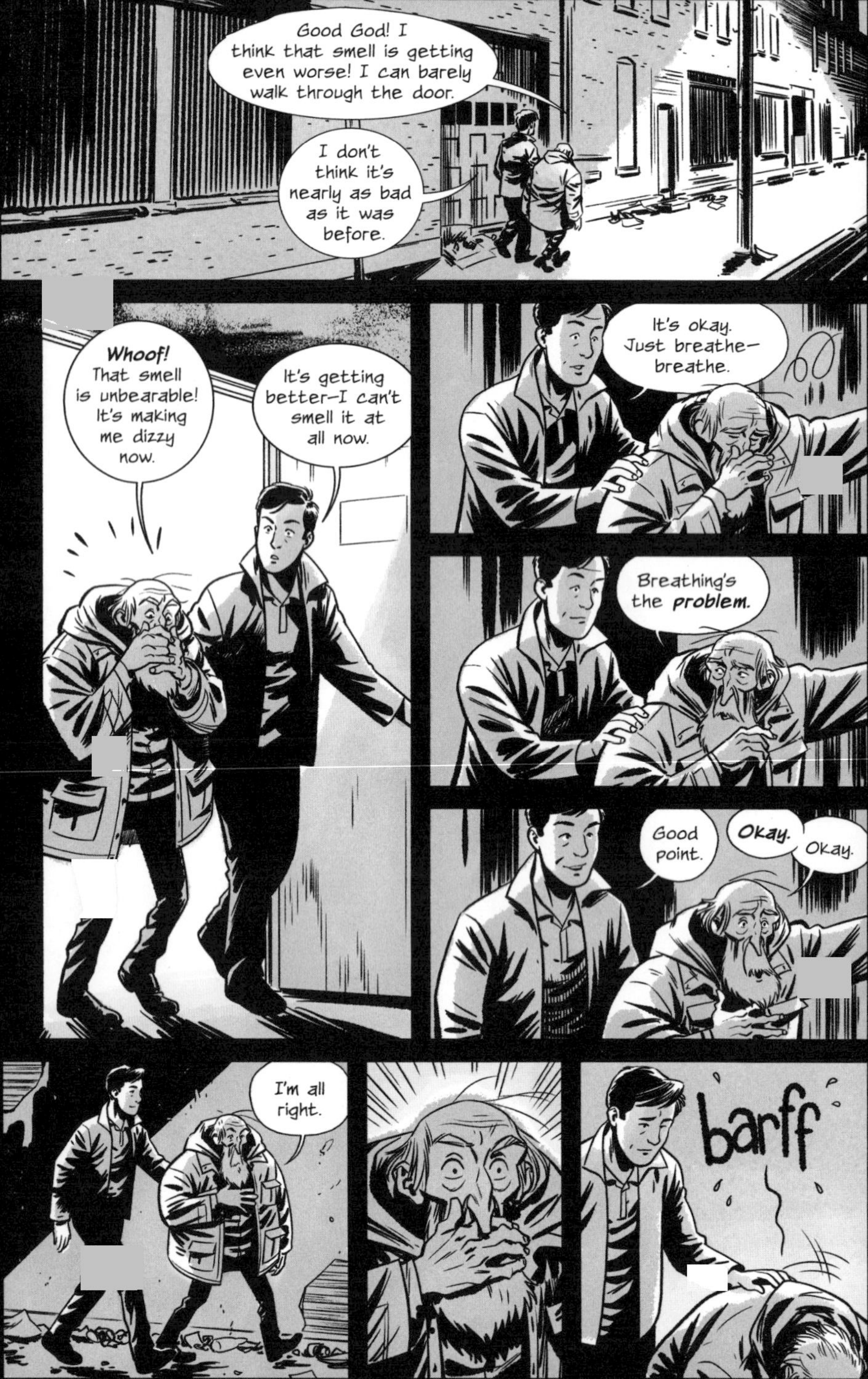
Good God! I think that smell is getting even worse! I can barely walk through the door.
I don't think it's nearly as bad as it was before.
Whoof! That smell is unbearable! It's making me dizzy now.
It's getting better—I can't smell it at all now.
It's okay. Just breathe—breathe.
Breathing's the ***problem.***
Good point.
Okay.
Okay.
I'm all right.
barff

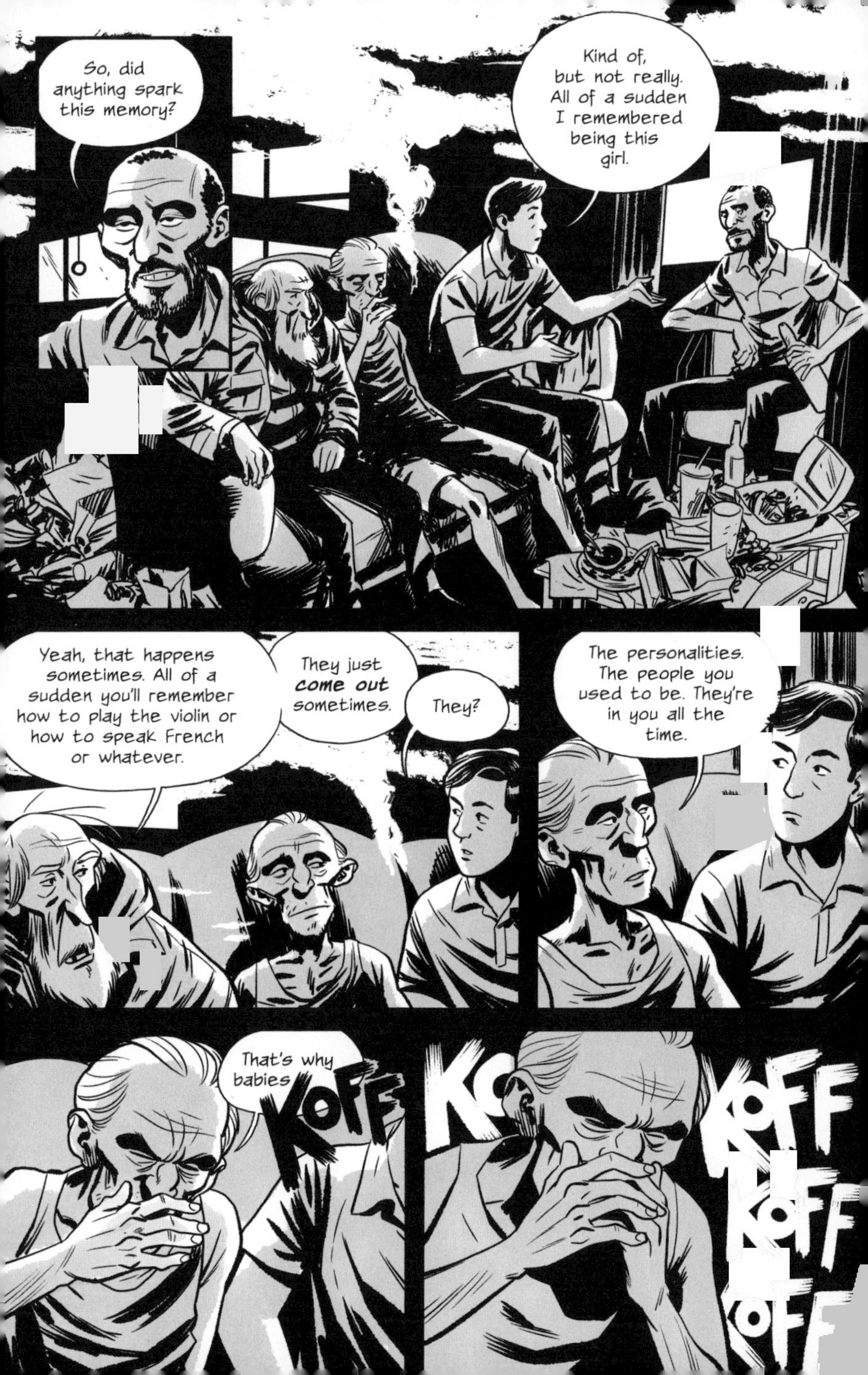
So, did anything spark this memory?
Kind of, but not really. All of a sudden I remembered being this girl.
Yeah, that happens sometimes. All of a sudden you'll remember how to play the violin or how to speak French or whatever.
They just **come out** sometimes.
They?
The personalities. The people you used to be. They're in you all the time.
That's why babies
KOFF
KOFF
KOFF
KOFF

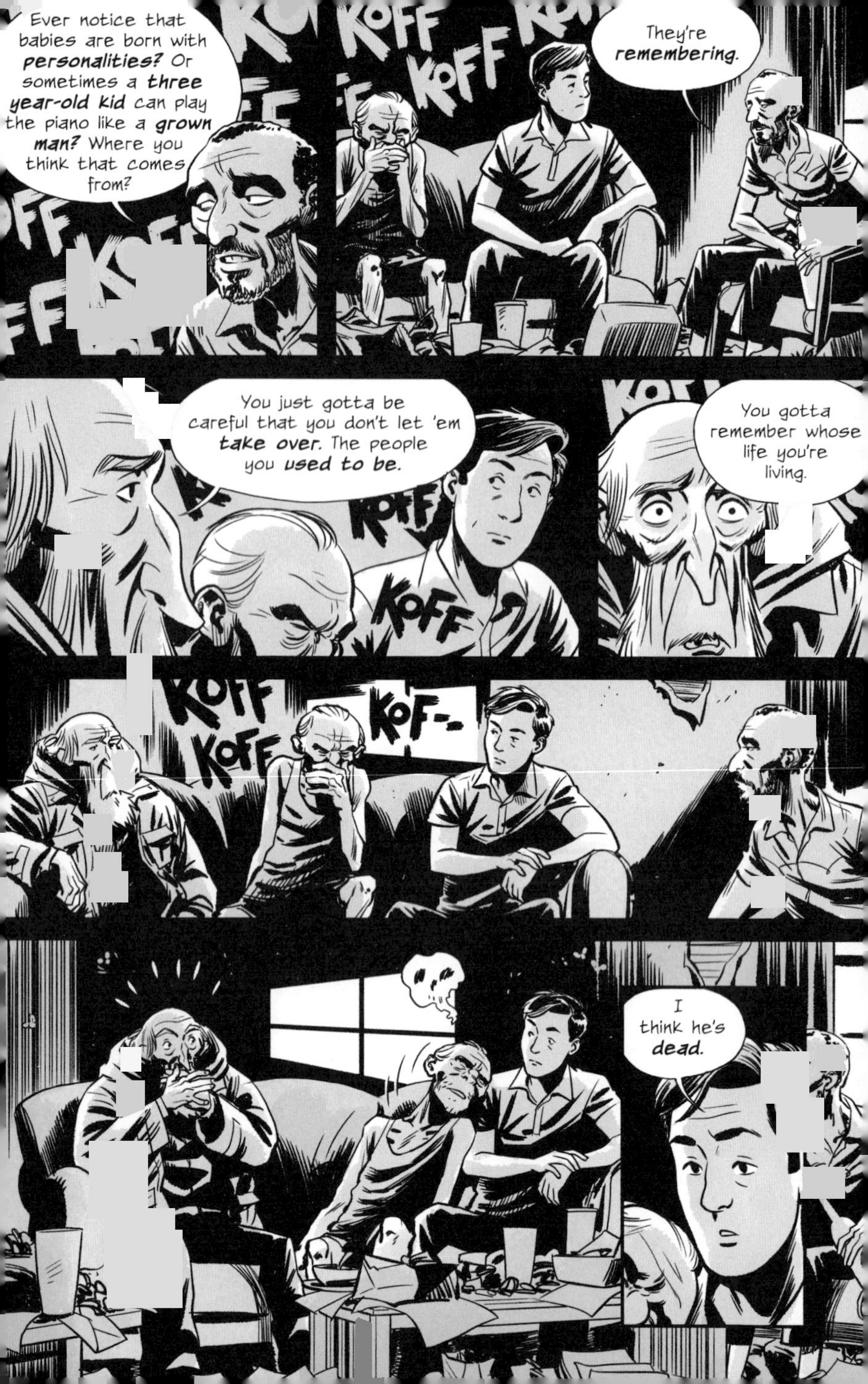

Ever notice that babies are born with **personalities?** Or sometimes a **three year-old kid** can play the piano like a **grown man?** Where you think that comes from?
KOFF
KOFF
KOFF KOFF
They're **remembering.**
You just gotta be careful that you don't let 'em **take over.** The people you **used to be.**
KOFF
KOFF
You gotta remember whose life you're living.
KOFF
KOFF
KOF-
I think he's **dead.**

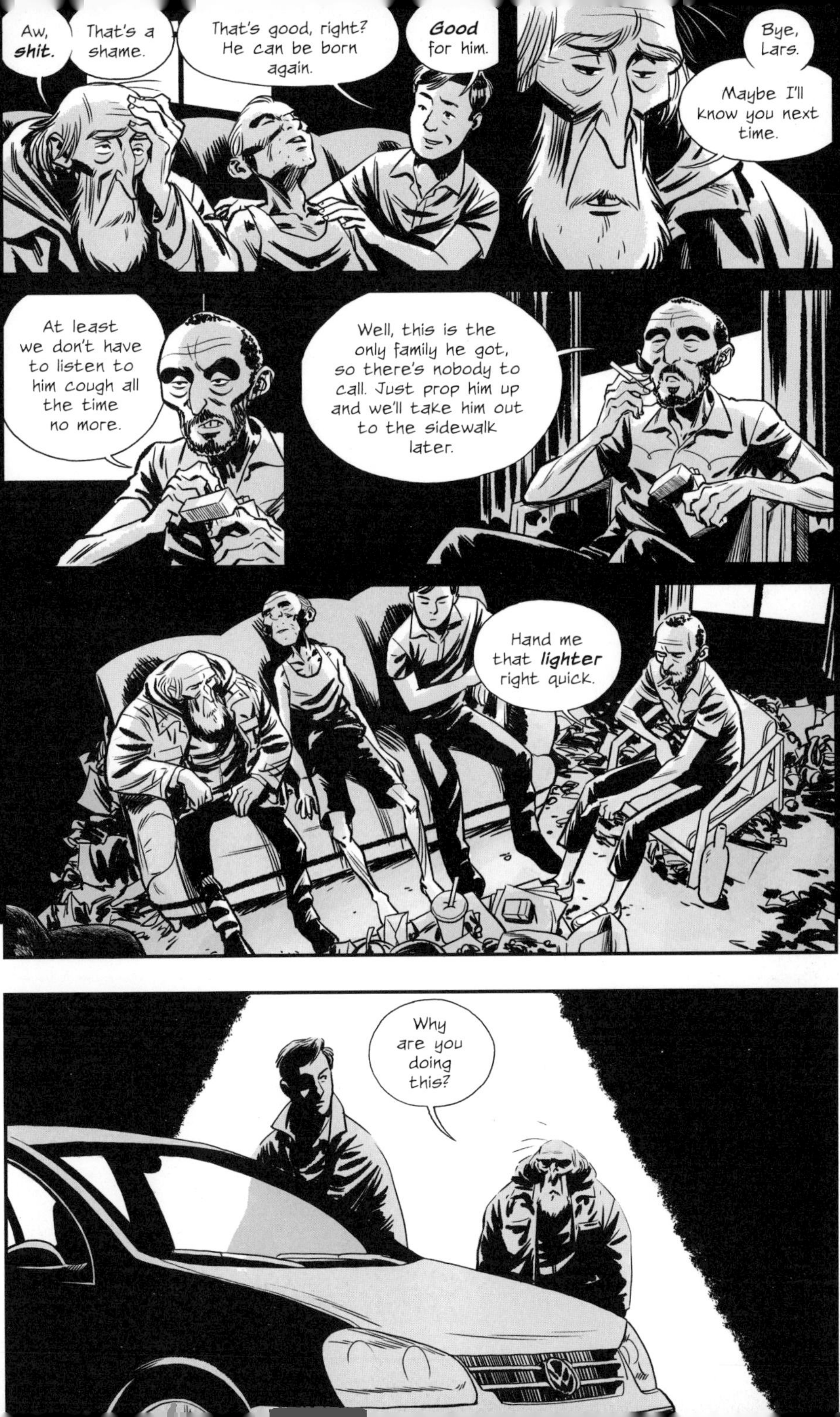
Aw, **shit.**
That's a shame.
That's good, right? He can be born again.
Good for him.
Bye, Lars.
Maybe I'll know you next time.
At least we don't have to listen to him cough all the time no more.
Well, this is the only family he got, so there's nobody to call. Just prop him up and we'll take him out to the sidewalk later.
Hand me that **lighter** right quick.
Why are you doing this?

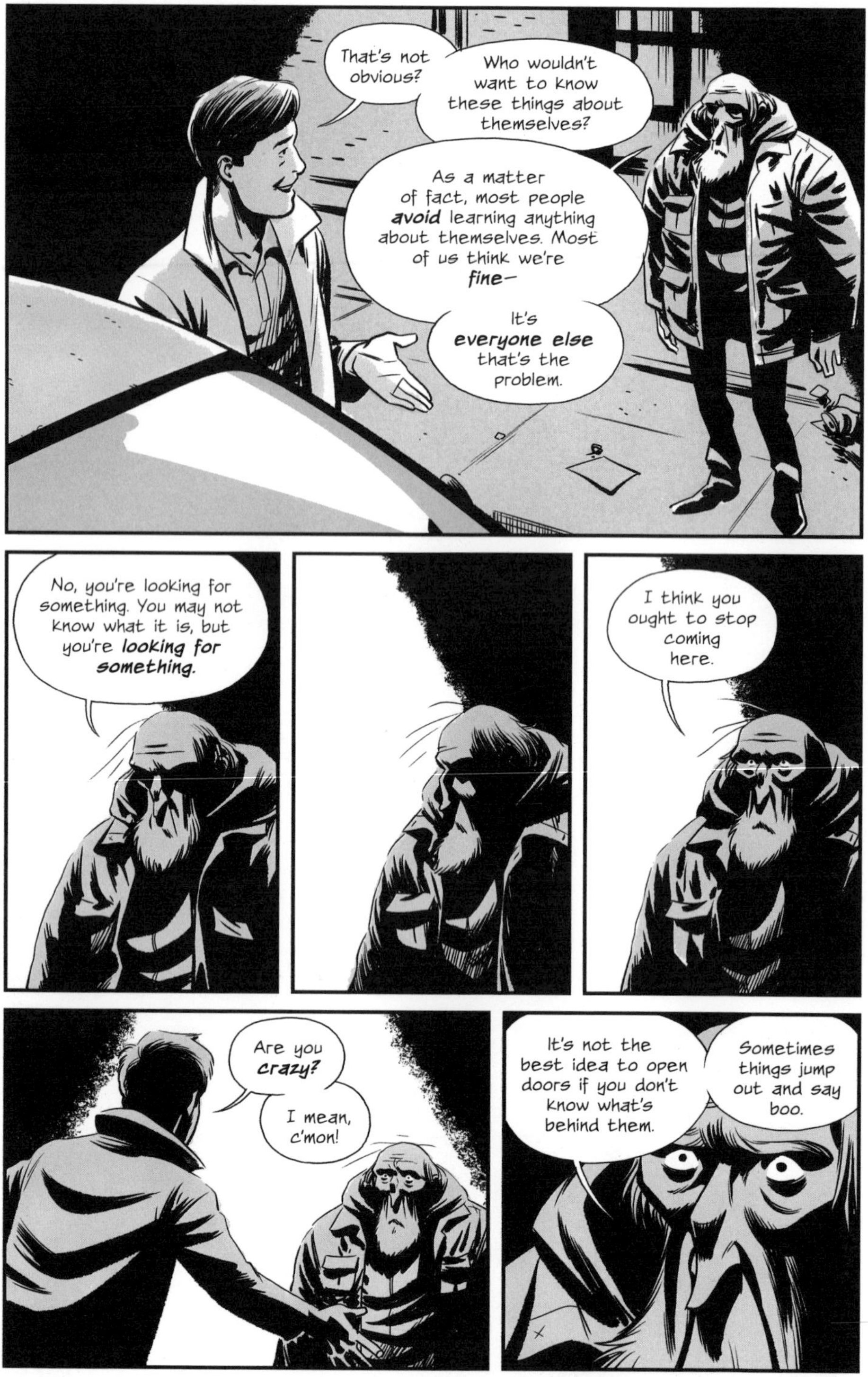
That's not obvious?
Who wouldn't want to know these things about themselves?
As a matter of fact, most people **avoid** learning anything about themselves. Most of us think we're ***fine***–
It's **everyone else** that's the problem.
No, you're looking for something. You may not know what it is, but you're **looking for something.**
I think you ought to stop coming here.
Are you ***crazy?***
I mean, c'mon!
It's not the best idea to open doors if you don't know what's behind them.
Sometimes things jump out and say boo.

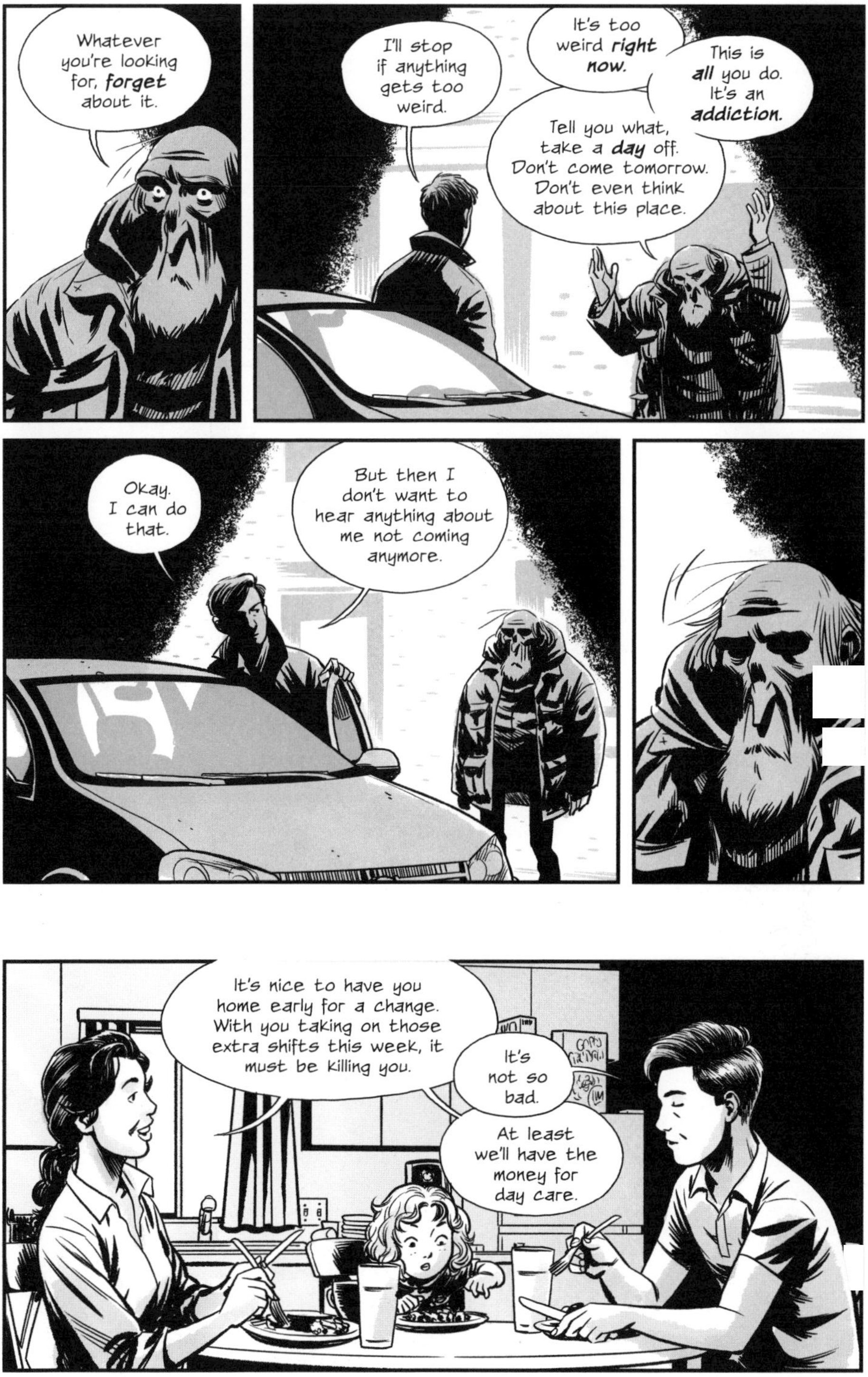
Whatever you're looking for, **forget** about it.
I'll stop if anything gets too weird.
It's too weird **right now.**
This is **all** you do. It's an **addiction.**
Tell you what, take a **day** off. Don't come tomorrow. Don't even think about this place.
Okay. I can do that.
But then I don't want to hear anything about me not coming anymore.
It's nice to have you home early for a change. With you taking on those extra shifts this week, it must be killing you.
It's not so bad.
At least we'll have the money for day care.

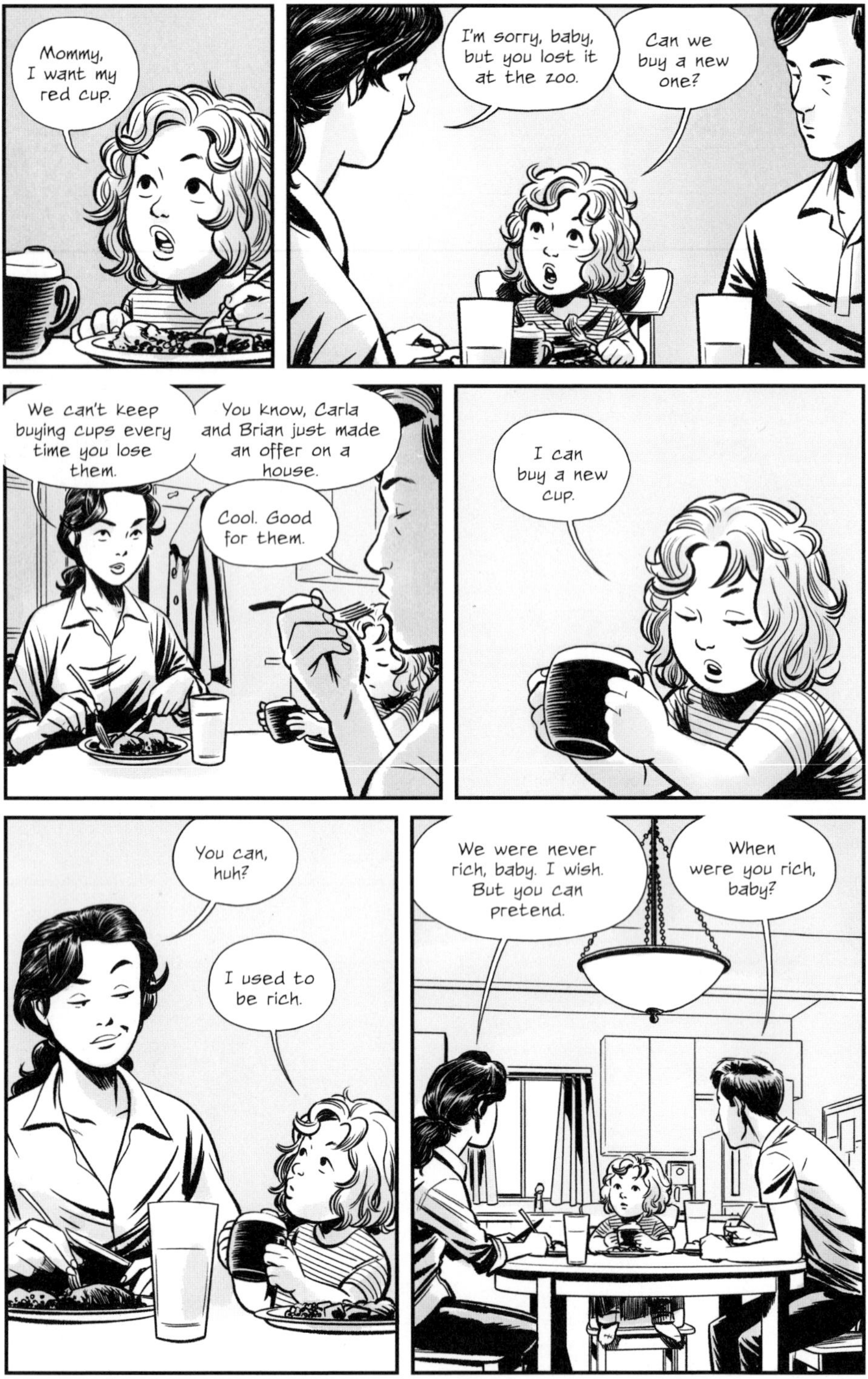
Mommy, I want my red cup.
I'm sorry, baby, but you lost it at the zoo.
Can we buy a new one?
We can't keep buying cups every time you lose them.
You know, Carla and Brian just made an offer on a house.
Cool. Good for them.
I can buy a new cup.
You can, huh?
I used to be rich.
We were never rich, baby. I wish. But you can pretend.
When were you rich, baby?

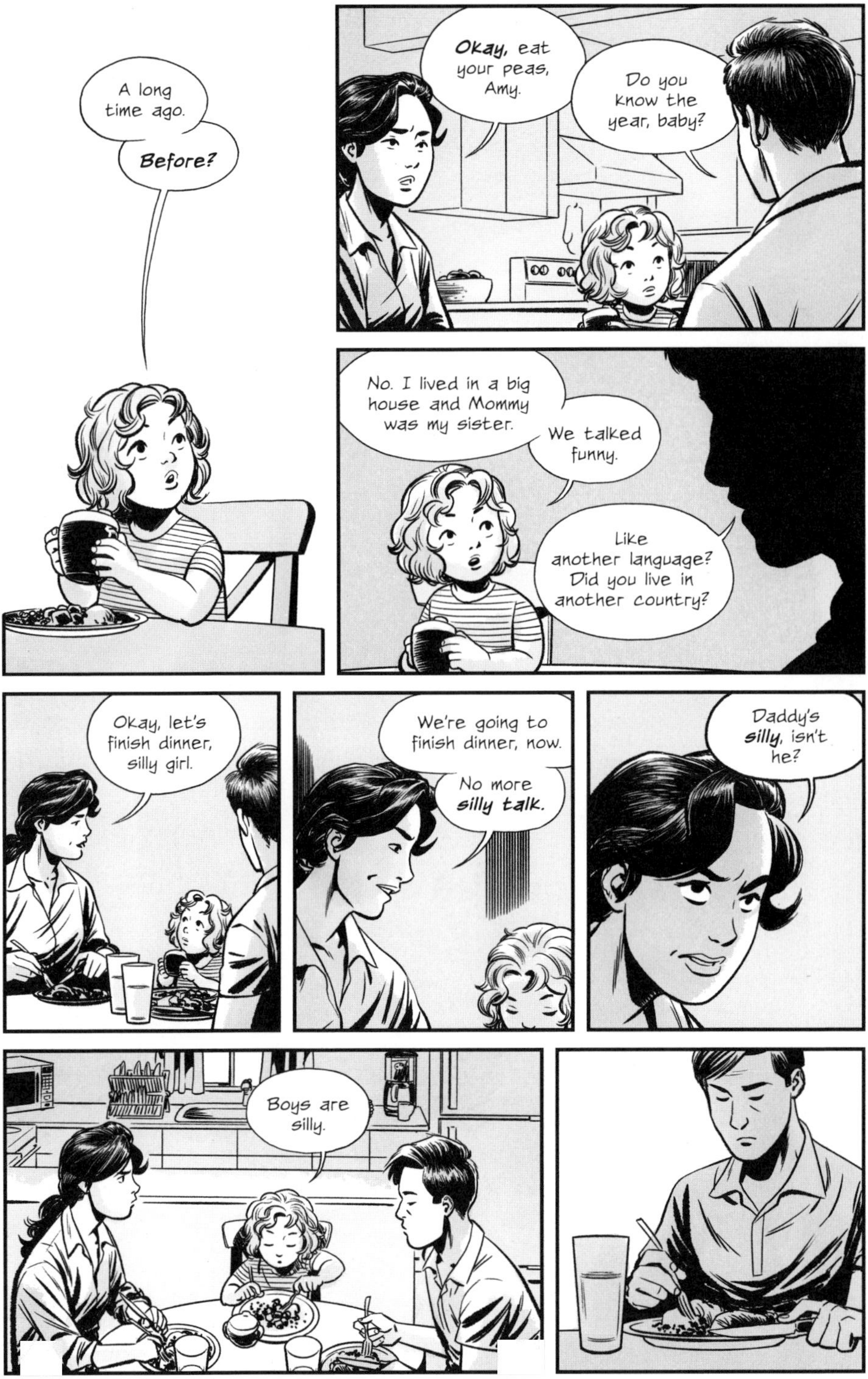
A long time ago.
Before?
Okay, eat your peas, Amy.
Do you know the year, baby?
No. I lived in a big house and Mommy was my sister.
We talked funny.
Like another language? Did you live in another country?
Okay, let's finish dinner, silly girl.
We're going to finish dinner, now.
No more silly talk.
Daddy's silly, isn't he?
Boys are silly.

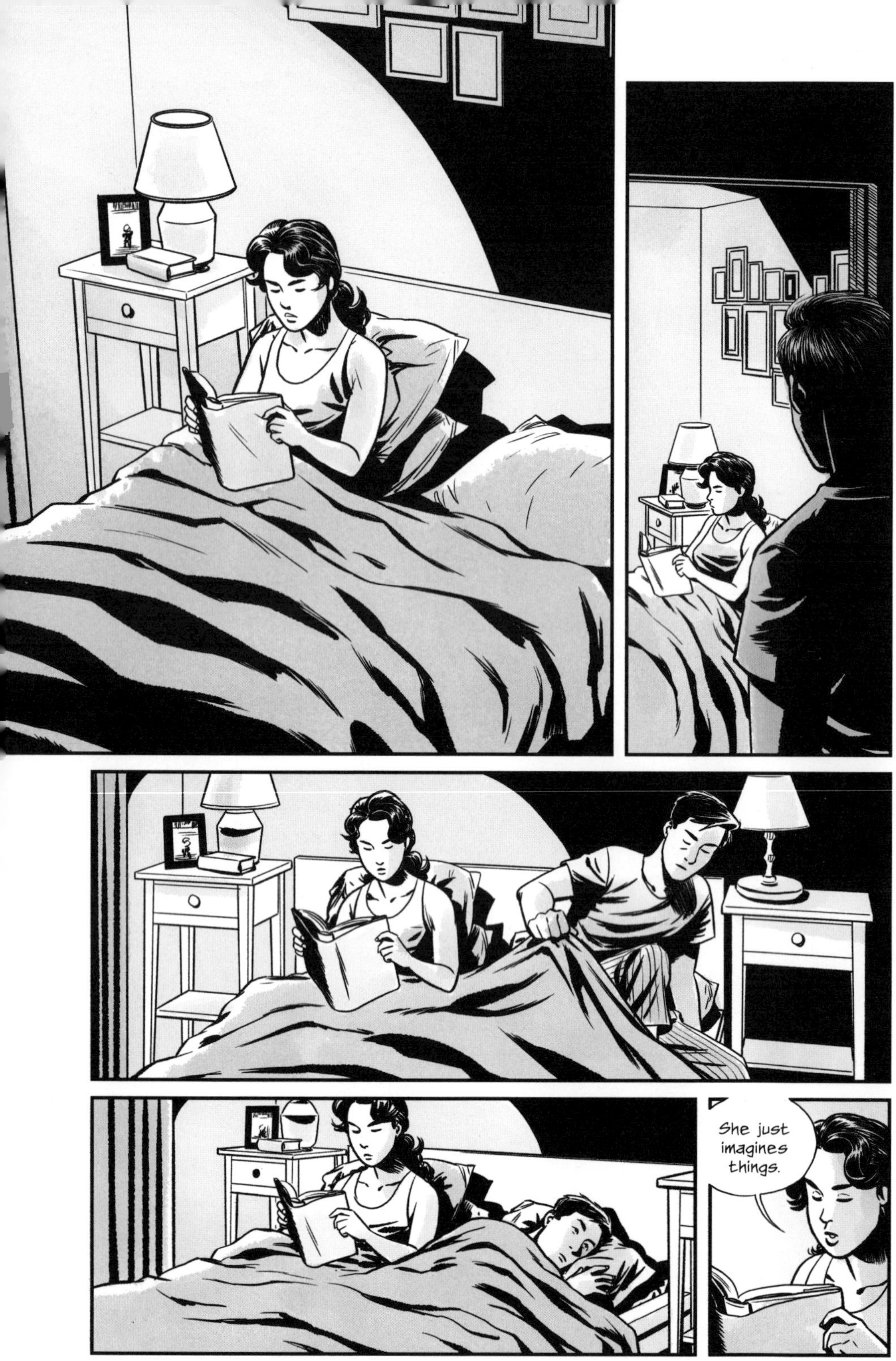
She just imagines things.

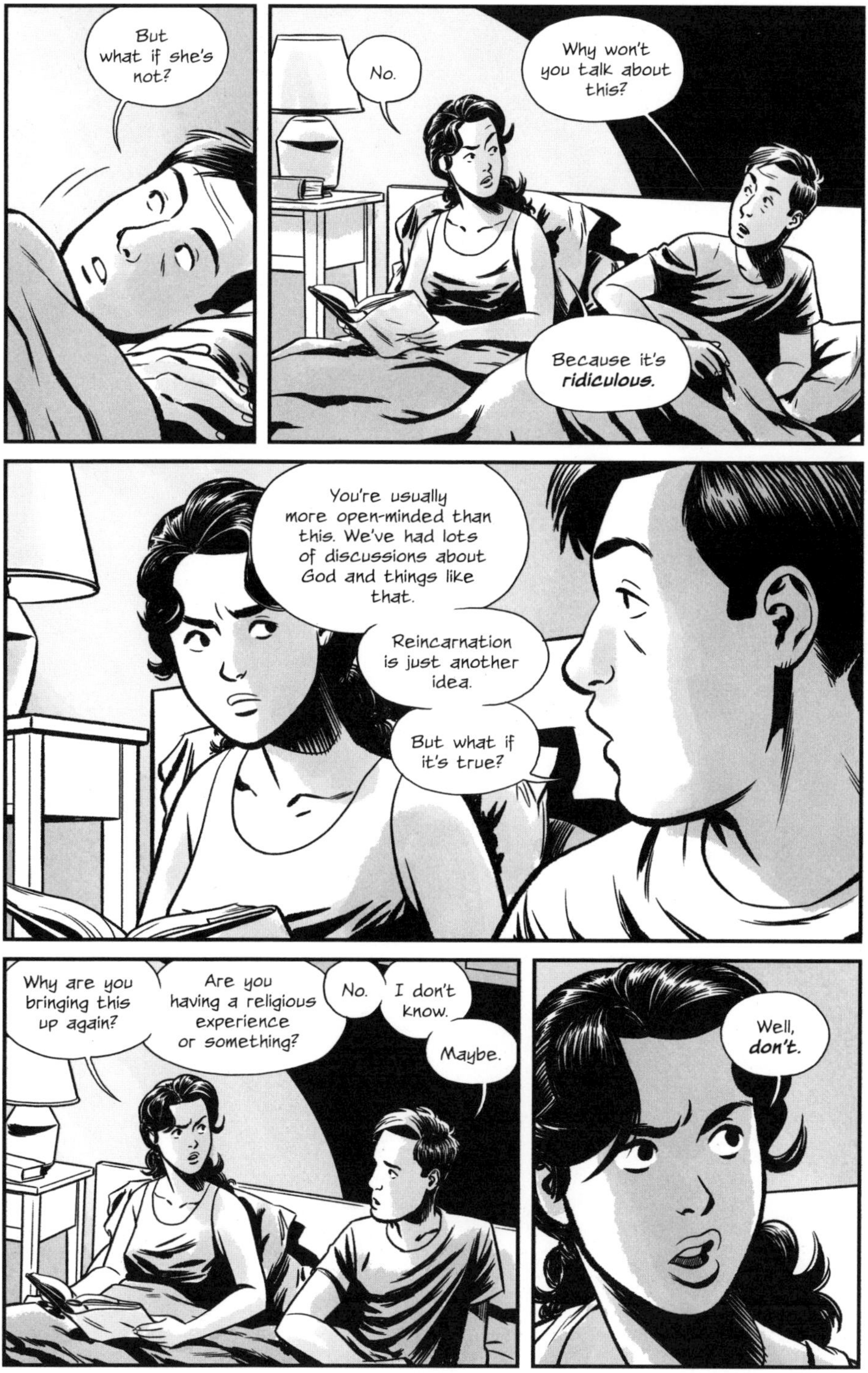
But what if she's not?
No.
Why won't you talk about this?
Because it's ***ridiculous.***
You're usually more open-minded than this. We've had lots of discussions about God and things like that.
Reincarnation is just another idea.
But what if it's true?
Why are you bringing this up again?
Are you having a religious experience or something?
No.
I don't know.
Maybe.
Well, ***don't.***

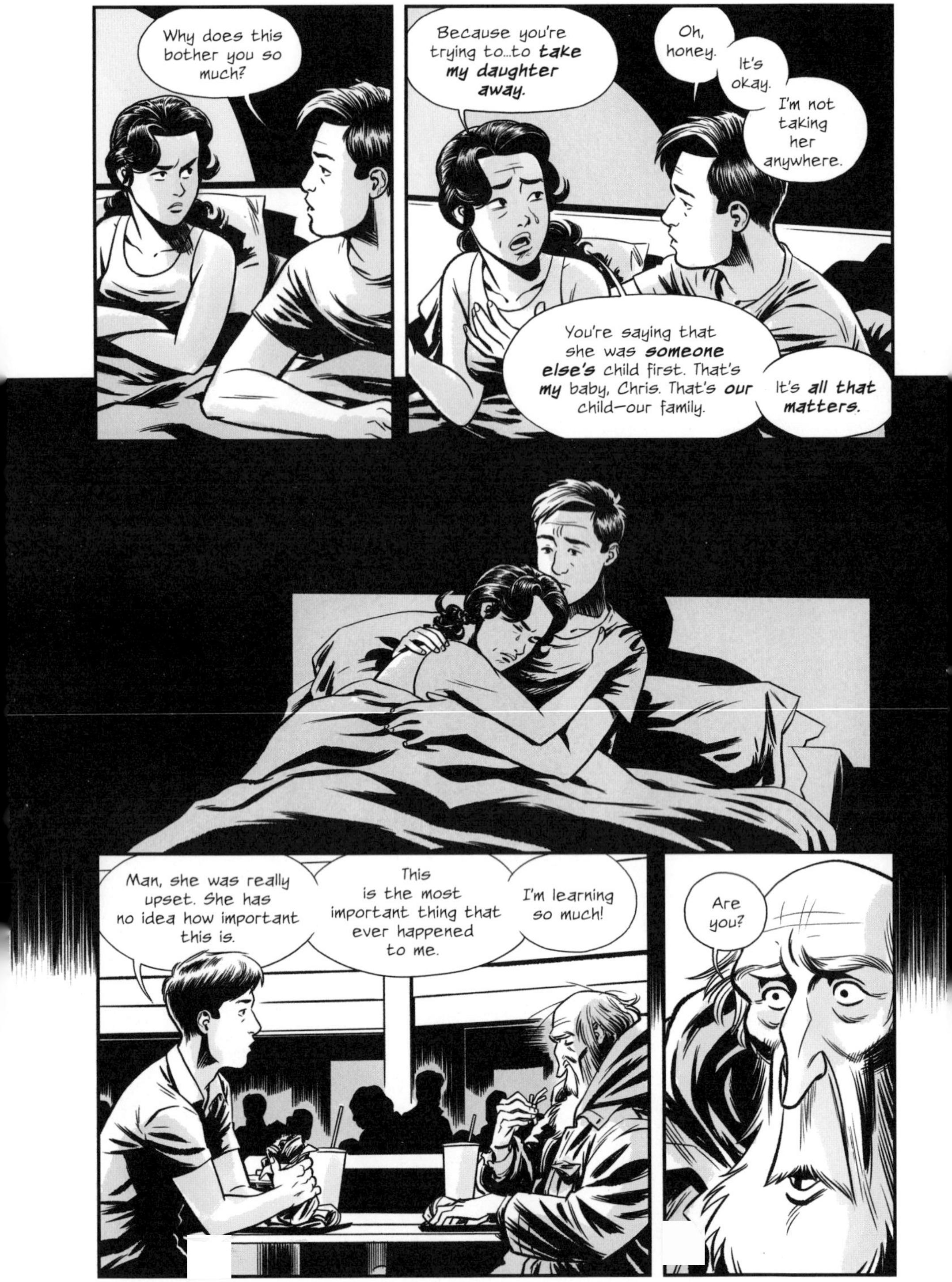
Why does this bother you so much?
Because you're trying to...to **take my daughter away.**
Oh, honey.
It's okay.
I'm not taking her anywhere.
You're saying that she was **someone else's** child first. That's **my** baby, Chris. That's **our** child—our family.
It's **all that matters.**
Man, she was really upset. She has no idea how important this is.
This is the most important thing that ever happened to me.
I'm learning so much!
Are you?

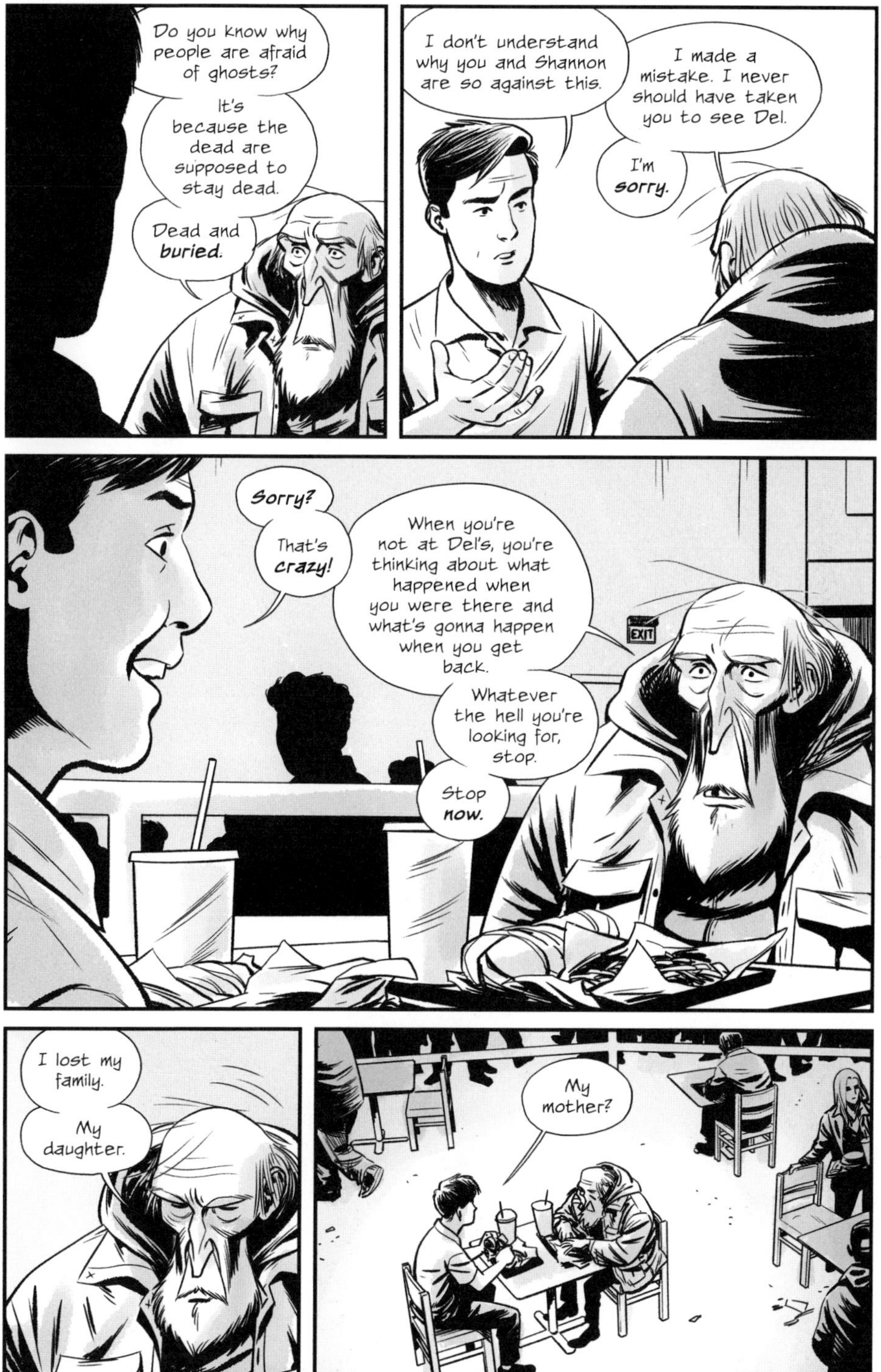
Do you know why people are afraid of ghosts?
It's because the dead are supposed to stay dead.
Dead and **buried.**
I don't understand why you and Shannon are so against this.
I made a mistake. I never should have taken you to see Del.
I'm **sorry.**
Sorry?
That's **crazy!**
When you're not at Del's, you're thinking about what happened when you were there and what's gonna happen when you get back.
Whatever the hell you're looking for, stop.
Stop **now.**
EXIT
I lost my family.
My daughter.
My mother?

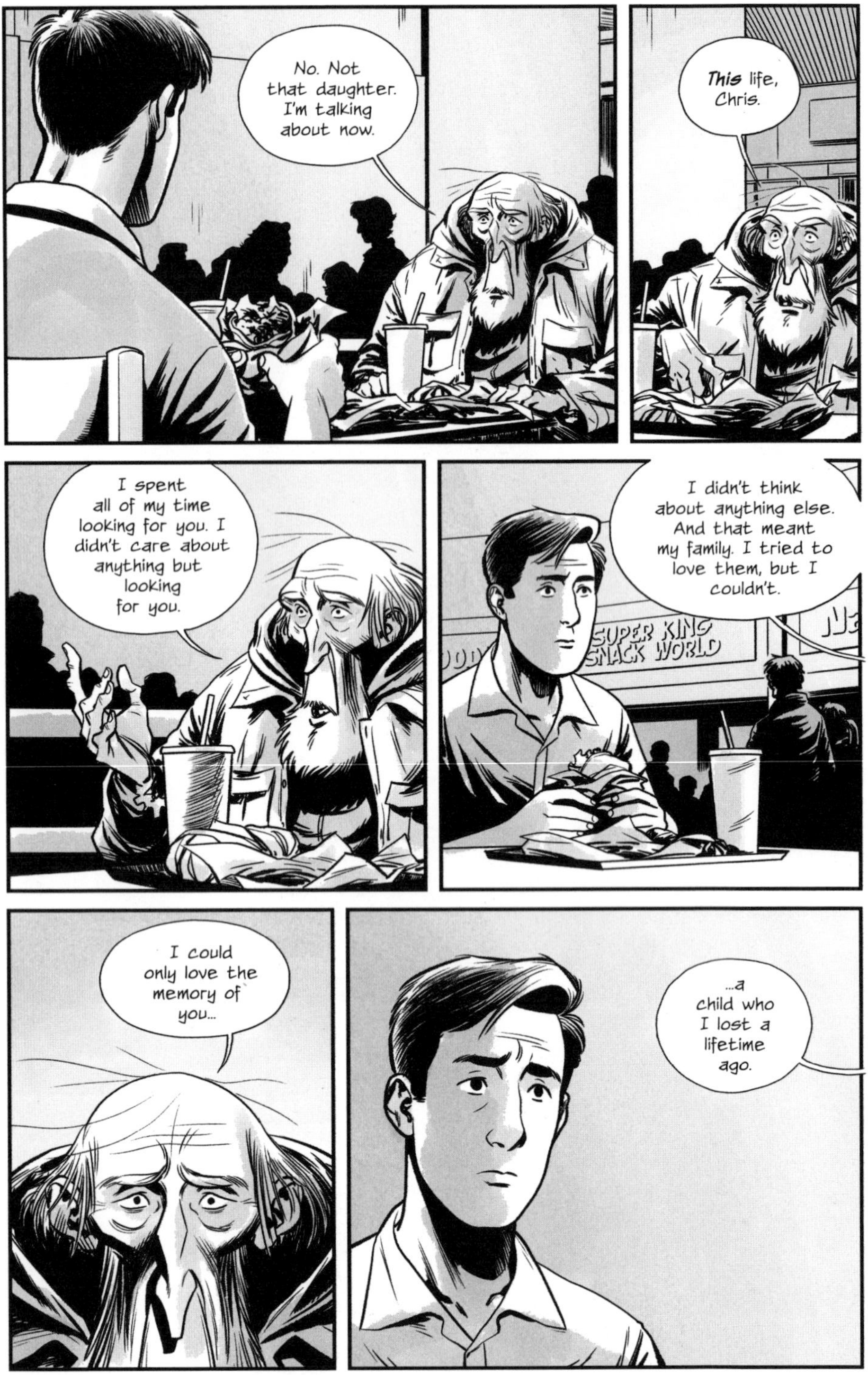
No. Not that daughter. I'm talking about now.
This life, Chris.
I spent all of my time looking for you. I didn't care about anything but looking for you.
I didn't think about anything else. And that meant my family. I tried to love them, but I couldn't.
SUPER KING SNACK WORLD
I could only love the memory of you...
...a child who I lost a lifetime ago.

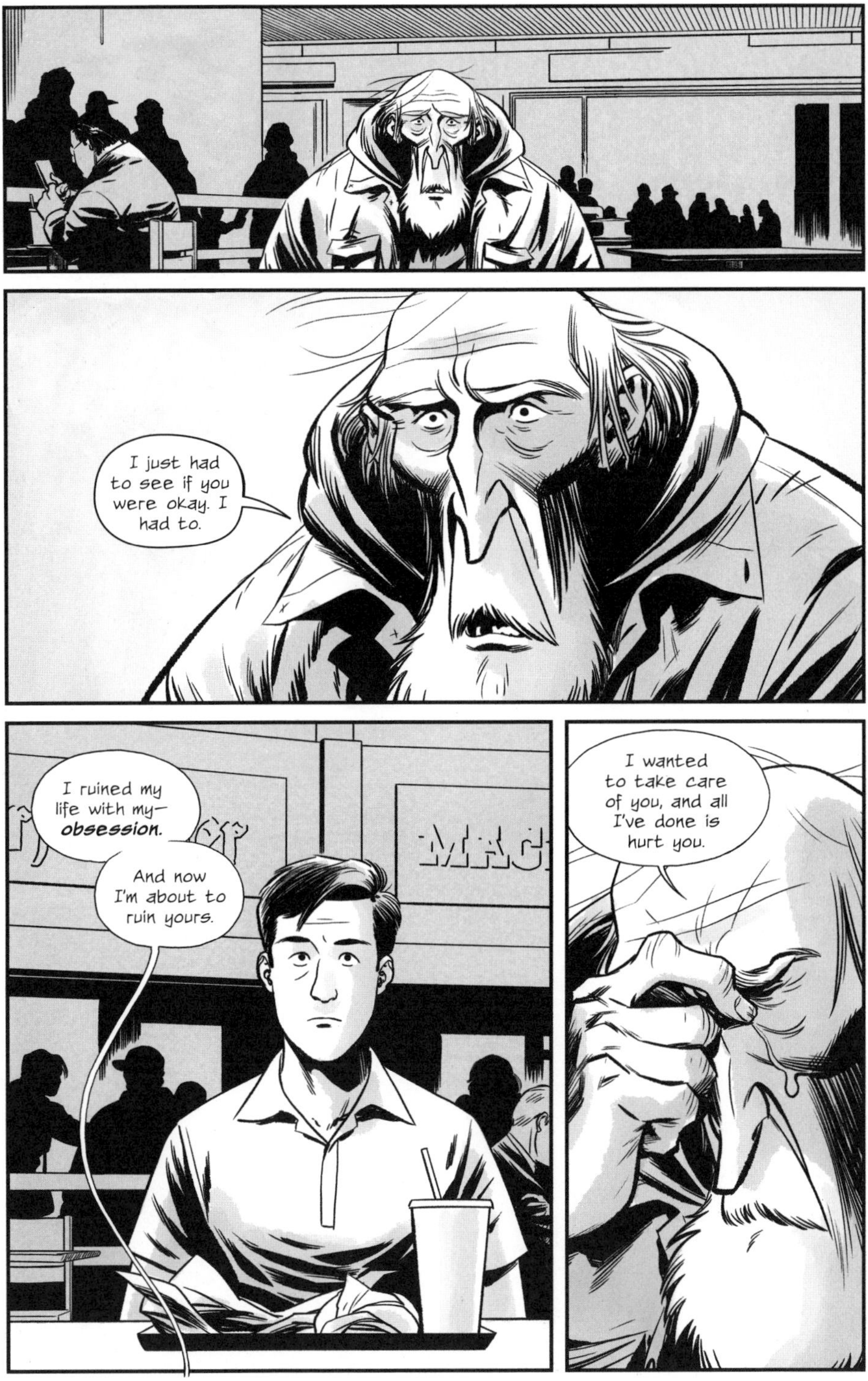
I just had to see if you were okay. I had to.
I ruined my life with my— obsession.
And now I'm about to ruin yours.
I wanted to take care of you, and all I've done is hurt you.

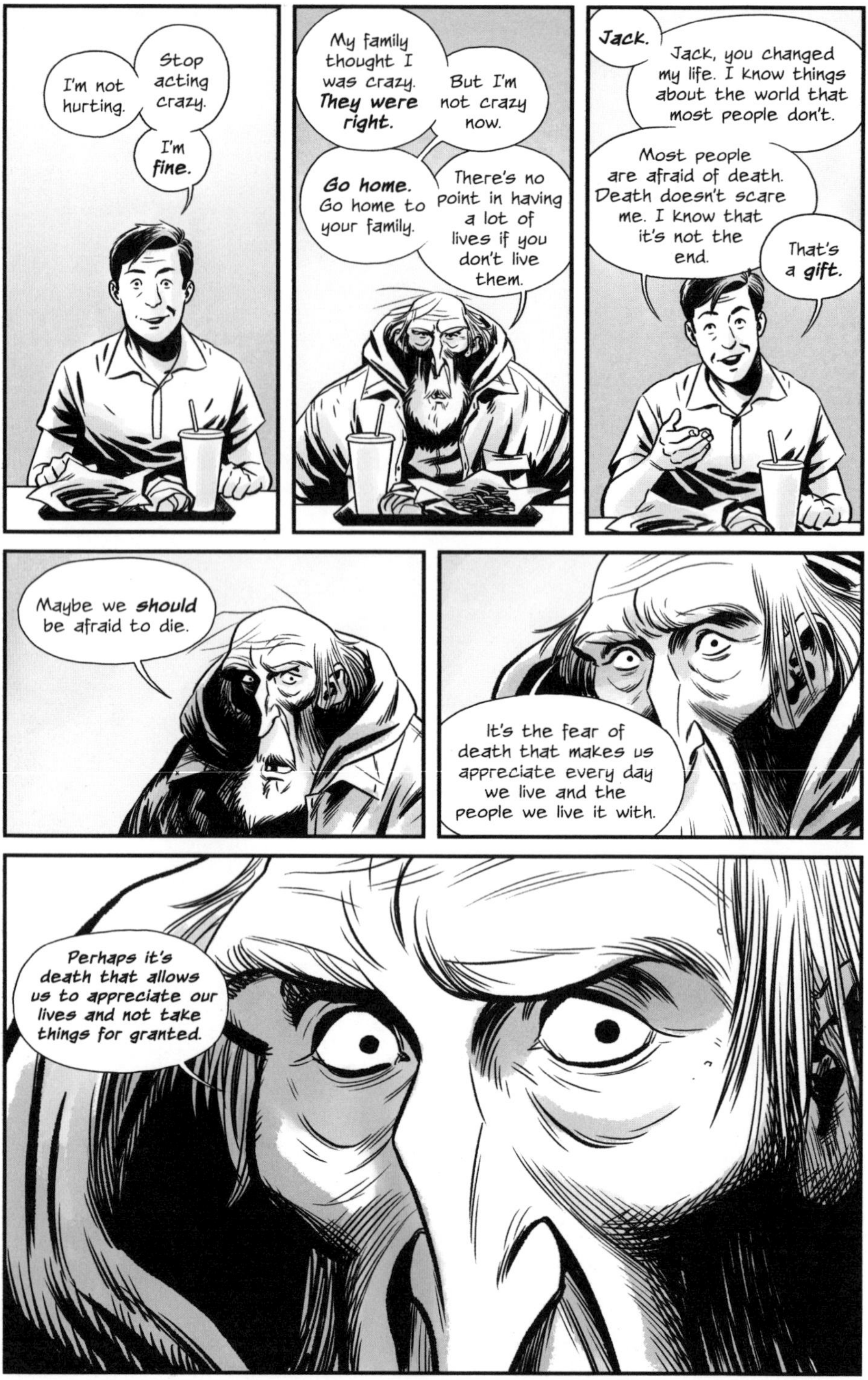
I'm not hurting.
Stop acting crazy.
I'm **fine.**
My family thought I was crazy. **They were right.**
But I'm not crazy now.
Go home. Go home to your family.
There's no point in having a lot of lives if you don't live them.
Jack.
Jack, you changed my life. I know things about the world that most people don't.
Most people are afraid of death. Death doesn't scare me. I know that it's not the end.
That's a **gift.**
Maybe we **should** be afraid to die.
It's the fear of death that makes us appreciate every day we live and the people we live it with.
Perhaps it's death that allows us to appreciate our lives and not take things for granted.

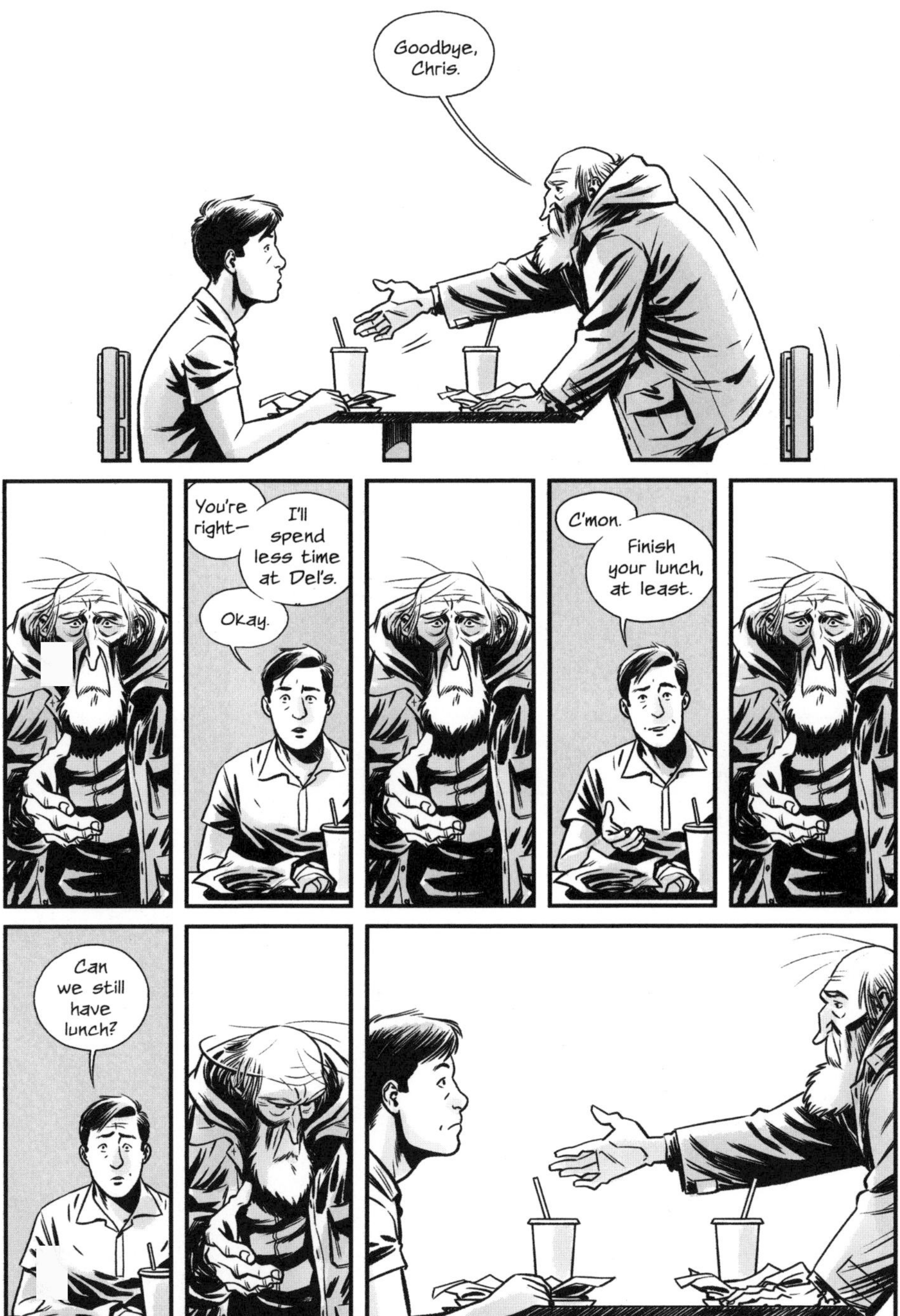
Goodbye, Chris.
You're right—
I'll spend less time at Del's.
Okay.
C'mon.
Finish your lunch, at least.
Can we still have lunch?

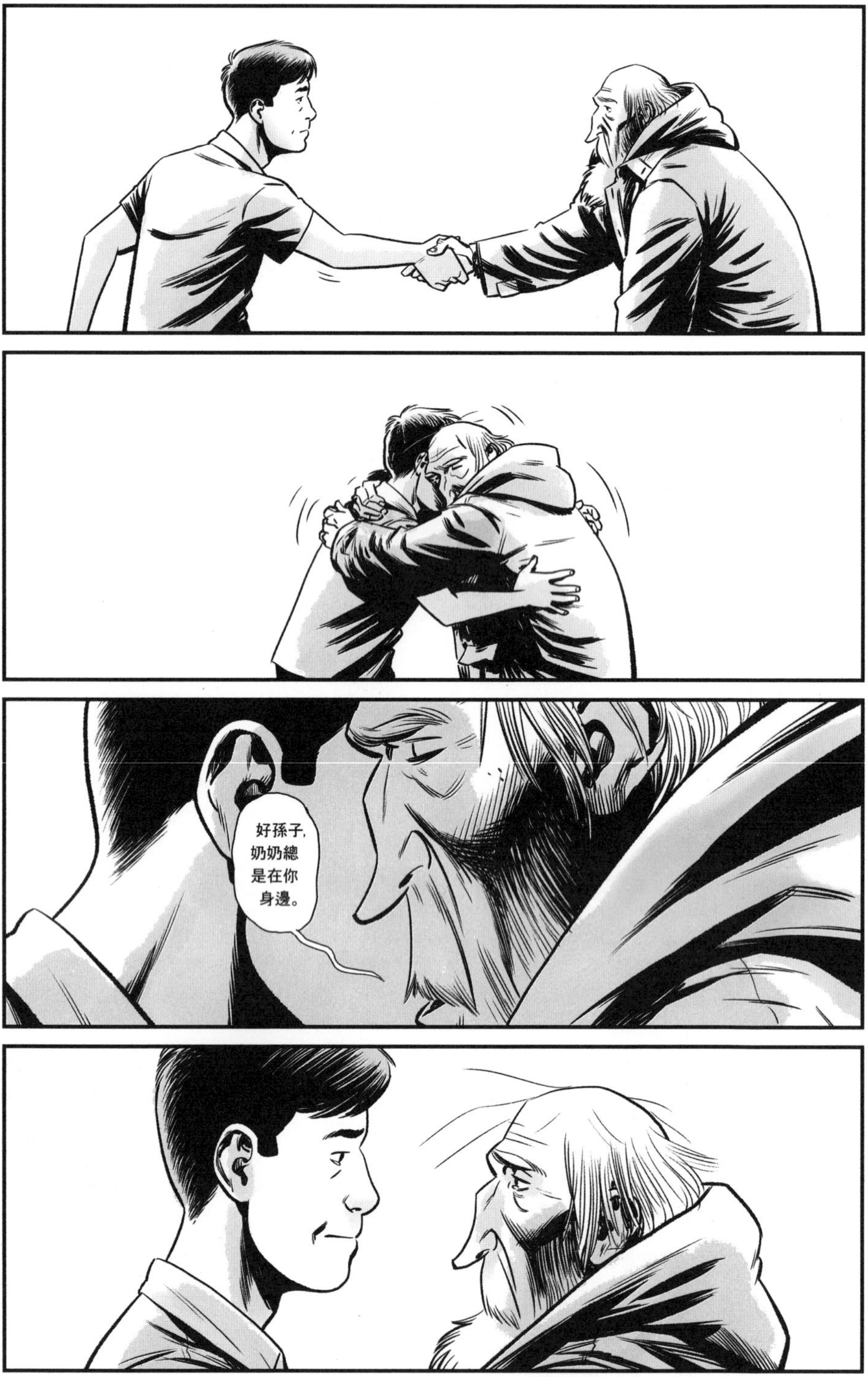
好孫子,奶奶總是在你身邊。

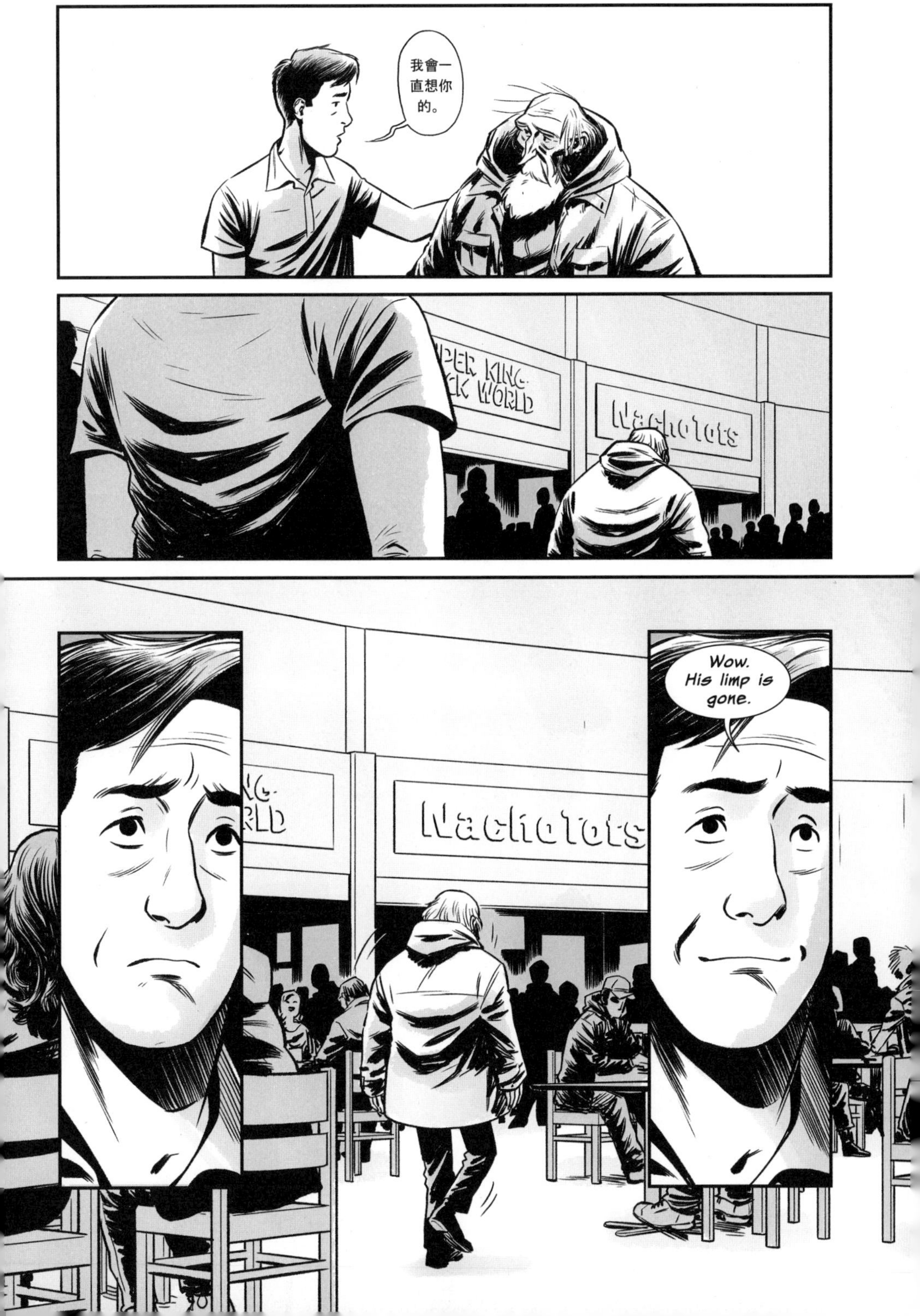
我會一直想你的。
Nachotots
Nachotots
Wow. His limp is gone.

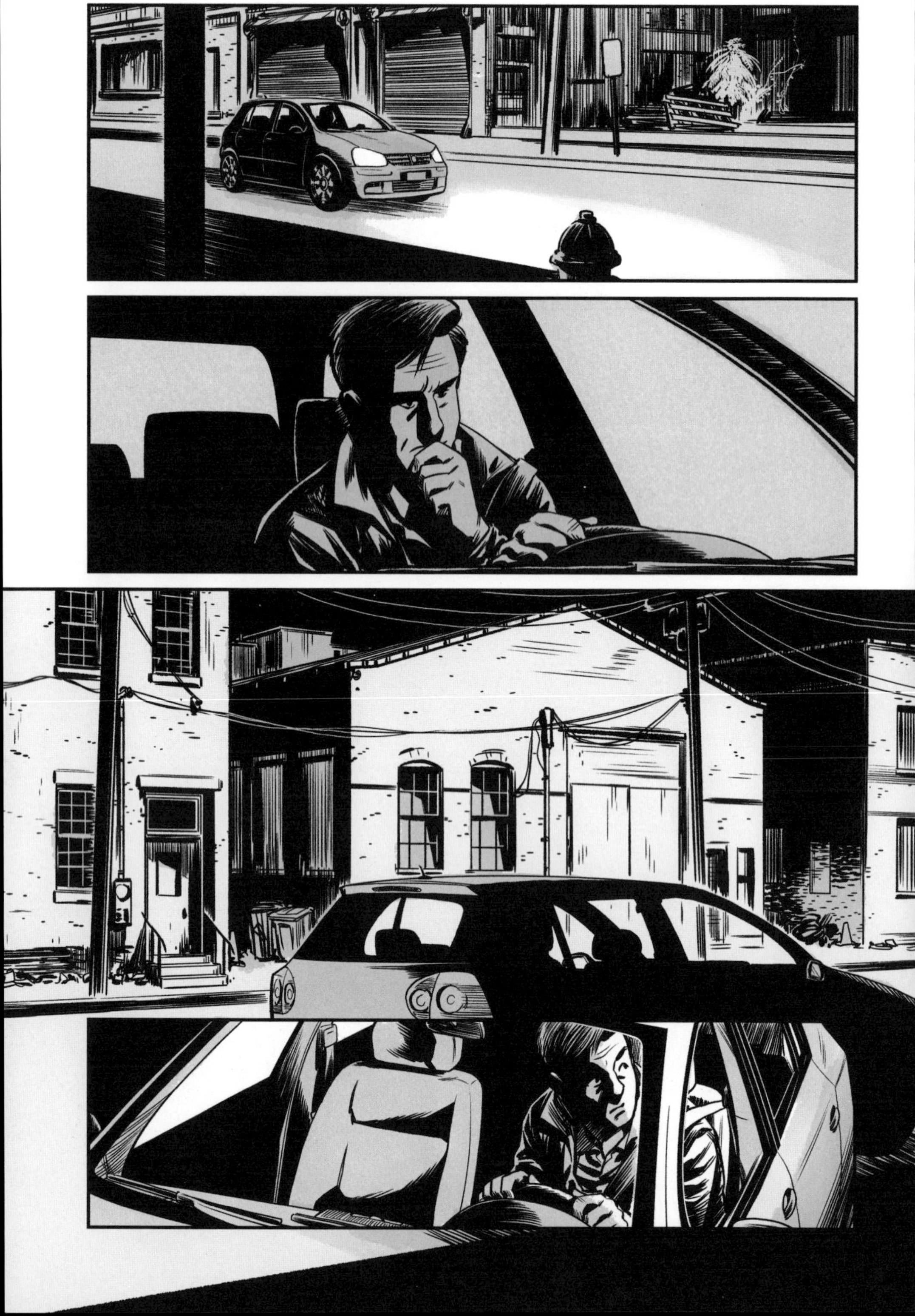

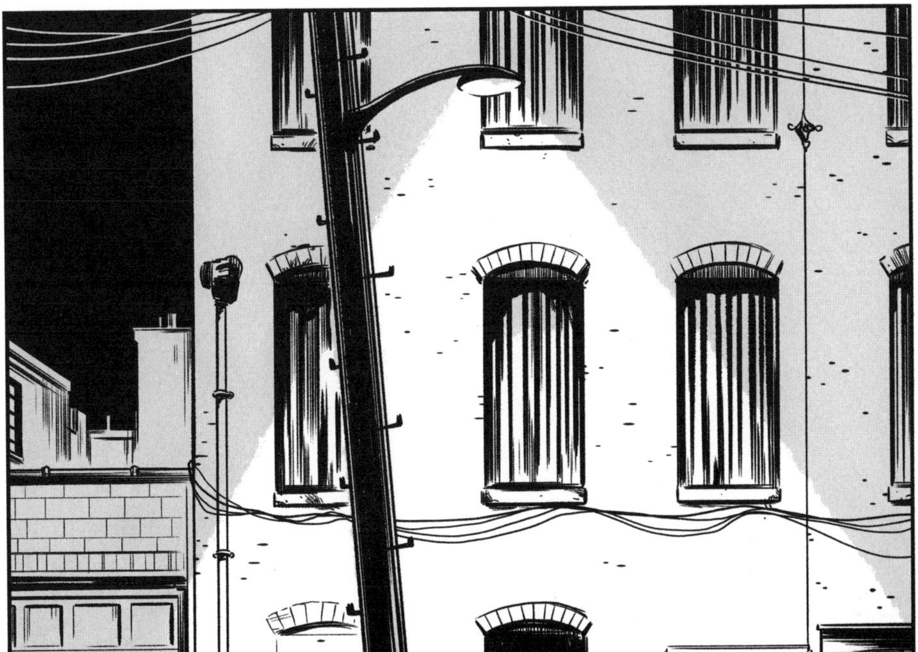

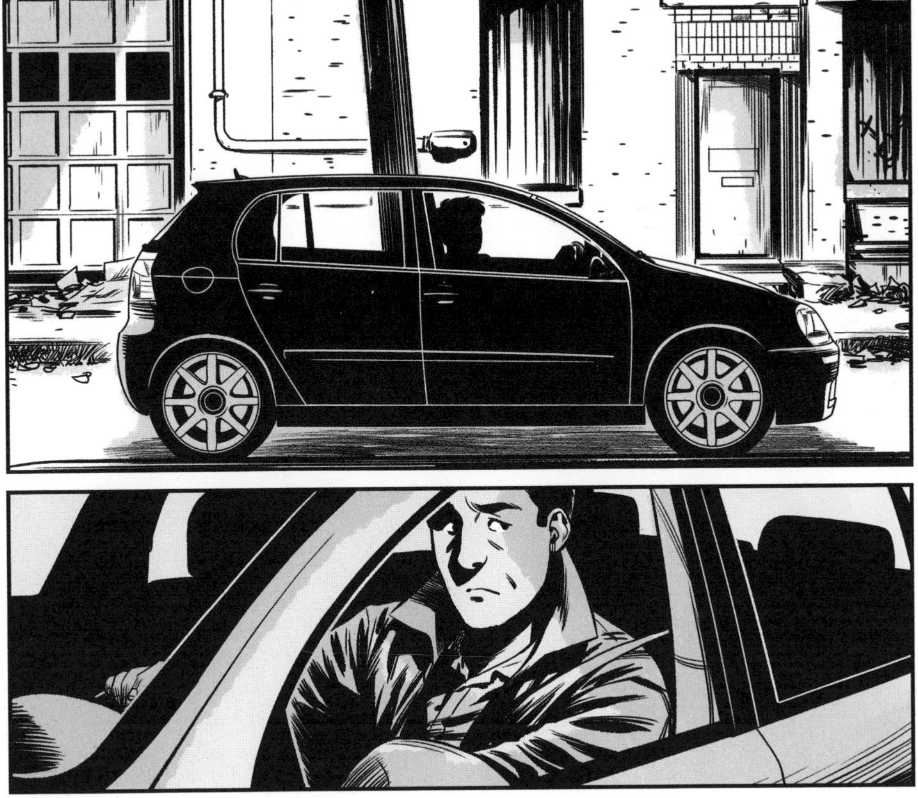

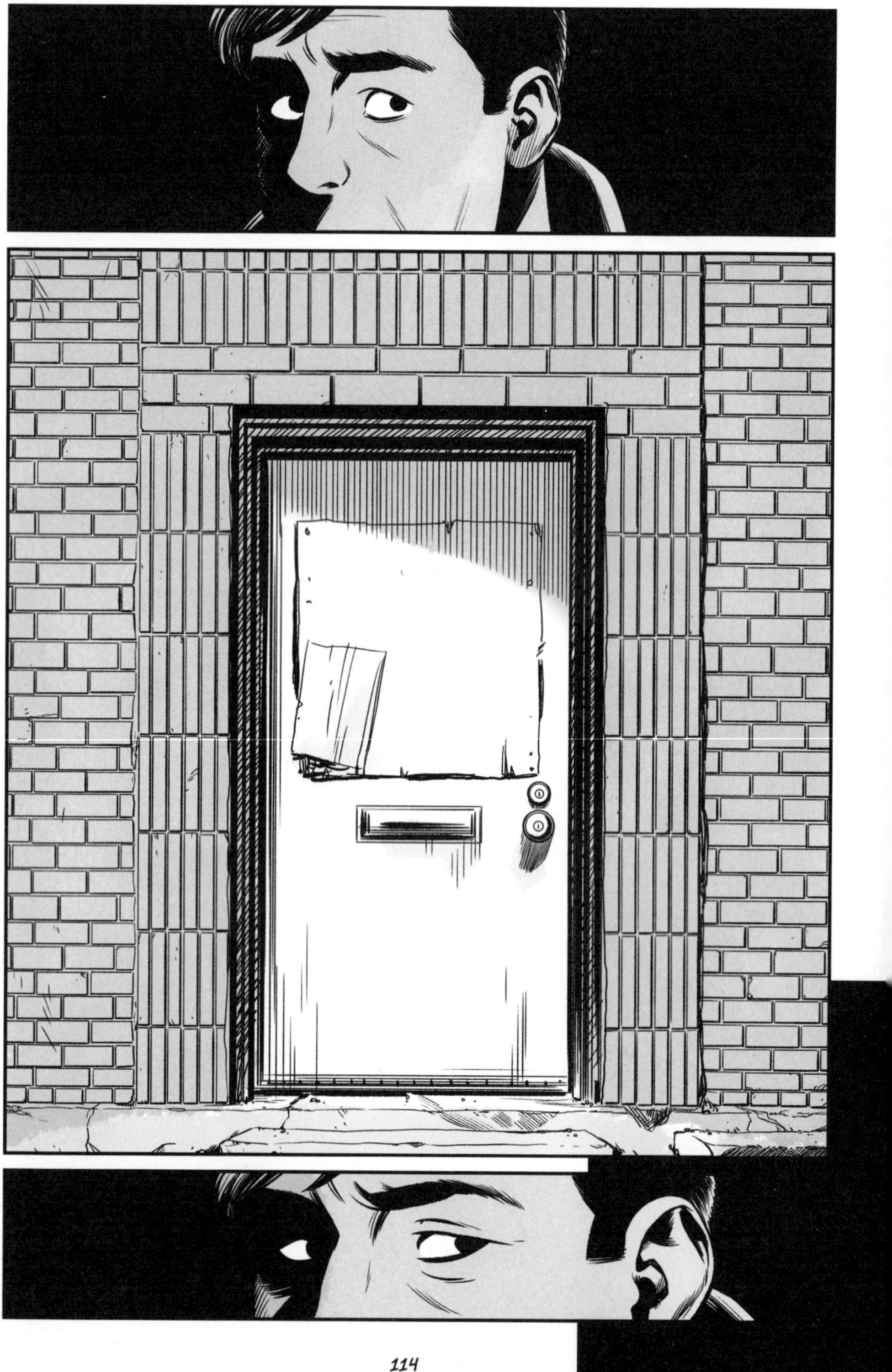

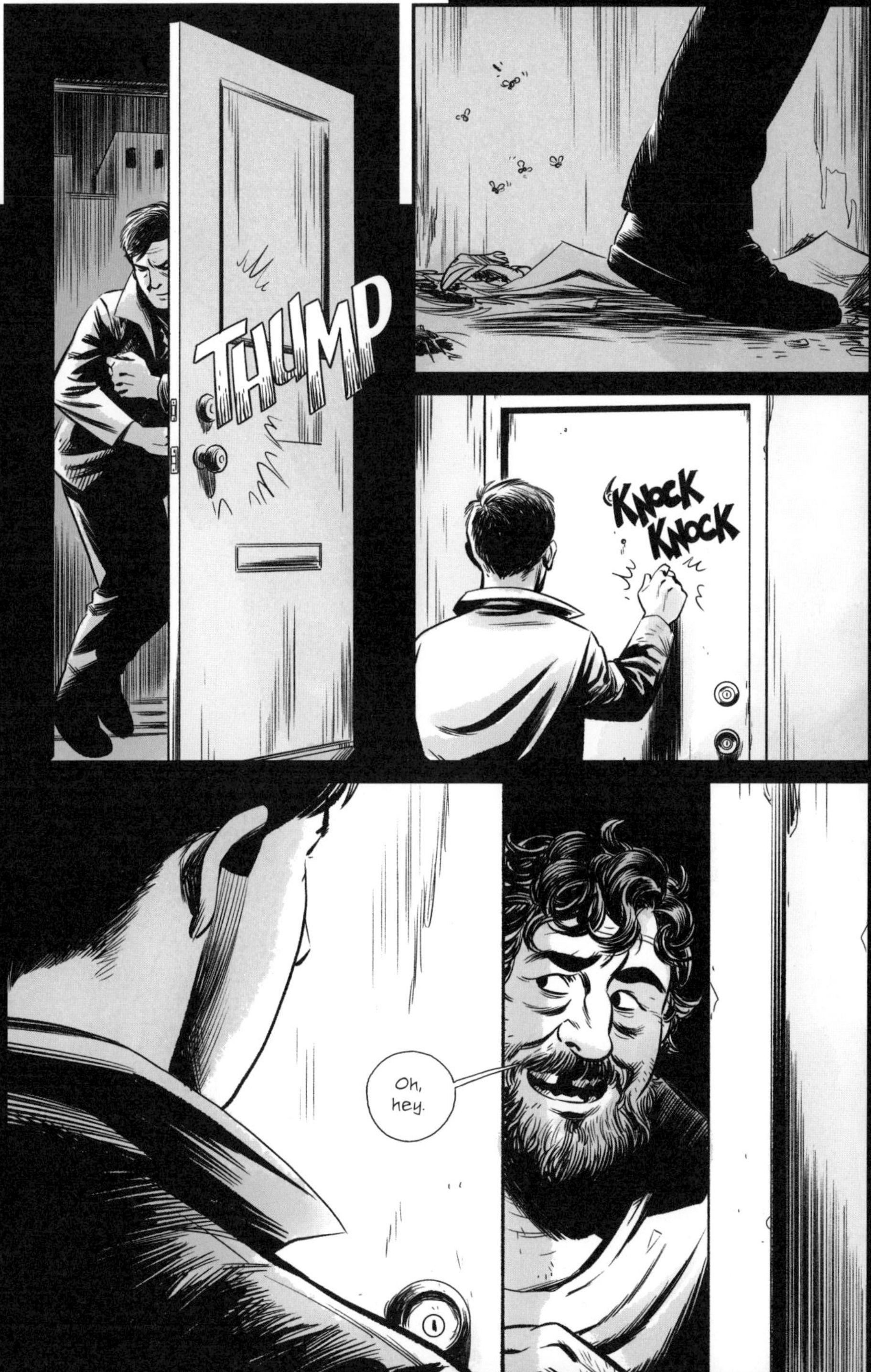
THUMP
KNOCK KNOCK
Oh, hey.

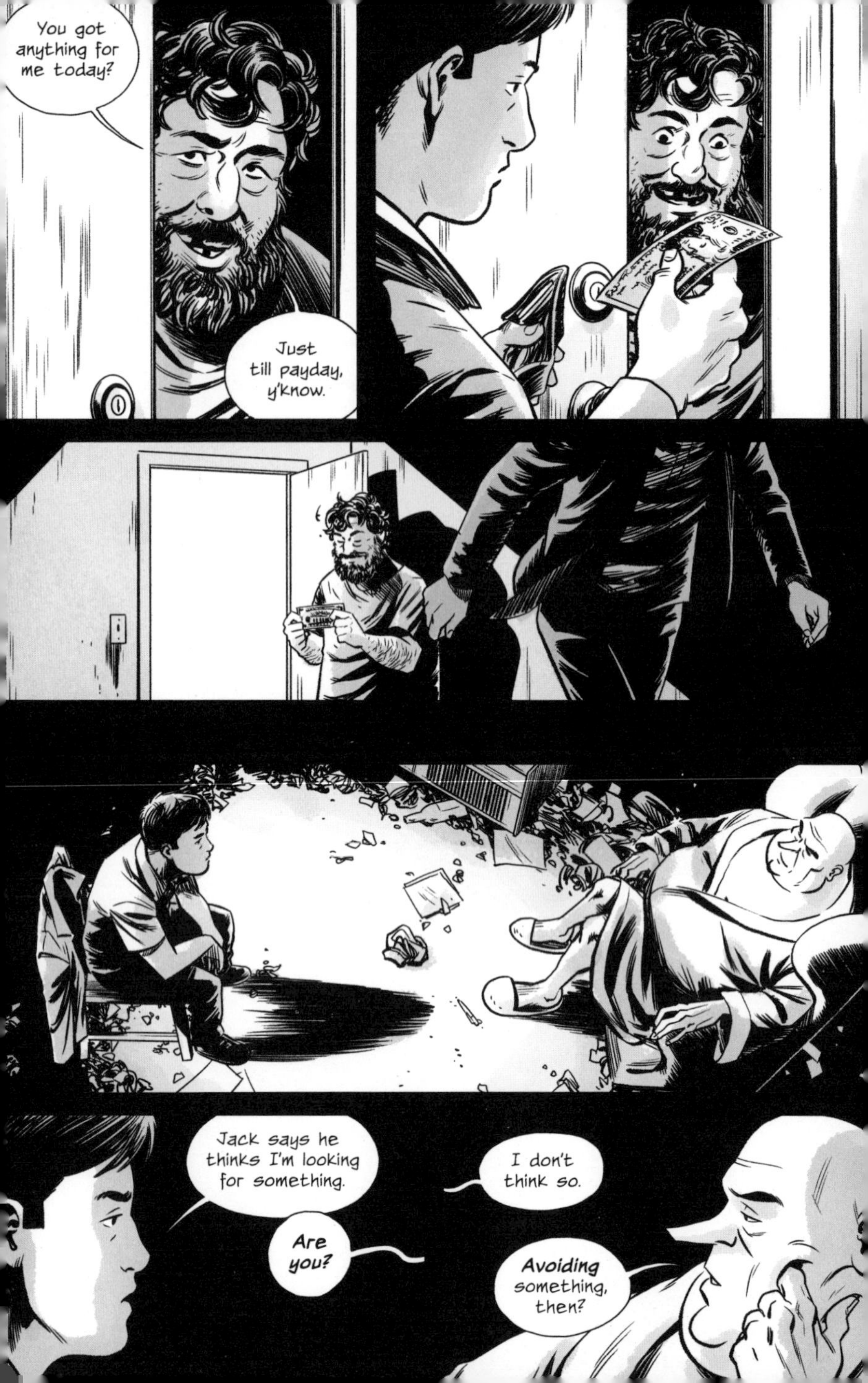

You got anything for me today?
Just till payday, y'know.
Jack says he thinks I'm looking for something.
Are you?
I don't think so.
Avoiding something, then?

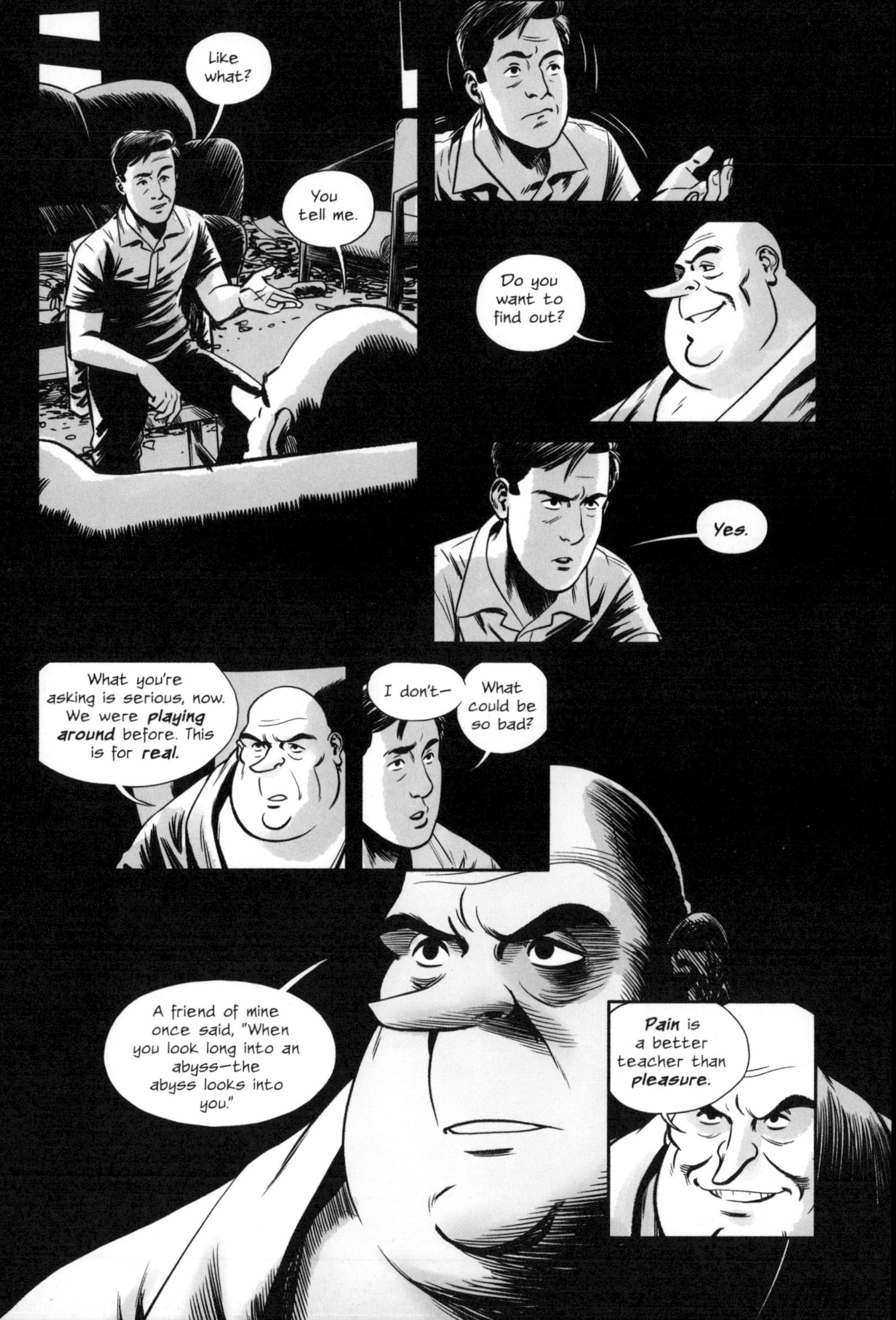
Like what?
You tell me.
Do you want to find out?
Yes.
What you're asking is serious, now. We were **playing around** before. This is for **real.**
I don't—
What could be so bad?
A friend of mine once said, "When you look long into an abyss—the abyss looks into you."
Pain is a better teacher than **pleasure.**

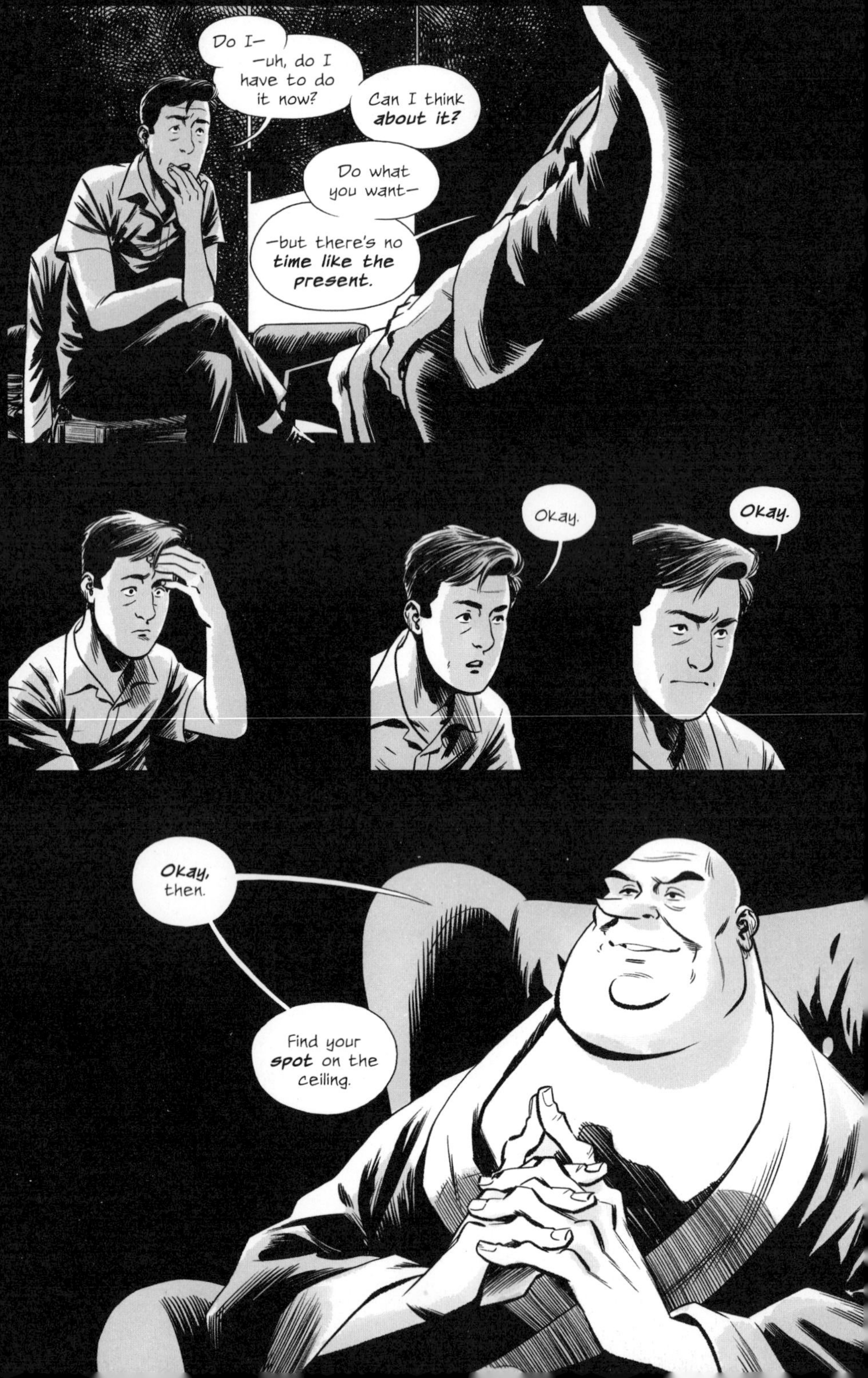
Do I—
—uh, do I have to do it now?
Can I think **about it?**
Do what you want—
—but there's no **time like the present.**
Okay.
Okay.
Okay, then.
Find your **spot** on the ceiling.

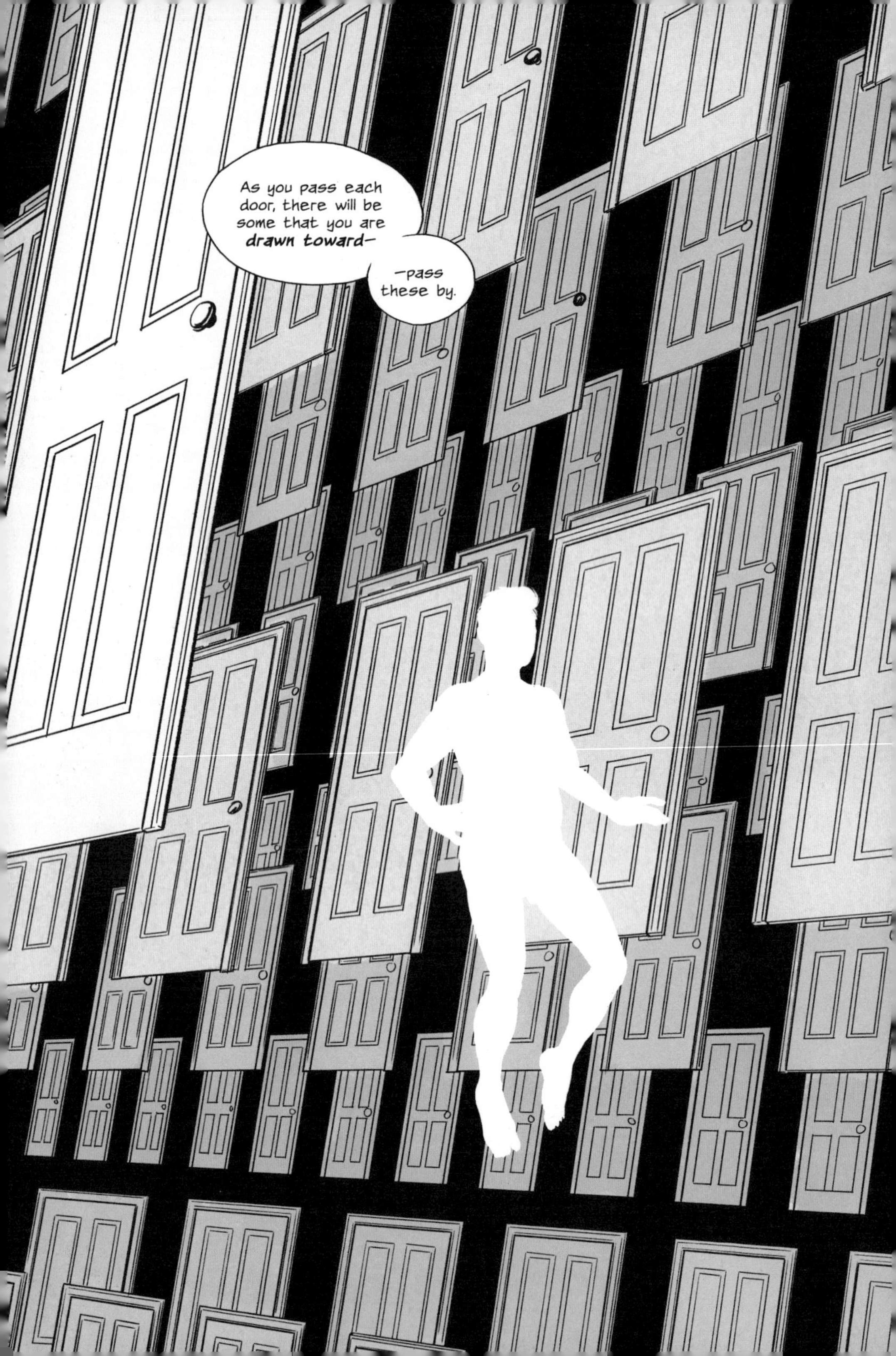
As you pass each door, there will be some that you are **drawn toward**—
—pass these by.

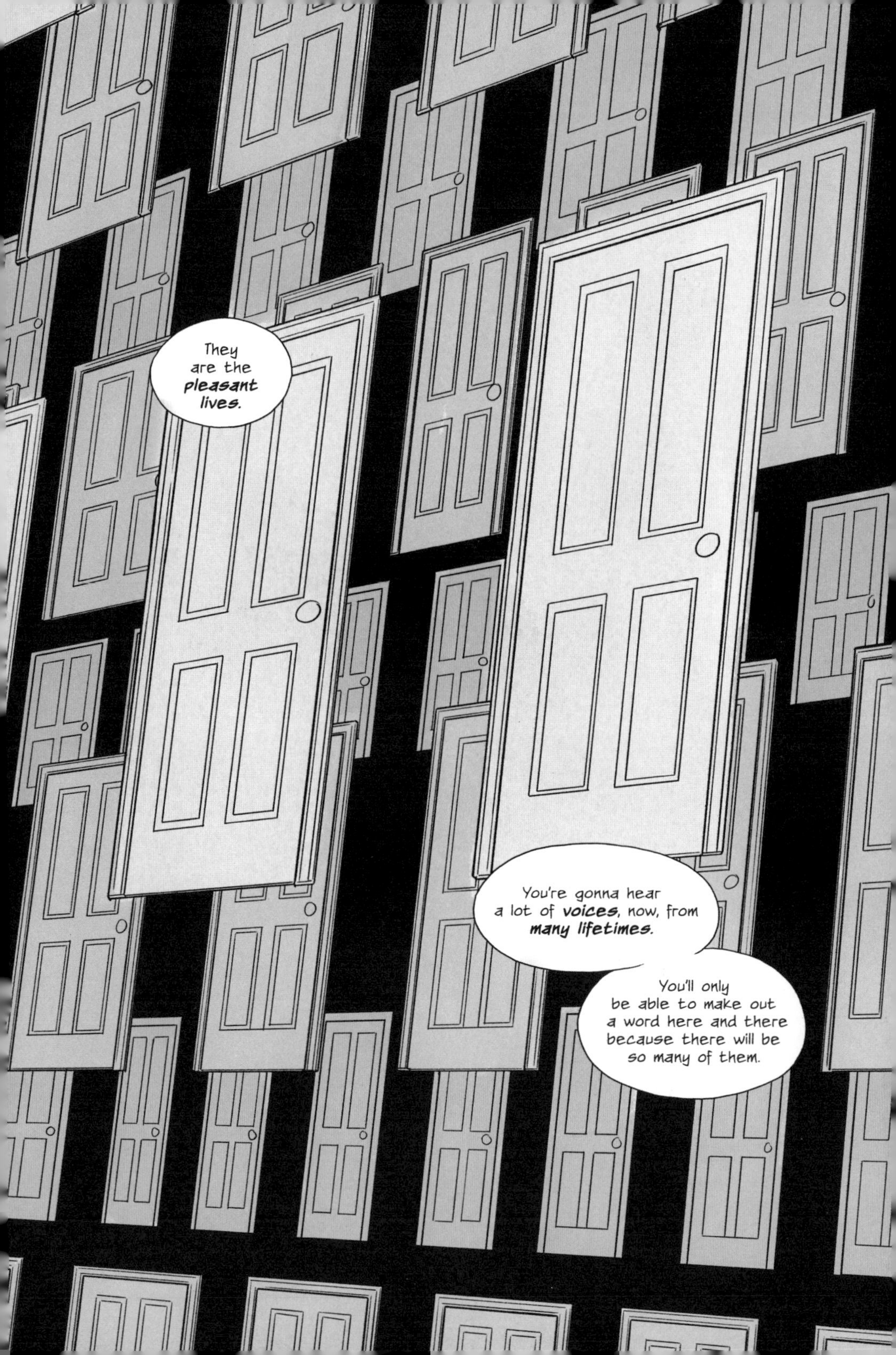
They are the pleasant lives.
You're gonna hear a lot of voices, now, from many lifetimes.
You'll only be able to make out a word here and there because there will be so many of them.

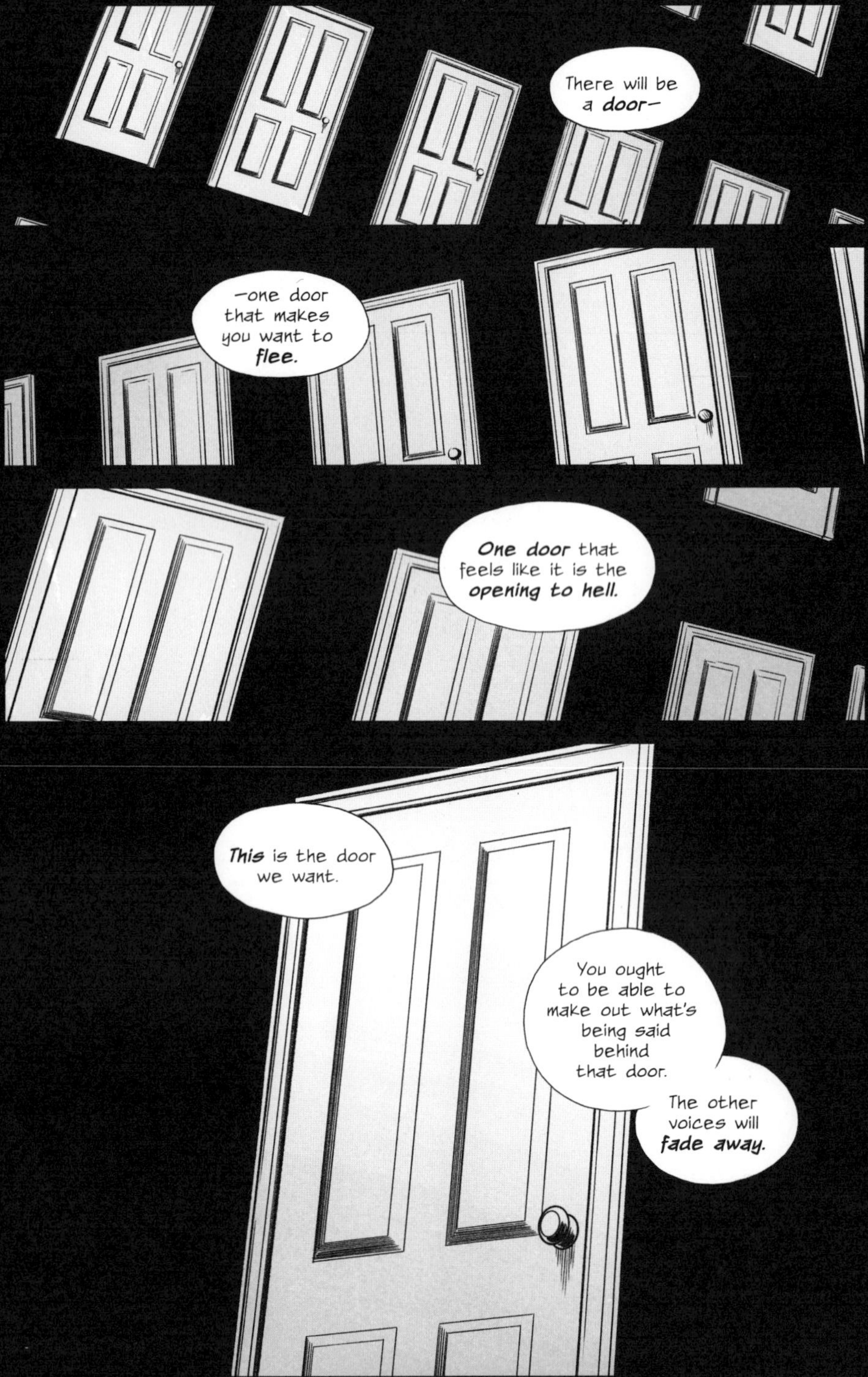
There will be a **door**—
—one door that makes you want to ***flee.***
One door that feels like it is the ***opening to hell.***
This is the door we want.
You ought to be able to make out what's being said behind that door.
The other voices will ***fade away.***

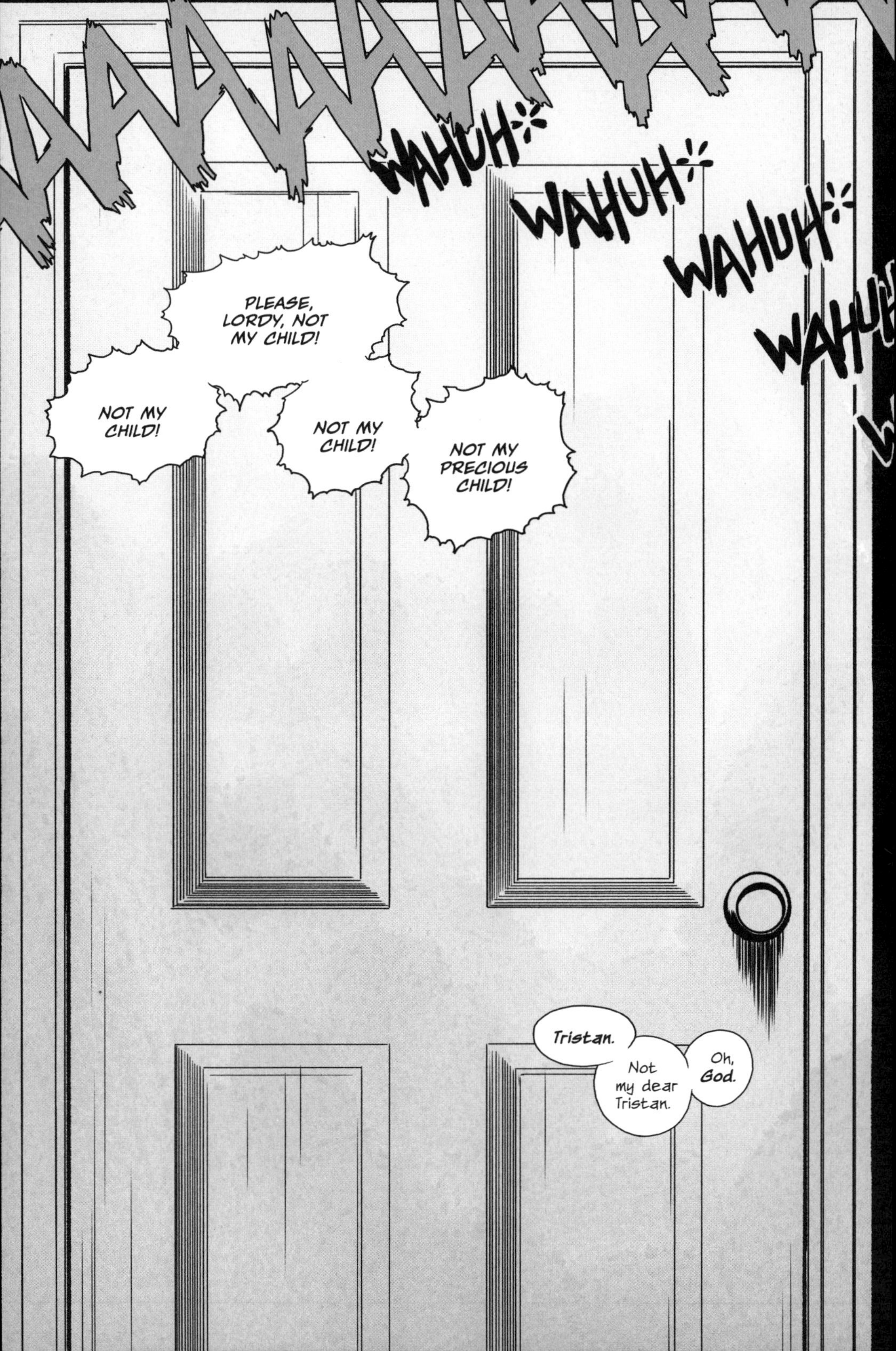

WAAAAAAAAAAA
WAHUH
WAHUH
WAHUH
PLEASE, LORDY, NOT MY CHILD!
NOT MY CHILD!
NOT MY CHILD!
NOT MY PRECIOUS CHILD!
Tristan.
Not my dear Tristan.
Oh, God.

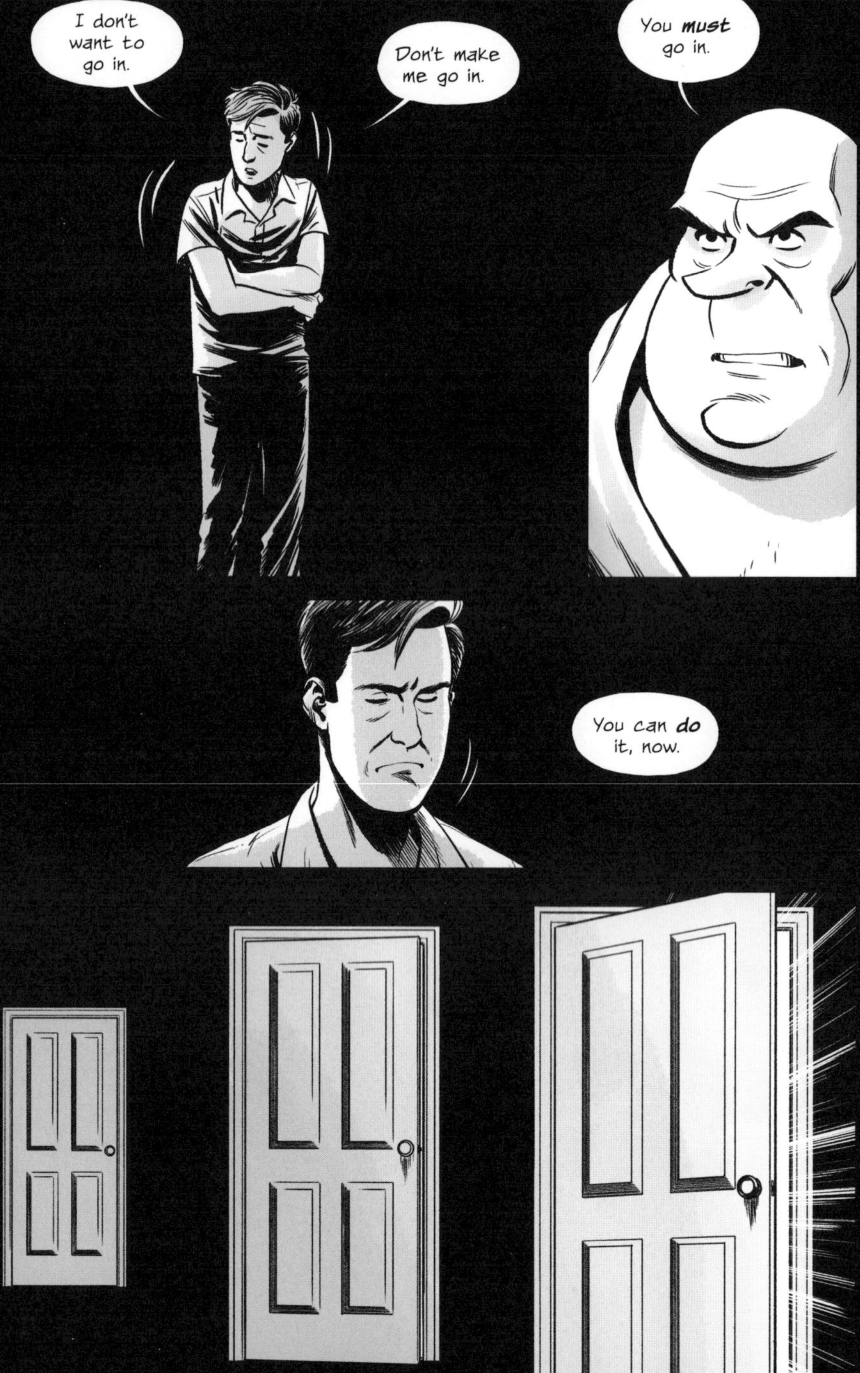
I don't want to go in.
Don't make me go in.
You **must** go in.
You can **do** it, now.

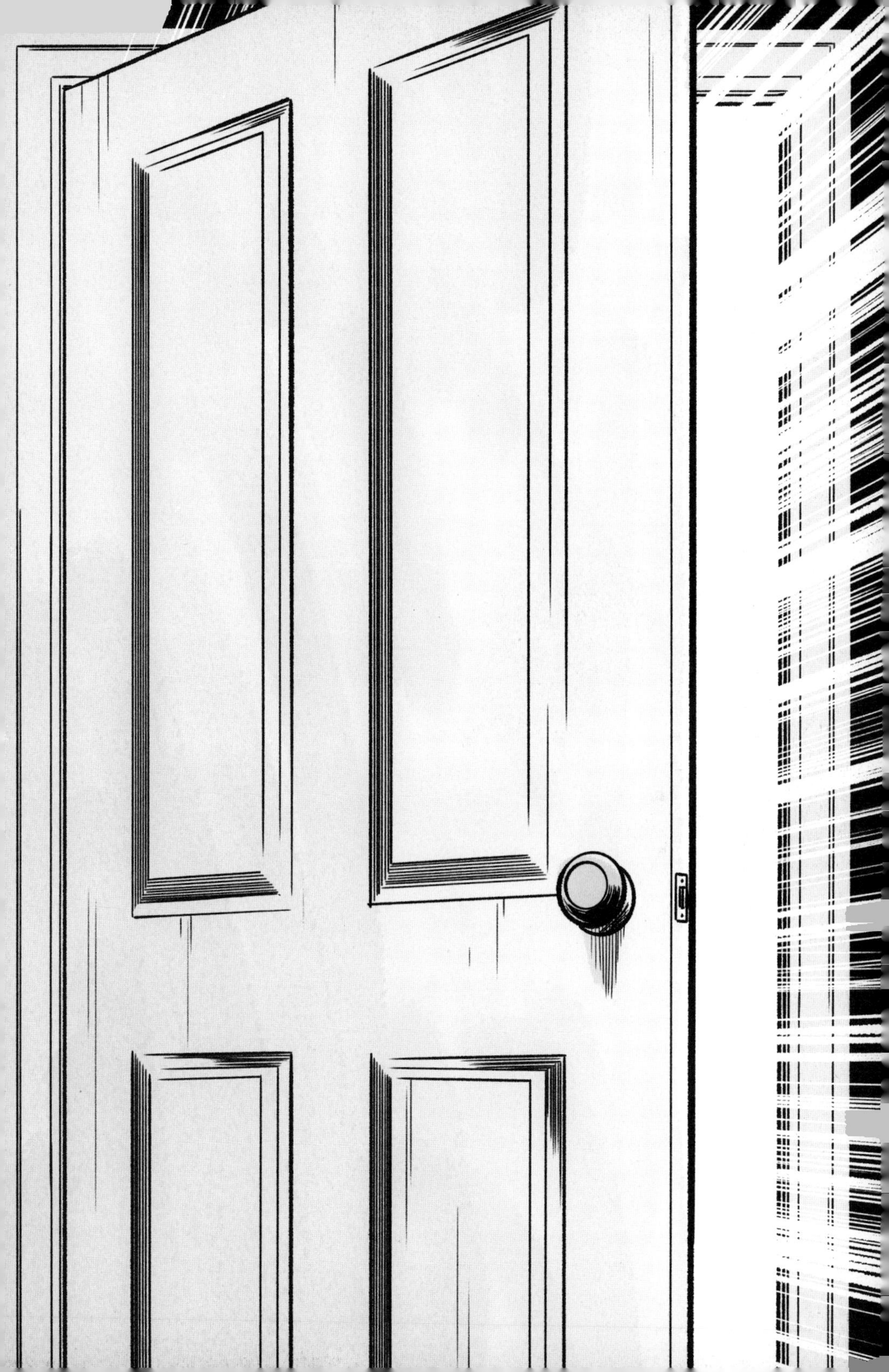

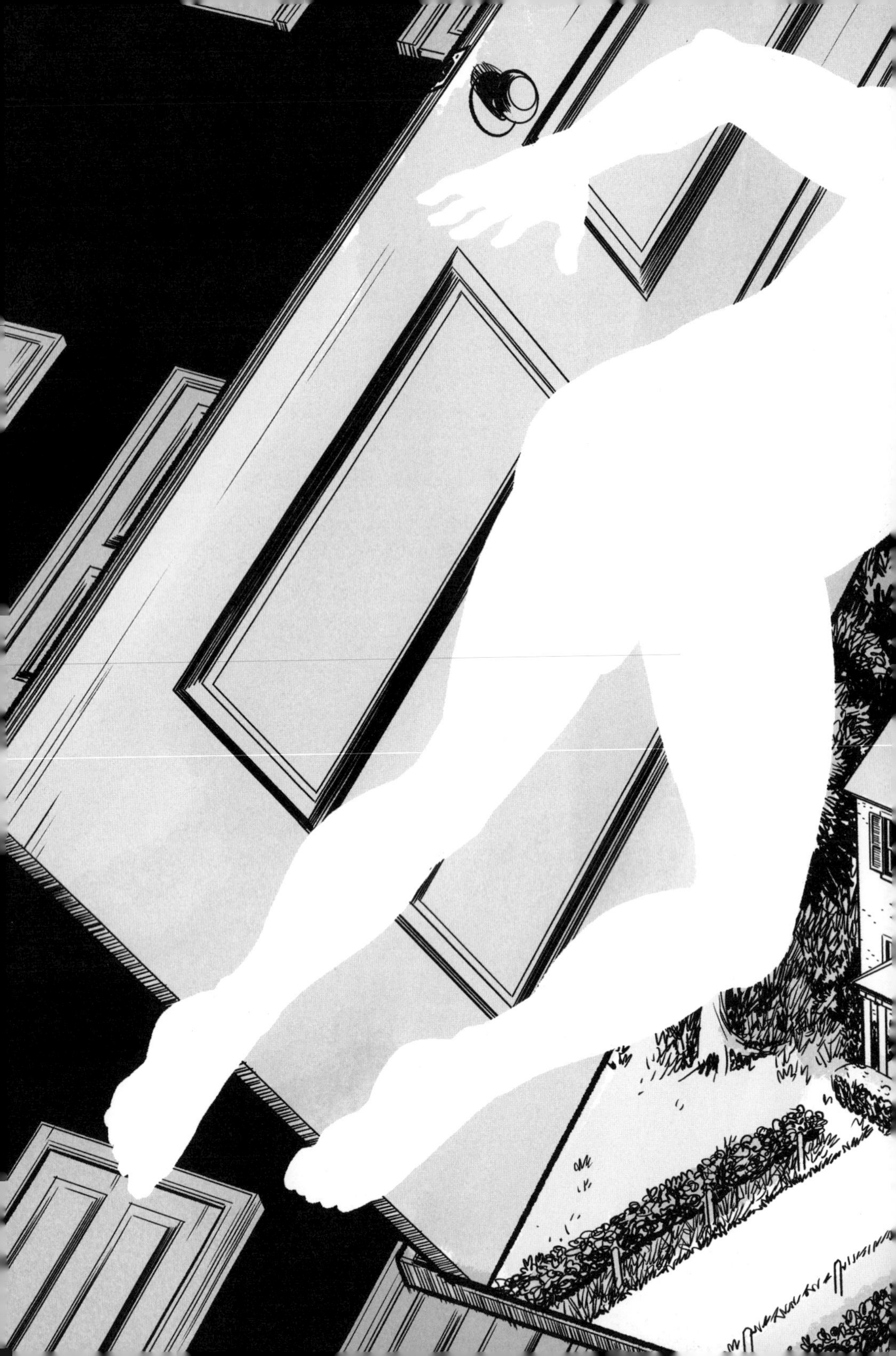

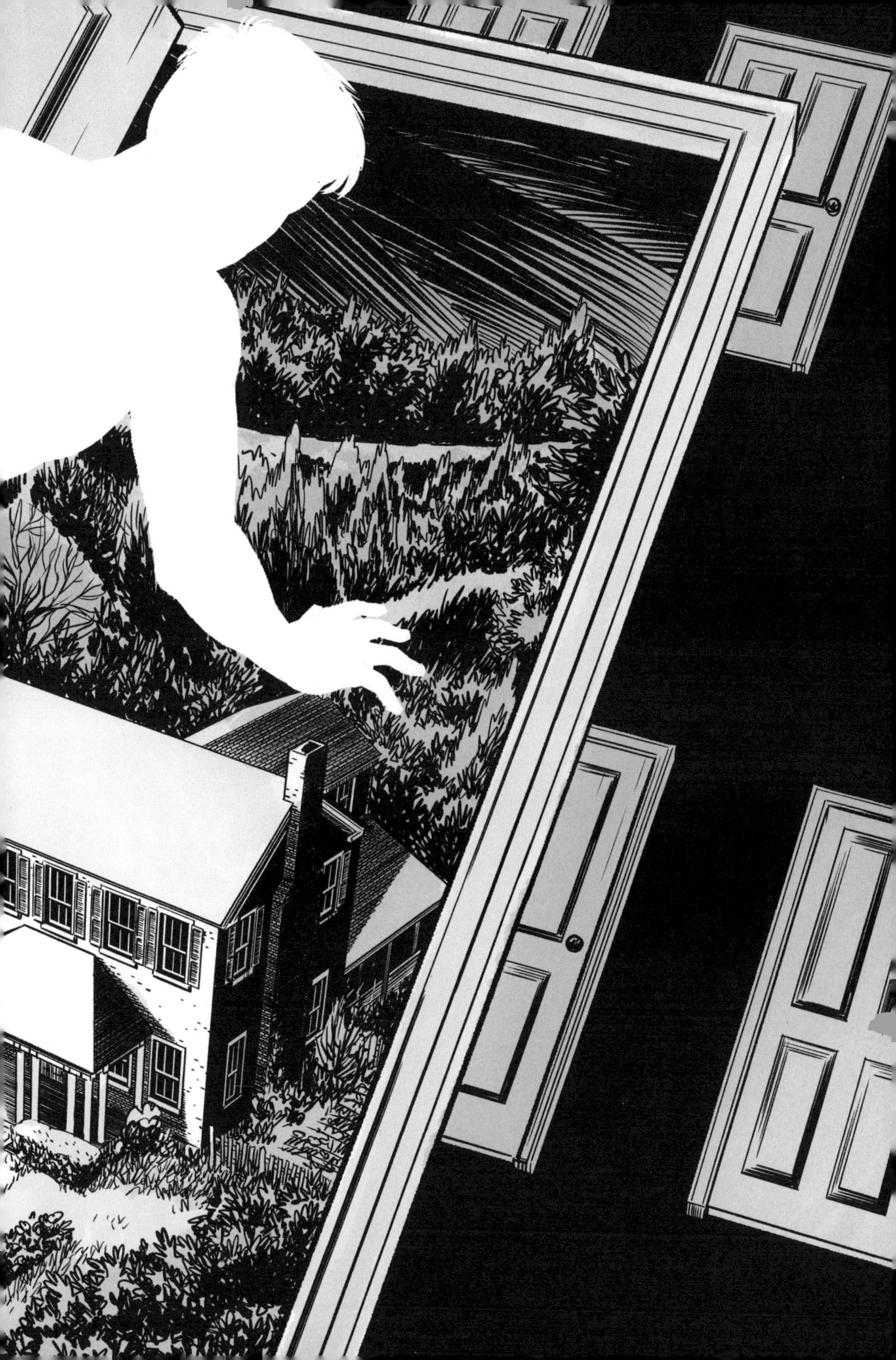

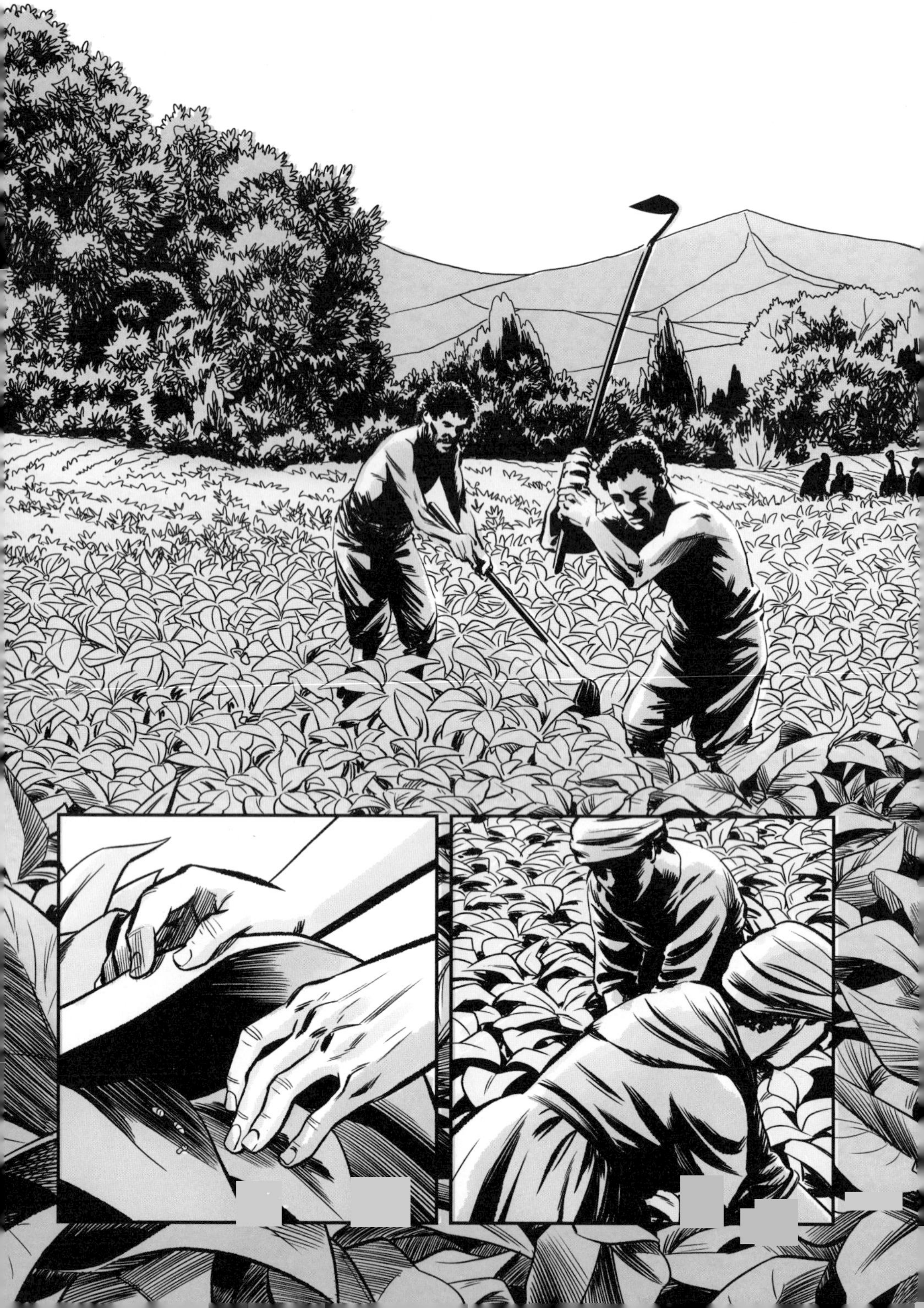

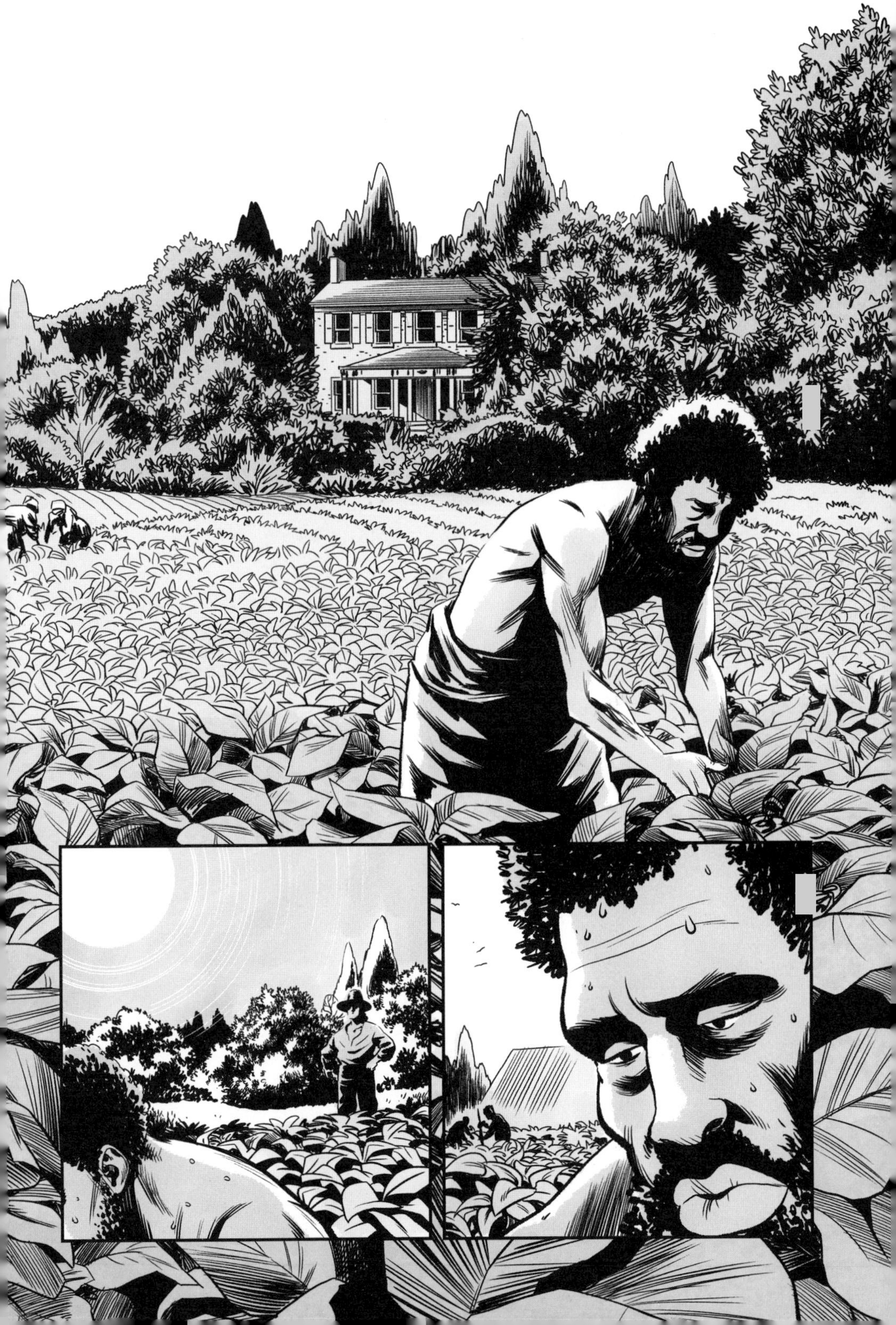

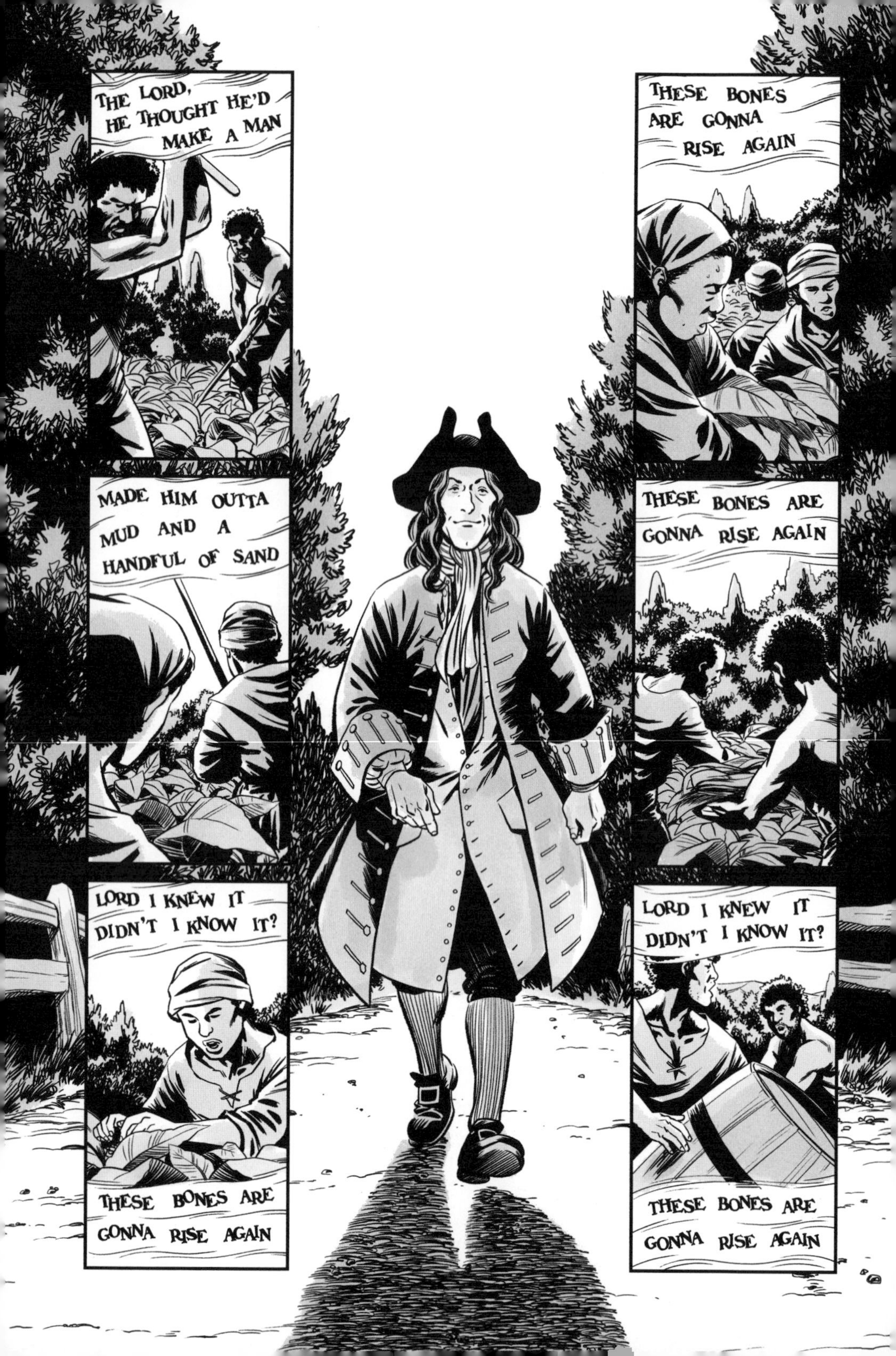
THE LORD, HE THOUGHT HE'D MAKE A MAN
THESE BONES ARE GONNA RISE AGAIN
MADE HIM OUTTA MUD AND A HANDFUL OF SAND
THESE BONES ARE GONNA RISE AGAIN
LORD I KNEW IT DIDN'T I KNOW IT?
THESE BONES ARE GONNA RISE AGAIN
LORD I KNEW IT DIDN'T I KNOW IT?
THESE BONES ARE GONNA RISE AGAIN

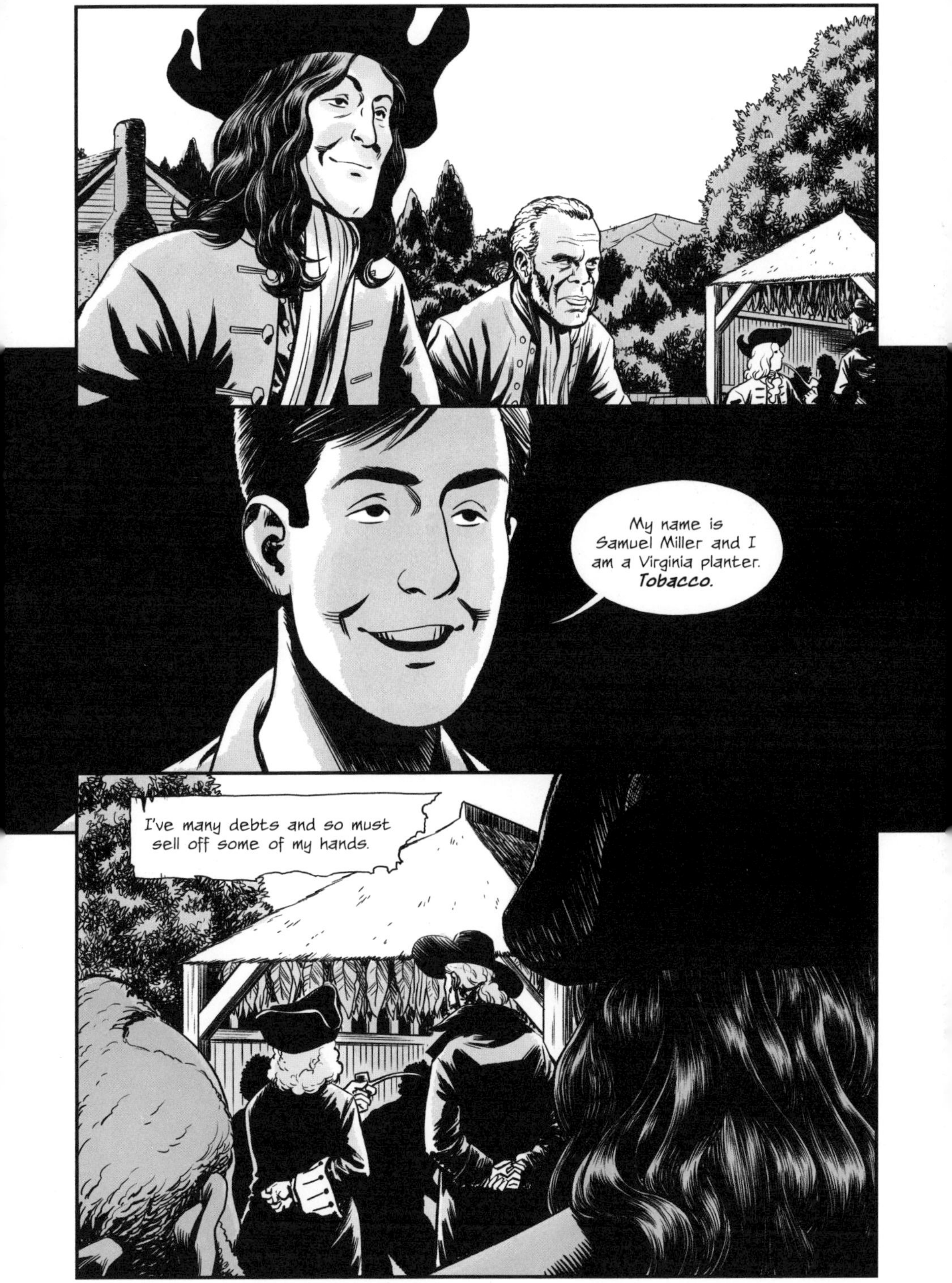
My name is Samuel Miller and I am a Virginia planter. *Tobacco.*
I've many debts and so must sell off some of my hands.

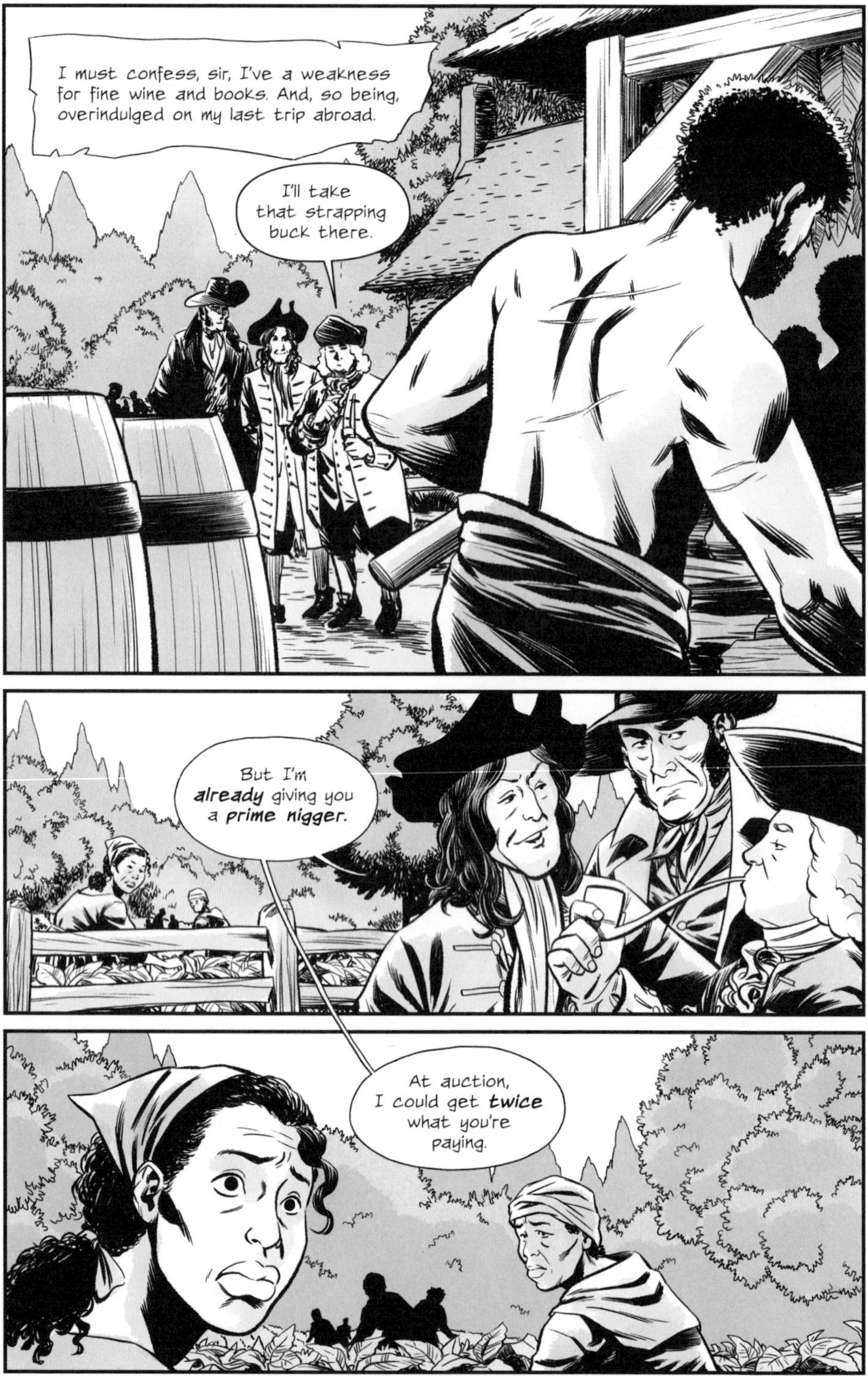
I must confess, sir, I've a weakness for fine wine and books. And, so being, overindulged on my last trip abroad.
I'll take that strapping buck there.
But I'm **already** giving you a **prime nigger.**
At auction, I could get **twice** what you're paying.

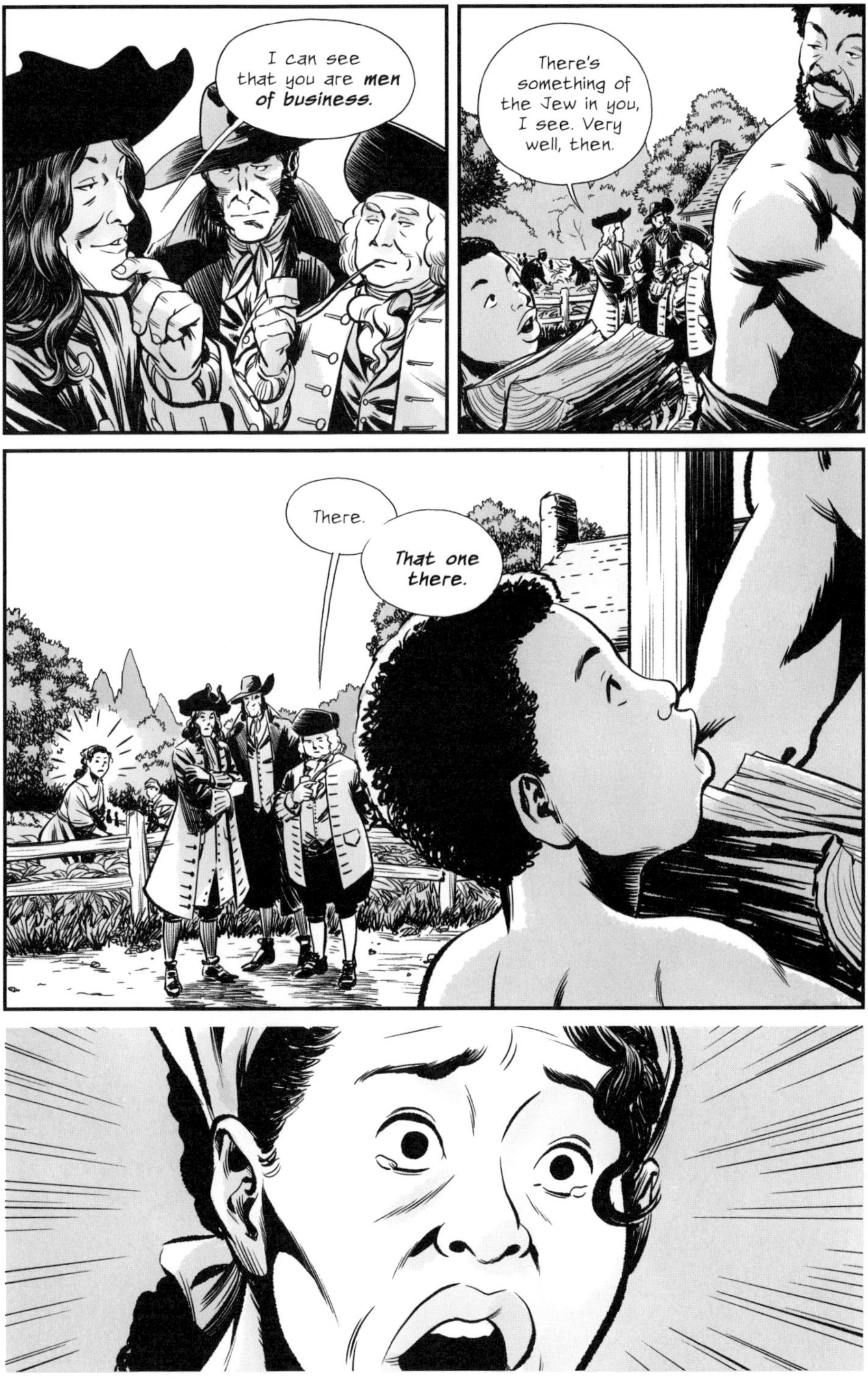
I can see that you are **men of business.**
There's something of the Jew in you, I see. Very well, then.
There.
That one there.

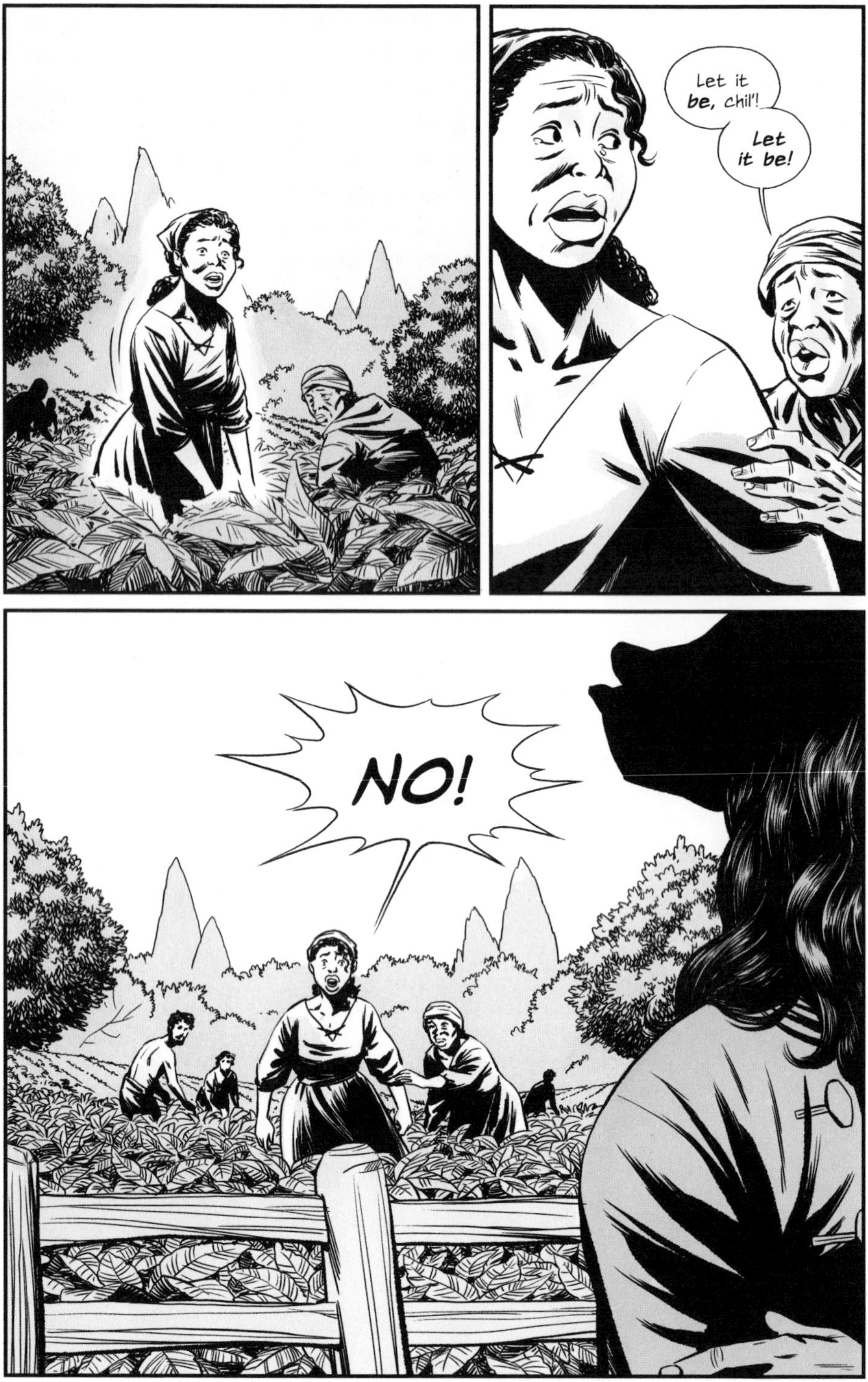
Let it be, chil'!
Let it be!
NO!

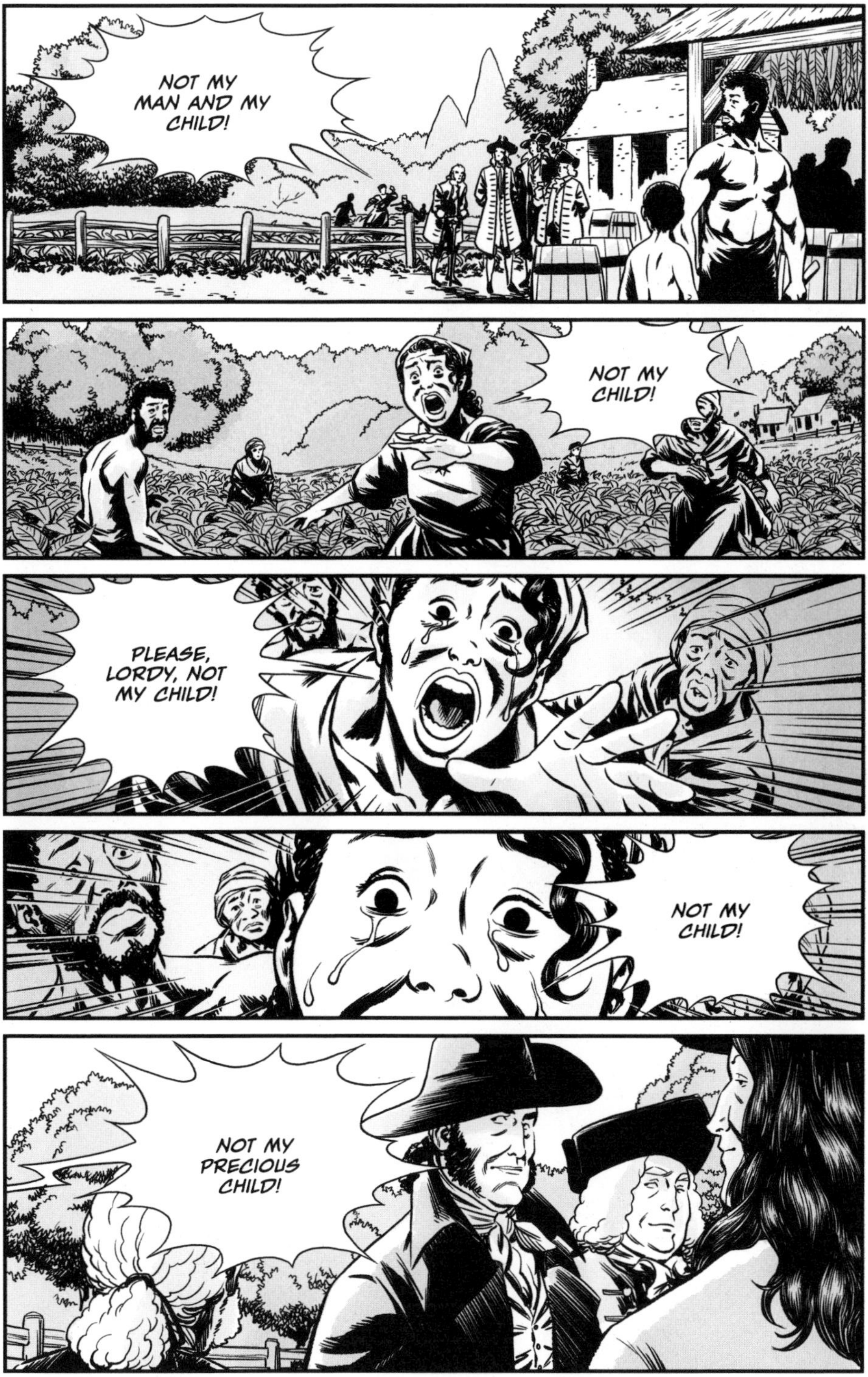
NOT MY MAN AND MY CHILD!
NOT MY CHILD!
PLEASE, LORDY, NOT MY CHILD!
NOT MY CHILD!
NOT MY PRECIOUS CHILD!

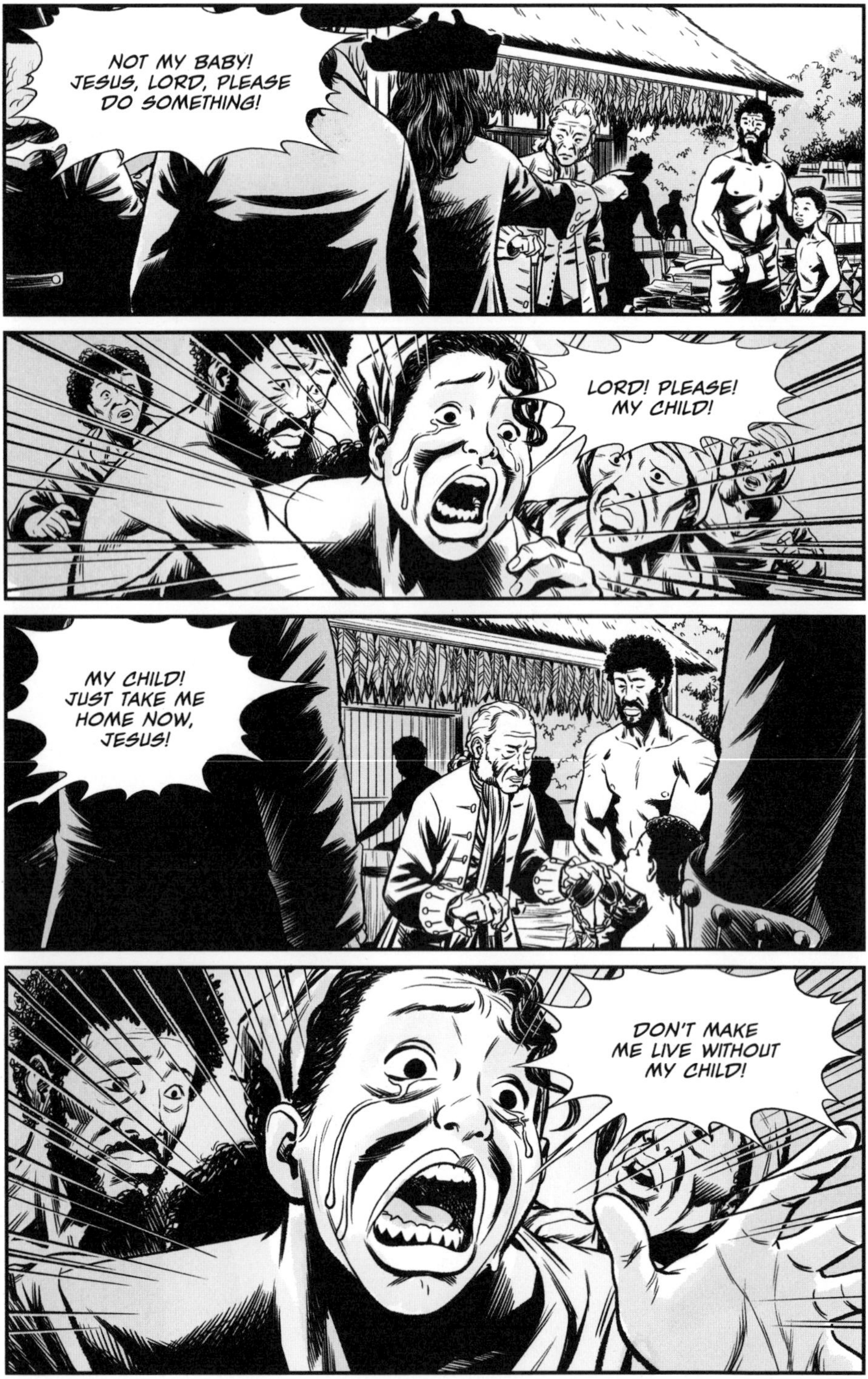
NOT MY BABY! JESUS, LORD, PLEASE DO SOMETHING!
LORD! PLEASE! MY CHILD!
MY CHILD! JUST TAKE ME HOME NOW, JESUS!
DON'T MAKE ME LIVE WITHOUT MY CHILD!

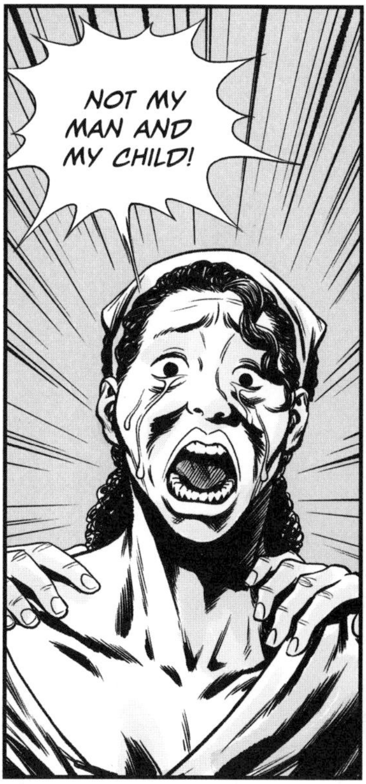
NOT MY MAN AND MY CHILD!

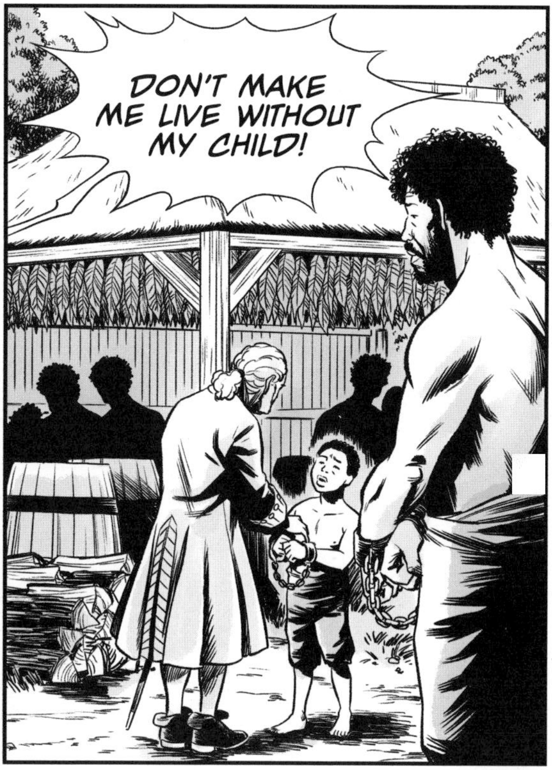
DON'T MAKE ME LIVE WITHOUT MY CHILD!

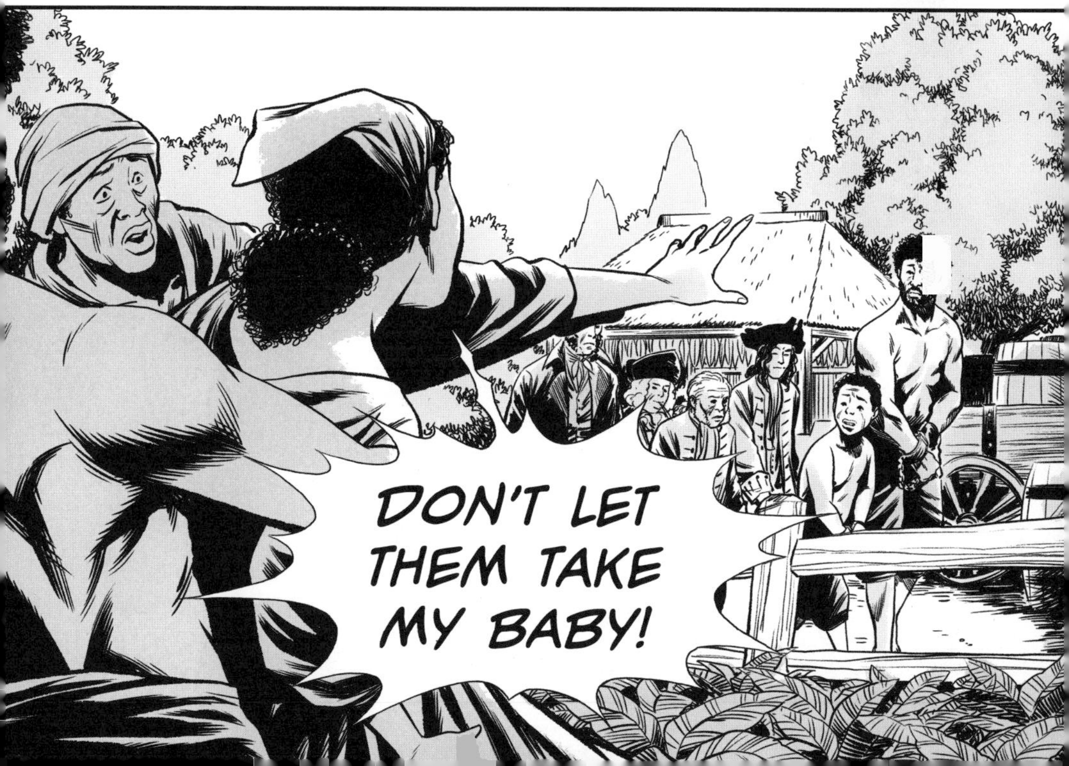
DON'T LET THEM TAKE MY BABY!

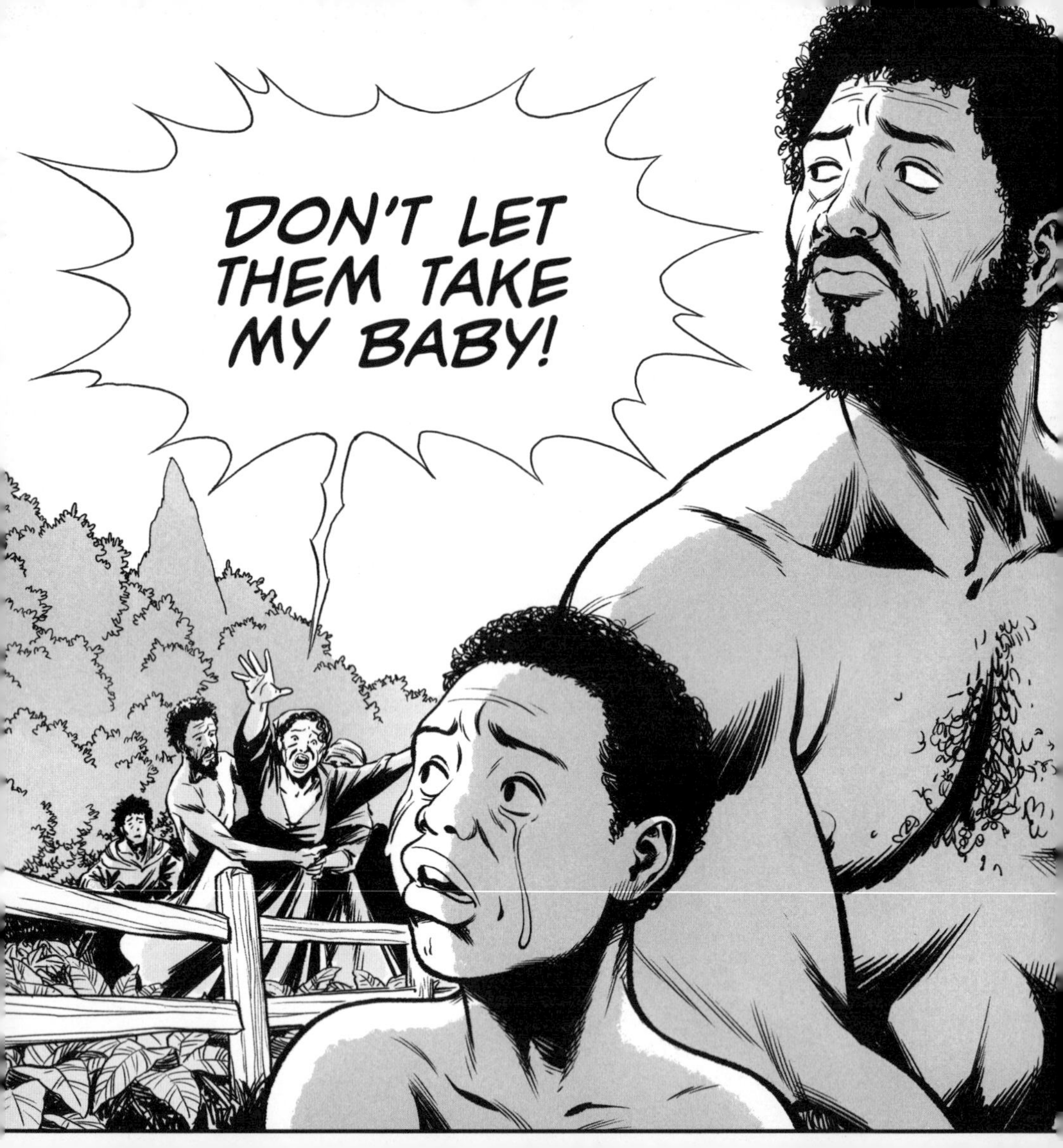
DON'T LET THEM TAKE MY BABY!

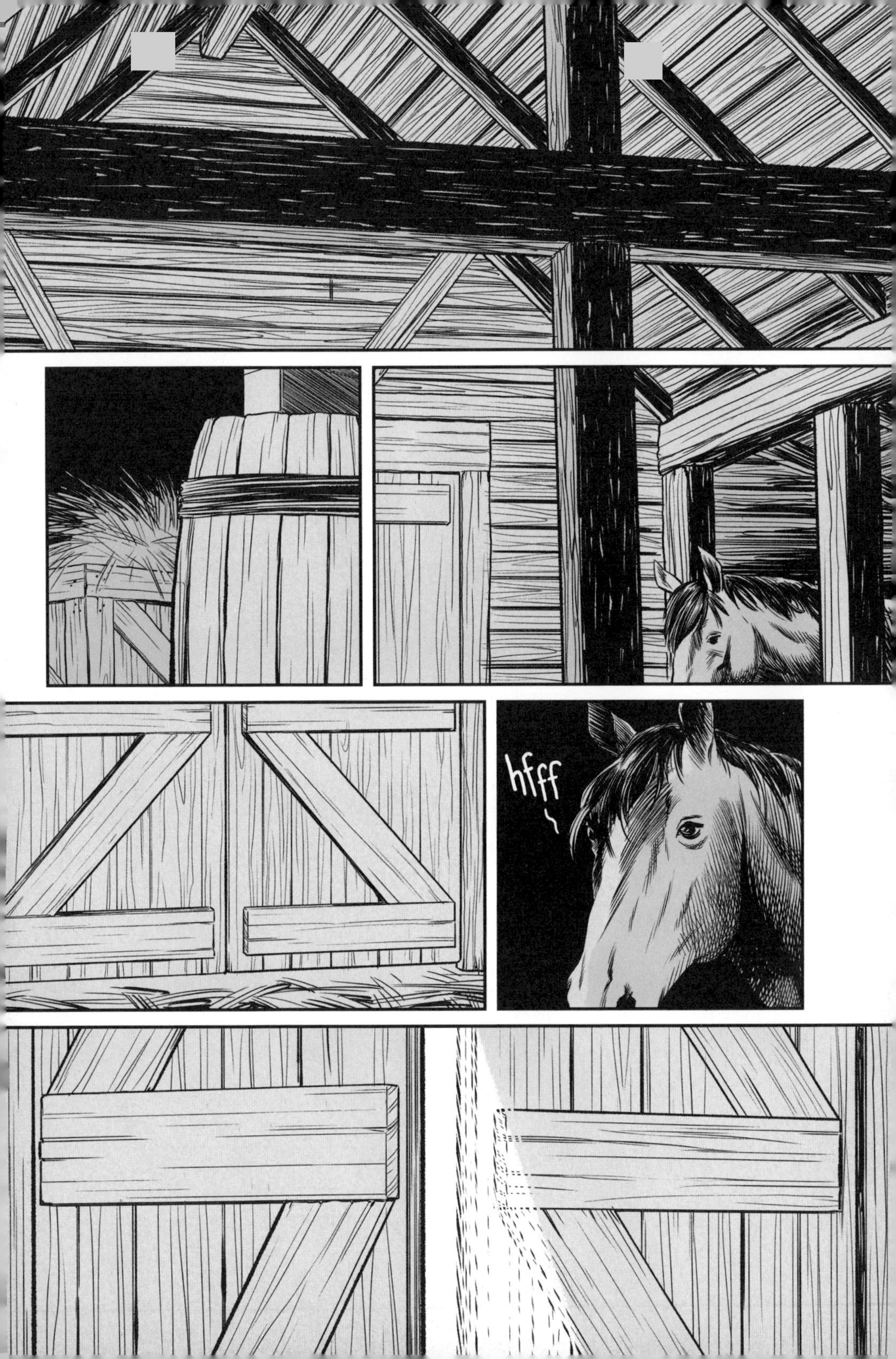
hfff

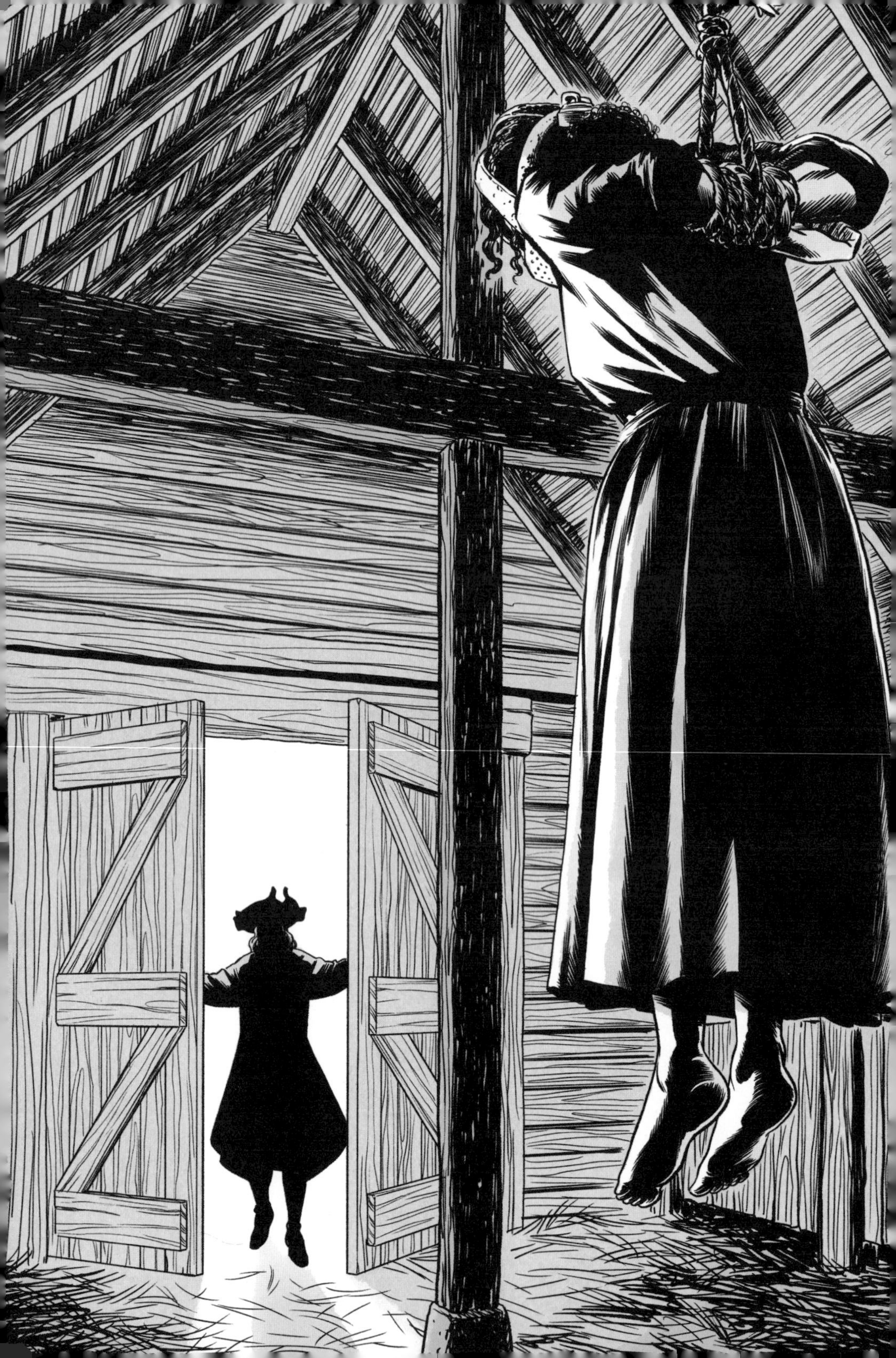

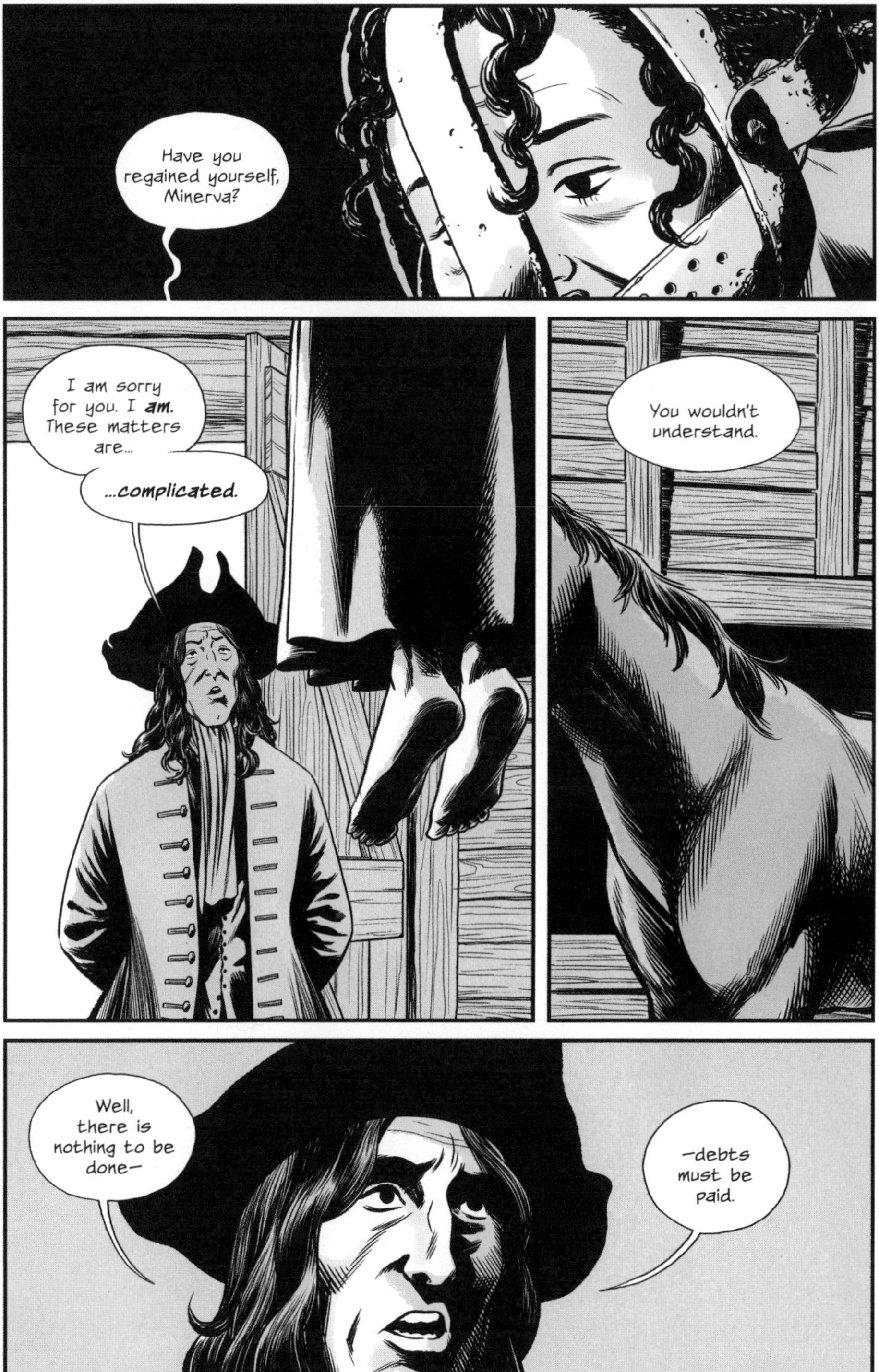
Have you regained yourself, Minerva?
I am sorry for you. I **am.** These matters are...
...**complicated.**
You wouldn't understand.
Well, there is nothing to be done—
—debts must be paid.

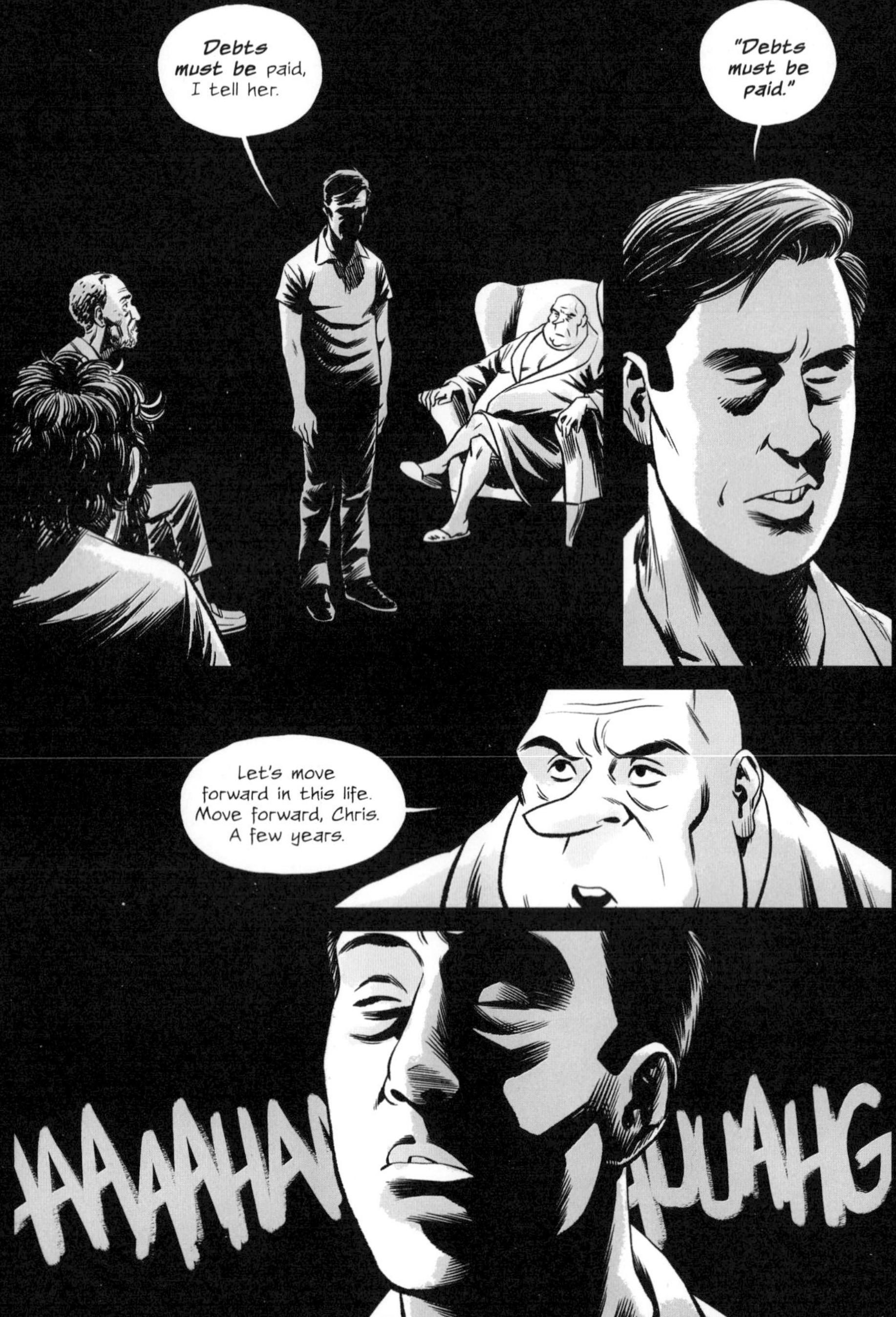
Debts must be paid, I tell her.
"Debts must be paid."
Let's move forward in this life. Move forward, Chris. A few years.
HAAAHAAUUAHG

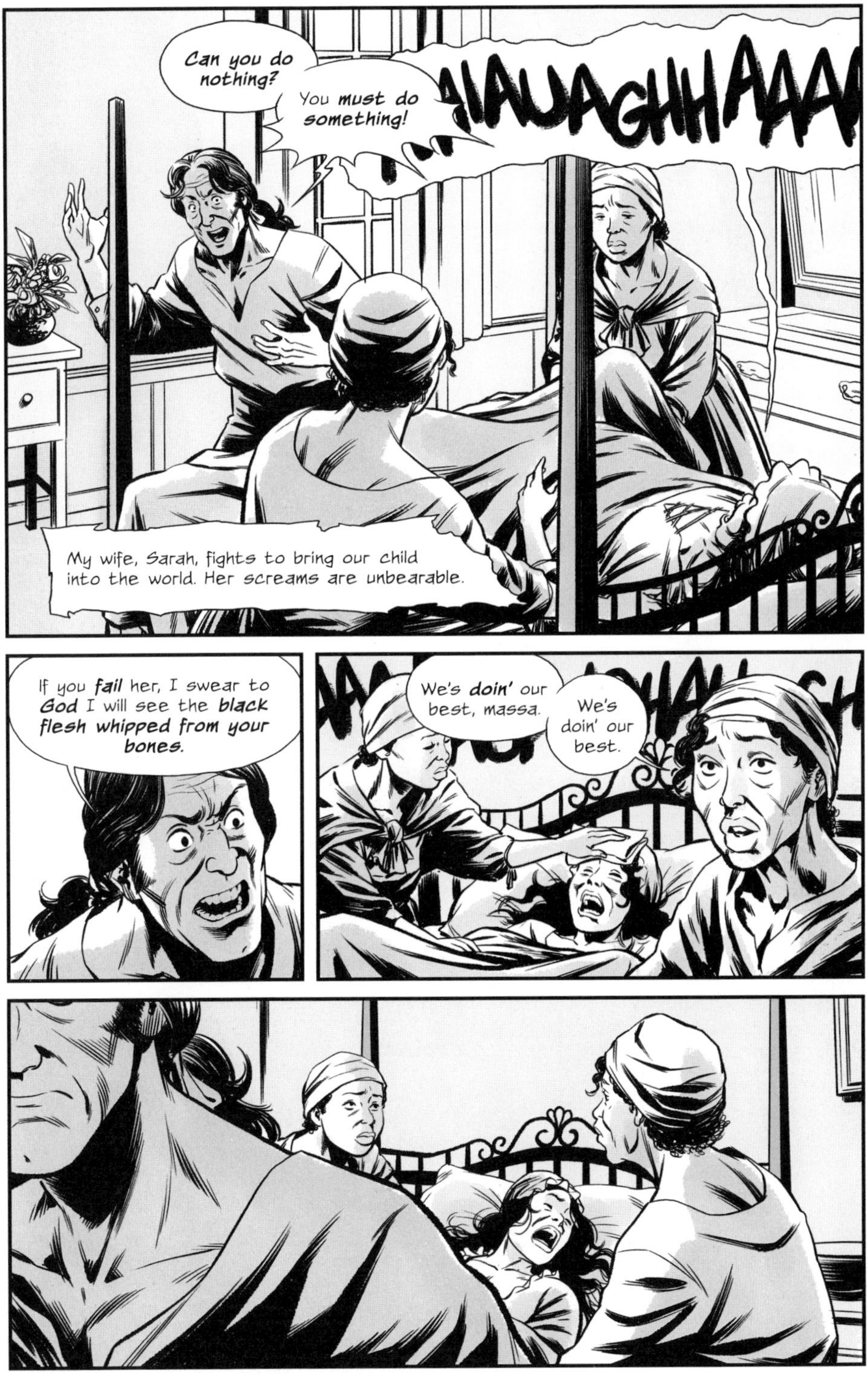
Can you do nothing?
You must do something!
AIAUAGHHAAAA
My wife, Sarah, fights to bring our child into the world. Her screams are unbearable.
If you fail her, I swear to God I will see the black flesh whipped from your bones.
We's doin' our best, massa.
We's doin' our best.

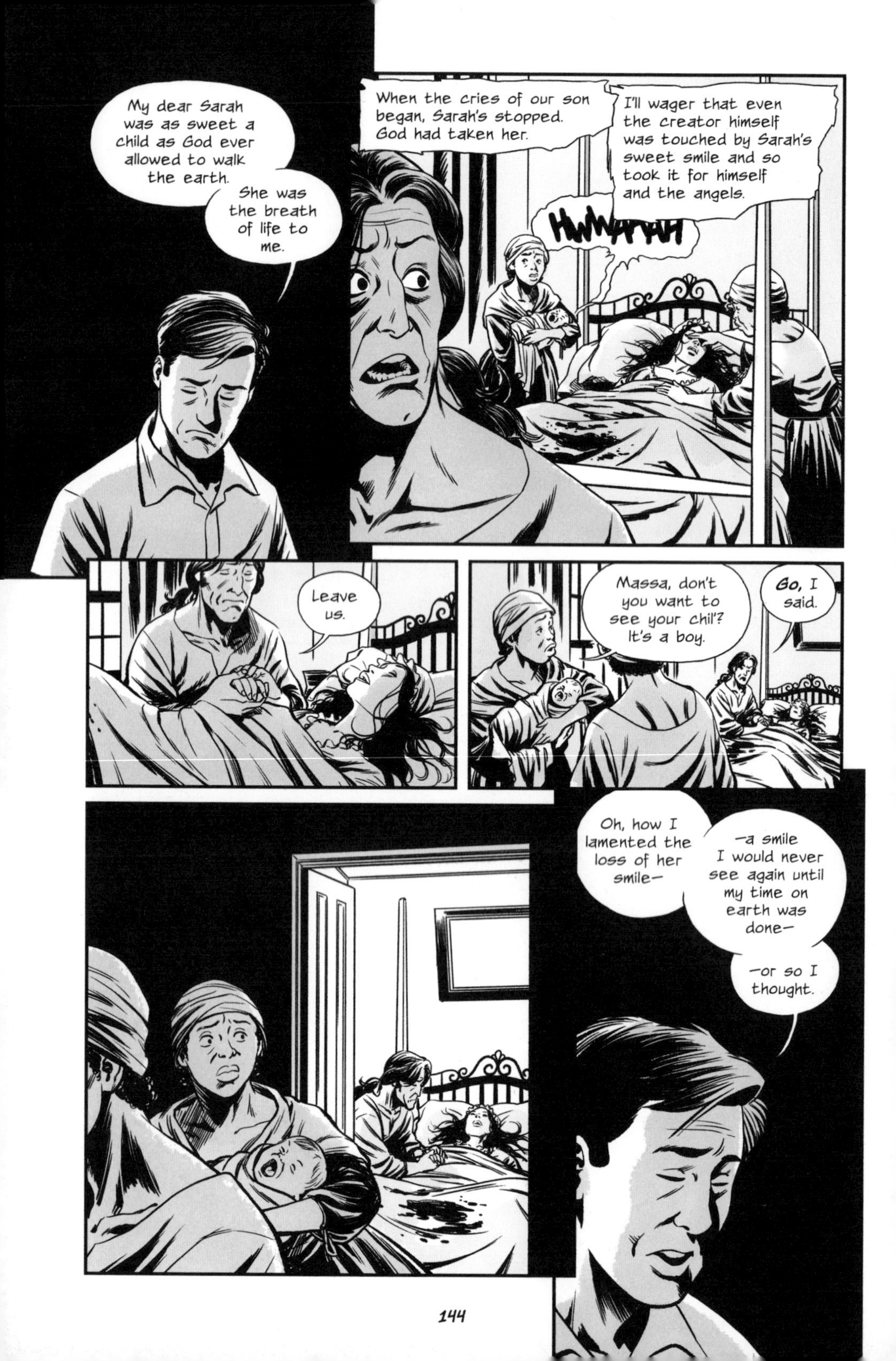
My dear Sarah was as sweet a child as God ever allowed to walk the earth.
She was the breath of life to me.
When the cries of our son began, Sarah's stopped. God had taken her.
I'll wager that even the creator himself was touched by Sarah's sweet smile and so took it for himself and the angels.
HWWAAAH
Leave us.
Massa, don't you want to see your chil'? It's a boy.
Go, I said.
Oh, how I lamented the loss of her smile—
—a smile I would never see again until my time on earth was done—
—or so I thought.

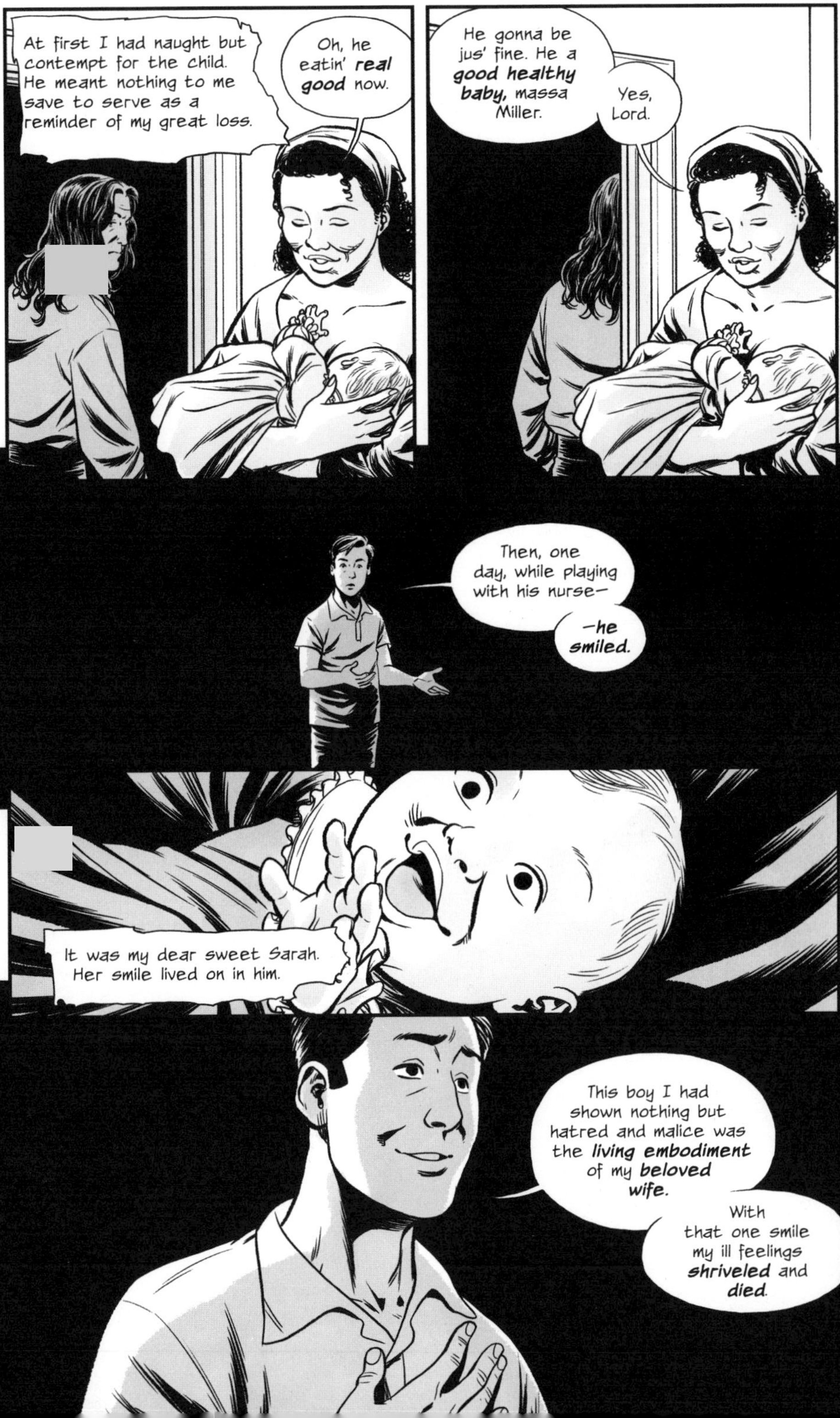
At first I had naught but contempt for the child. He meant nothing to me save to serve as a reminder of my great loss.
Oh, he eatin' **real good** now.
He gonna be jus' fine. He a **good healthy baby,** massa Miller.
Yes, Lord.
Then, one day, while playing with his nurse—
—**he smiled.**
It was my dear sweet Sarah. Her smile lived on in him.
This boy I had shown nothing but hatred and malice was the **living embodiment** of my **beloved wife.**
With that one smile my ill feelings **shriveled** and **died.**

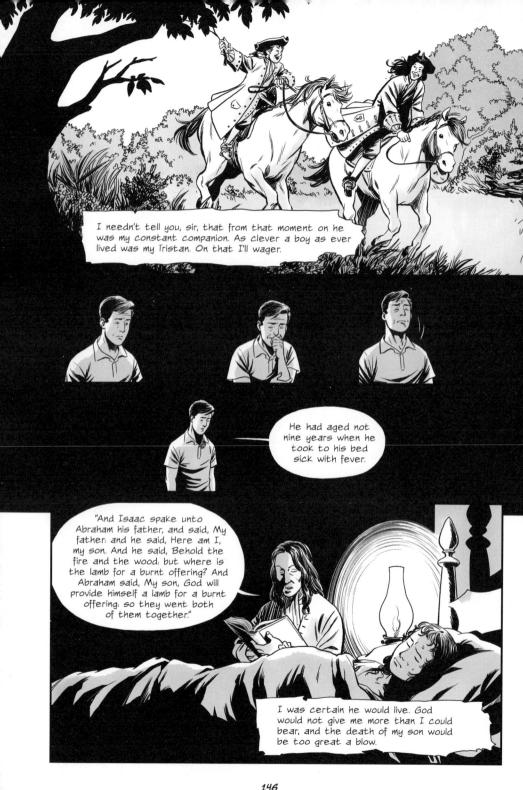

I needn't tell you, sir, that from that moment on he was my constant companion. As clever a boy as ever lived was my Tristan. On that I'll wager.

He had aged not nine years when he took to his bed sick with fever.

"And Isaac spake unto Abraham his father, and said, My father: and he said, Here am I, my son. And he said, Behold the fire and the wood: but where is the lamb for a burnt offering? And Abraham said, My son, God will provide himself a lamb for a burnt offering: so they went both of them together."

I was certain he would live. God would not give me more than I could bear, and the death of my son would be too great a blow.

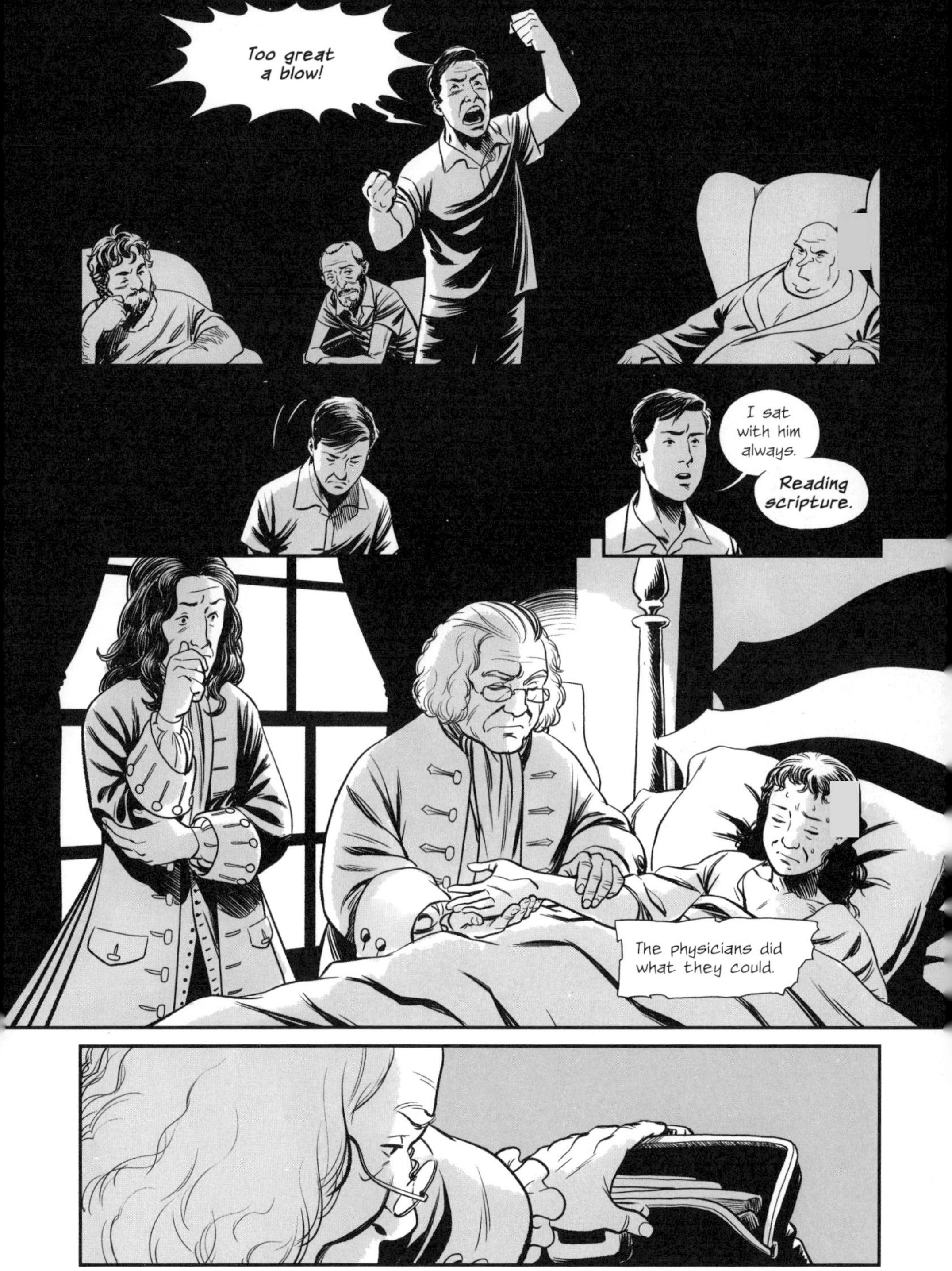
Too great a blow!
I sat with him always.
Reading scripture.
The physicians did what they could.

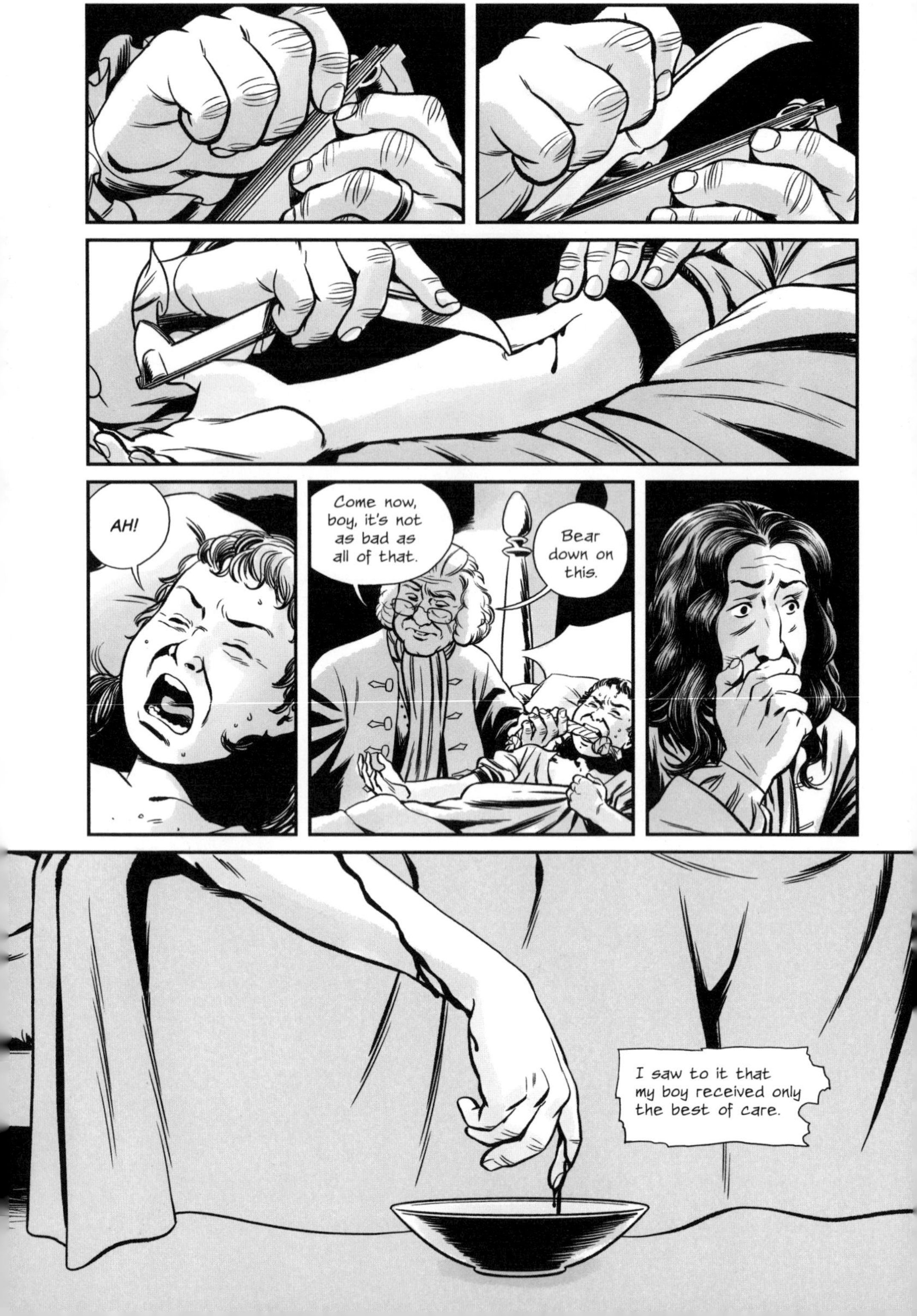
AH!
Come now, boy, it's not as bad as all of that.
Bear down on this.
I saw to it that my boy received only the best of care.

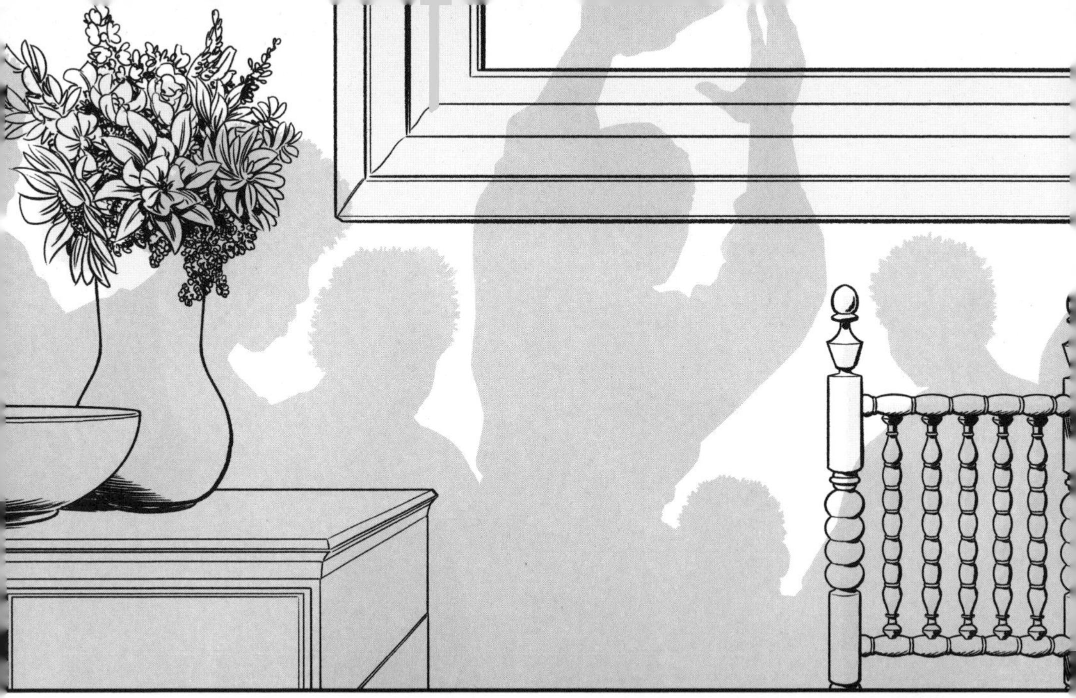

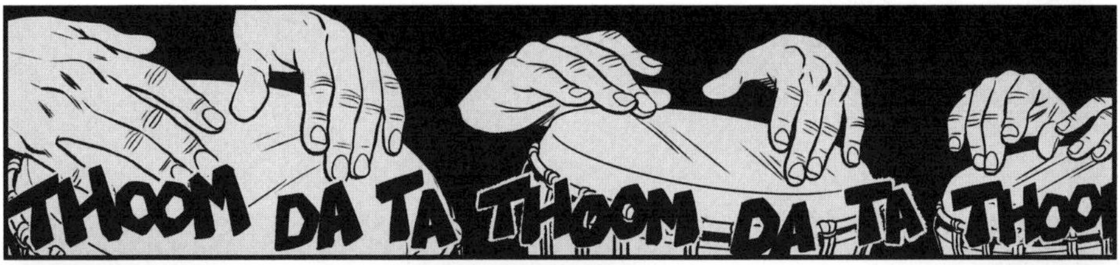
THOOM DA TA THOOM DA TA THOO

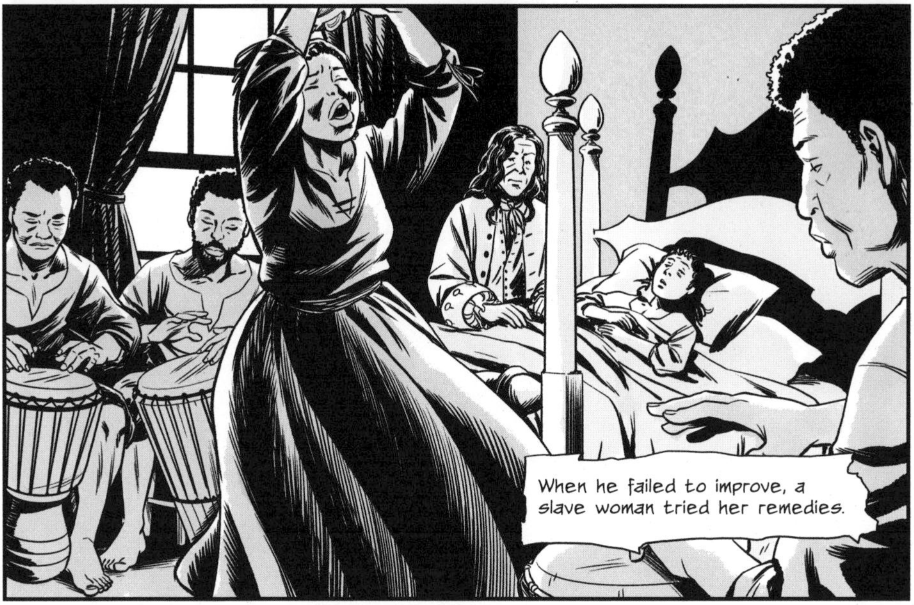
When he failed to improve, a slave woman tried her remedies.

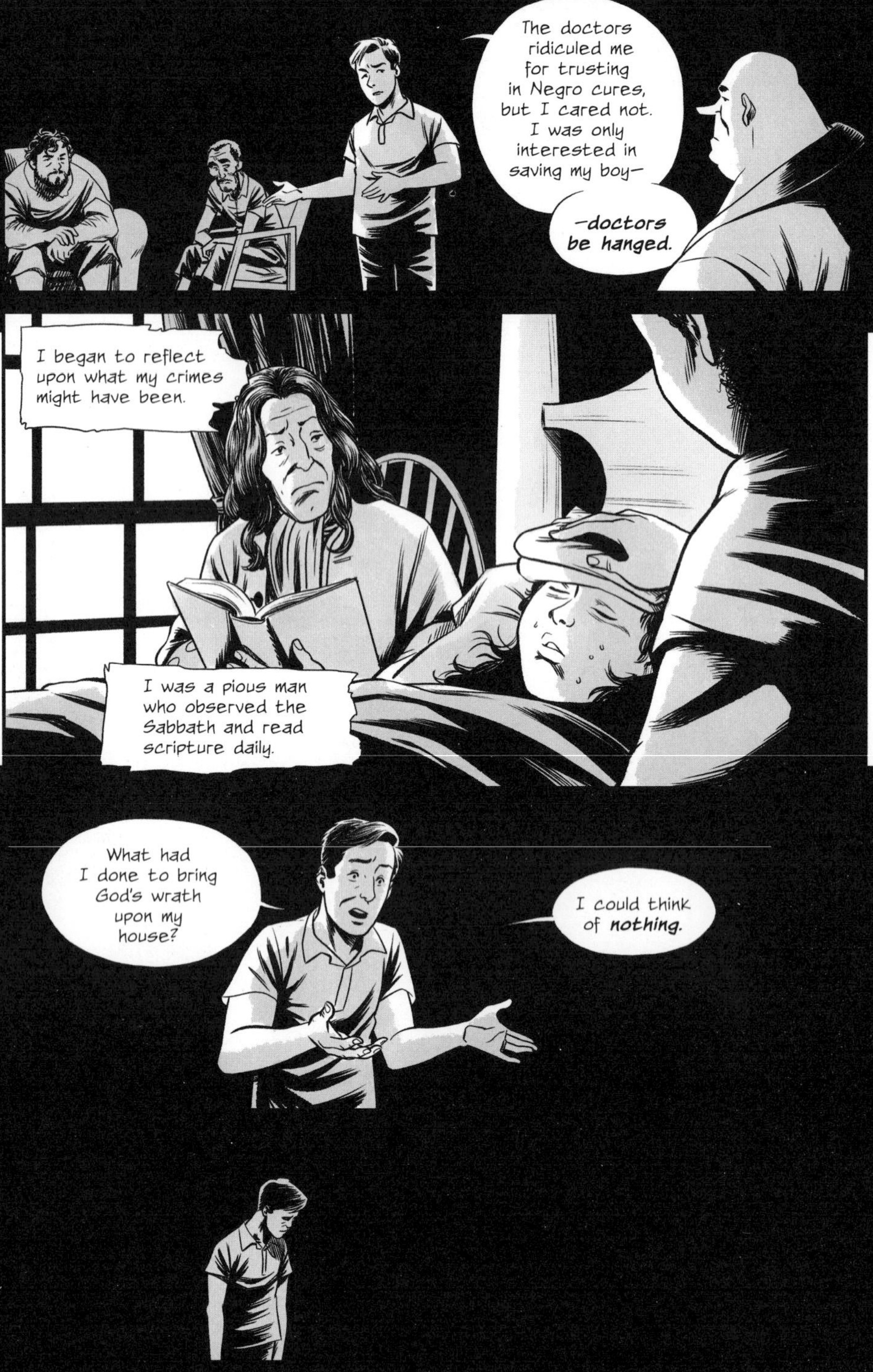

The doctors ridiculed me for trusting in Negro cures, but I cared not. I was only interested in saving my boy—
—doctors be hanged.
I began to reflect upon what my crimes might have been.
I was a pious man who observed the Sabbath and read scripture daily.
What had I done to bring God's wrath upon my house?
I could think of nothing.

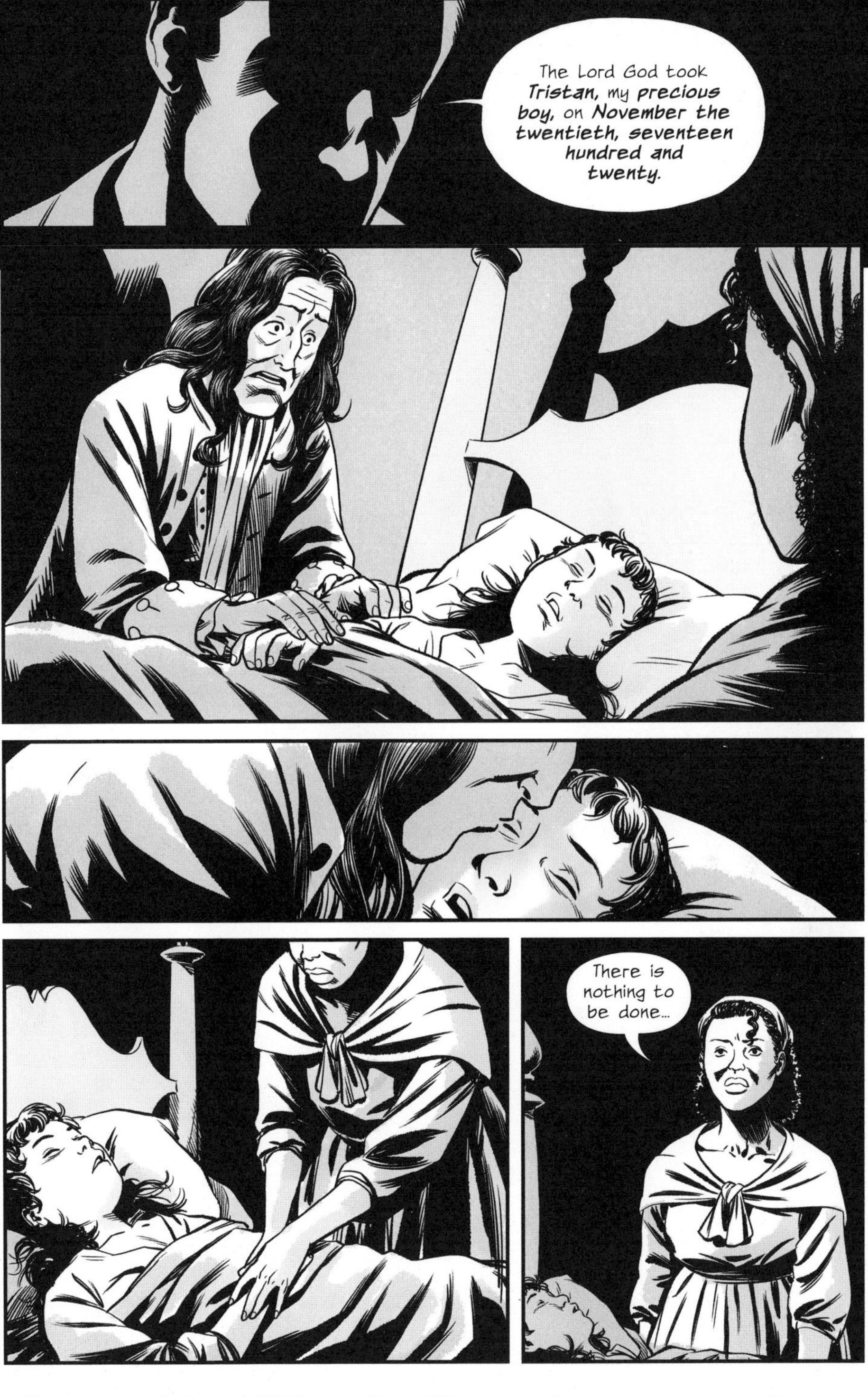
The Lord God took **Tristan,** my **precious boy,** on **November the twentieth, seventeen hundred and twenty.**
There is nothing to be done...

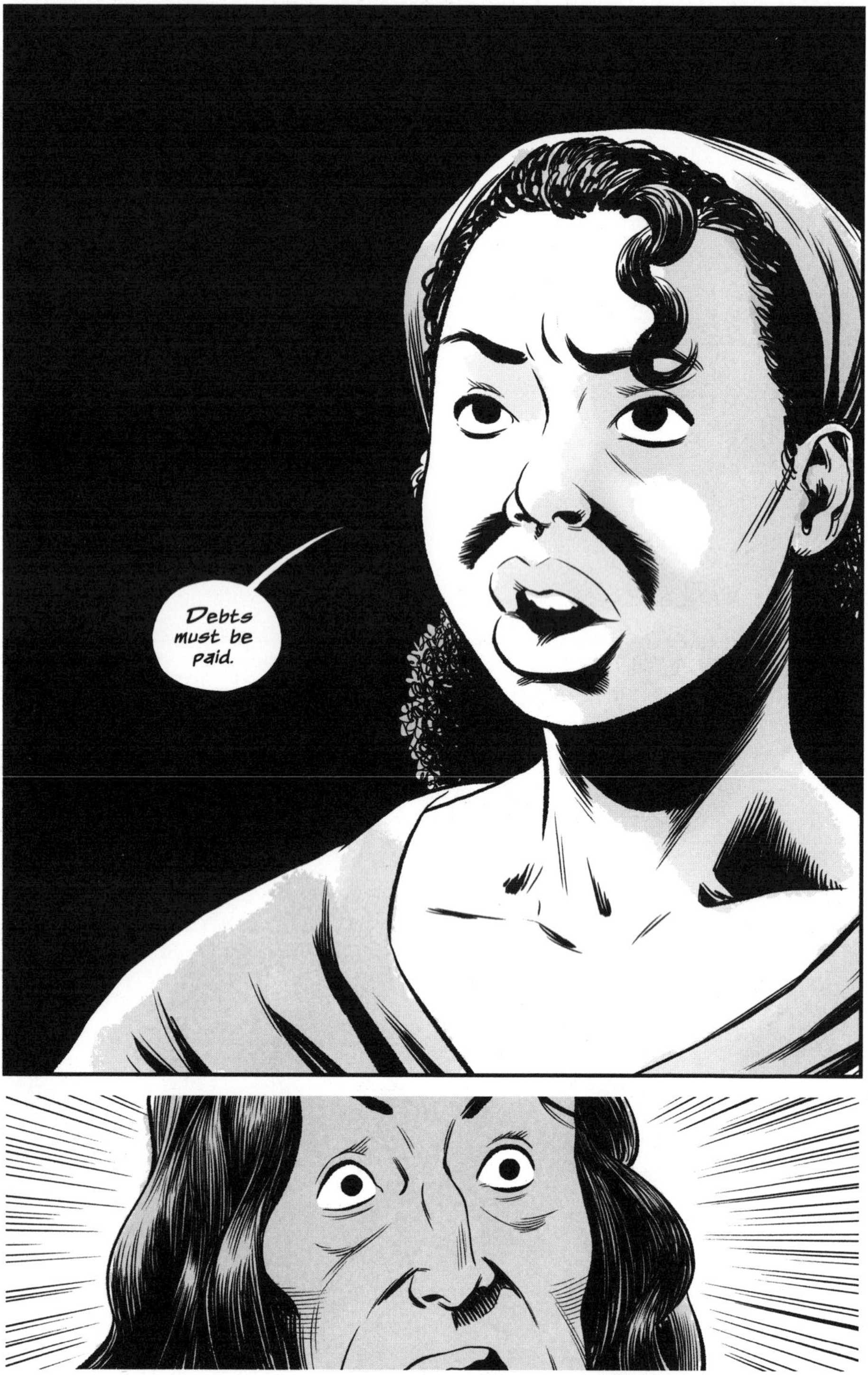
Debts must be paid.

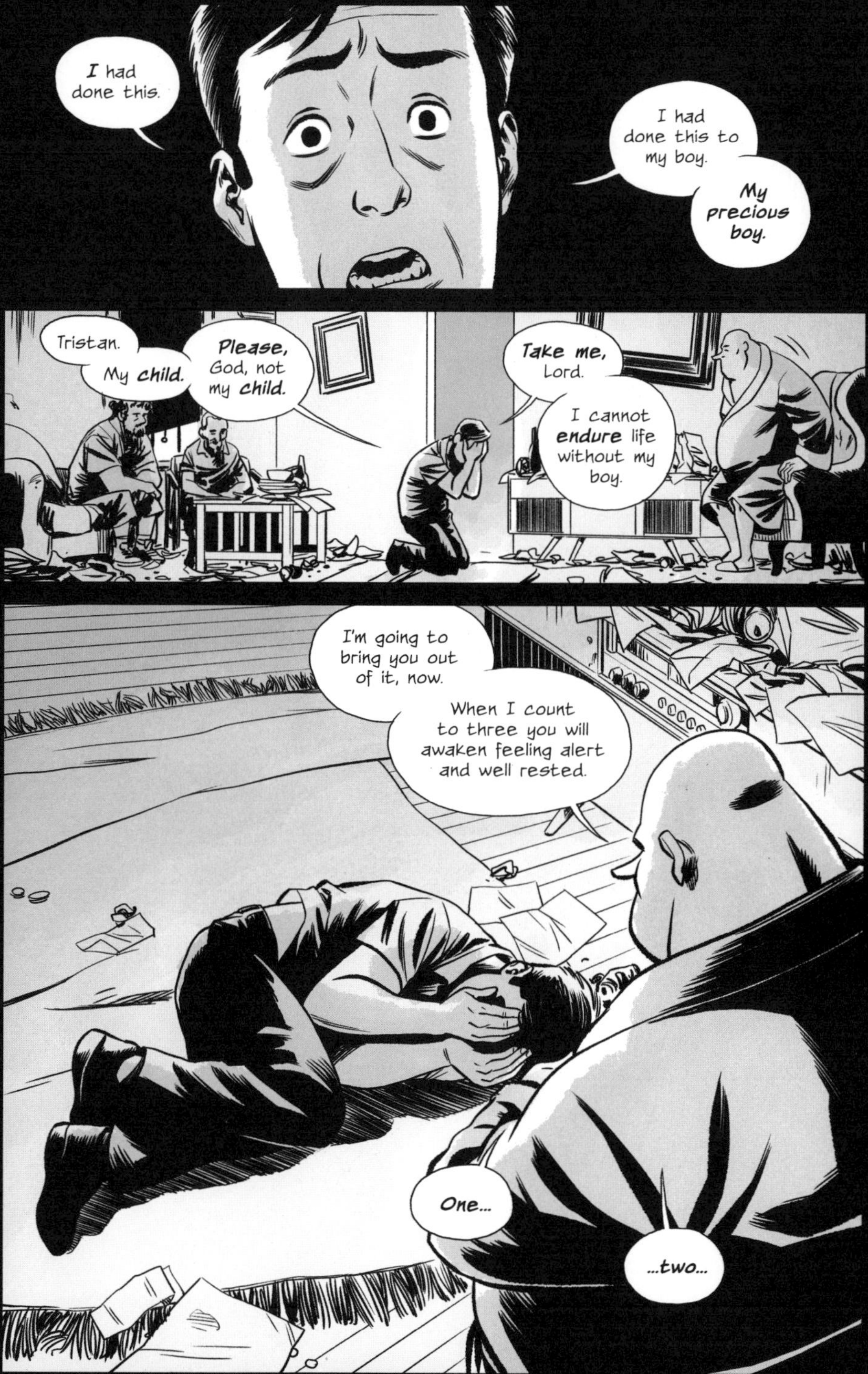
I had done this.
I had done this to my boy.
My precious boy.
Tristan.
My child.
Please, God, not my child.
Take me, Lord.
I cannot endure life without my boy.
I'm going to bring you out of it, now.
When I count to three you will awaken feeling alert and well rested.
One...
...two...

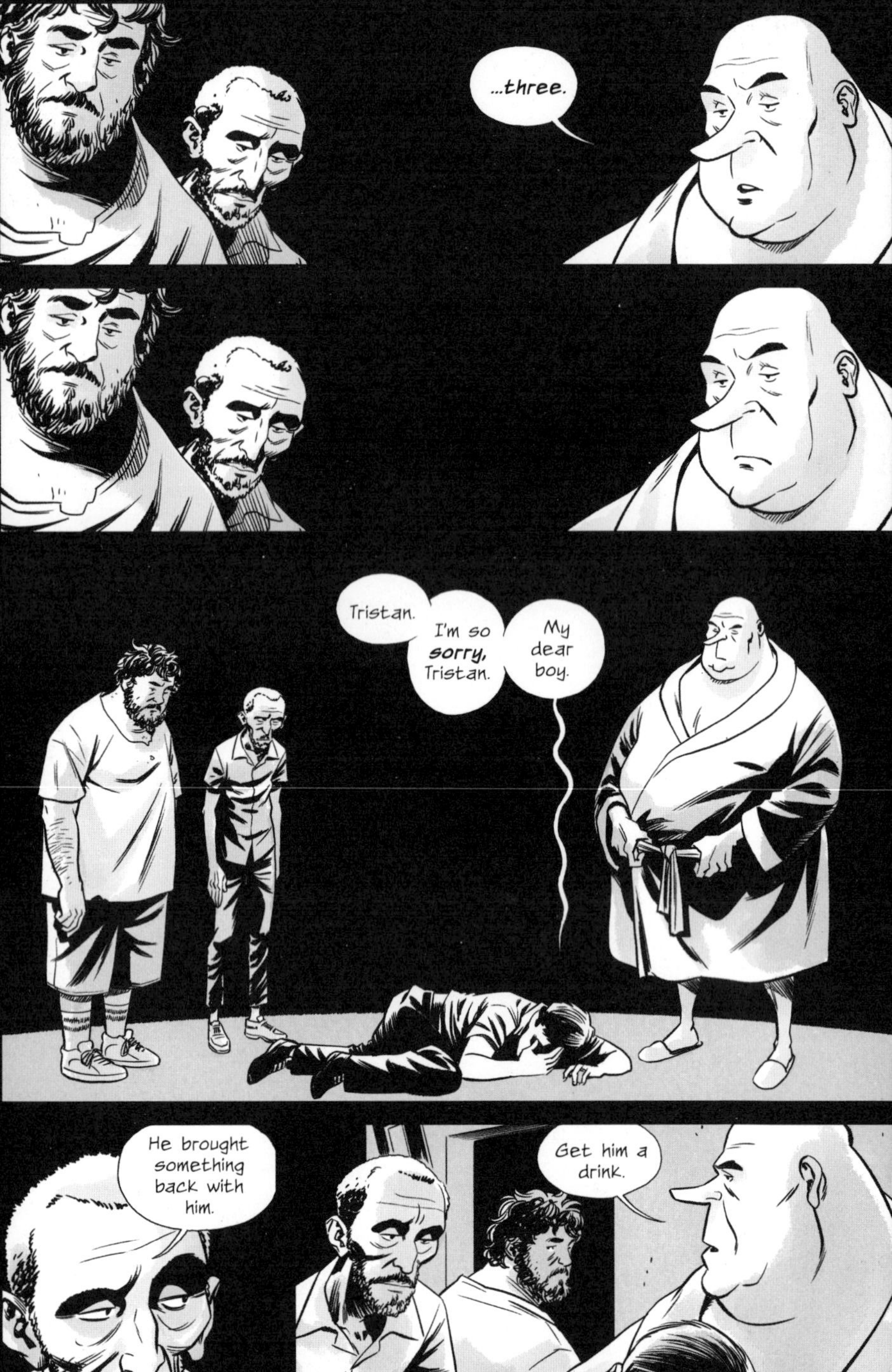

...three.
Tristan.
I'm so **sorry,** Tristan.
My dear boy.
He brought something back with him.
Get him a drink.

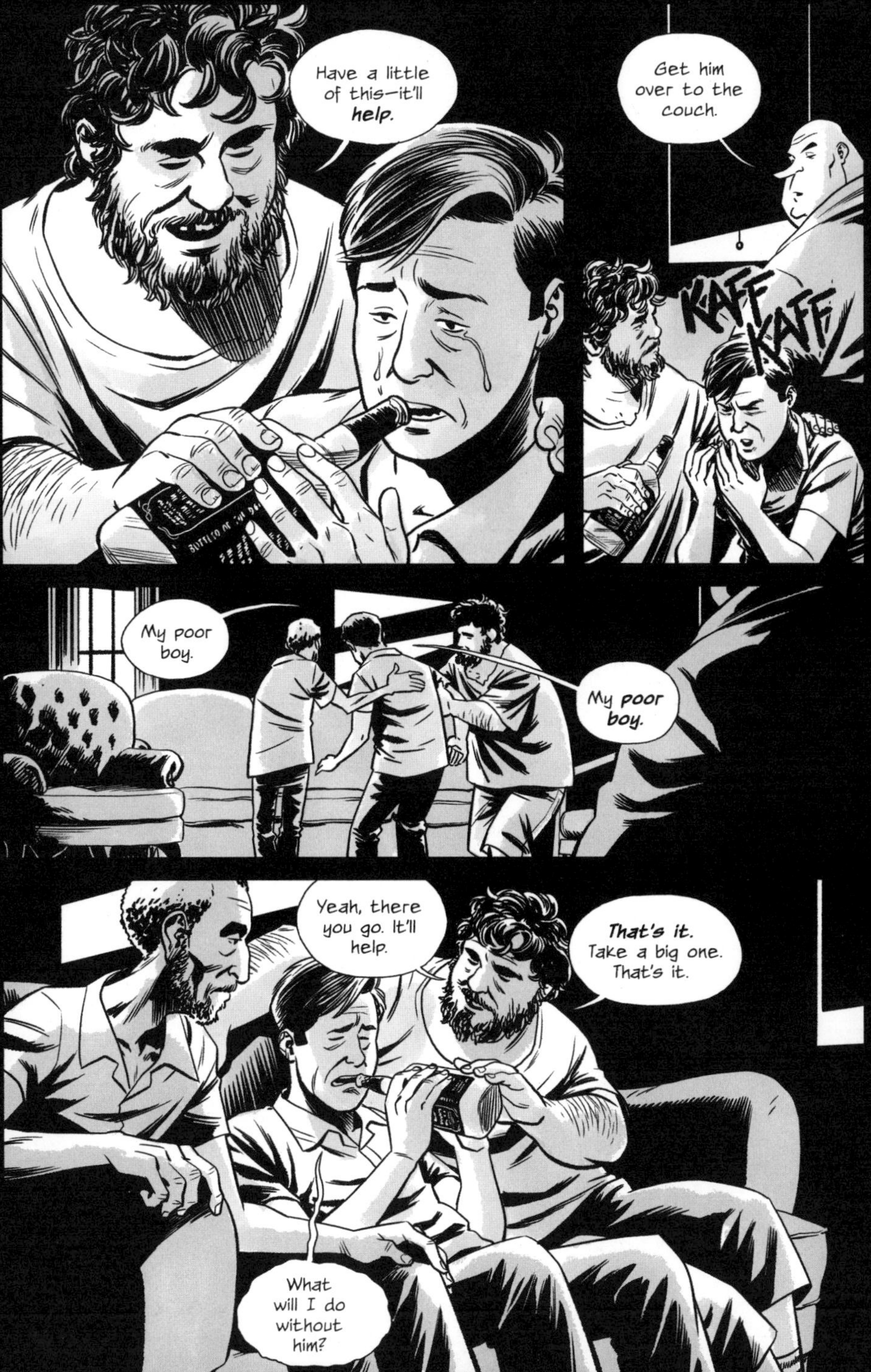
Have a little of this—it'll **help**.
Get him over to the couch.
KAFF KAFF
My poor boy.
My **poor boy**.
Yeah, there you go. It'll help.
That's it. Take a big one. That's it.
What will I do without him?

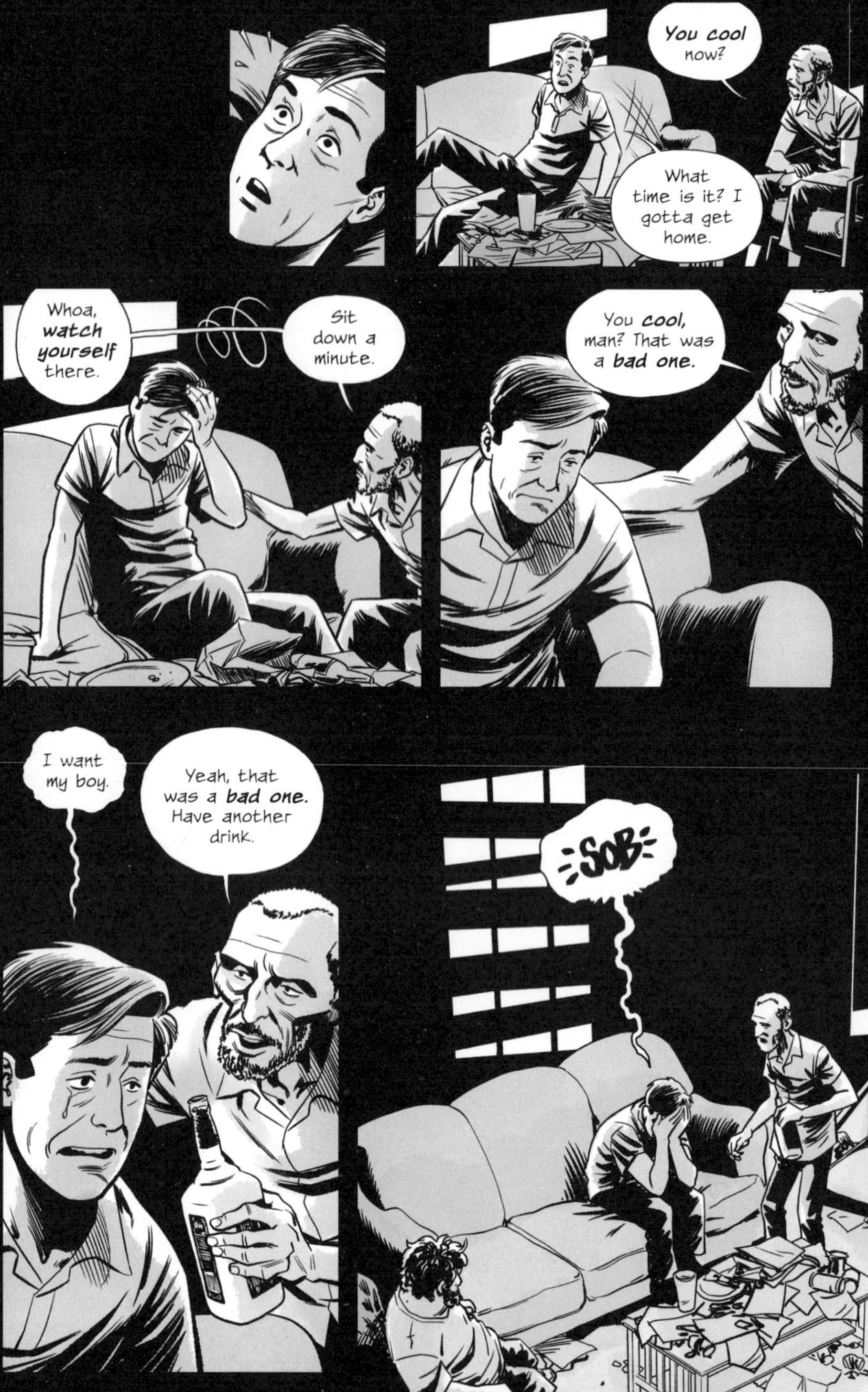

You cool now?
What time is it? I gotta get home.
Whoa, watch yourself there.
Sit down a minute.
You cool, man? That was a bad one.
I want my boy.
Yeah, that was a bad one. Have another drink.
SOB

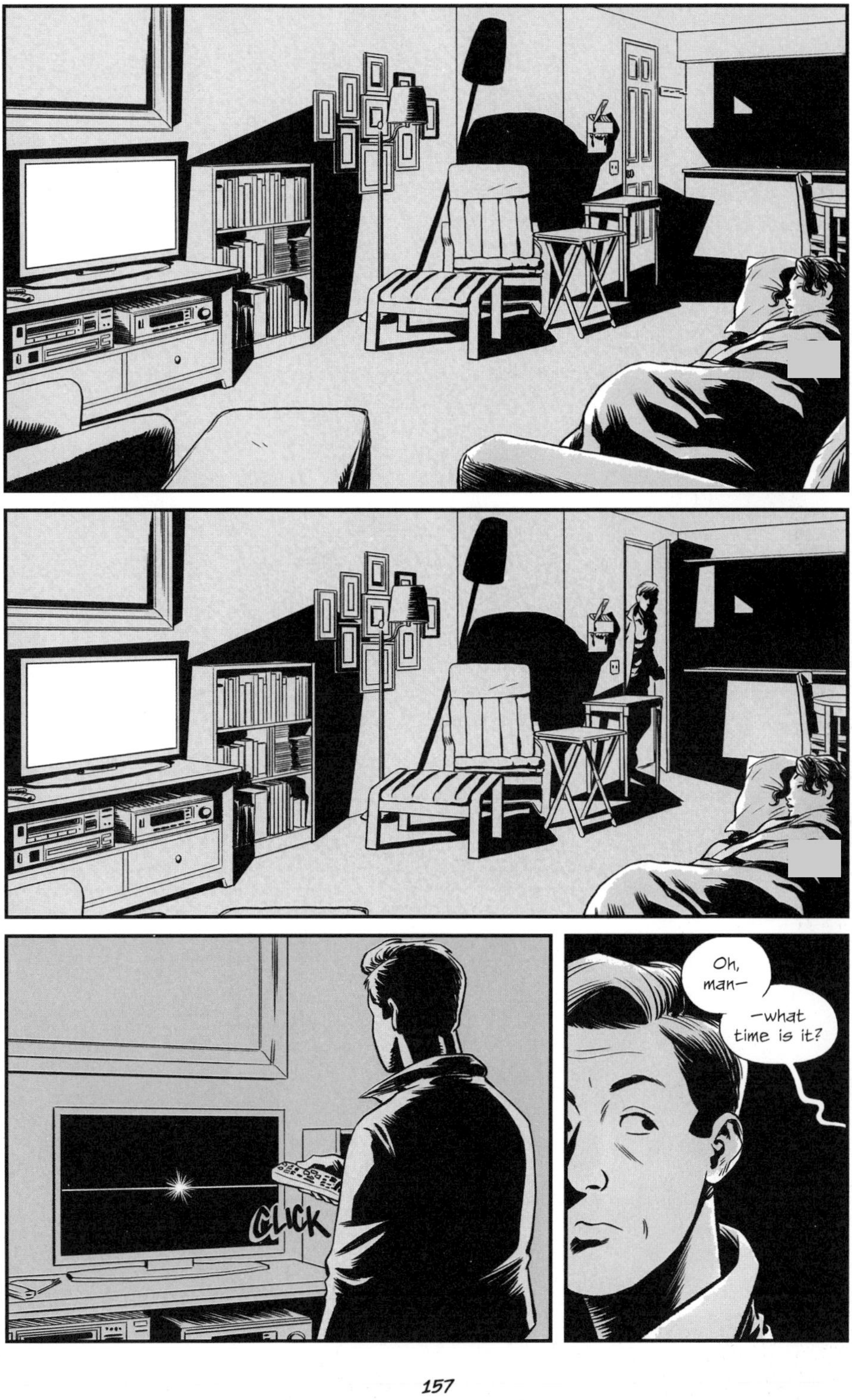
CLICK
Oh, man—
—what time is it?

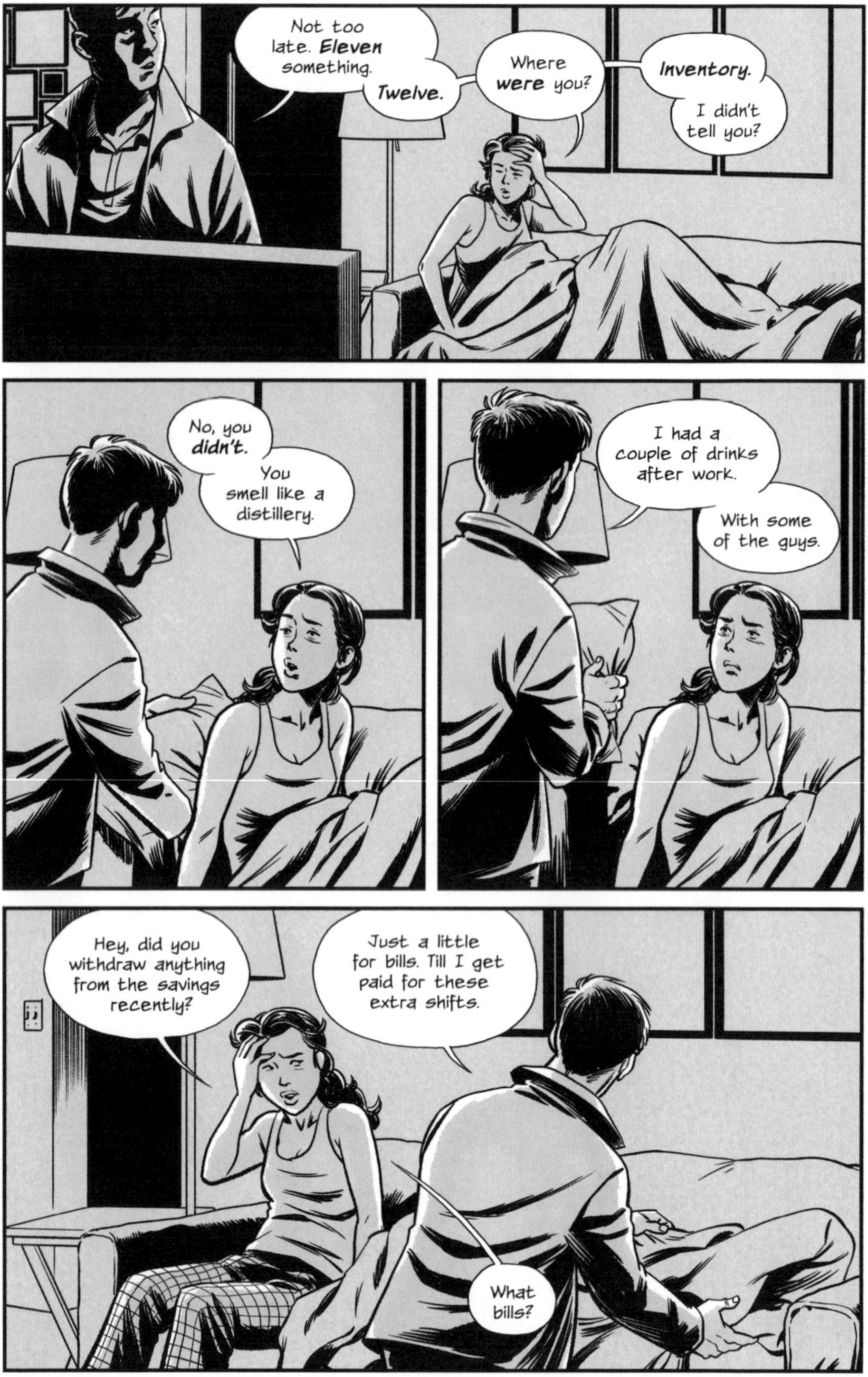
Not too late. **Eleven** something.
Twelve.
Where **were** you?
Inventory.
I didn't tell you?
No, you **didn't.**
You smell like a distillery.
I had a couple of drinks after work.
With some of the guys.
Hey, did you withdraw anything from the savings recently?
Just a little for bills. Till I get paid for these extra shifts.
What bills?

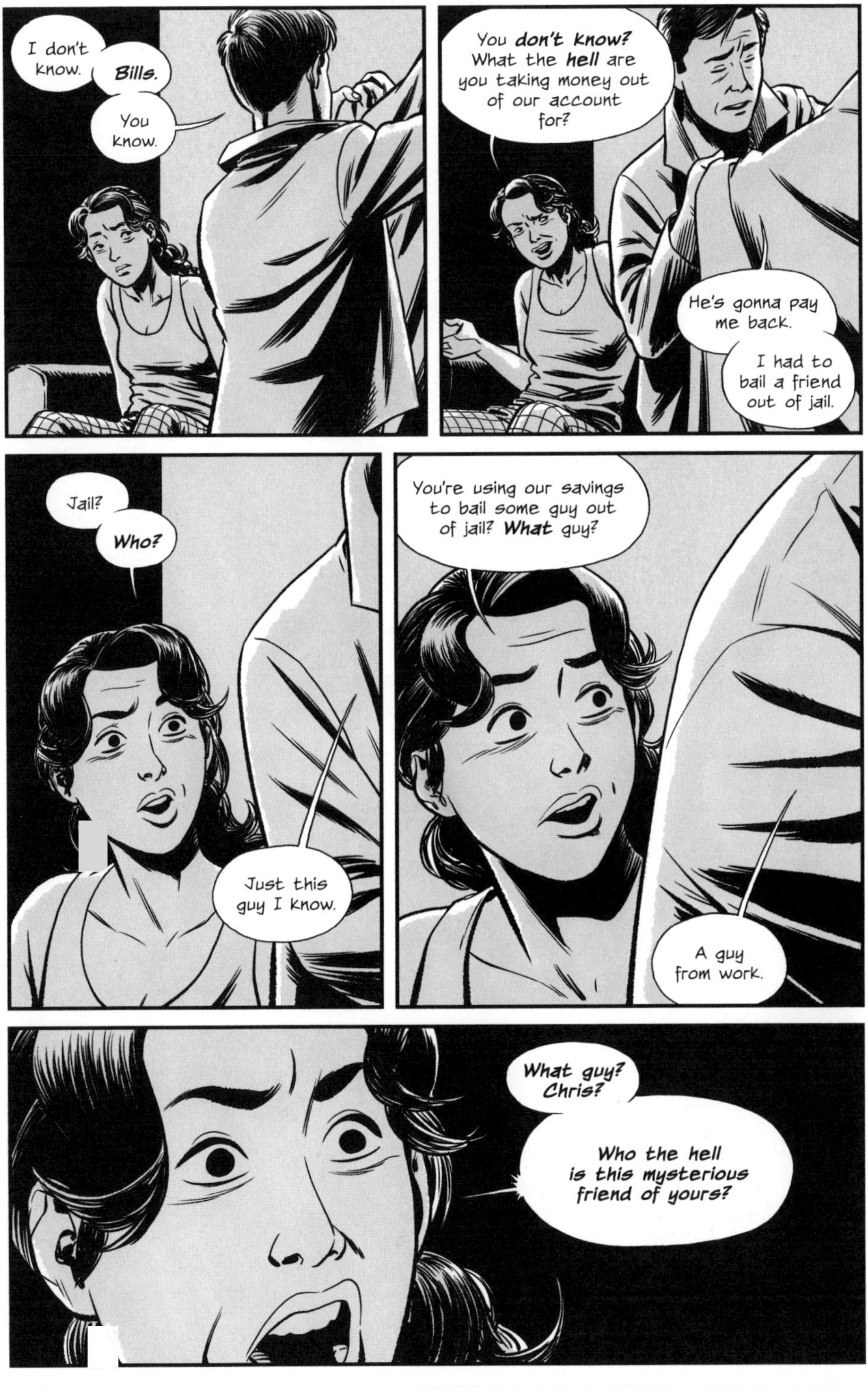
I don't know.
Bills.
You know.
You don't know? What the hell are you taking money out of our account for?
He's gonna pay me back.
I had to bail a friend out of jail.
Jail?
Who?
Just this guy I know.
You're using our savings to bail some guy out of jail? What guy?
A guy from work.
What guy? Chris?
Who the hell is this mysterious friend of yours?

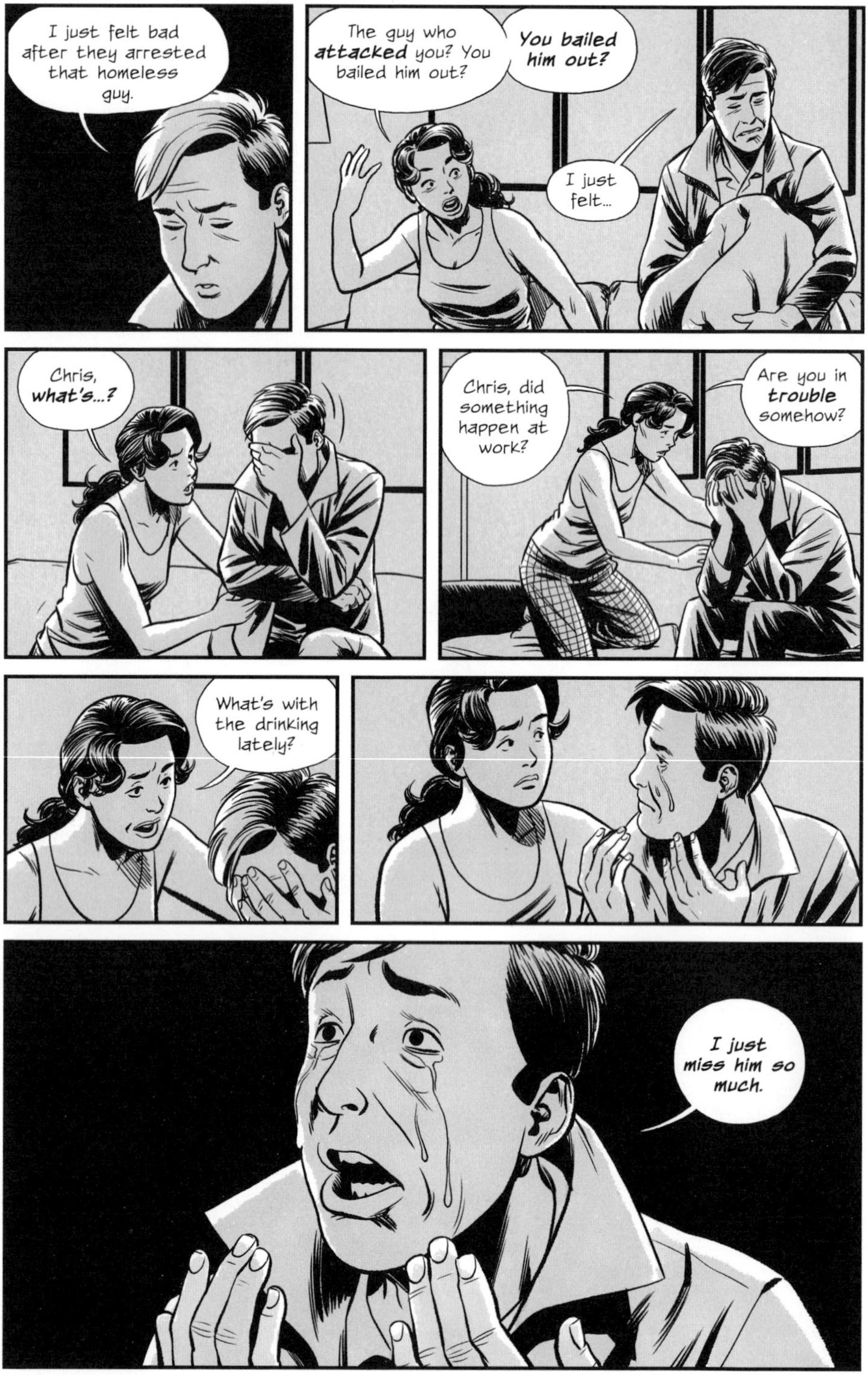
I just felt bad after they arrested that homeless guy.
The guy who **attacked** you? You bailed him out?
You bailed him out?
I just felt...
Chris, **what's...?**
Chris, did something happen at work?
Are you in **trouble** somehow?
What's with the drinking lately?
I just miss him so much.

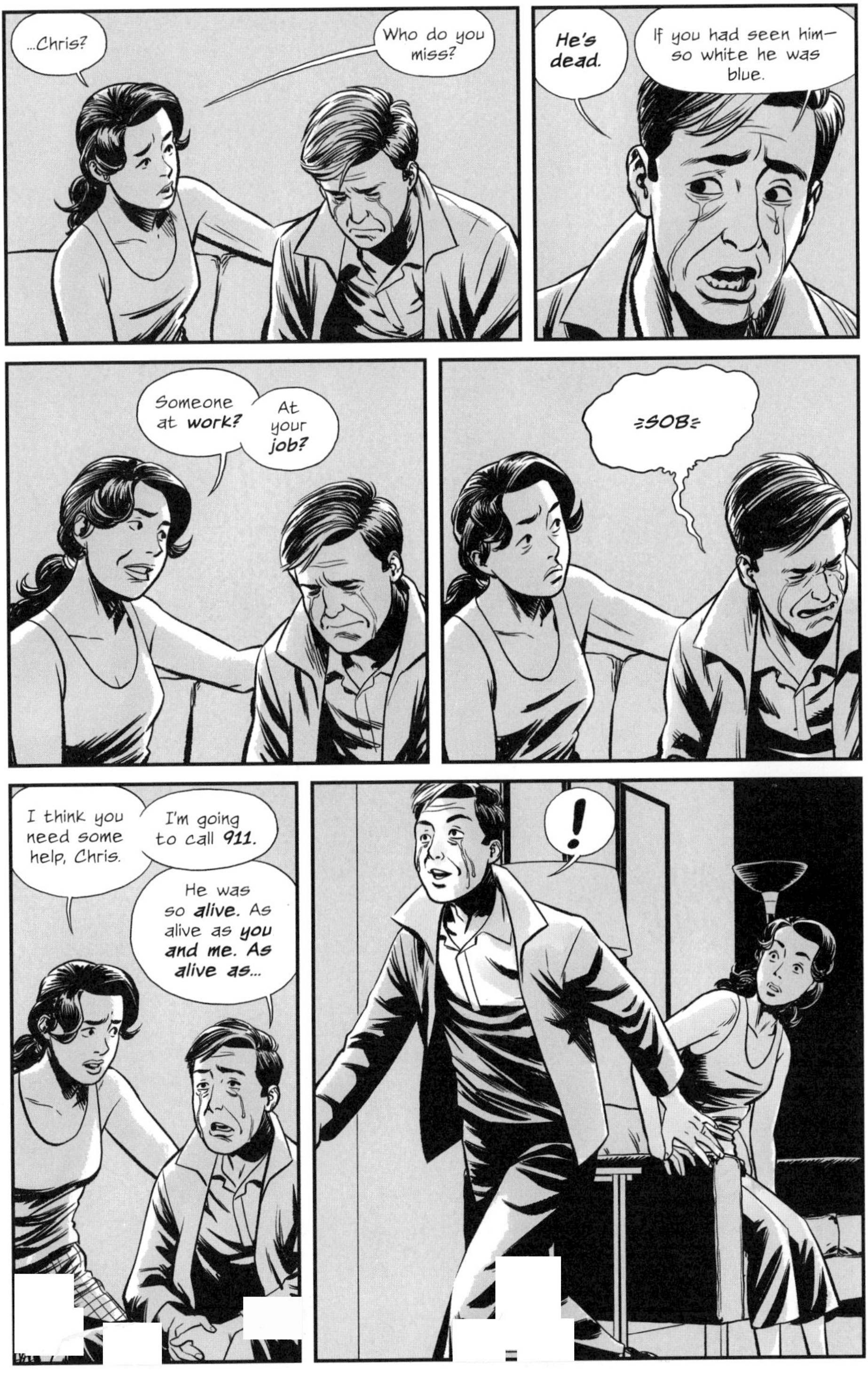
...Chris?
Who do you miss?
He's dead.
If you had seen him— so white he was blue.
Someone at work?
At your job?
=SOB=
I think you need some help, Chris.
I'm going to call 911.
He was so alive. As alive as you and me. As alive as...
!

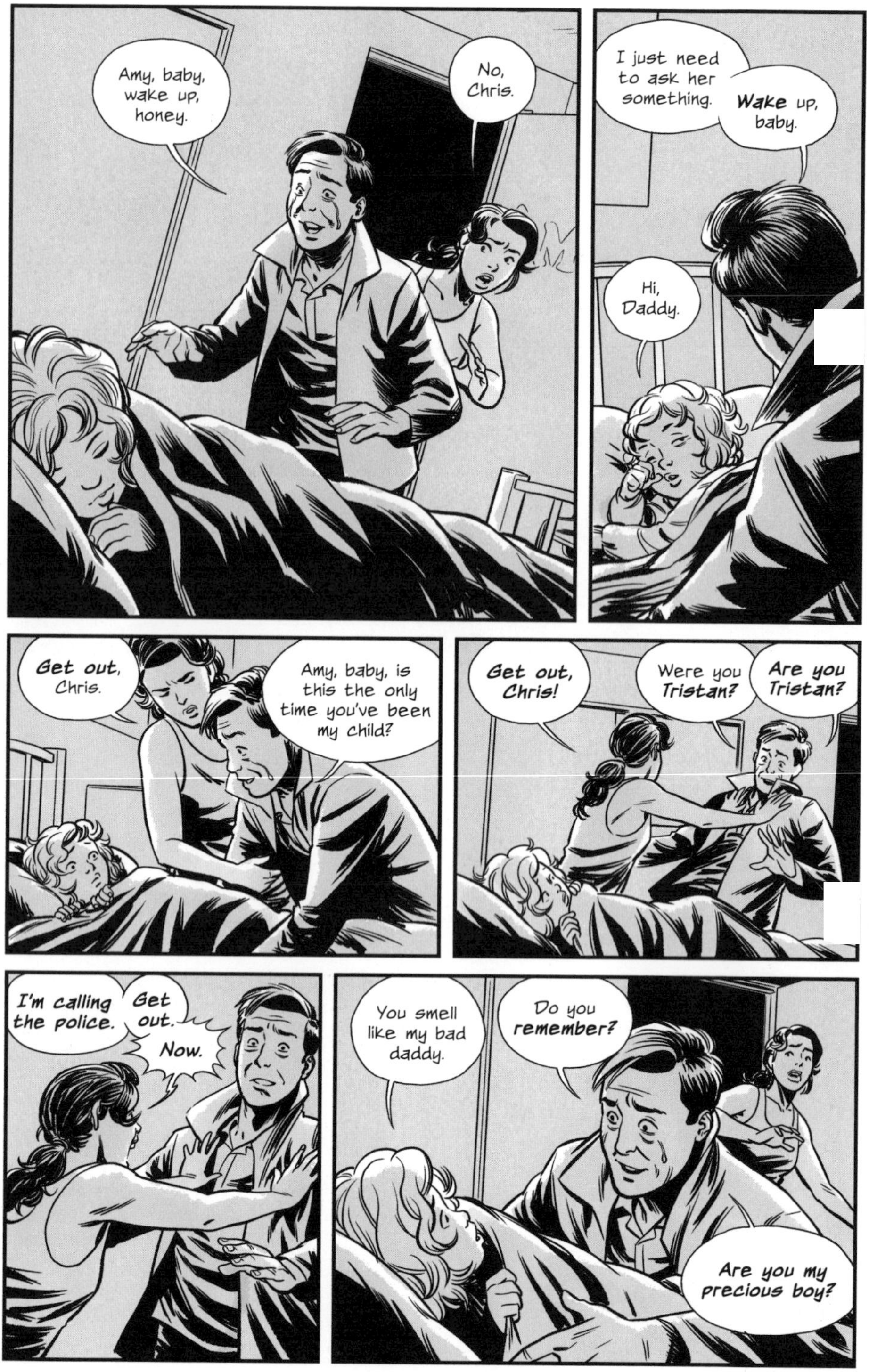
Amy, baby, wake up, honey.
No, Chris.
I just need to ask her something.
Wake up, baby.
Hi, Daddy.
Get out, Chris.
Amy, baby, is this the only time you've been my child?
Get out, Chris!
Were you Tristan?
Are you Tristan?
I'm calling the police.
Get out.
Now.
You smell like my bad daddy.
Do you remember?
Are you my precious boy?

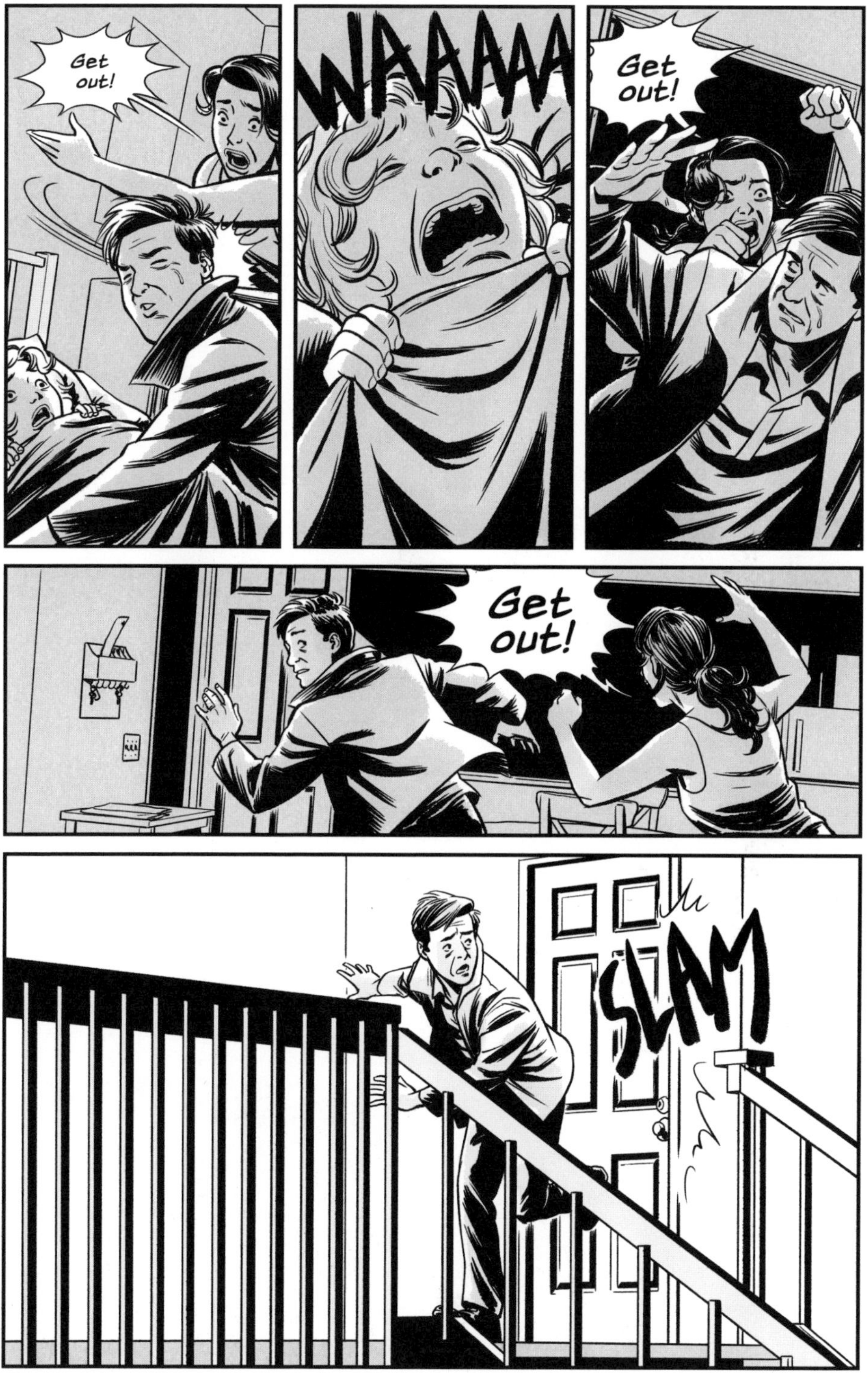
Get out!
WAAAAA
Get out!
Get out!
SLAM

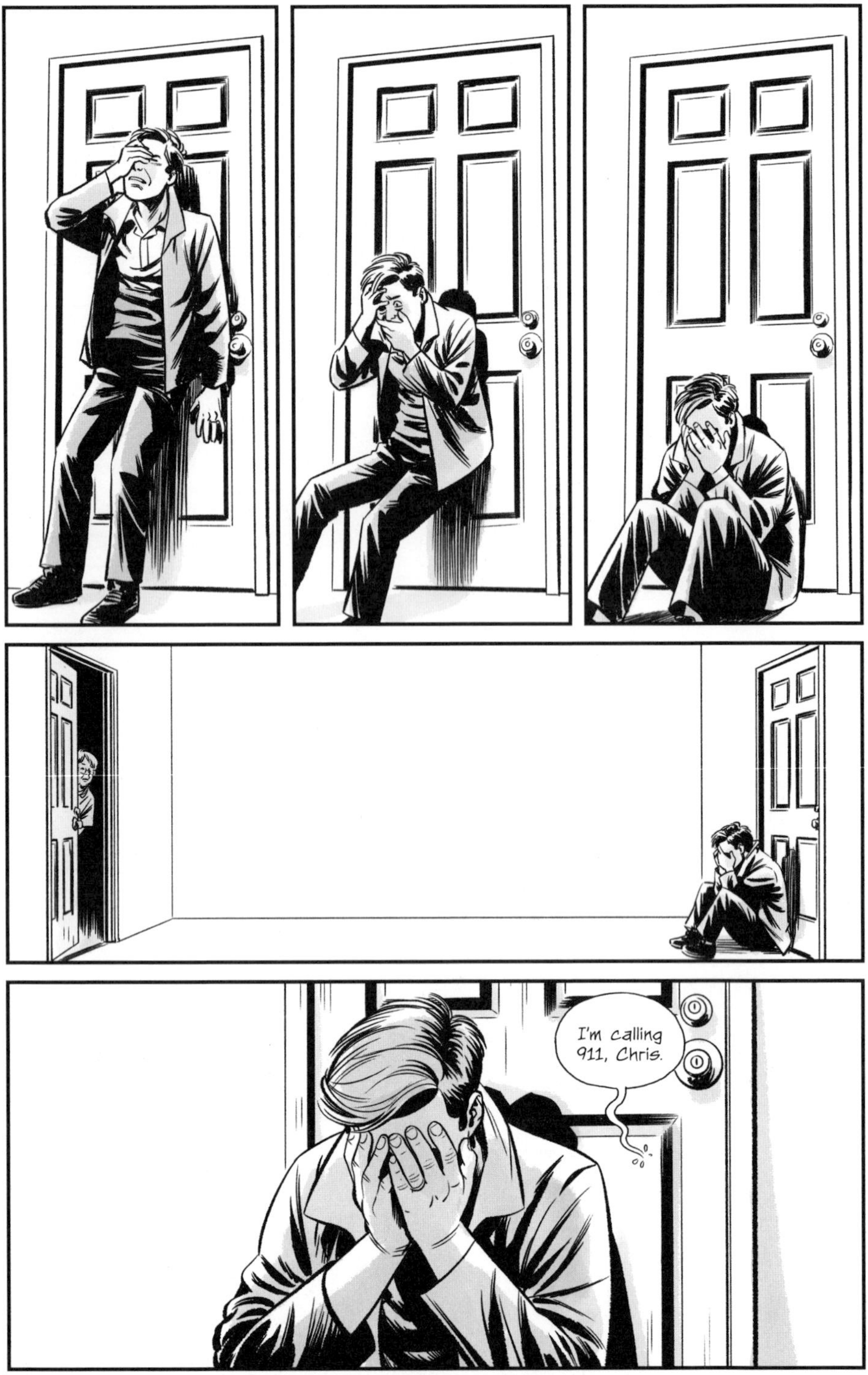
I'm calling
911, Chris.

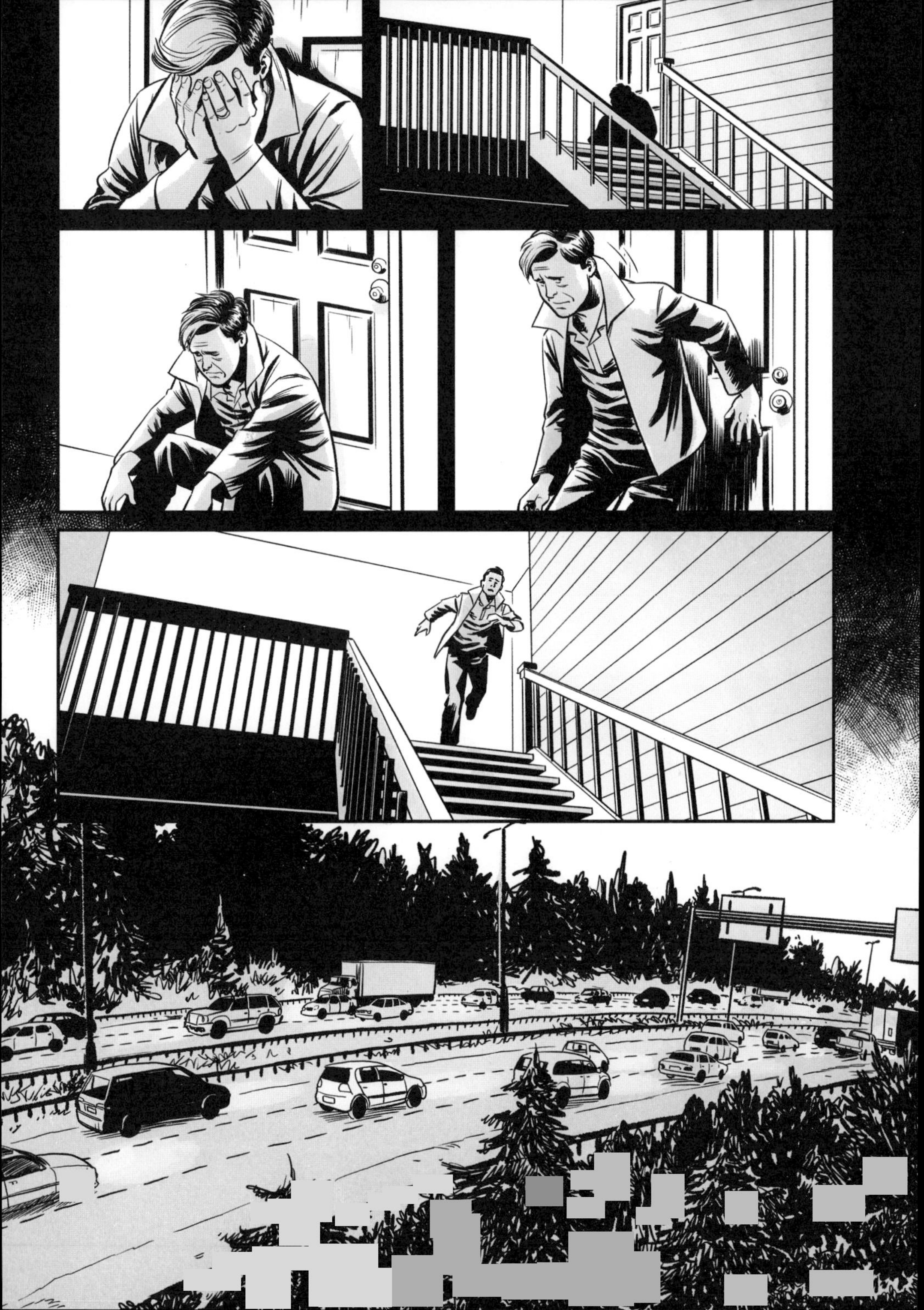

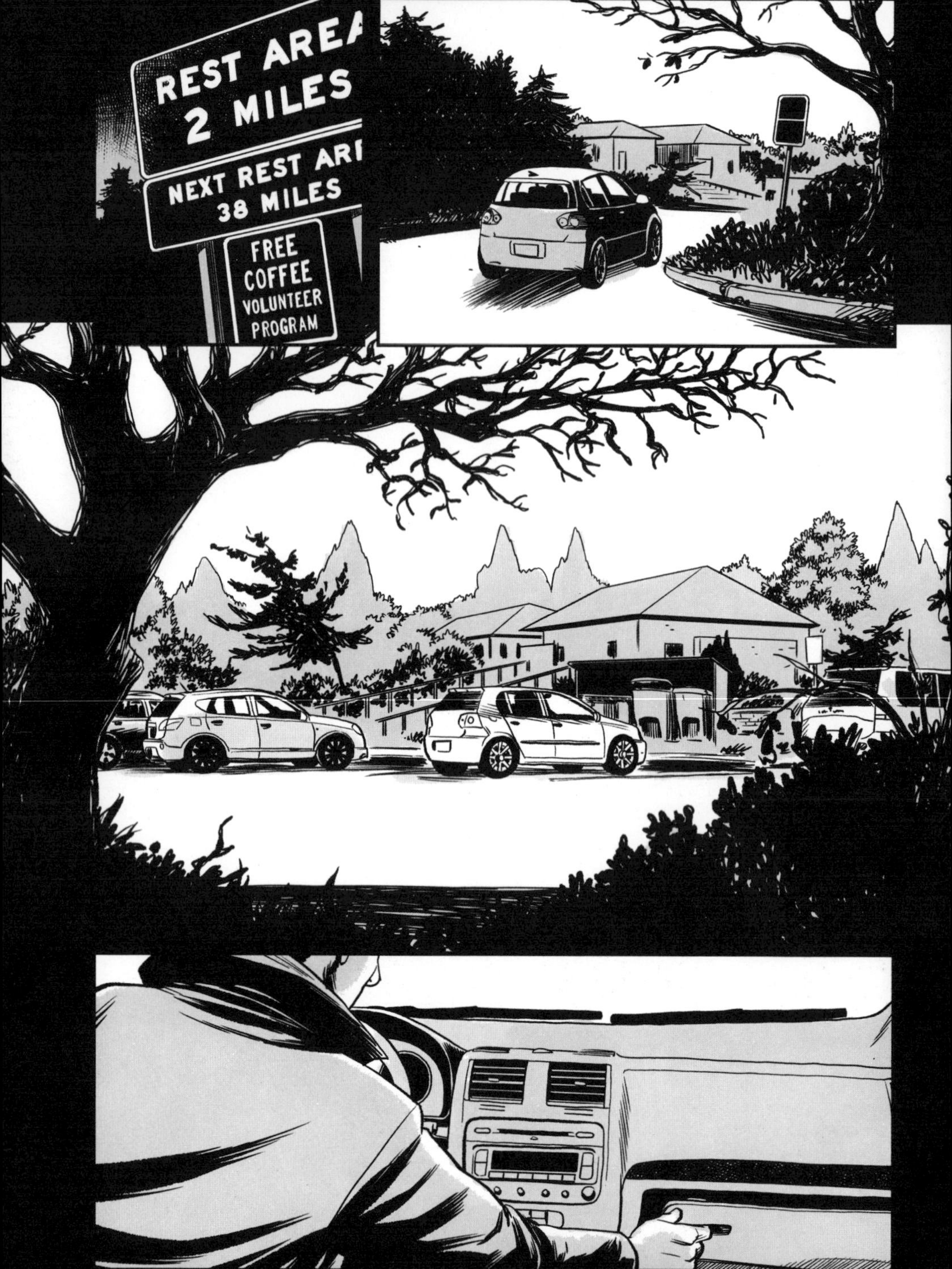
REST AREA
2 MILES
NEXT REST AR
38 MILES
FREE
COFFEE
VOLUNTEER
PROGRAM

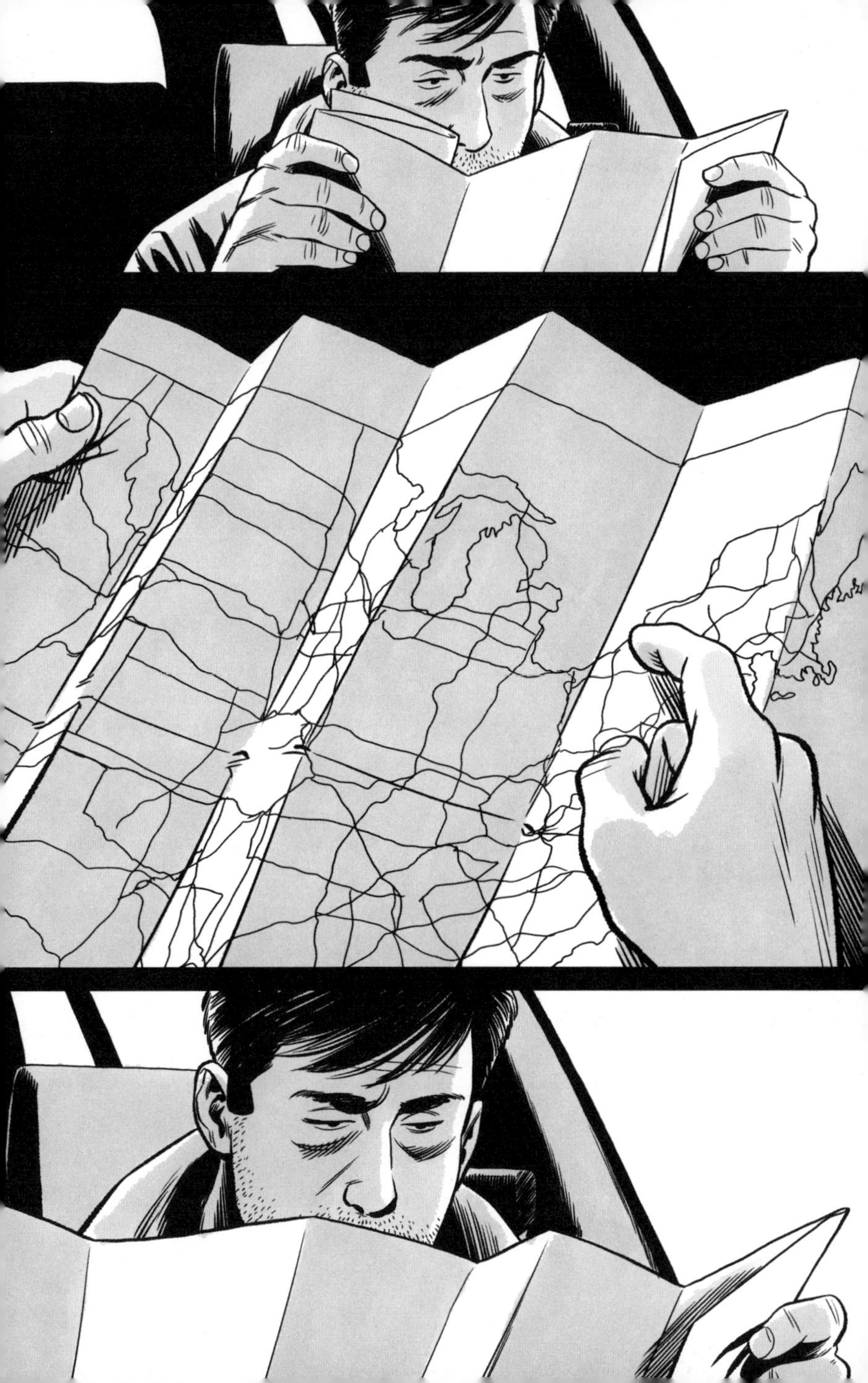

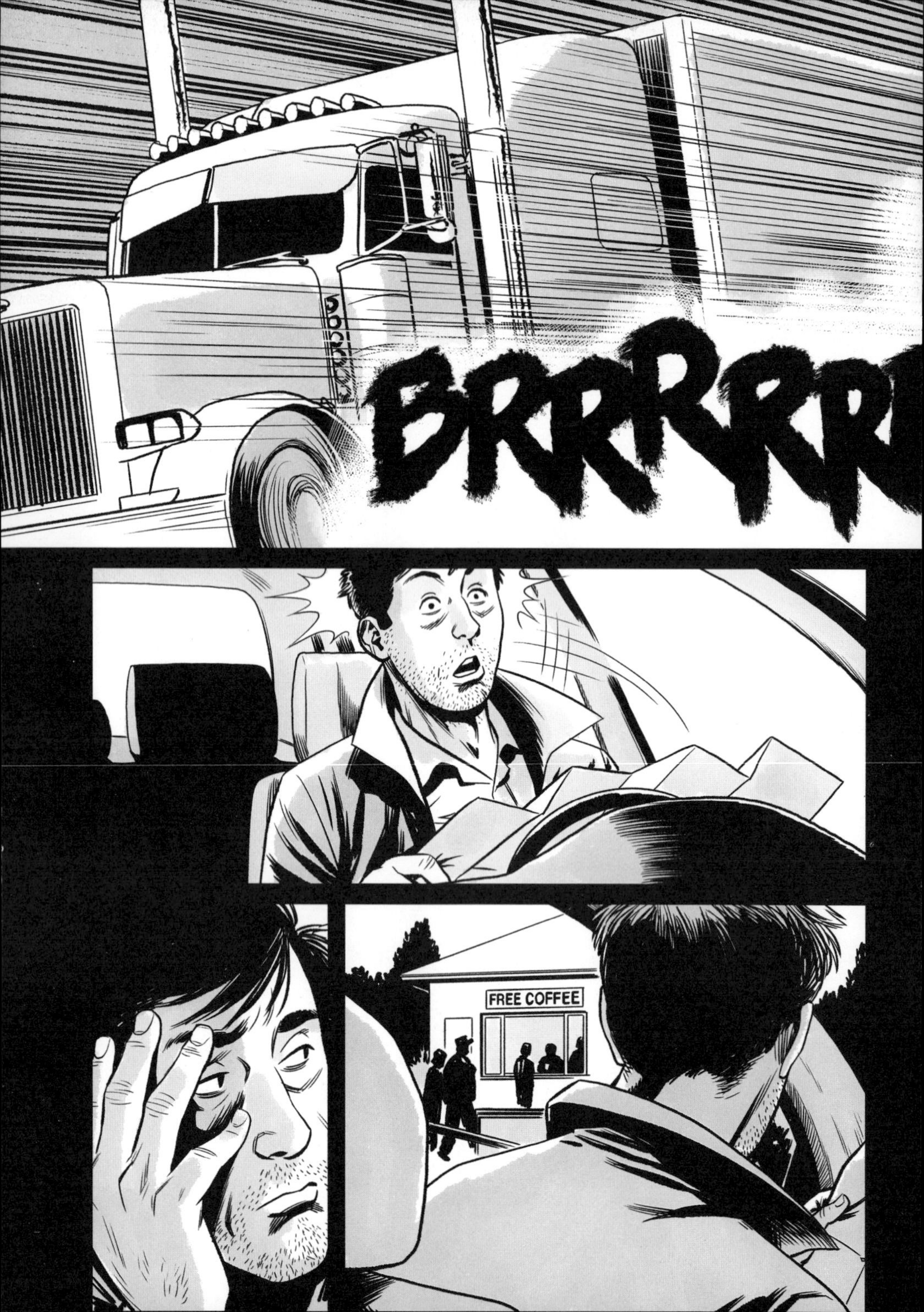
BRRRRRR
FREE COFFEE

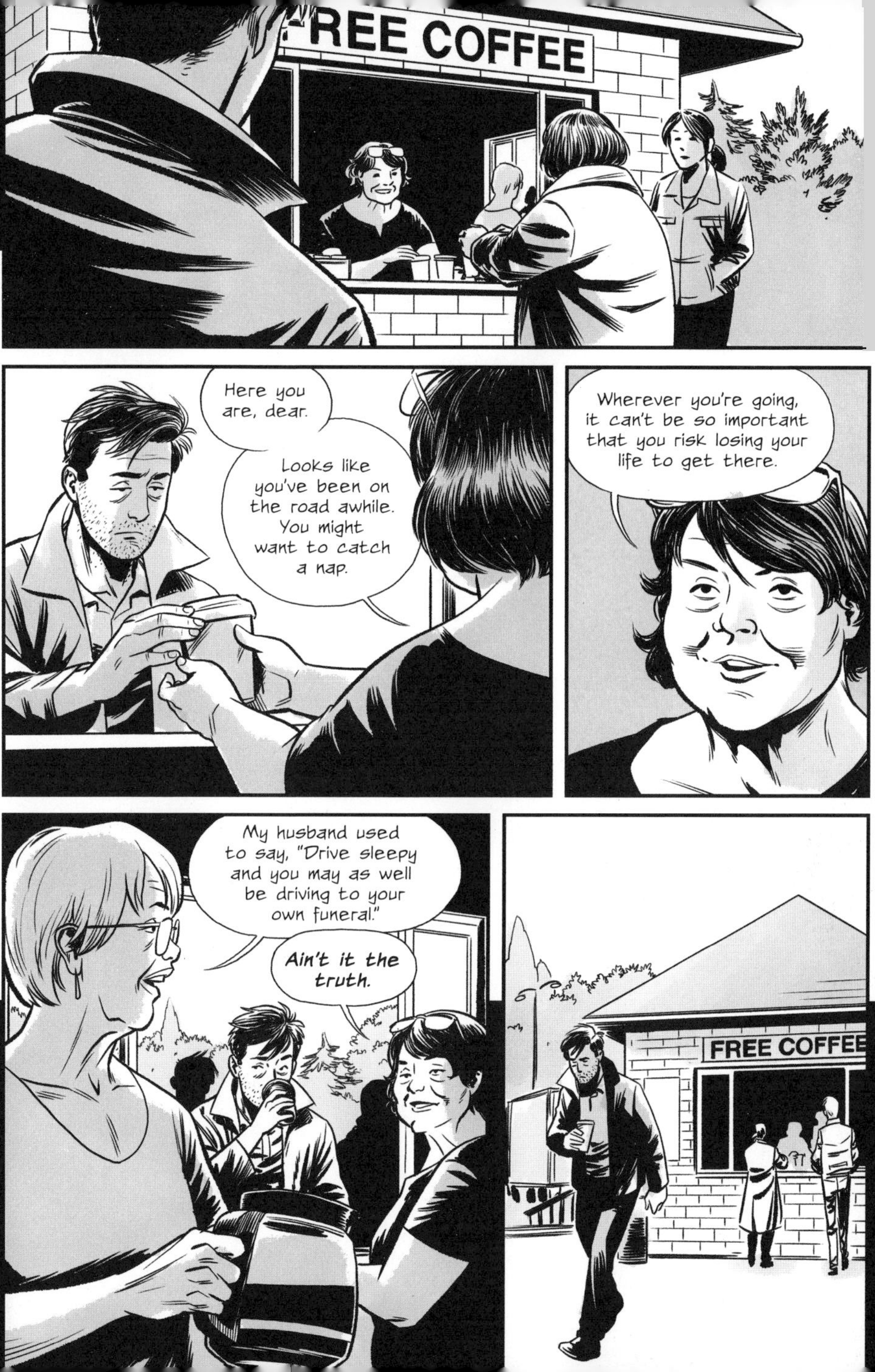
FREE COFFEE
Here you are, dear.
Looks like you've been on the road awhile. You might want to catch a nap.
Wherever you're going, it can't be so important that you risk losing your life to get there.
My husband used to say, "Drive sleepy and you may as well be driving to your own funeral."
Ain't it the truth.
FREE COFFEE

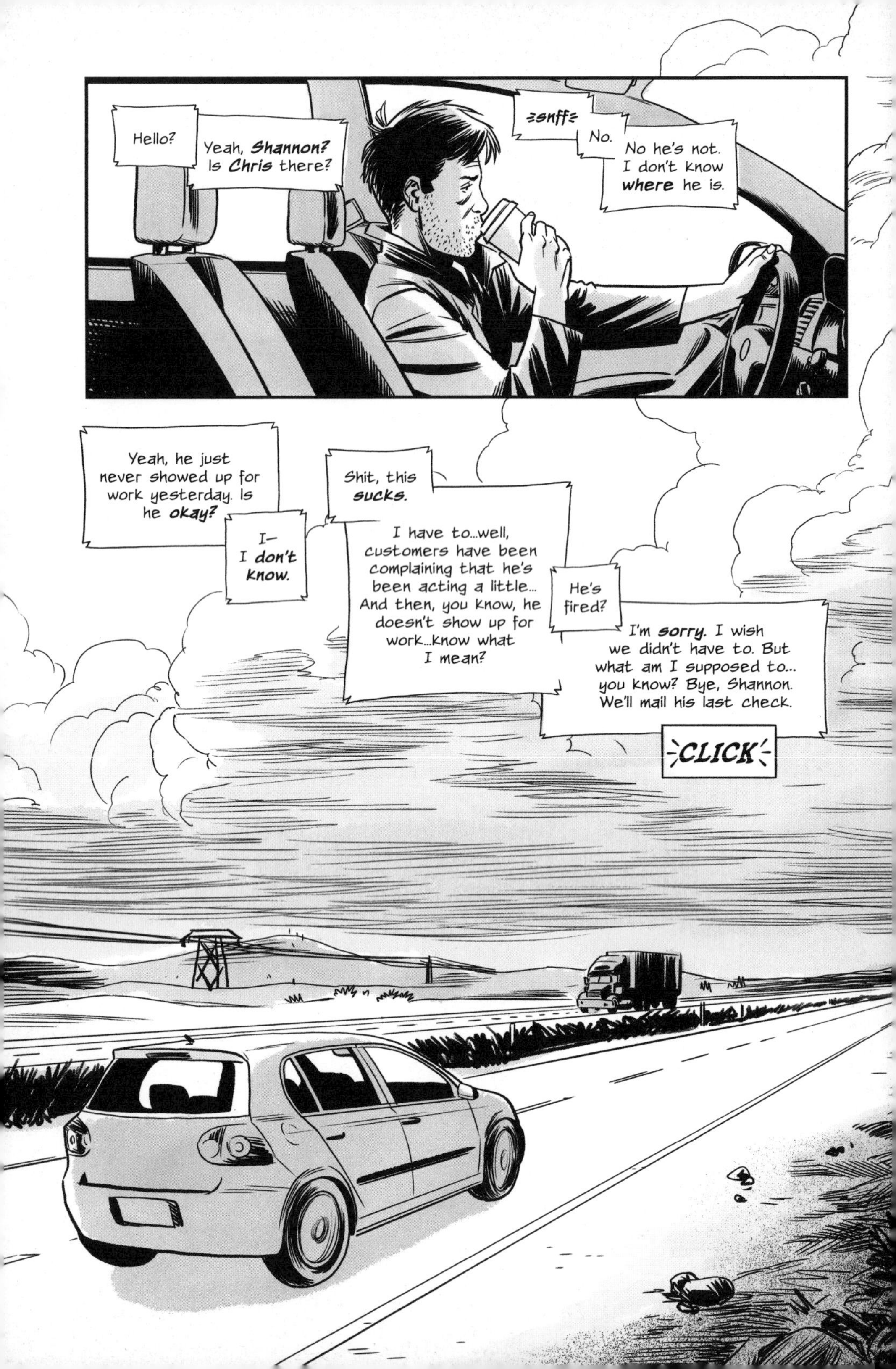
Hello?
Yeah, Shannon? Is Chris there?
=snff=
No.
No he's not. I don't know where he is.
Yeah, he just never showed up for work yesterday. Is he okay?
I— I don't know.
Shit, this sucks.
I have to...well, customers have been complaining that he's been acting a little... And then, you know, he doesn't show up for work...know what I mean?
He's fired?
I'm sorry. I wish we didn't have to. But what am I supposed to... you know? Bye, Shannon. We'll mail his last check.
CLICK

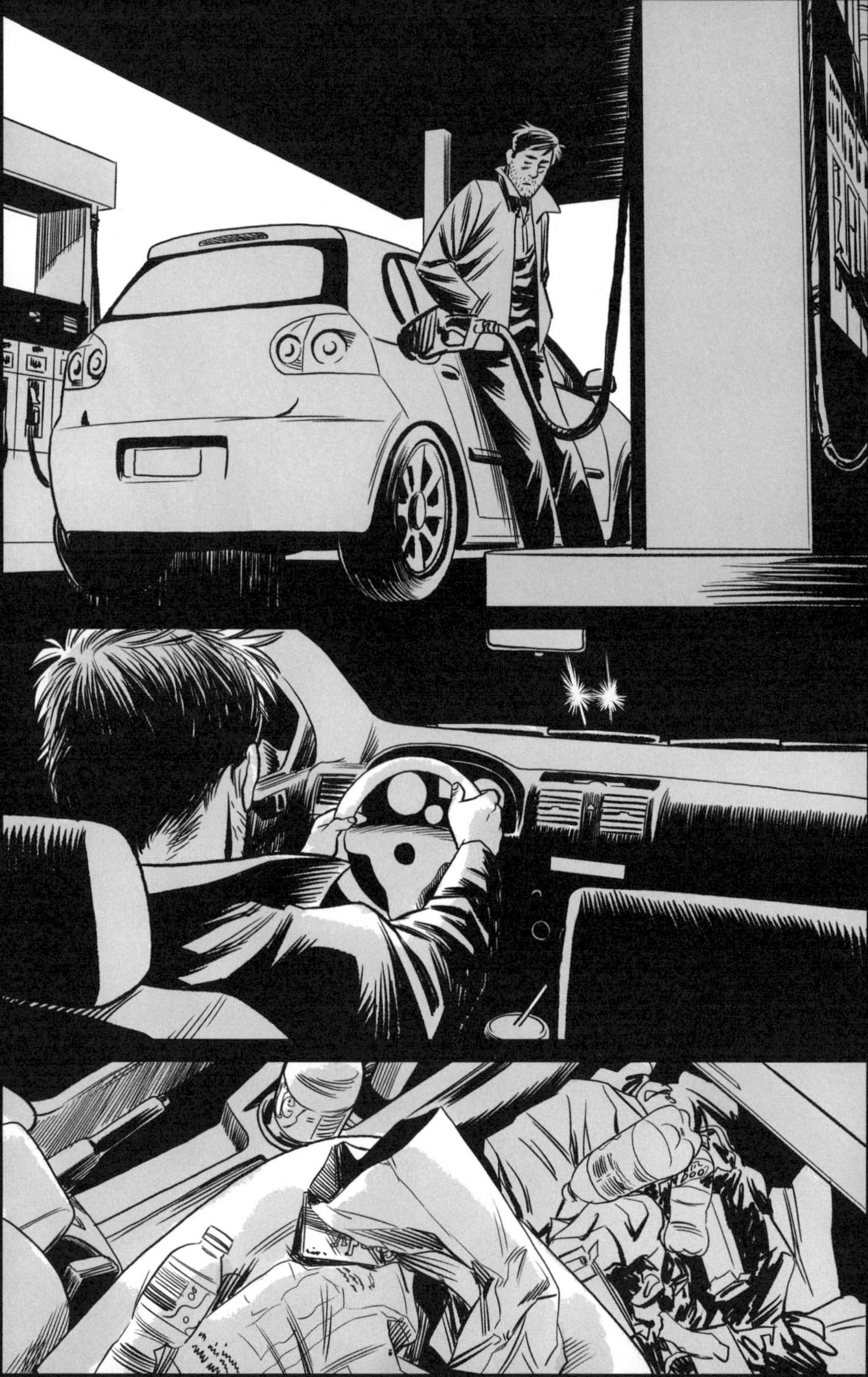

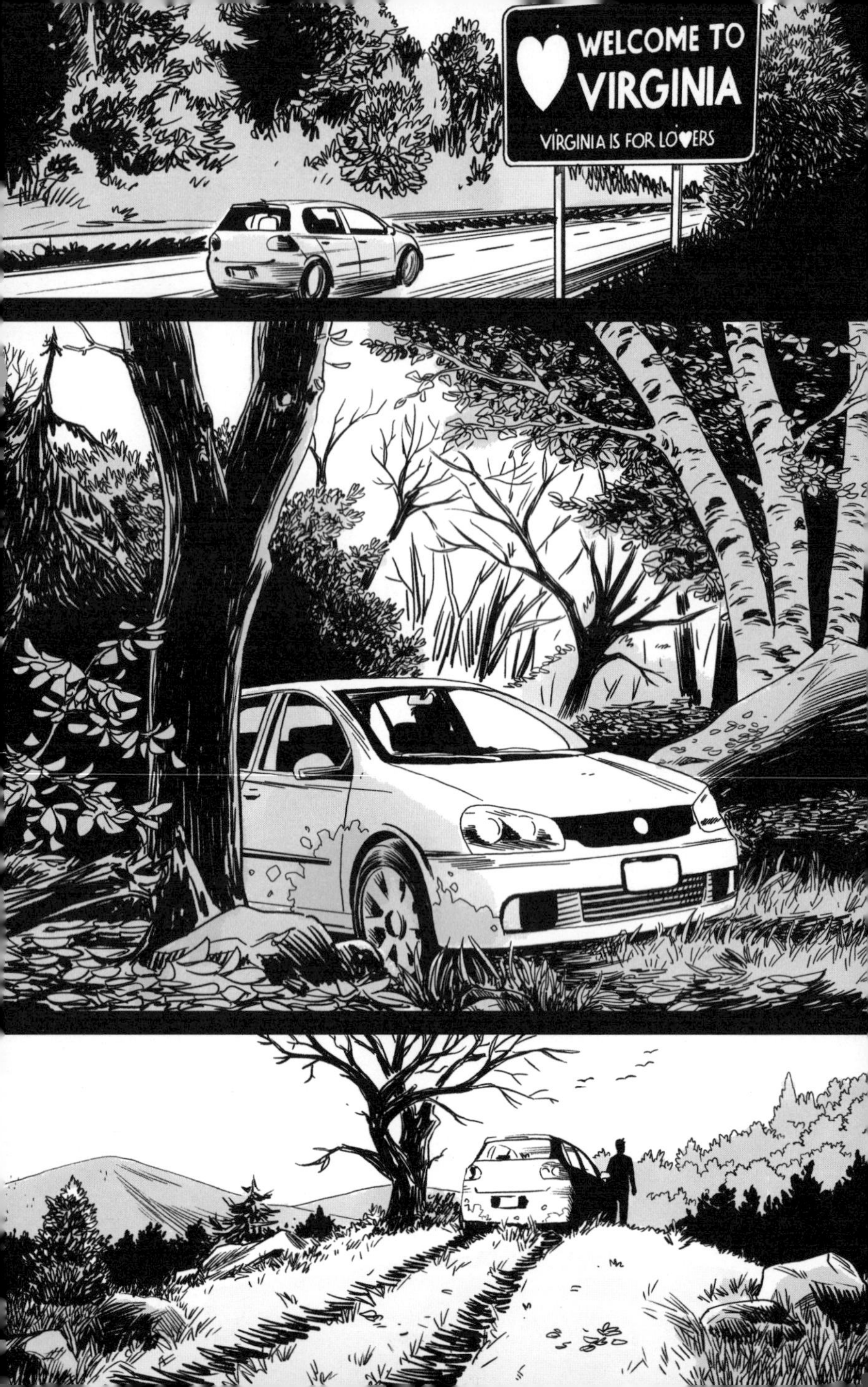
WELCOME TO
VIRGINIA
VIRGINIA IS FOR LOVERS

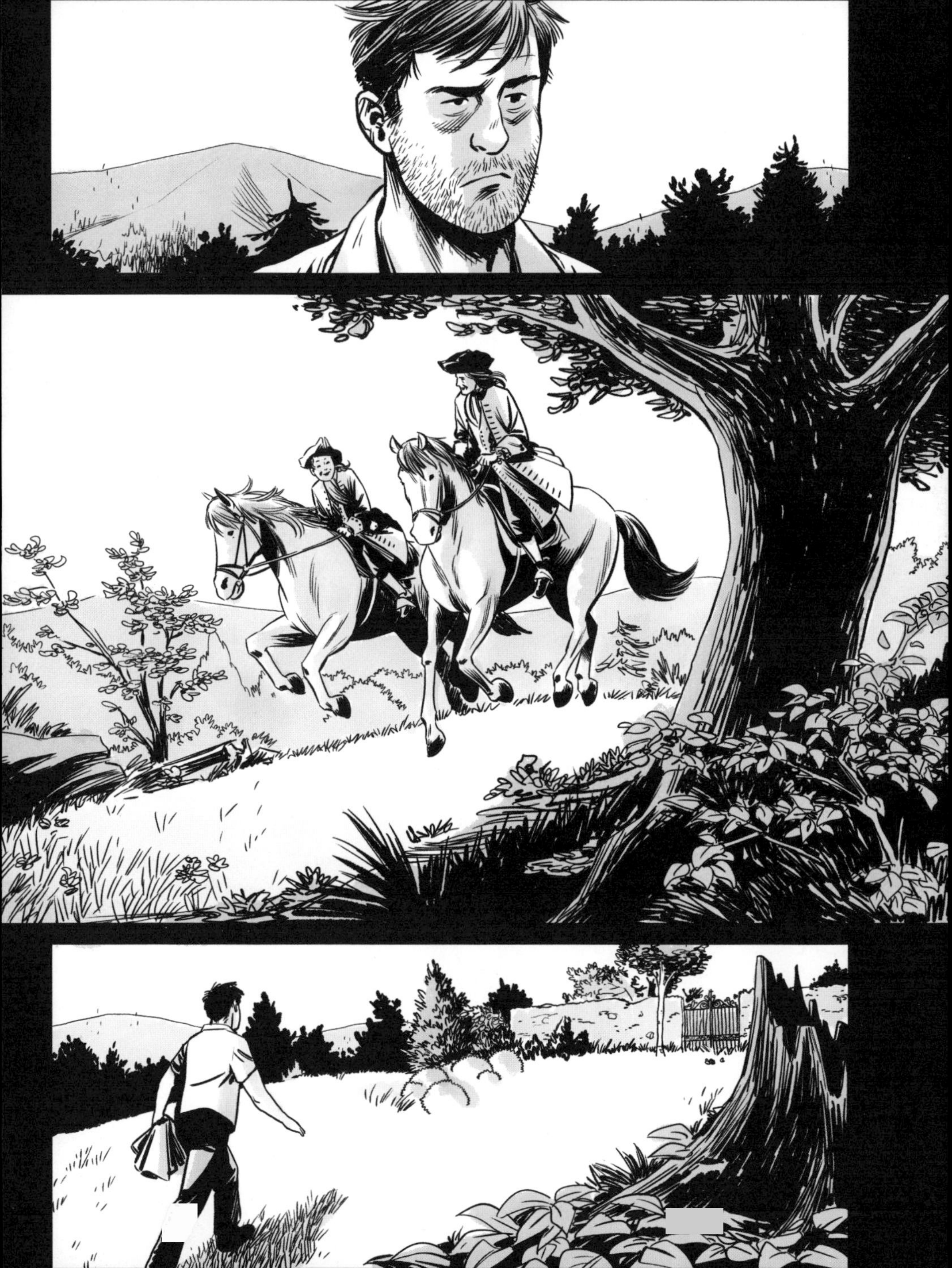

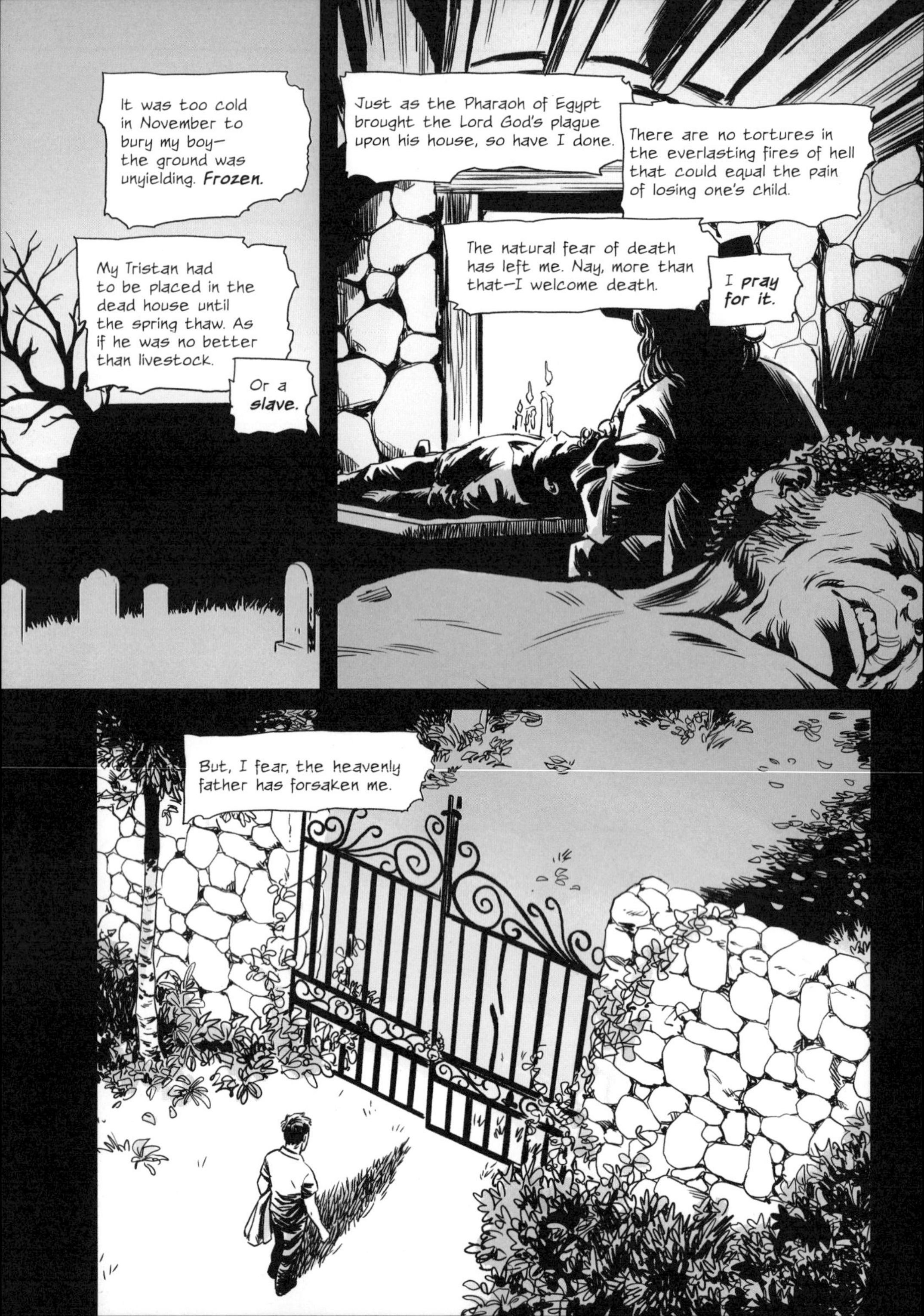
It was too cold in November to bury my boy—the ground was unyielding. Frozen.
My Tristan had to be placed in the dead house until the spring thaw. As if he was no better than livestock.
Or a slave.
Just as the Pharaoh of Egypt brought the Lord God's plague upon his house, so have I done.
There are no tortures in the everlasting fires of hell that could equal the pain of losing one's child.
The natural fear of death has left me. Nay, more than that—I welcome death.
I pray for it.
But, I fear, the heavenly father has forsaken me.

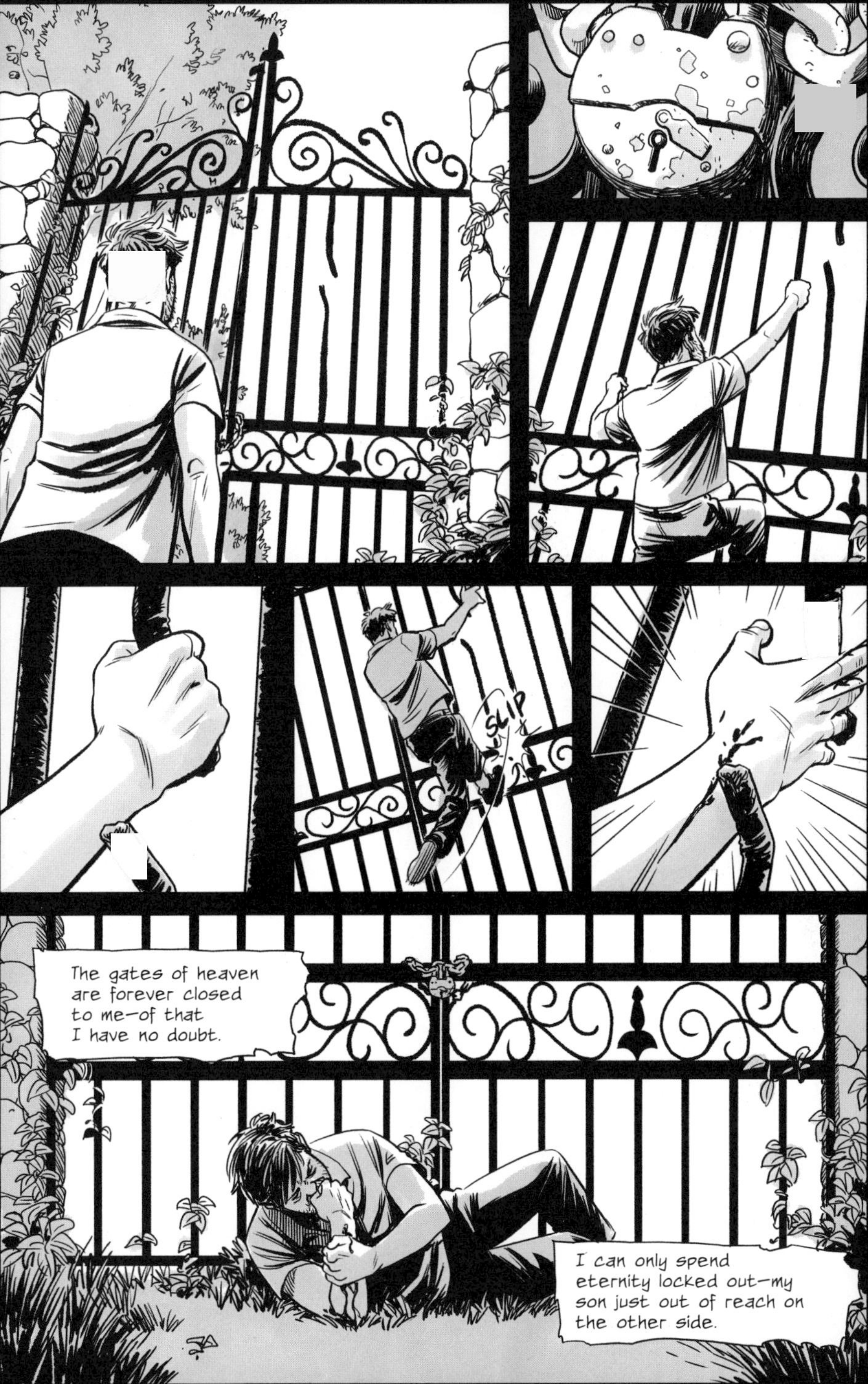
SLIP
The gates of heaven are forever closed to me—of that I have no doubt.
I can only spend eternity locked out—my son just out of reach on the other side.

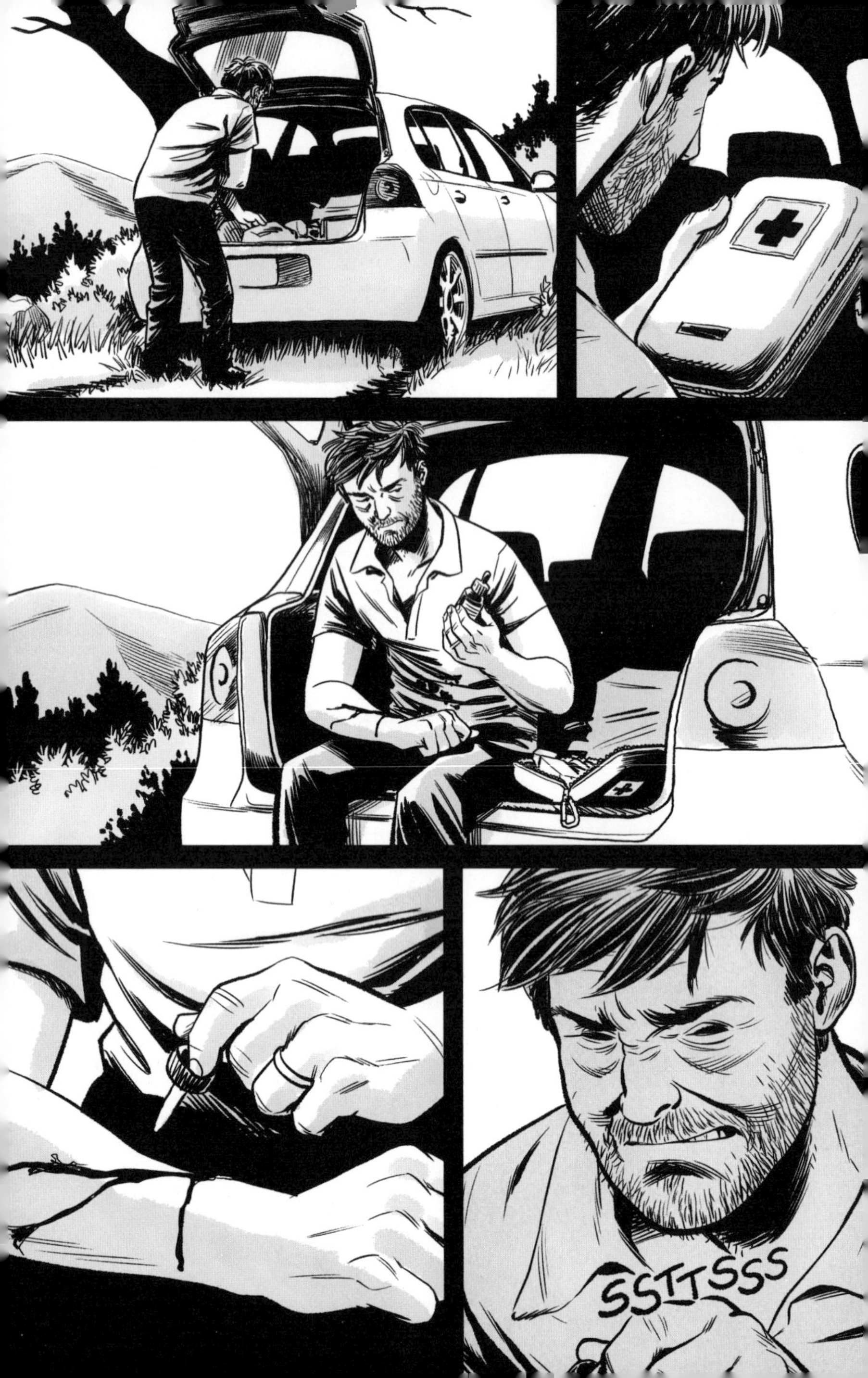
SSTTSSS

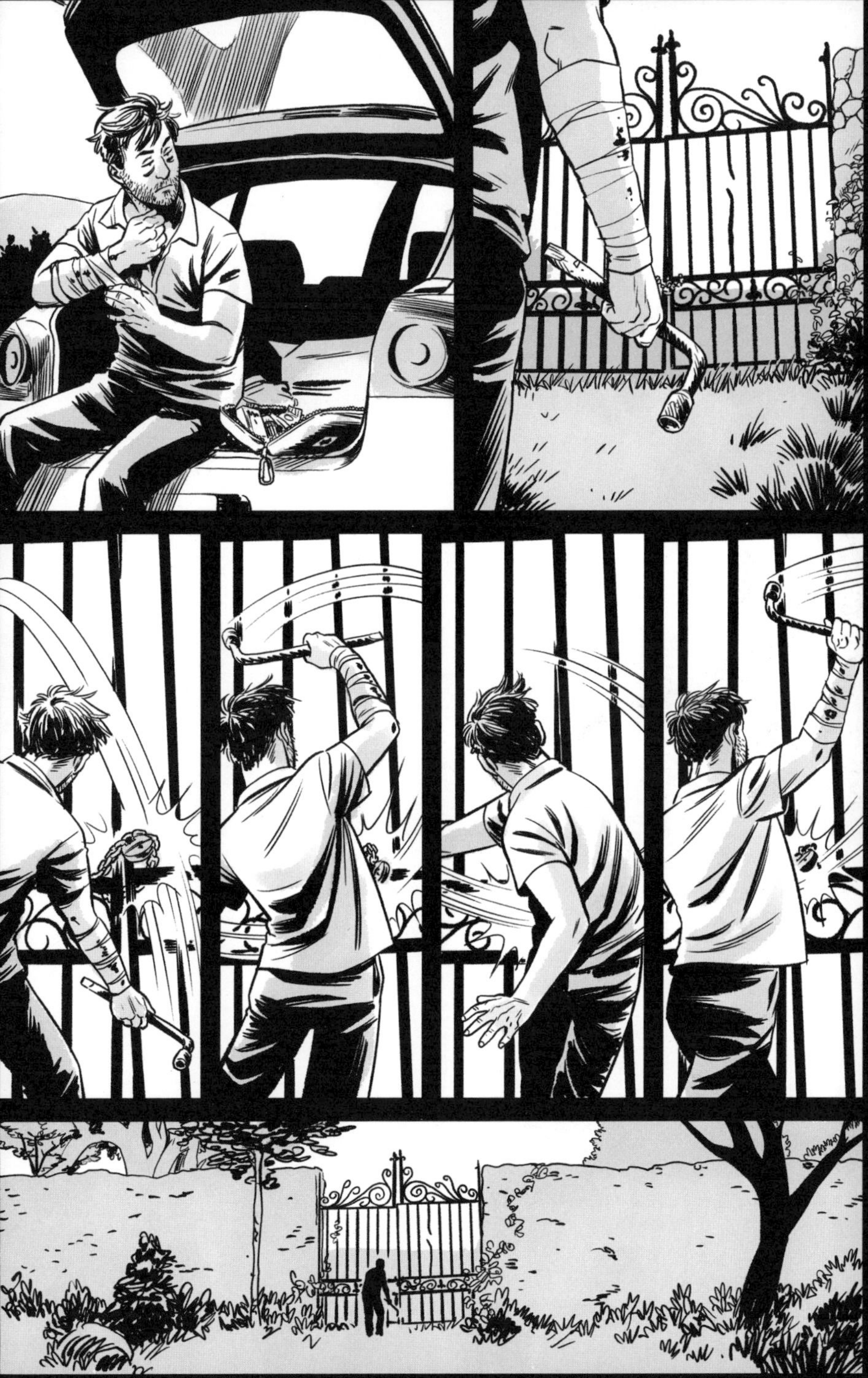

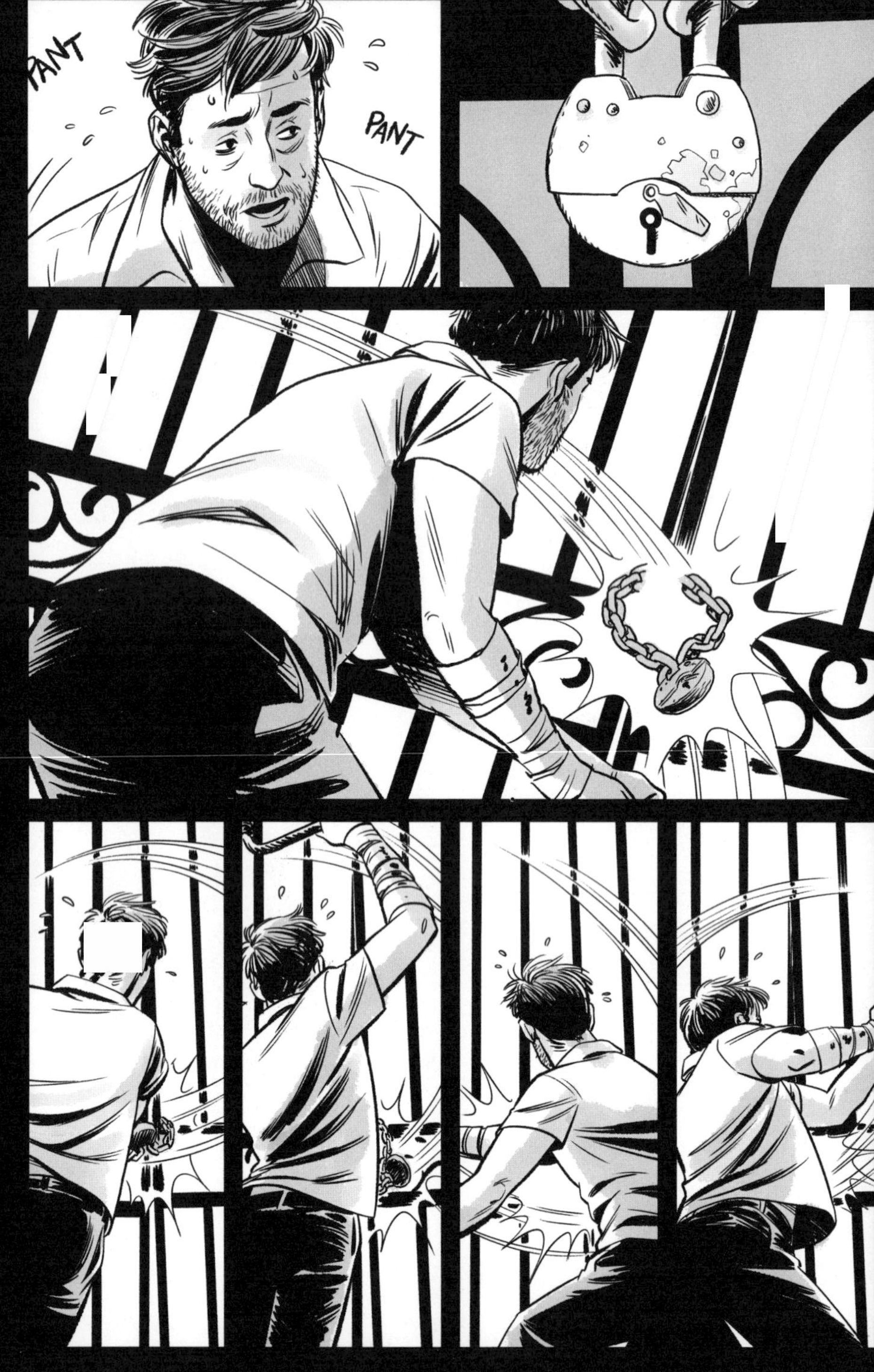
PANT
PANT

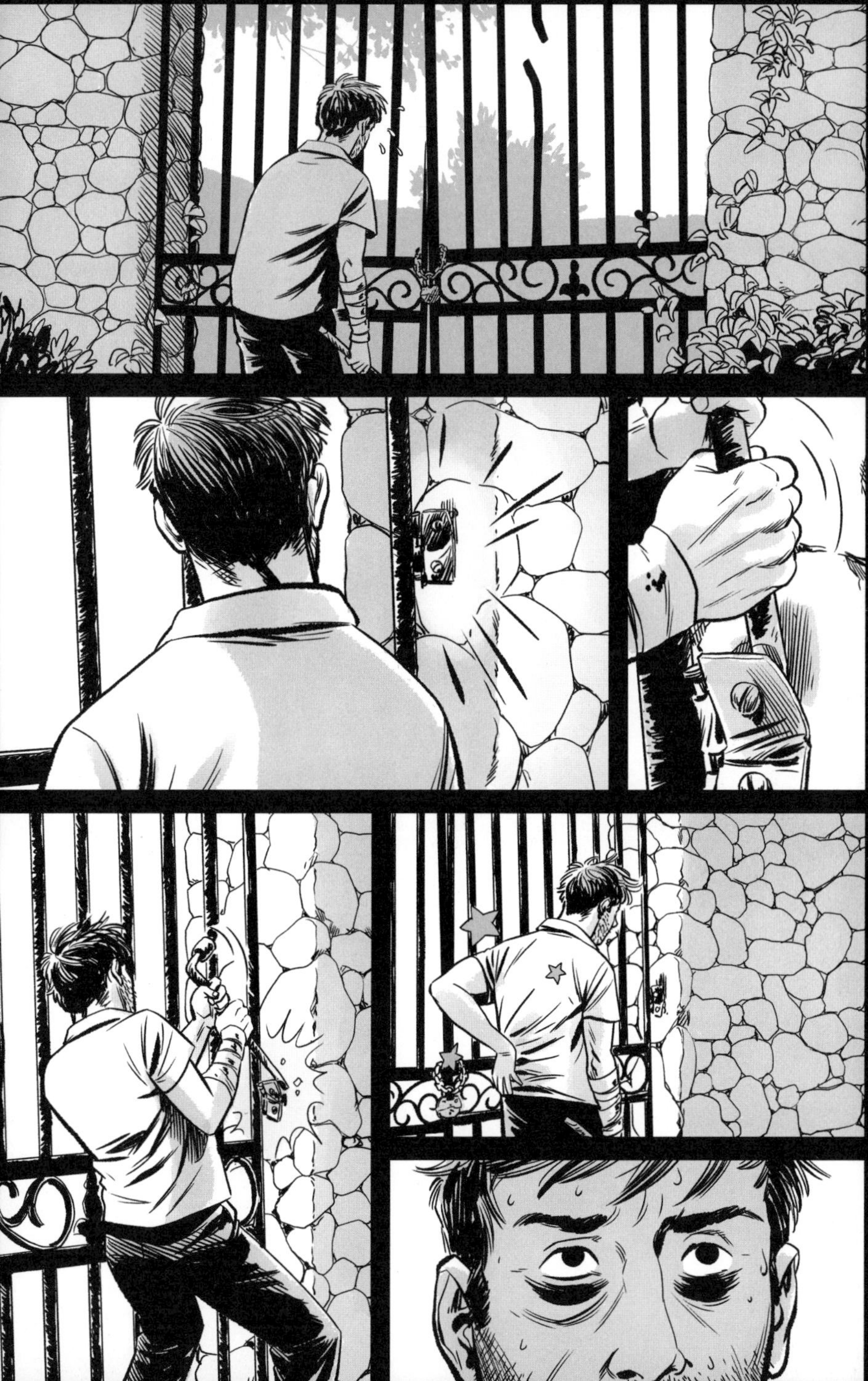

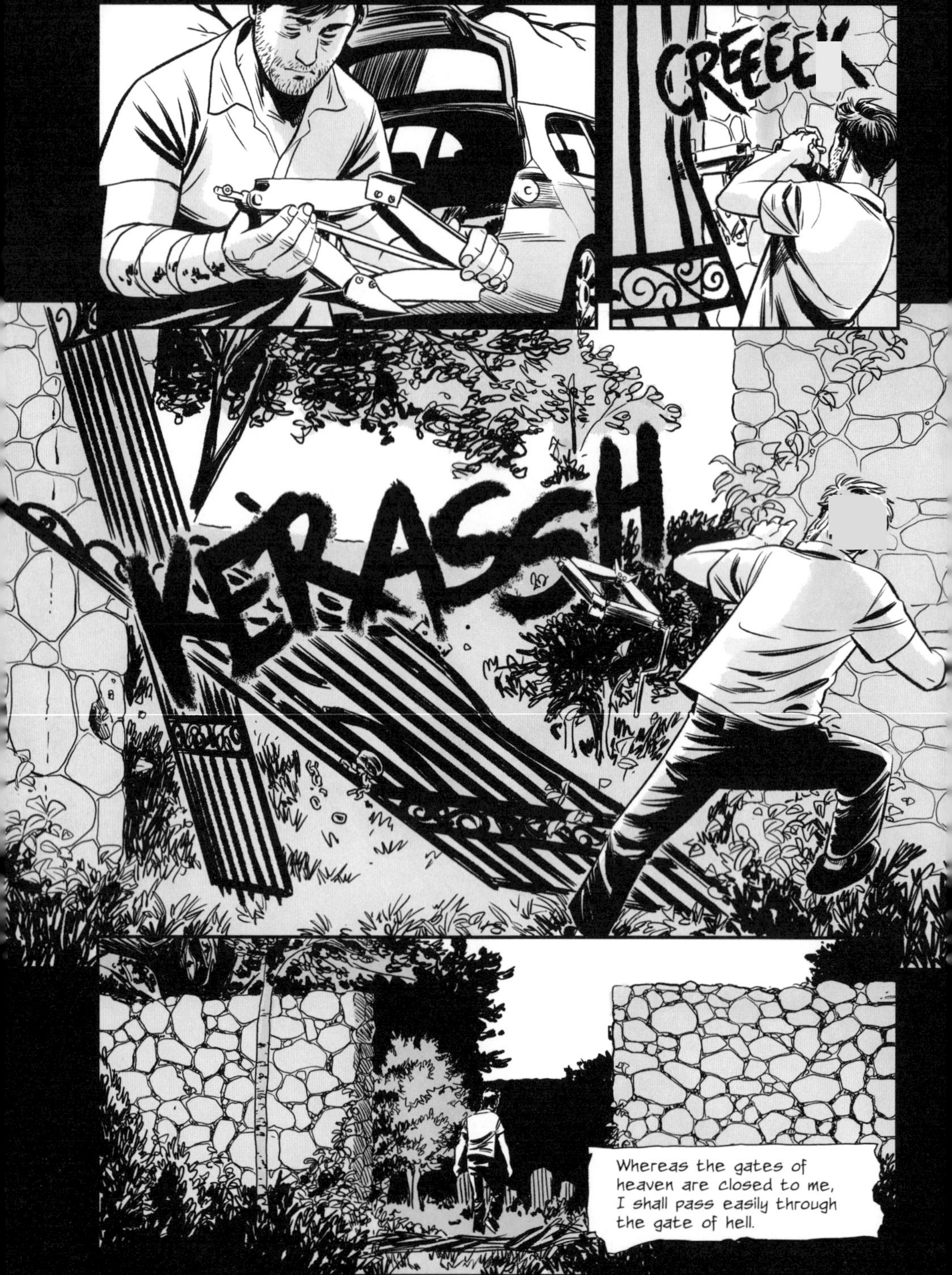
CREEEE
KRASCH
Whereas the gates of heaven are closed to me, I shall pass easily through the gate of hell.

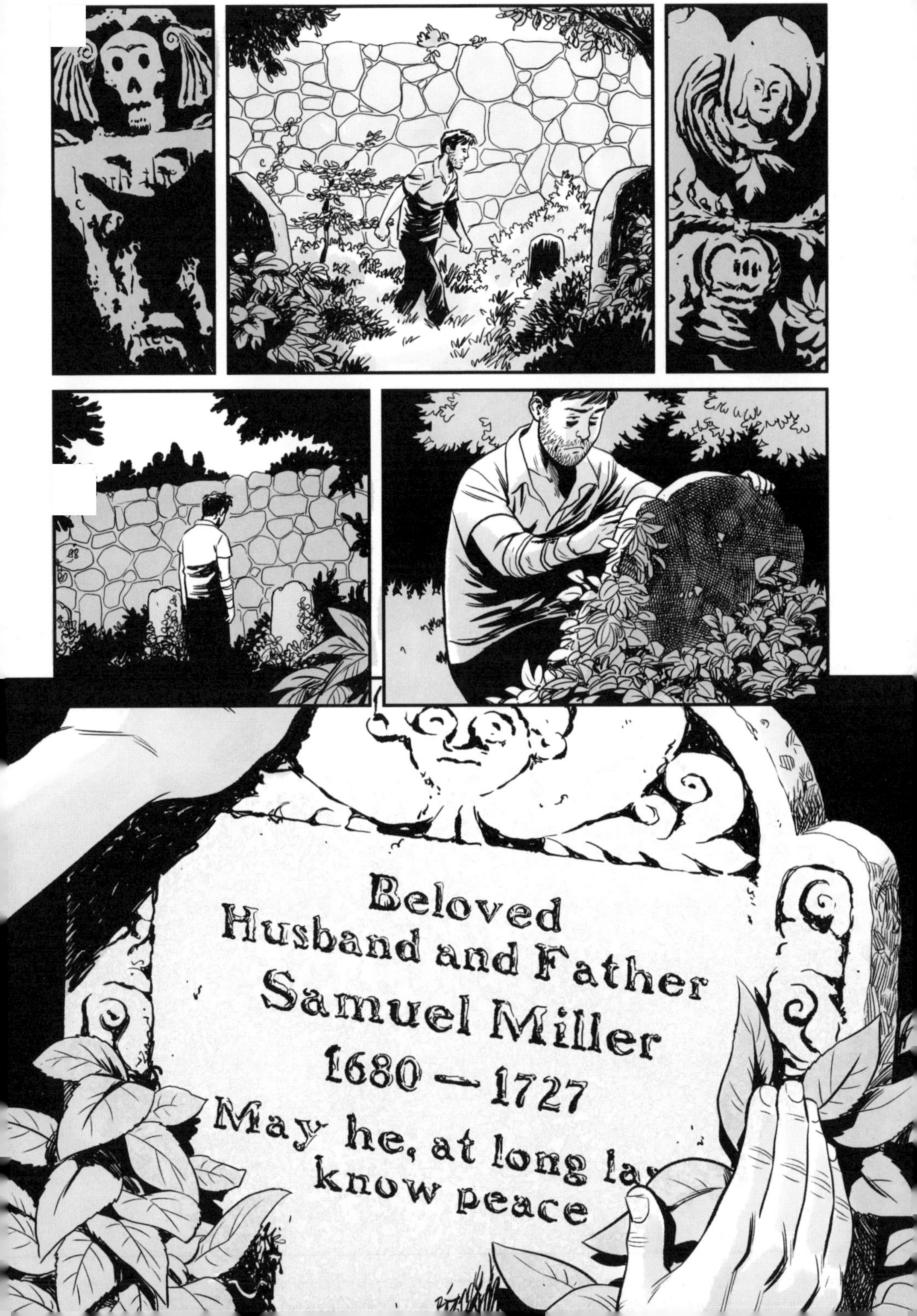
Beloved
Husband and Father
Samuel Miller
1680 — 1727
May he, at long la
know peace

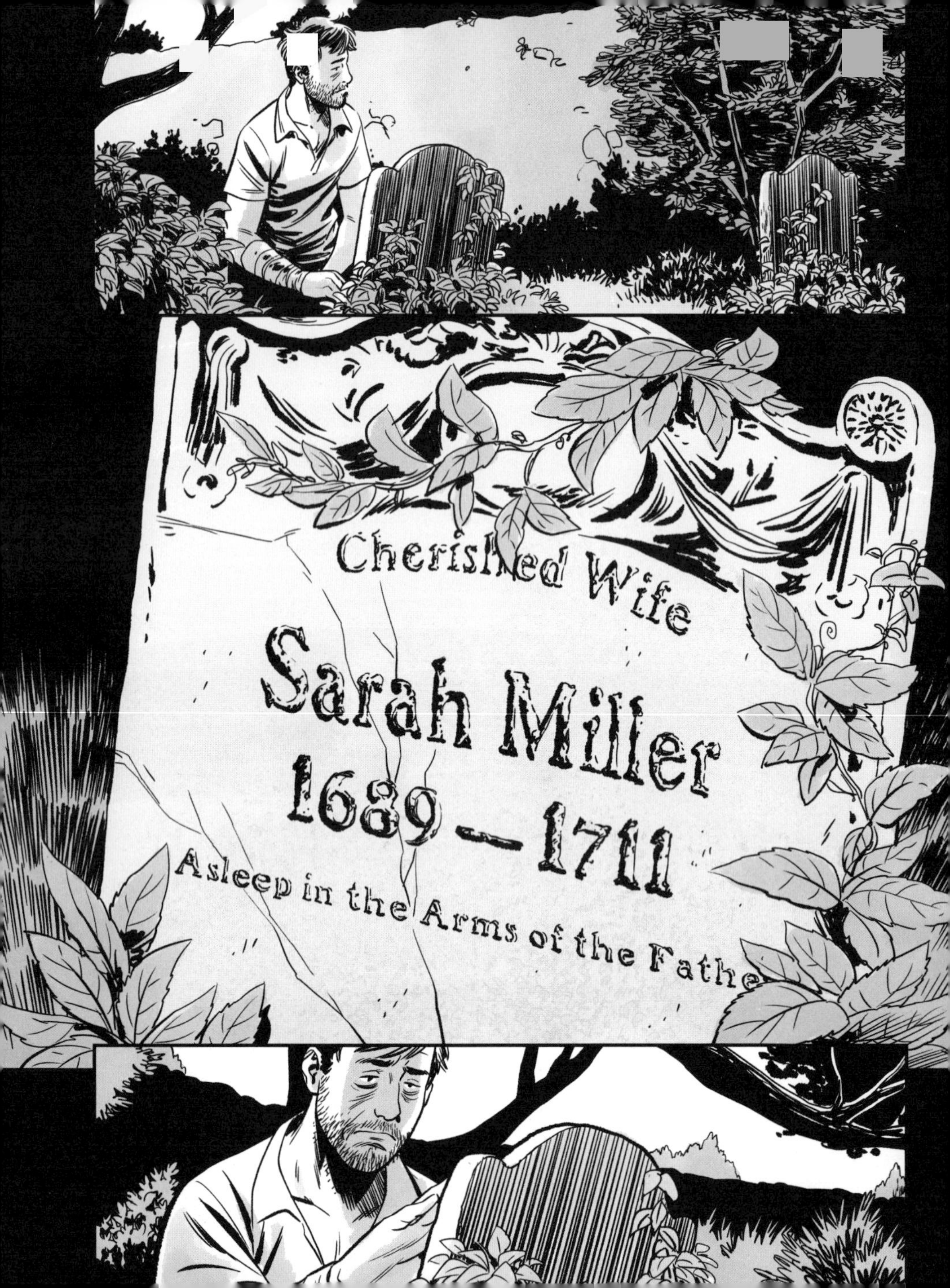
Cherished Wife
Sarah Miller
1689 — 1711
Asleep in the Arms of the Fathe

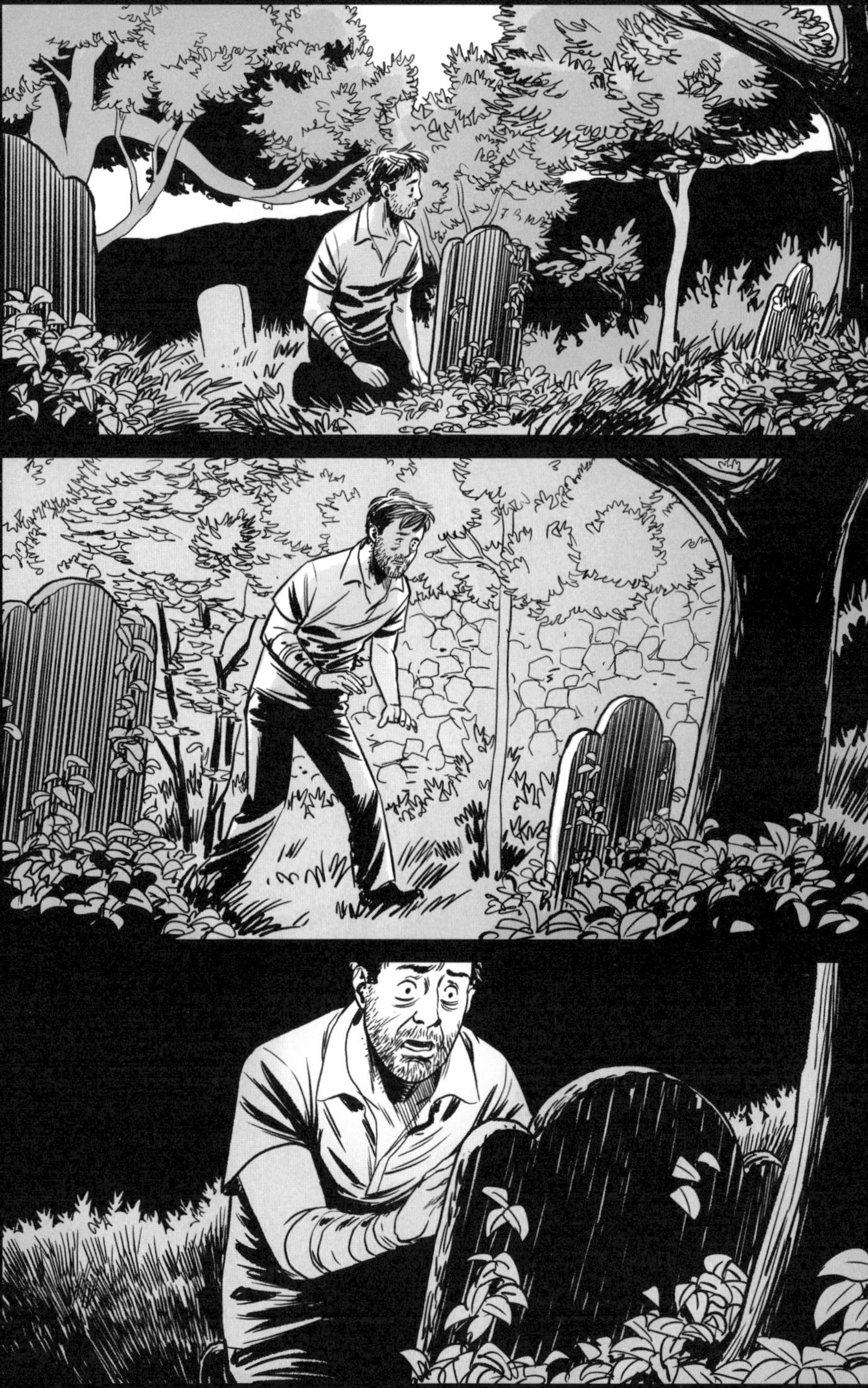

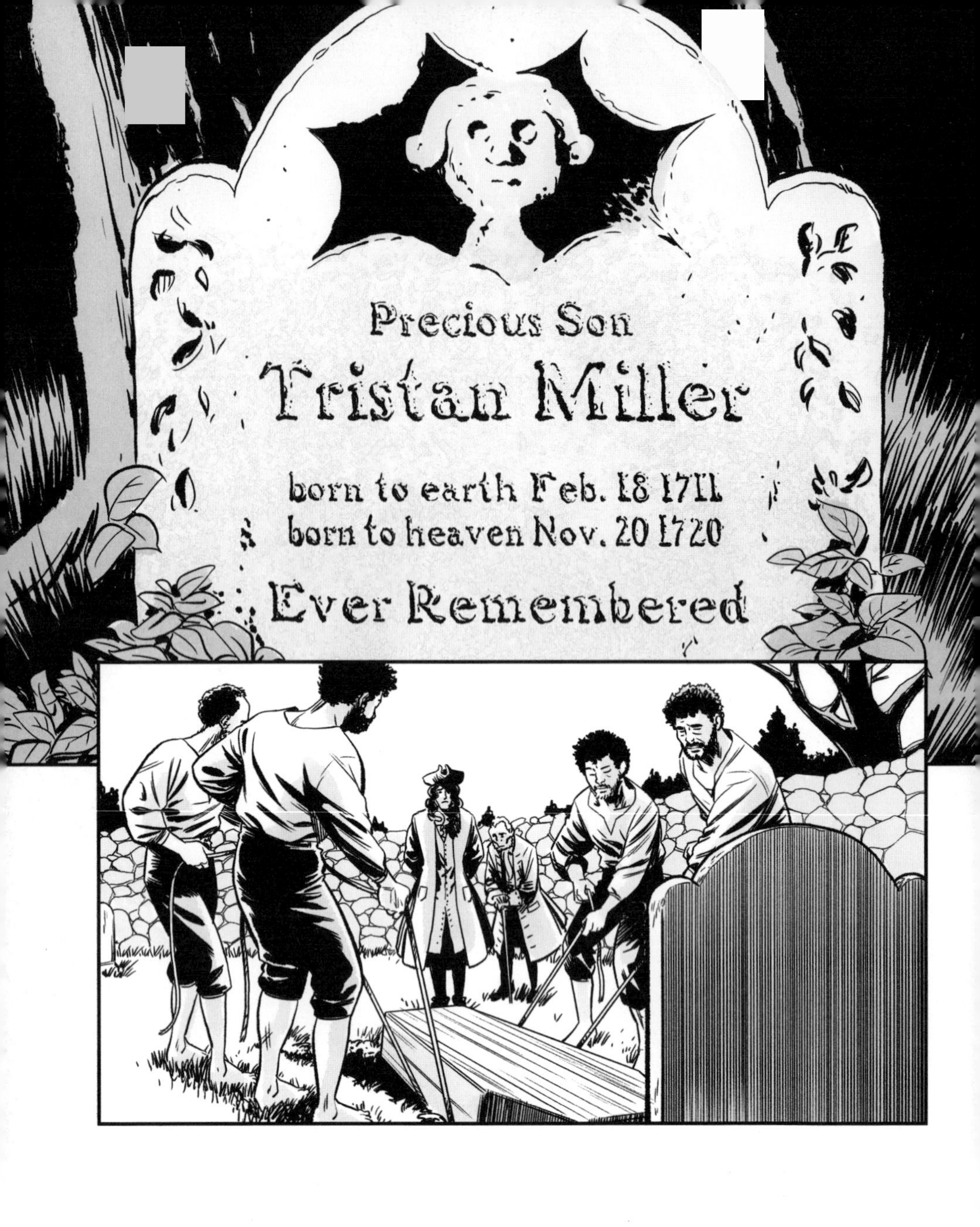
Precious Son
Tristan Miller
born to earth Feb. 18 1711
born to heaven Nov. 20 1720
Ever Remembered

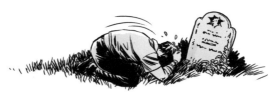

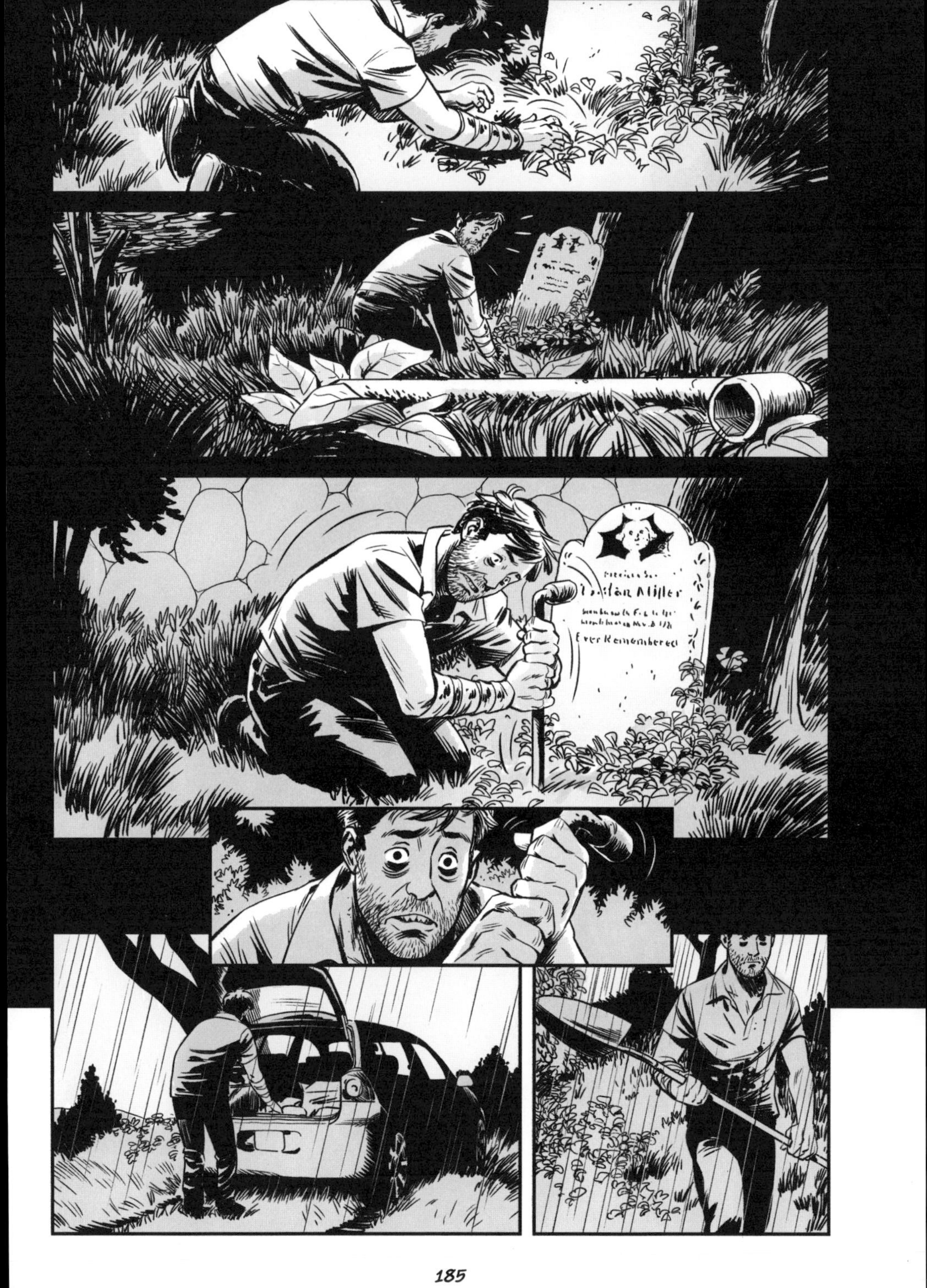
Ever Remembered

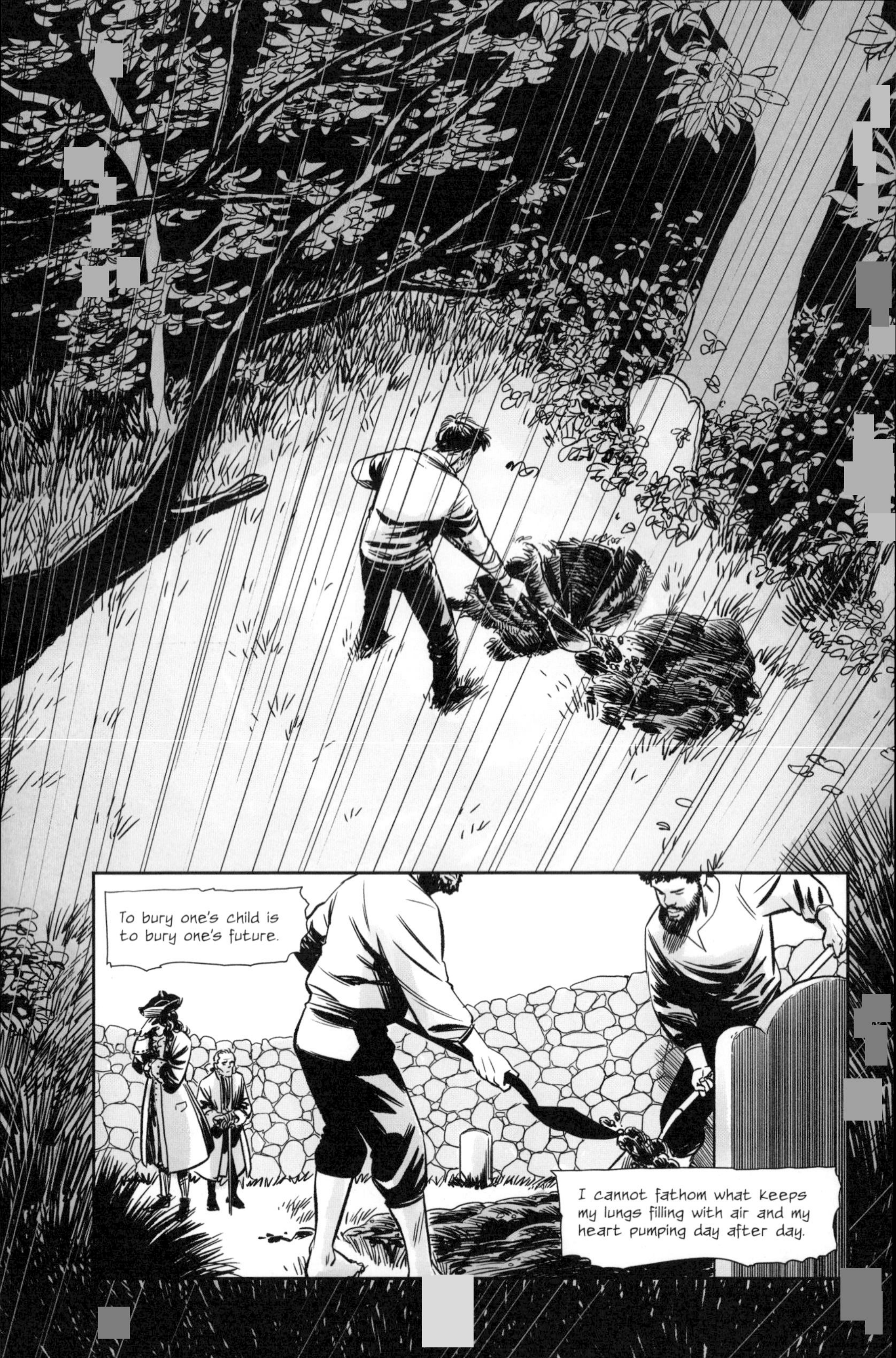
To bury one's child is to bury one's future.
I cannot fathom what keeps my lungs filling with air and my heart pumping day after day.

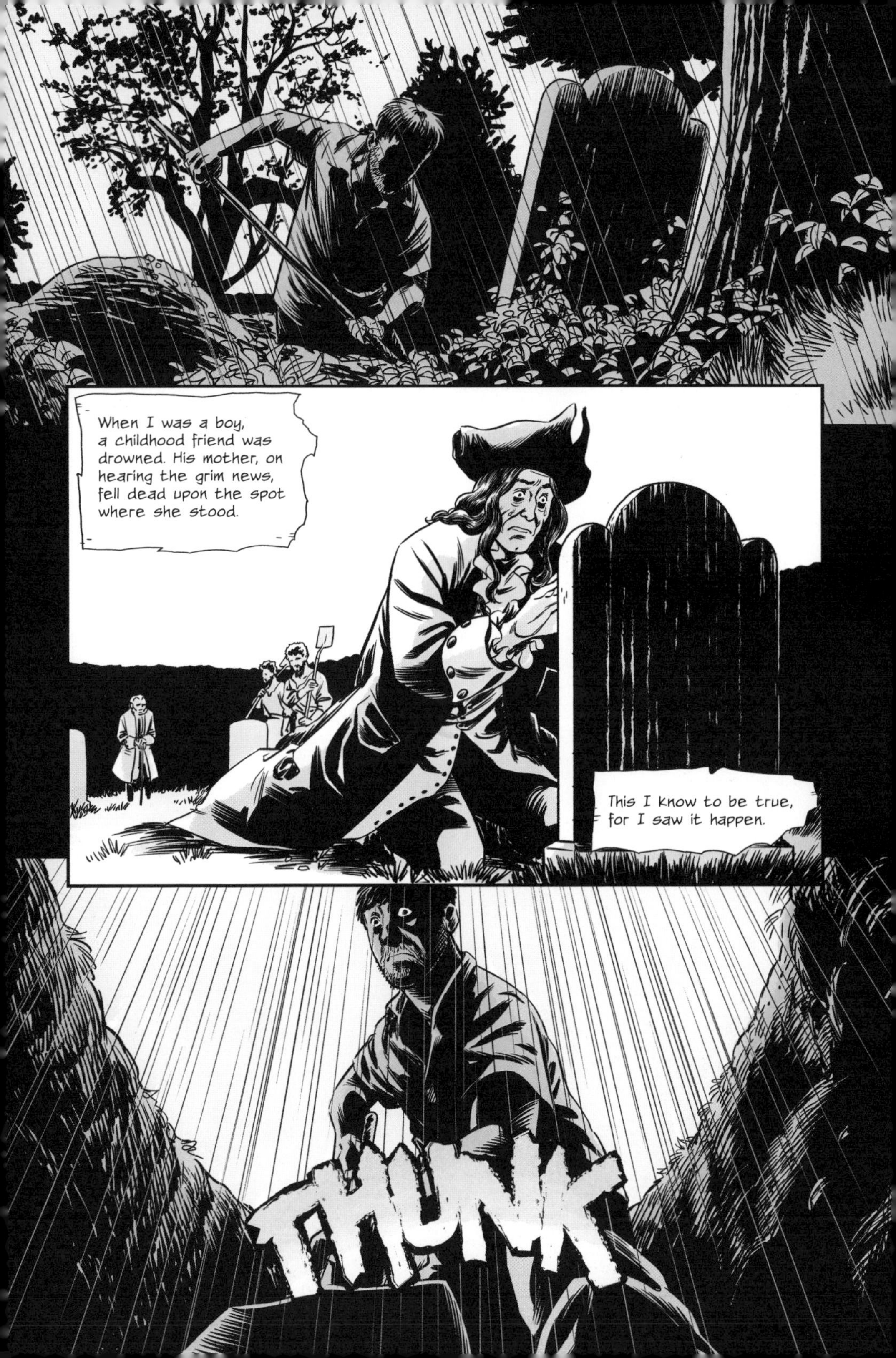
When I was a boy, a childhood friend was drowned. His mother, on hearing the grim news, fell dead upon the spot where she stood.
This I know to be true, for I saw it happen.
THUNK

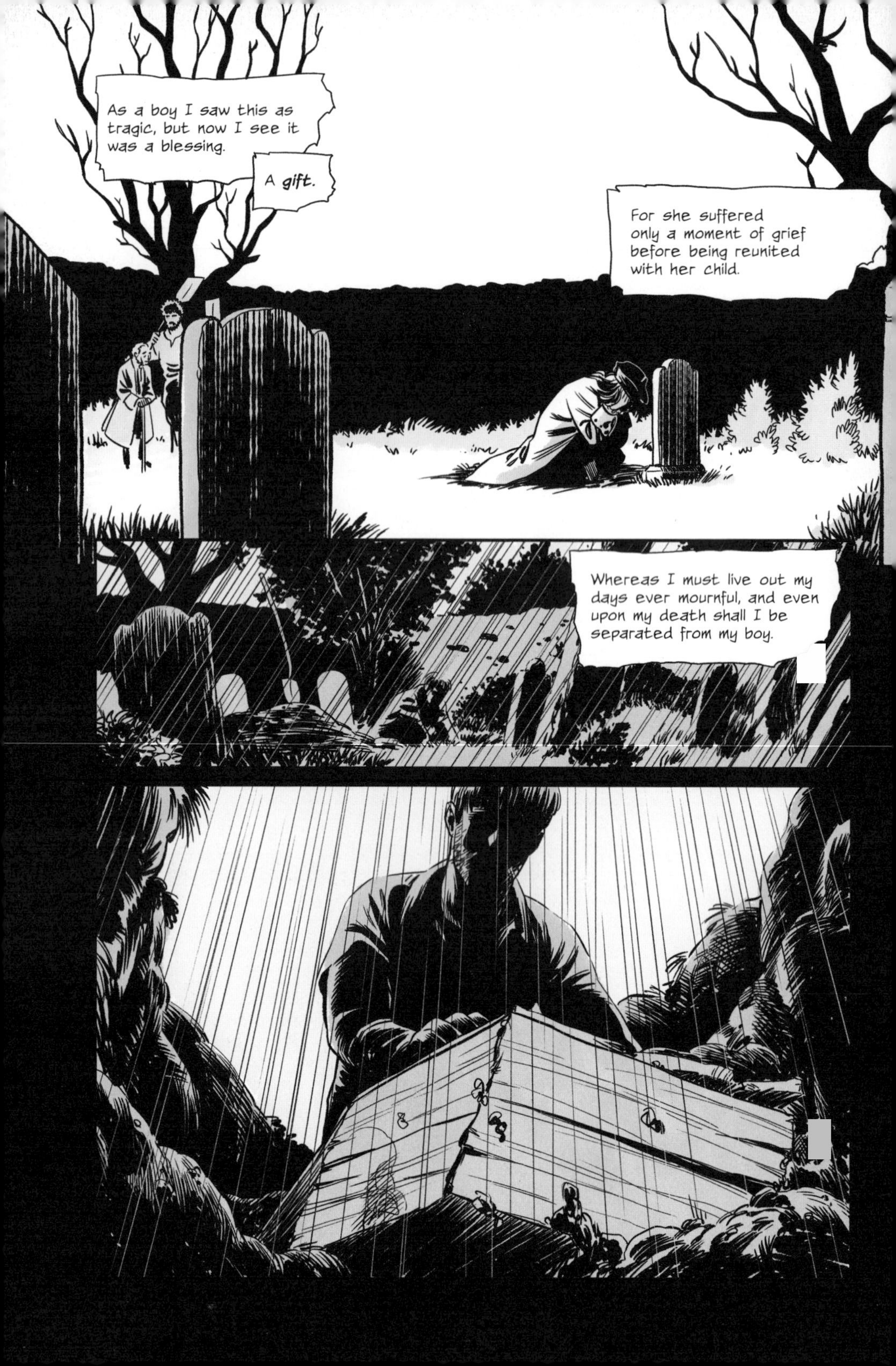
As a boy I saw this as tragic, but now I see it was a blessing.
A **gift.**
For she suffered only a moment of grief before being reunited with her child.
Whereas I must live out my days ever mournful, and even upon my death shall I be separated from my boy.

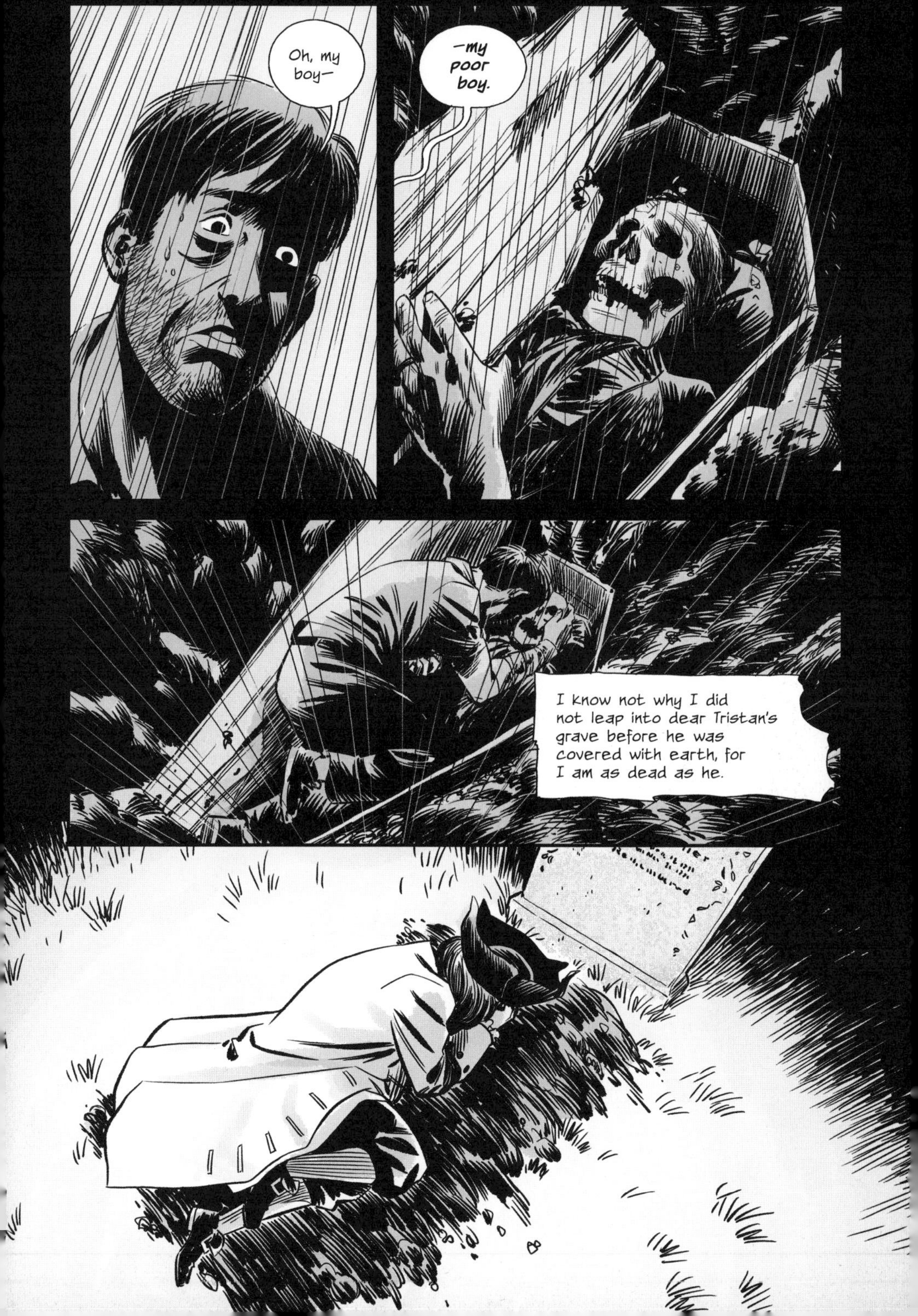
Oh, my boy—
—my poor boy.
I know not why I did not leap into dear Tristan's grave before he was covered with earth, for I am as dead as he.

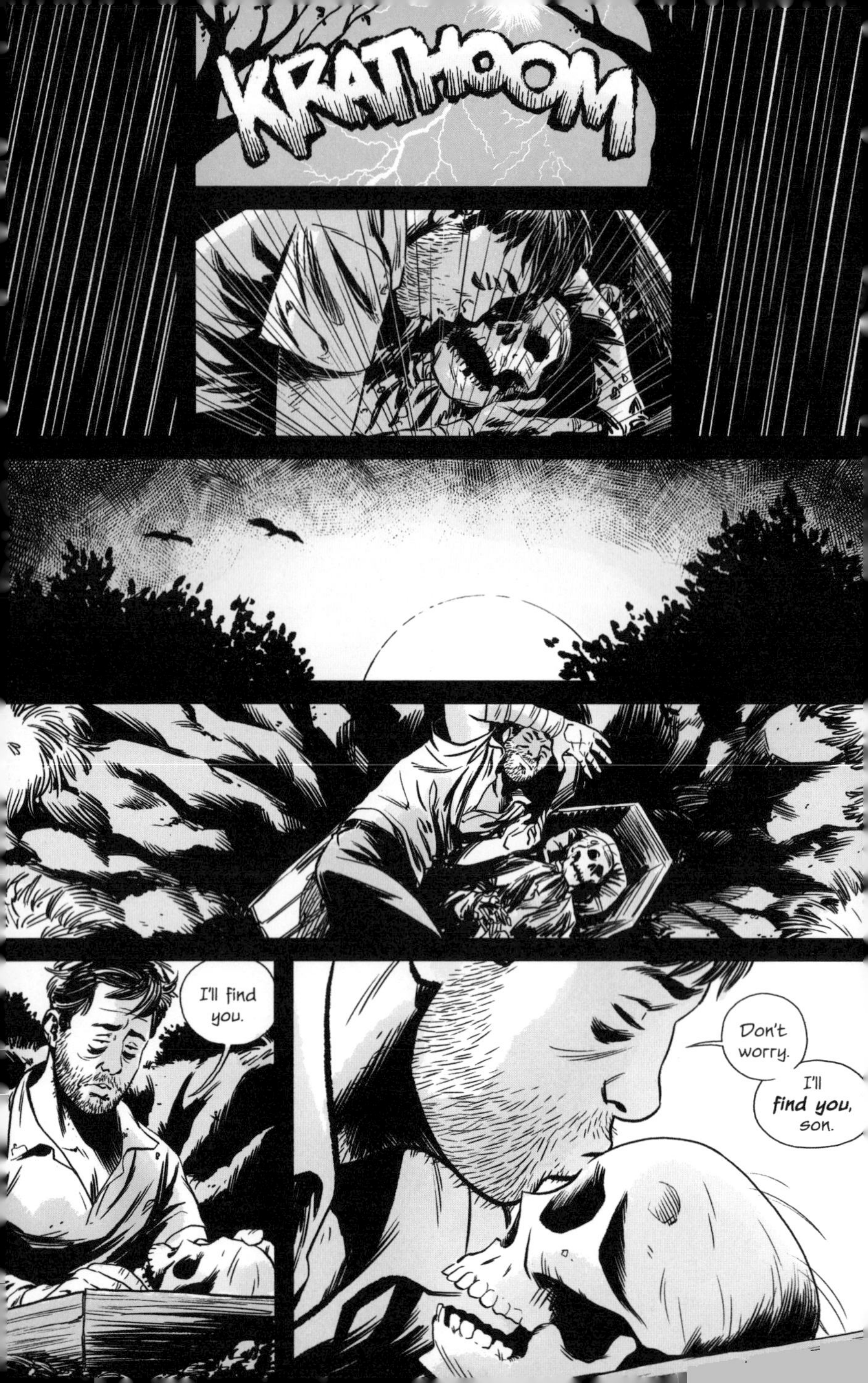
KRATHOOM
I'll find you.
Don't worry.
I'll find you, son.

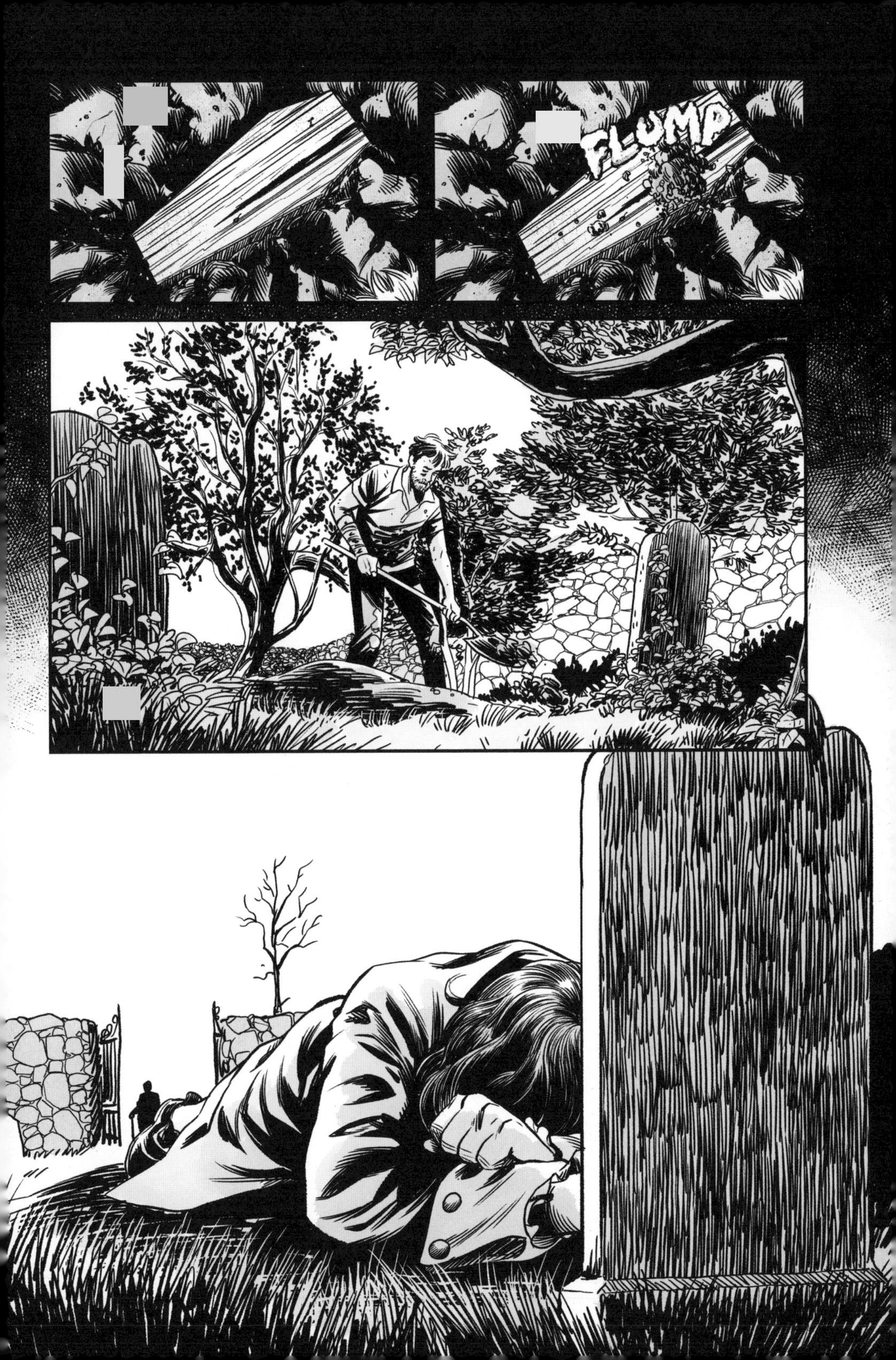
FLUMP

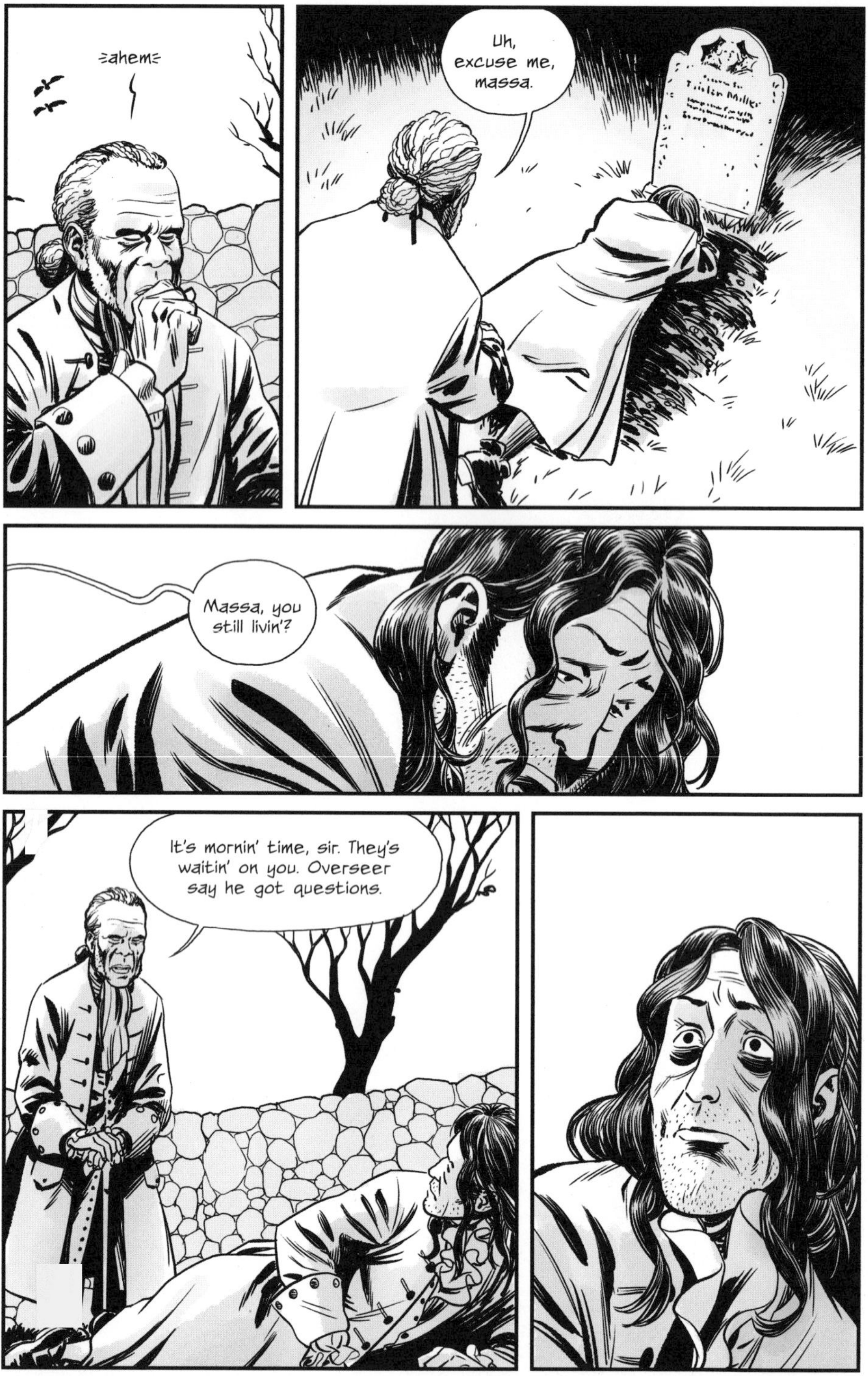
=ahem=
Uh, excuse me, massa.
Massa, you still livin'?
It's mornin' time, sir. They's waitin' on you. Overseer say he got questions.

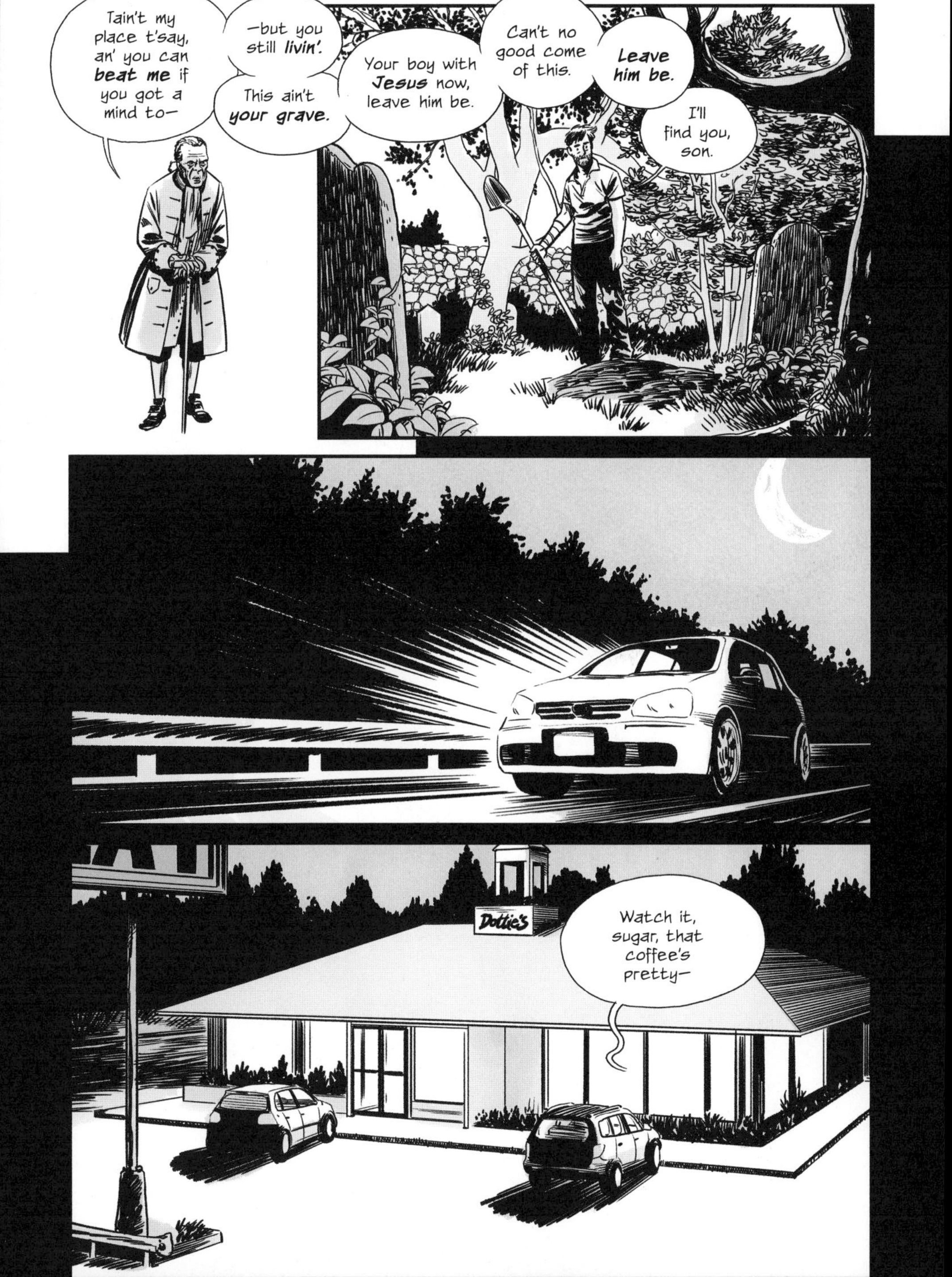

Tain't my place t'say, an' you can **beat me** if you got a mind to—
—but you still **livin'.**
This ain't **your grave.**
Your boy with **Jesus** now, leave him be.
Can't no good come of this.
Leave him be.
I'll find you, son.
Dottie's
Watch it, sugar, that coffee's pretty—

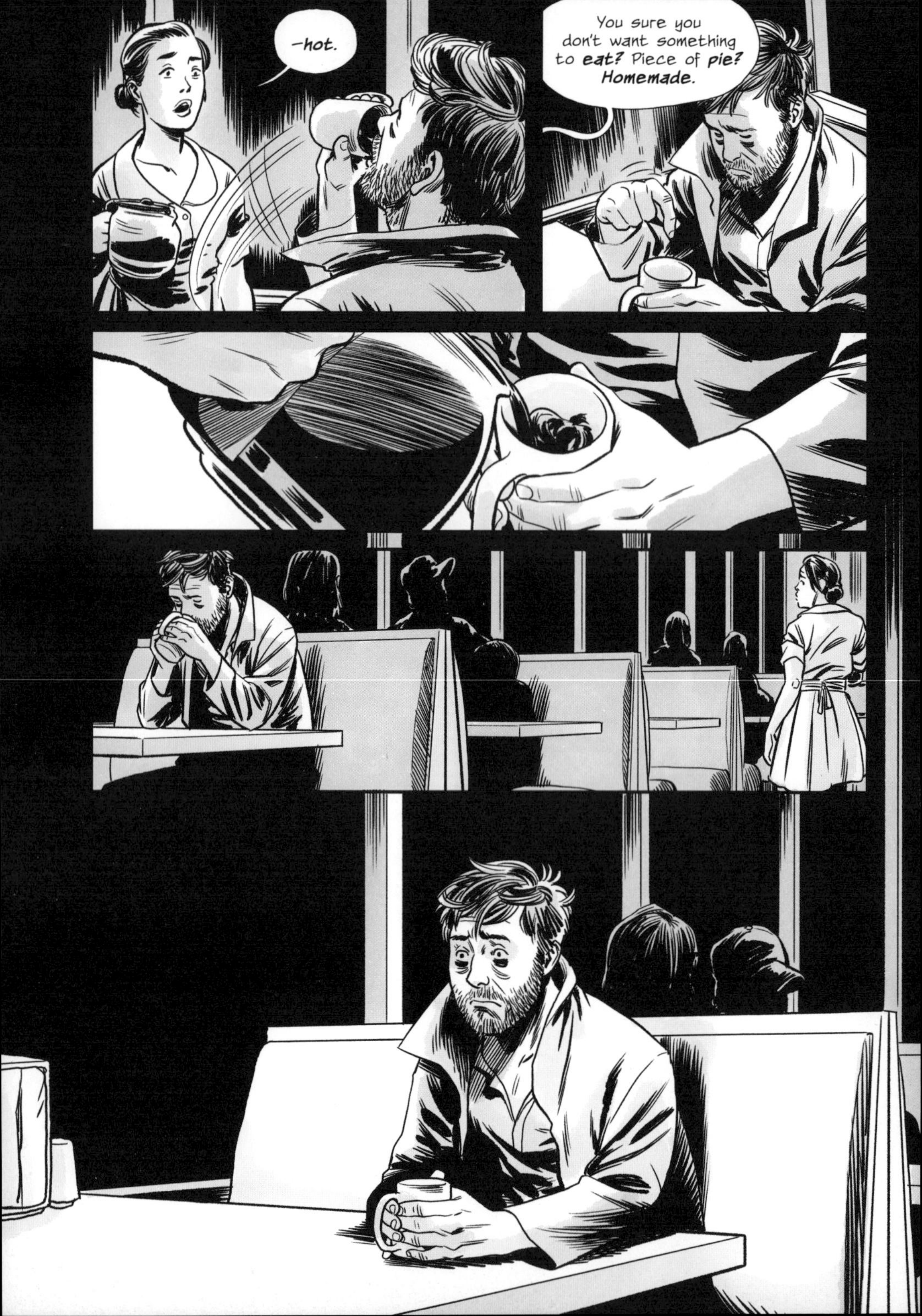

–hot.
You sure you don't want something to eat? Piece of pie? Homemade.

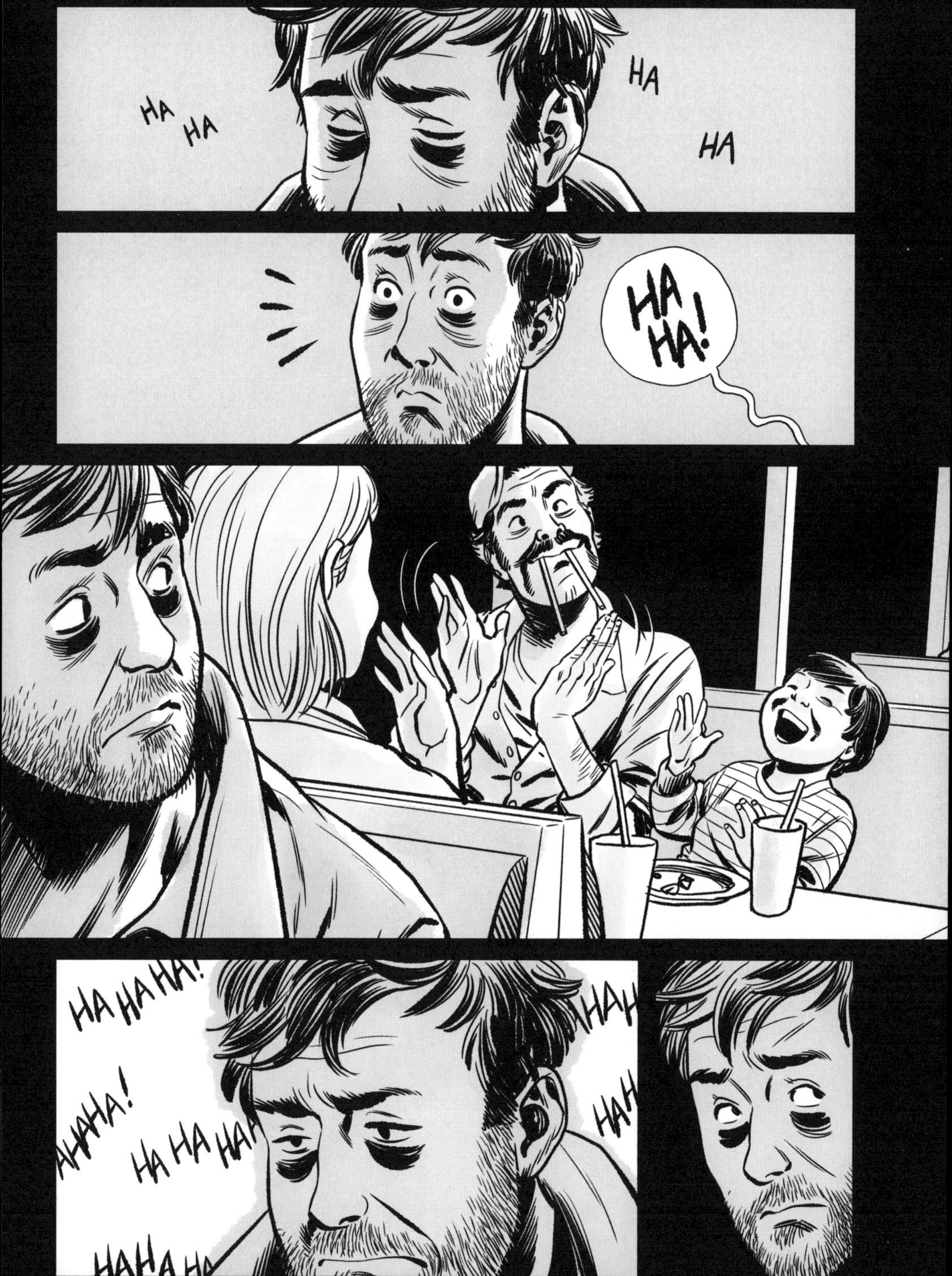
HA
HA
HA
HA
HA HA!
HA HA HA!
HAHAHA!
HA HA HA
HAHAHA

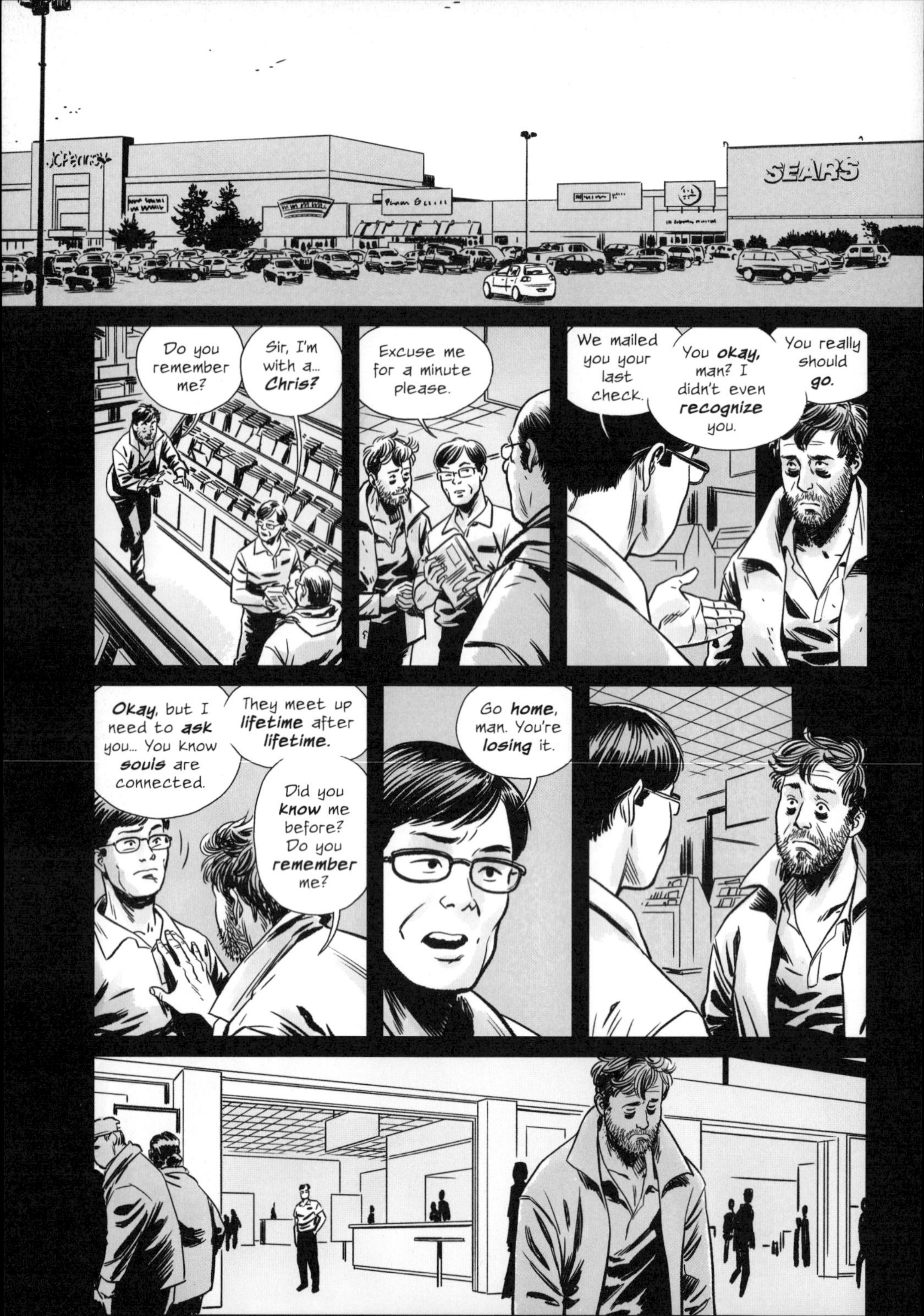

JCPenney
SEARS
Do you remember me?
Sir, I'm with a... Chris?
Excuse me for a minute please.
We mailed you your last check.
You okay, man? I didn't even recognize you.
You really should go.
Okay, but I need to ask you... You know souls are connected.
They meet up lifetime after lifetime.
Did you know me before? Do you remember me?
Go home, man. You're losing it.

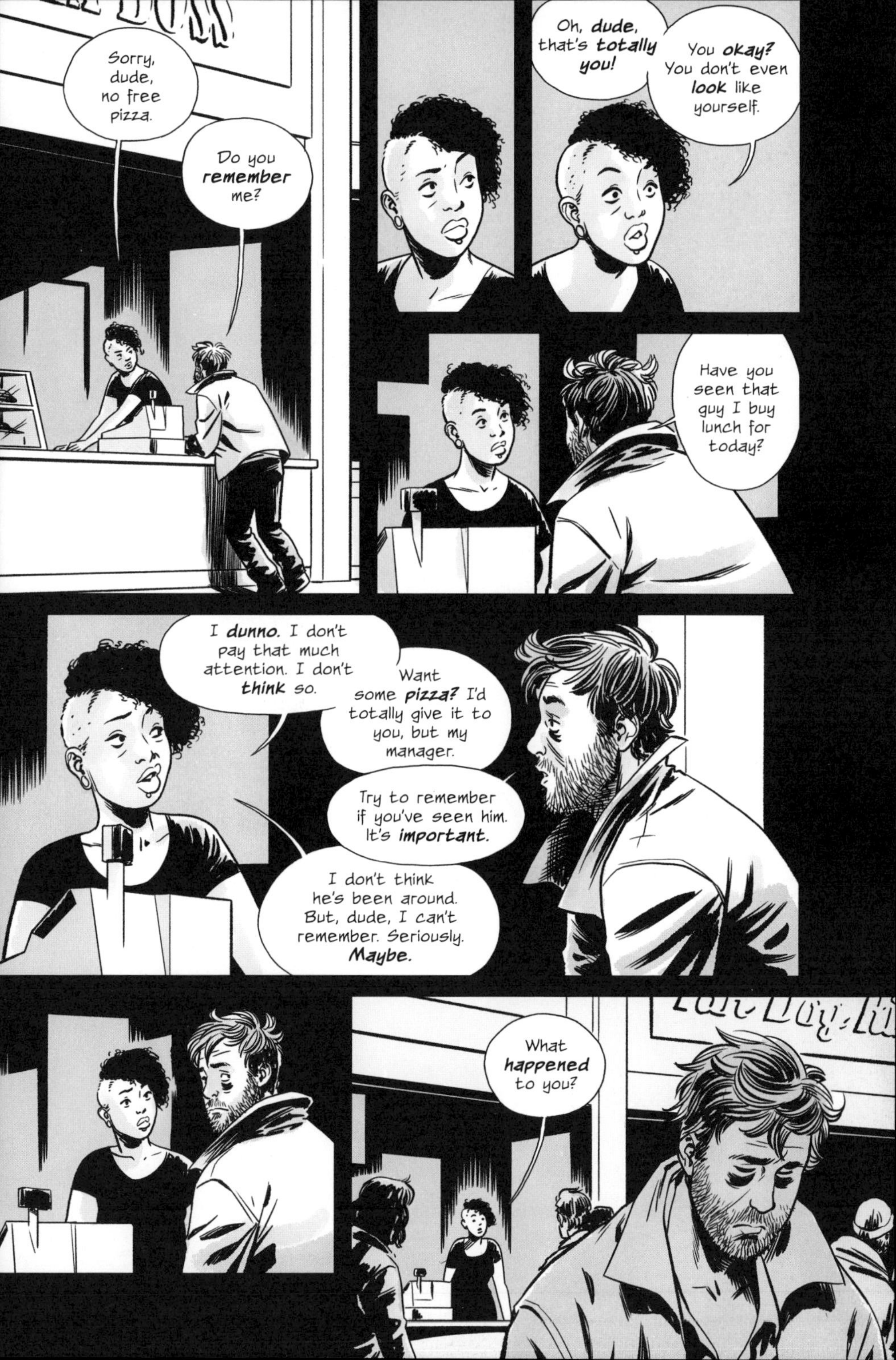
Sorry, dude, no free pizza.
Do you remember me?
Oh, dude, that's totally you!
You okay? You don't even look like yourself.
Have you seen that guy I buy lunch for today?
I dunno. I don't pay that much attention. I don't think so.
Want some pizza? I'd totally give it to you, but my manager.
Try to remember if you've seen him. It's important.
I don't think he's been around. But, dude, I can't remember. Seriously. Maybe.
What happened to you?

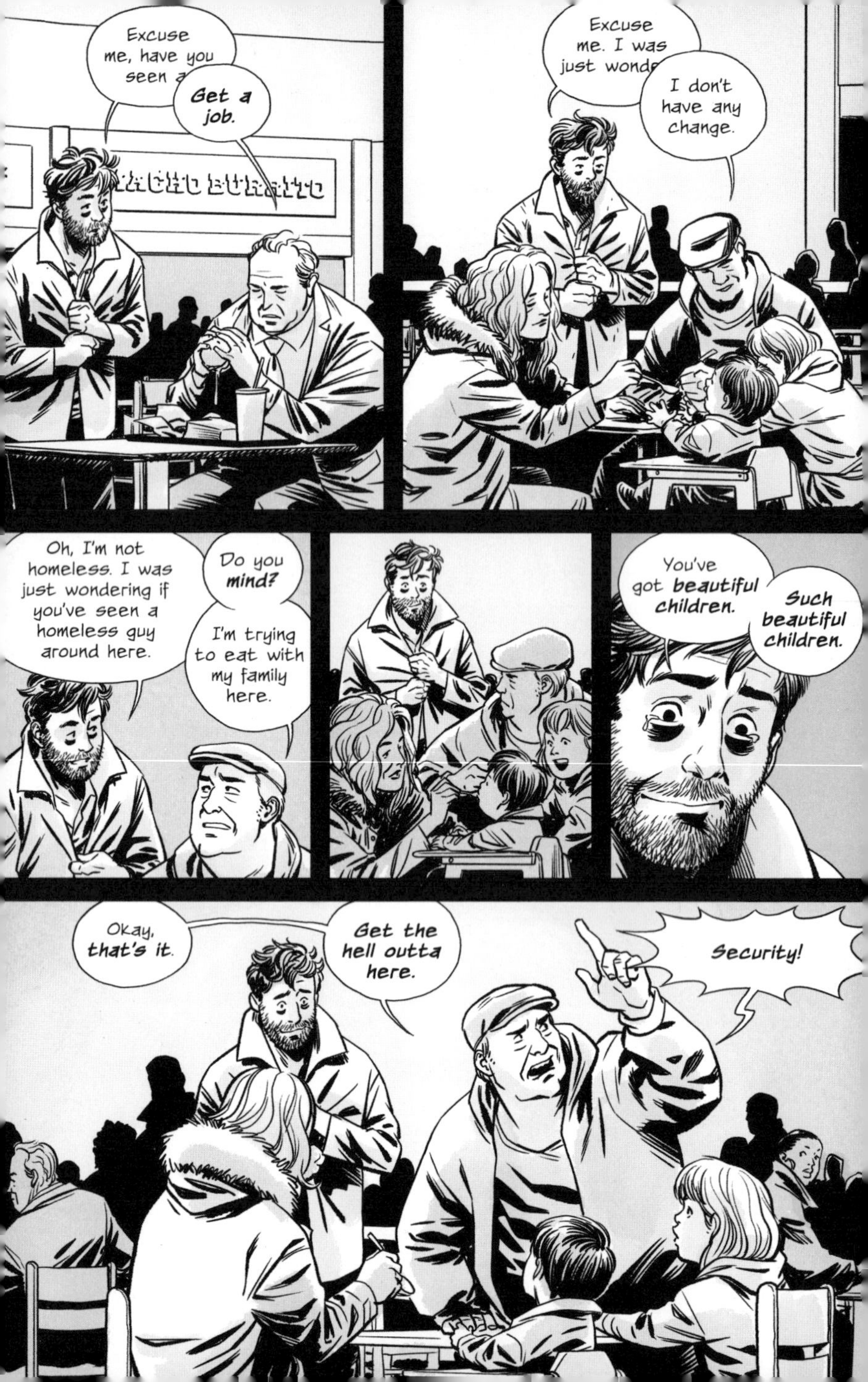
Excuse me, have you seen a
Get a job.
Excuse me. I was just wonde
I don't have any change.
Oh, I'm not homeless. I was just wondering if you've seen a homeless guy around here.
Do you mind?
I'm trying to eat with my family here.
You've got beautiful children.
Such beautiful children.
Okay, that's it.
Get the hell outta here.
Security!

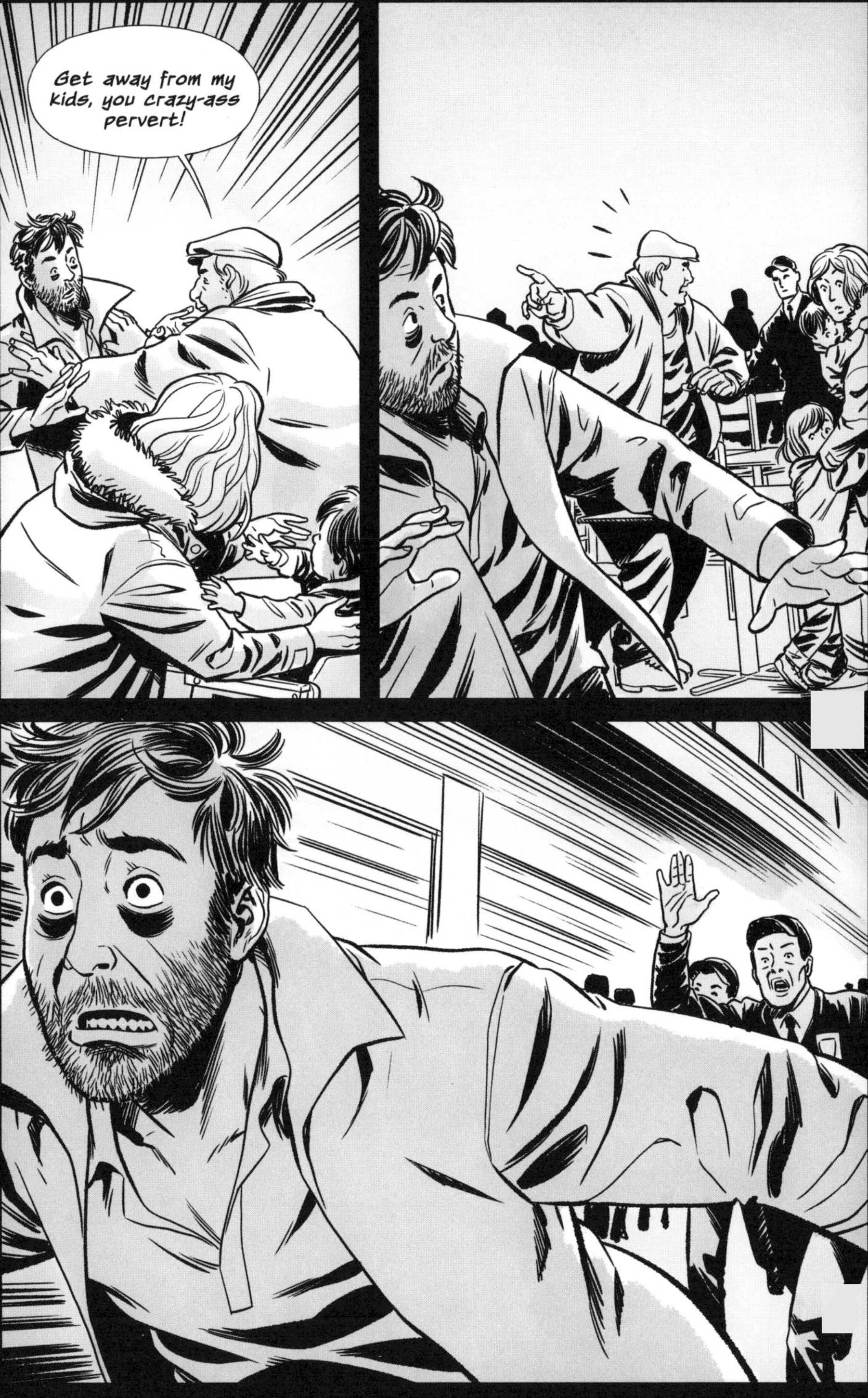
Get away from my kids, you crazy-ass pervert!

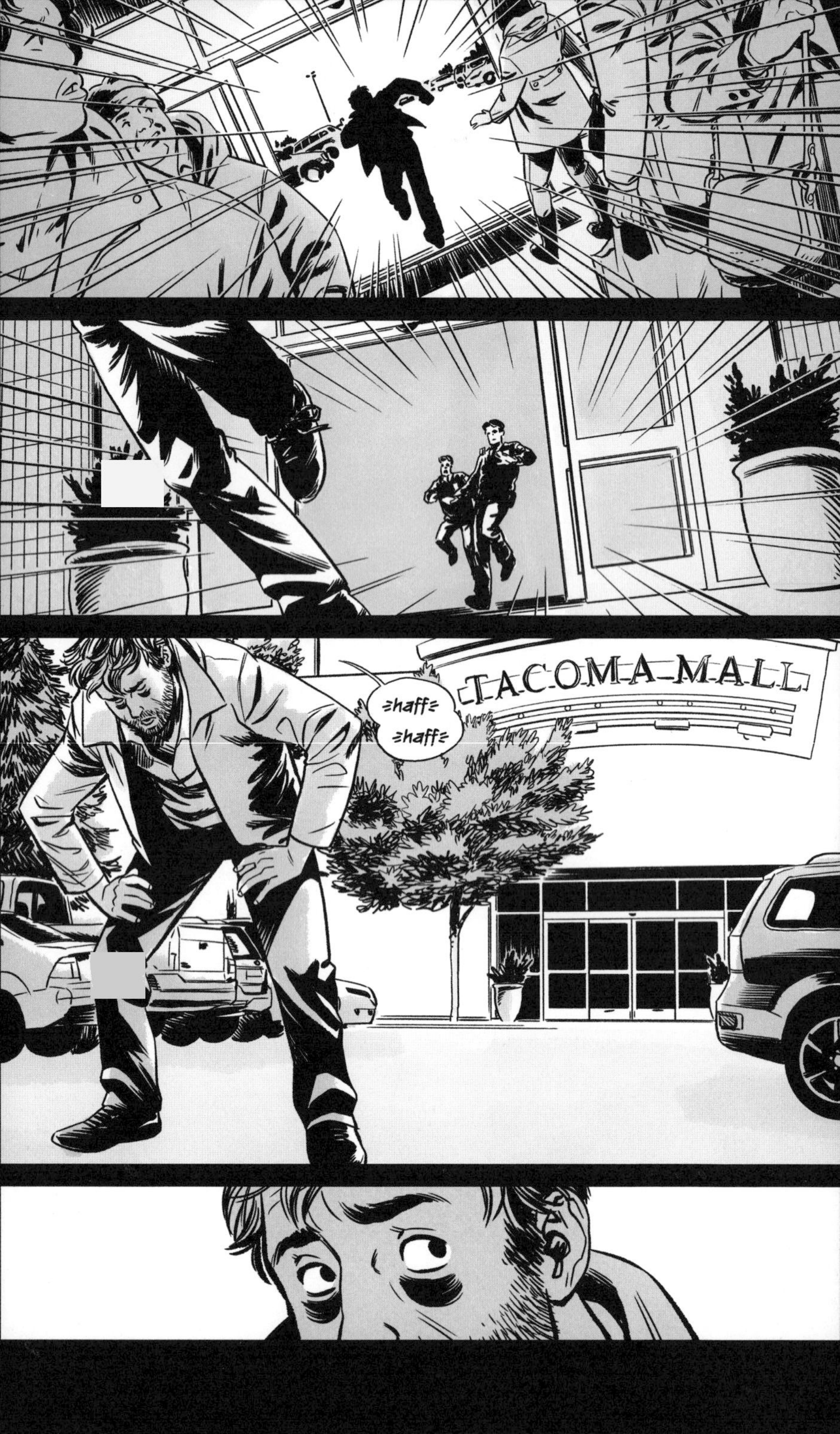
TACOMA MALL
haff haff

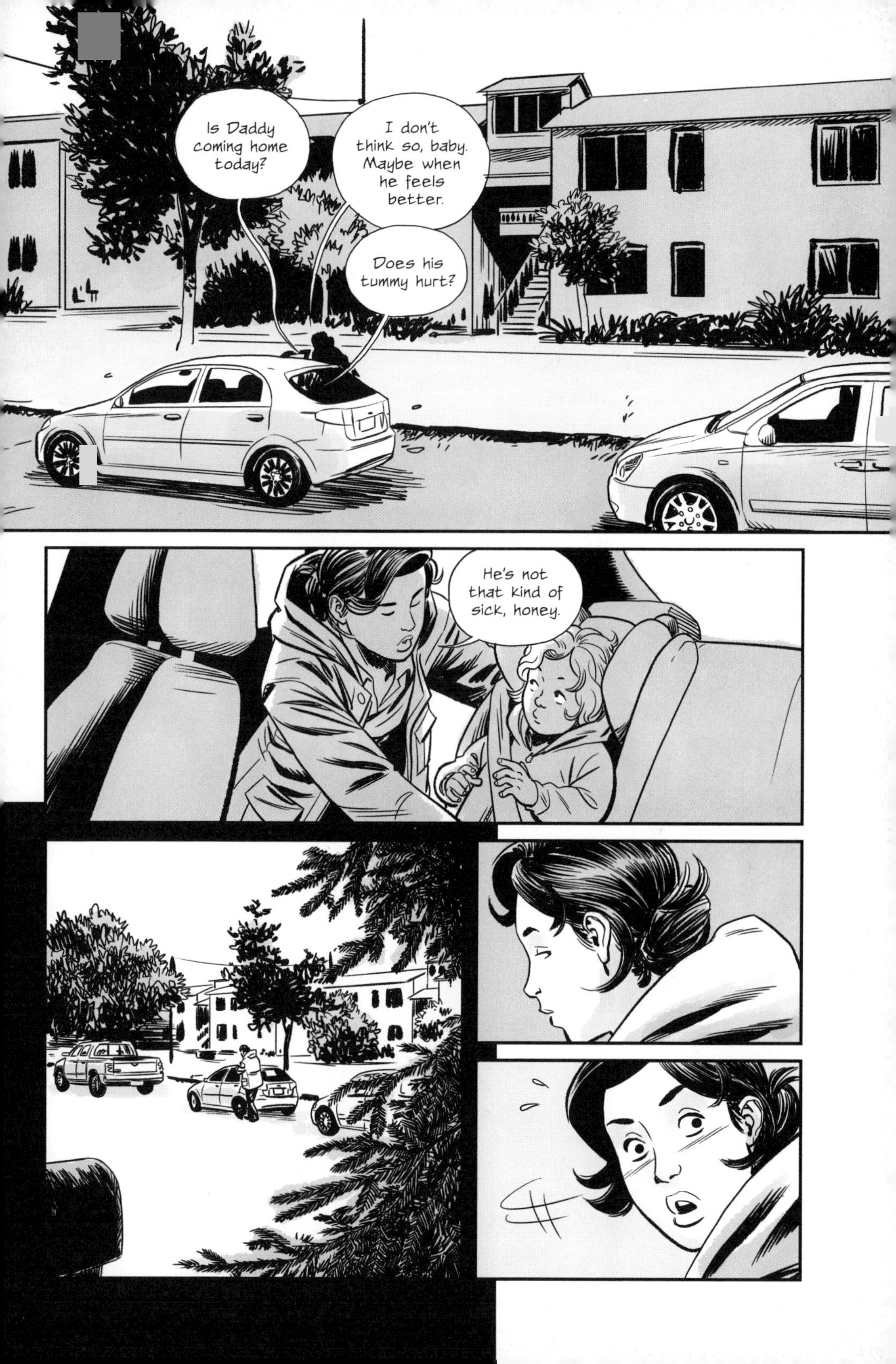
Is Daddy coming home today?
I don't think so, baby. Maybe when he feels better.
Does his tummy hurt?
He's not that kind of sick, honey.

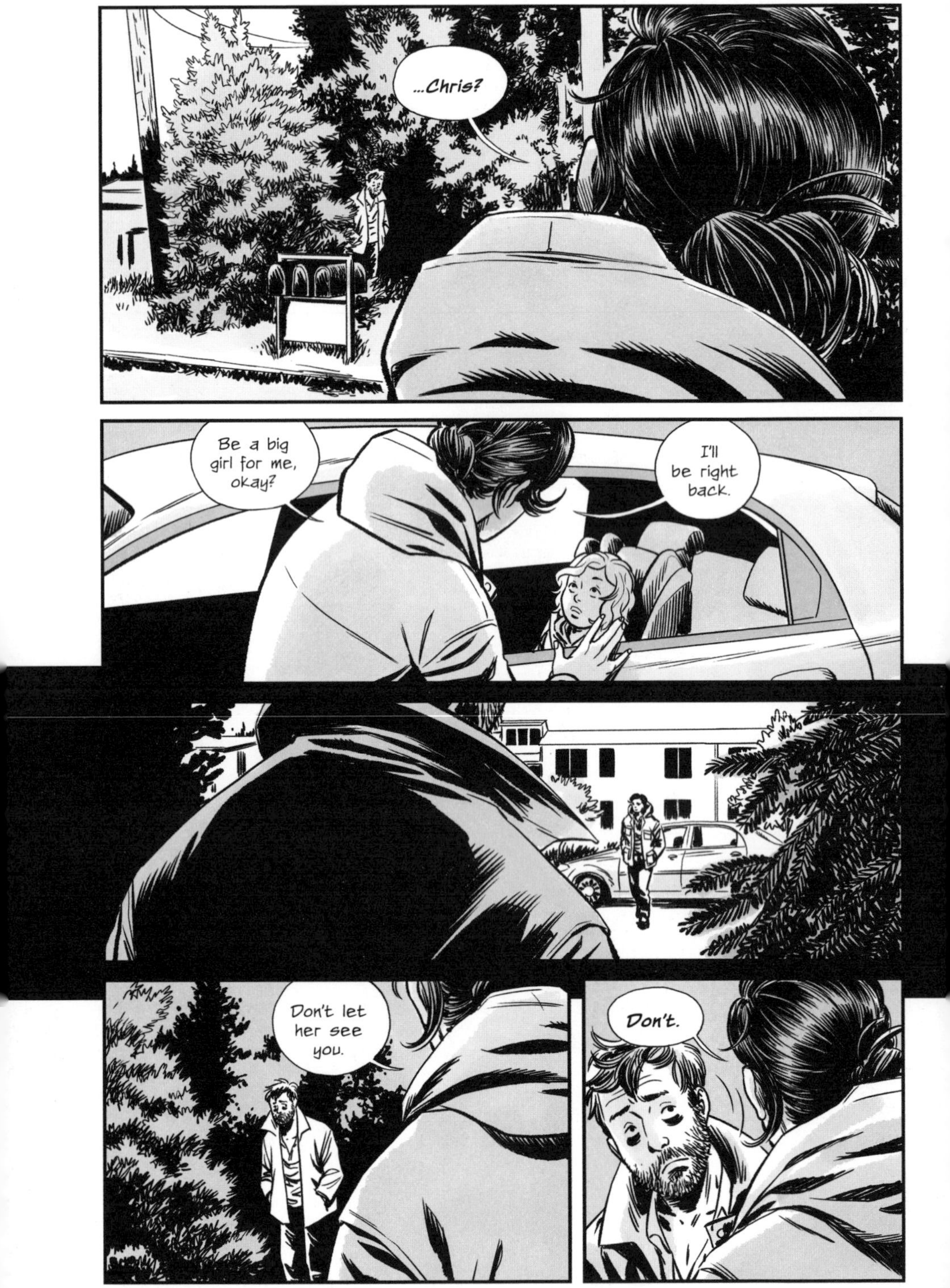
...Chris?
Be a big girl for me, okay?
I'll be right back.
Don't let her see you.
Don't.

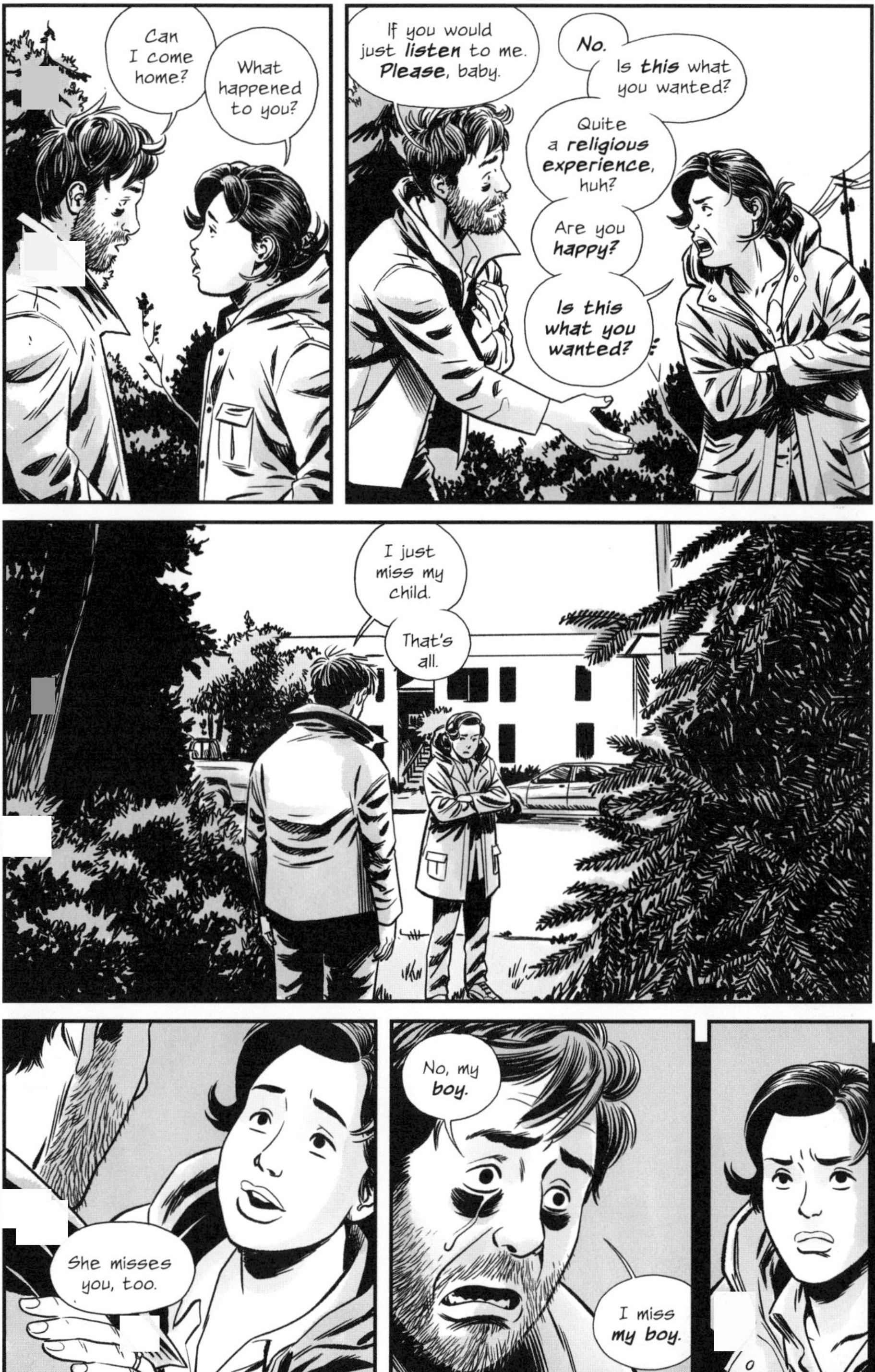
Can I come home?
What happened to you?
If you would just listen to me. Please, baby.
No.
Is this what you wanted?
Quite a religious experience, huh?
Are you happy?
Is this what you wanted?
I just miss my child.
That's all.
She misses you, too.
No, my boy.
I miss my boy.

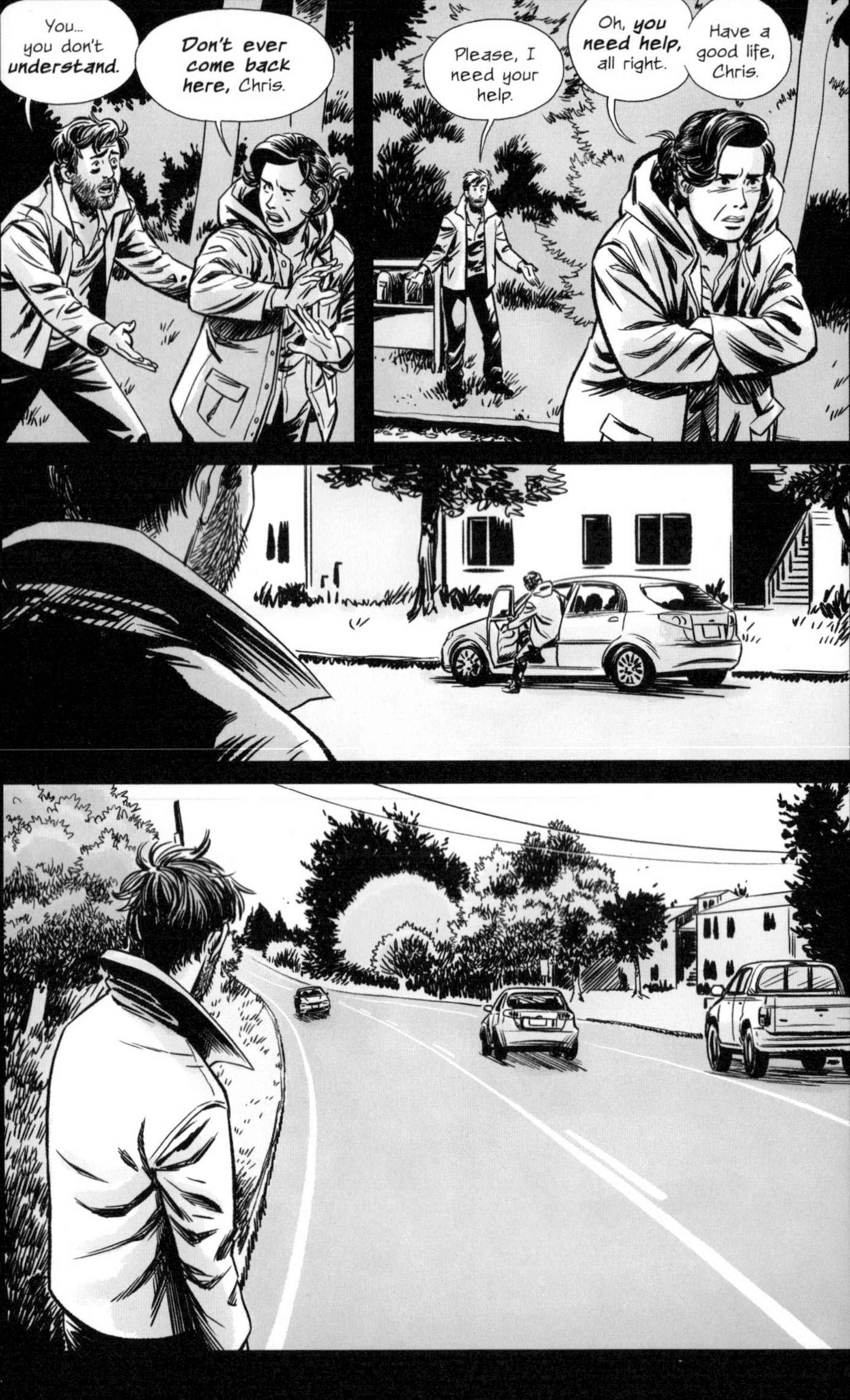
You... you don't **understand**.
Don't ever come back here, Chris.
Please, I need your help.
Oh, **you need help,** all right.
Have a good life, Chris.

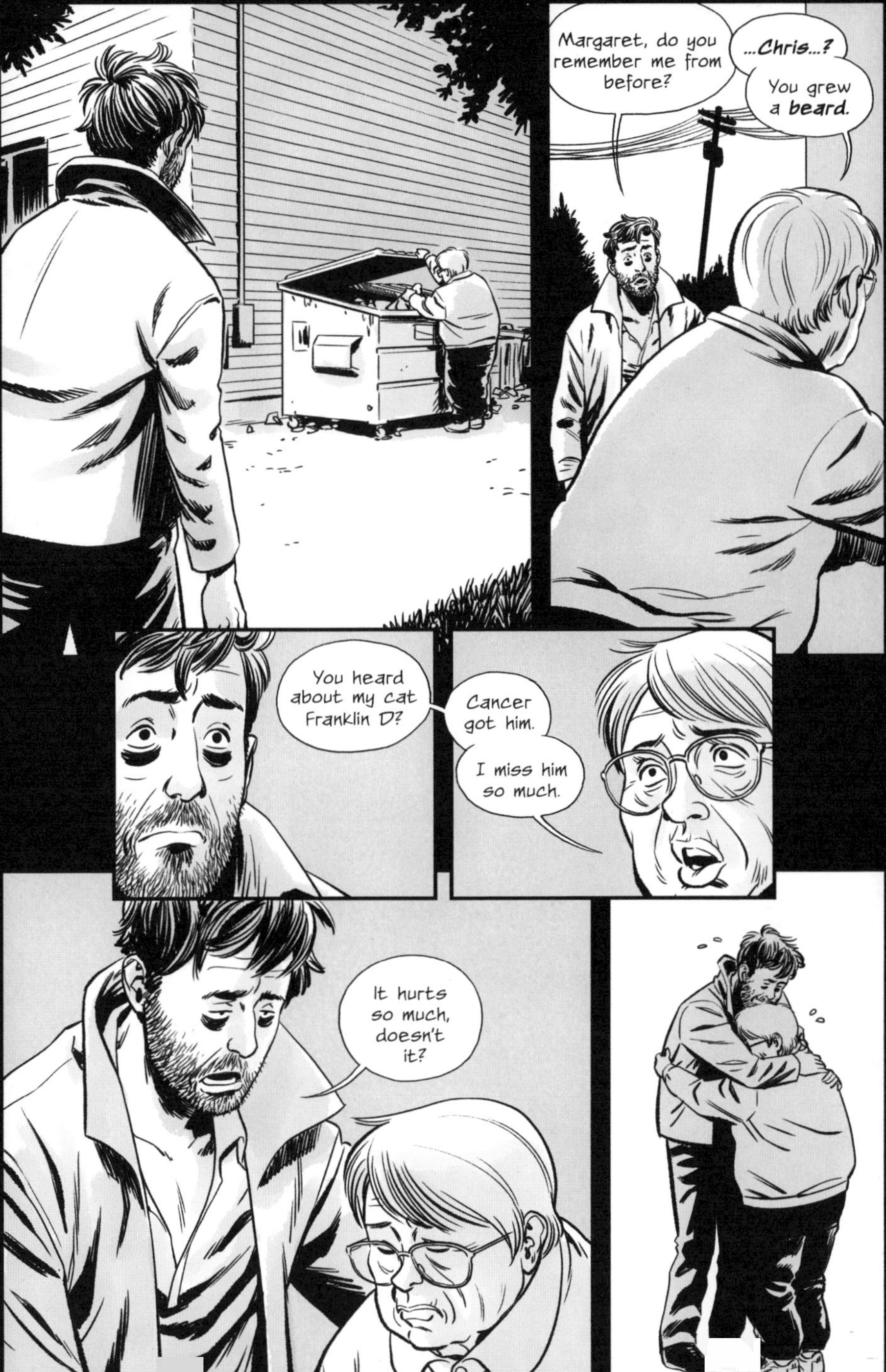
Margaret, do you remember me from before?
...**Chris**...?
You grew a **beard**.
You heard about my cat Franklin D?
Cancer got him.
I miss him so much.
It hurts so much, doesn't it?

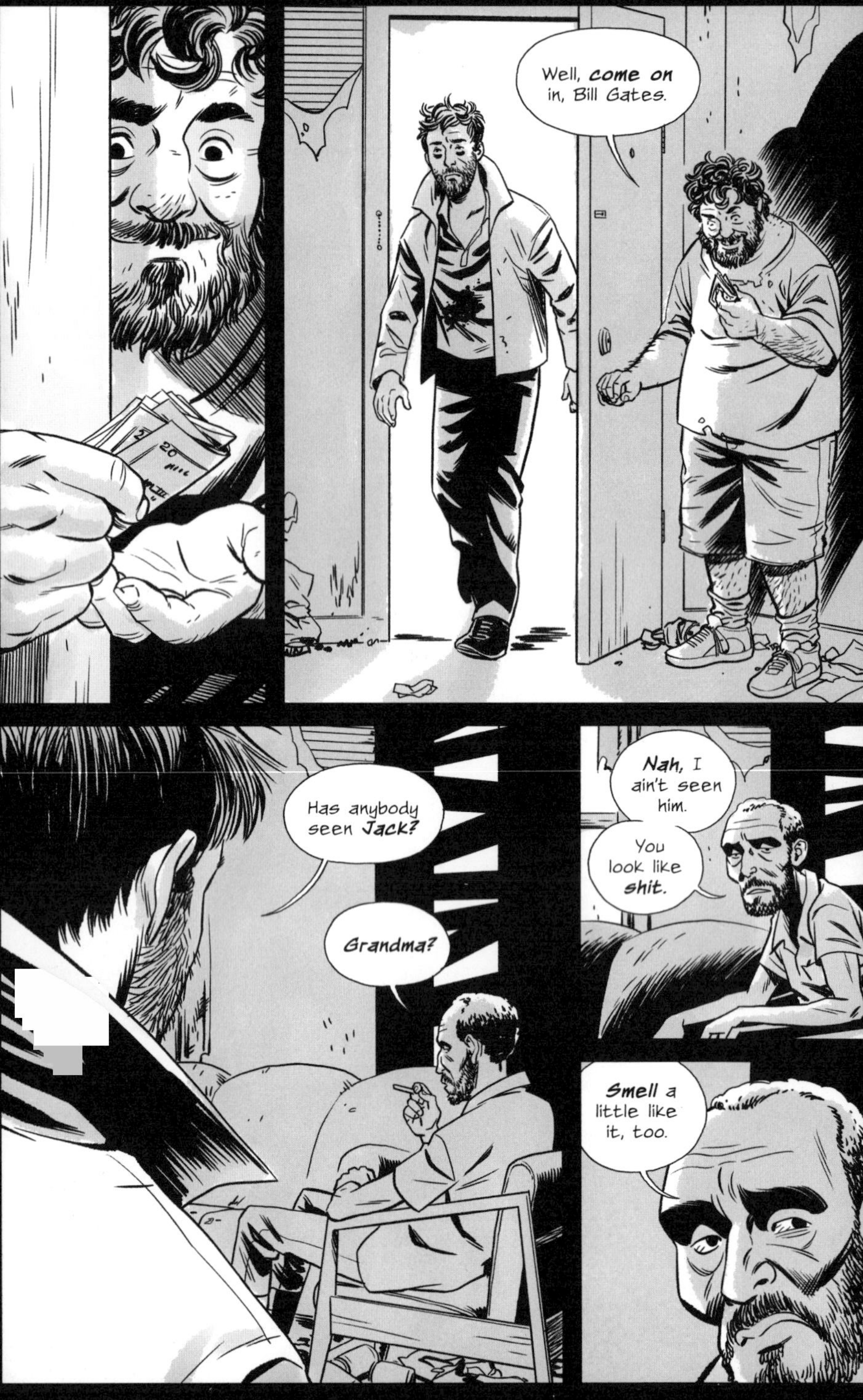
Well, come on in, Bill Gates.
Has anybody seen Jack?
Grandma?
Nah, I ain't seen him.
You look like shit.
Smell a little like it, too.

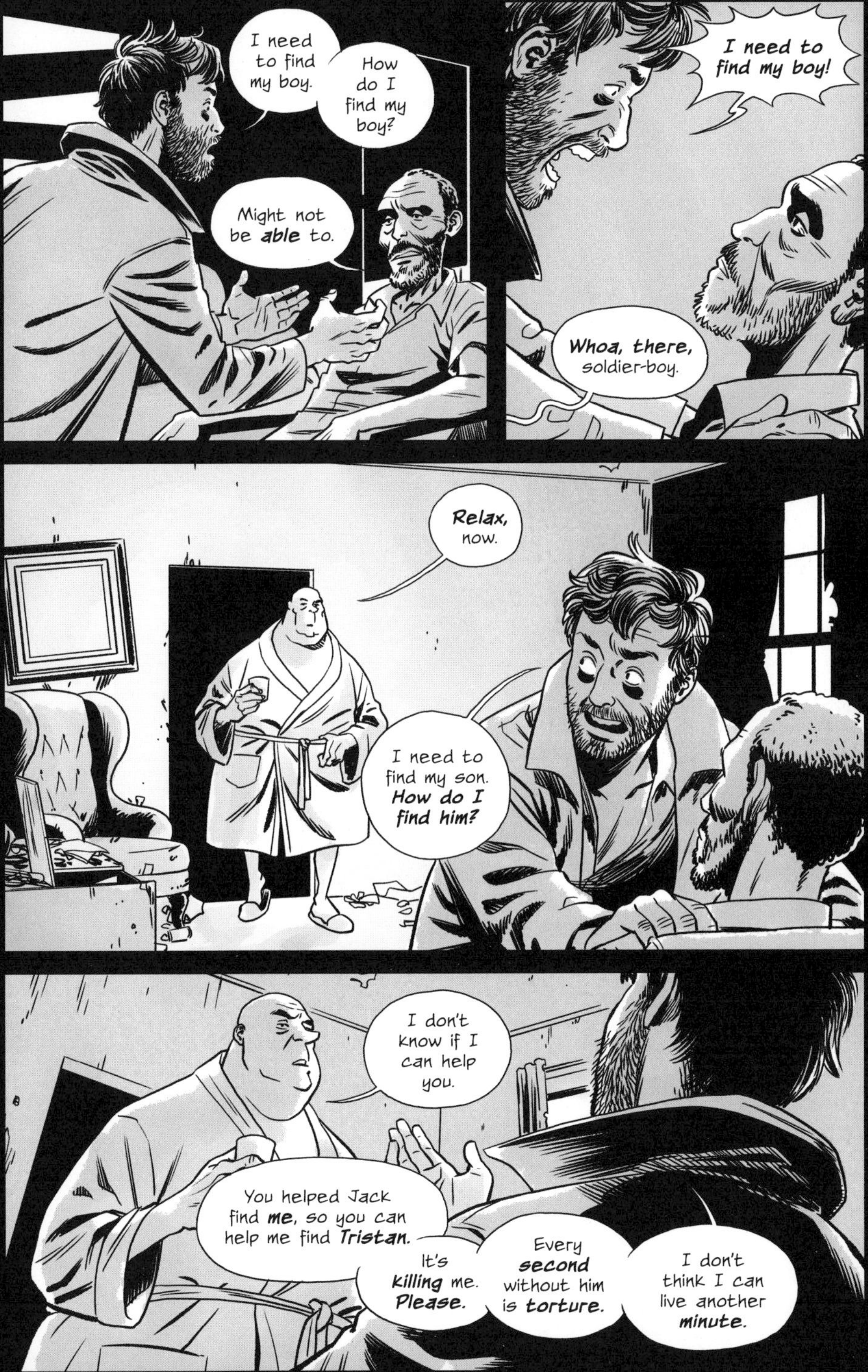
I need to find my boy.
How do I find my boy?
Might not be able to.
I need to find my boy!
Whoa, there, soldier-boy.
Relax, now.
I need to find my son. How do I find him?
I don't know if I can help you.
You helped Jack find me, so you can help me find Tristan.
It's killing me. Please.
Every second without him is torture.
I don't think I can live another minute.

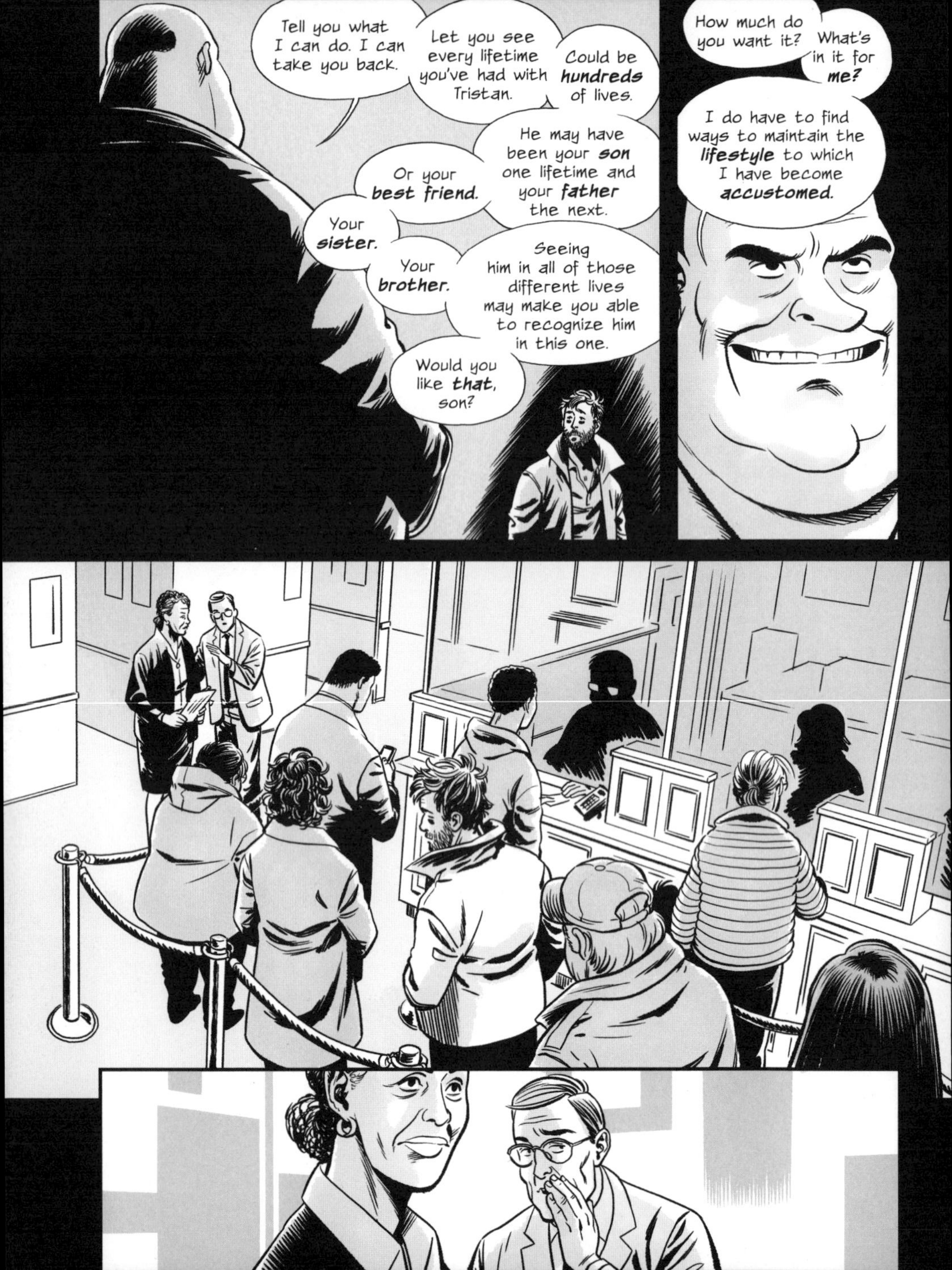
Tell you what I can do. I can take you back.
Let you see every lifetime you've had with Tristan.
Could be **hundreds** of lives.
He may have been your **son** one lifetime and your **father** the next.
Or your **best friend.**
Your **sister.**
Your **brother.**
Seeing him in all of those different lives may make you able to recognize him in this one.
Would you like **that,** son?
How much do you want it?
What's in it for **me?**
I do have to find ways to maintain the **lifestyle** to which I have become **accustomed.**

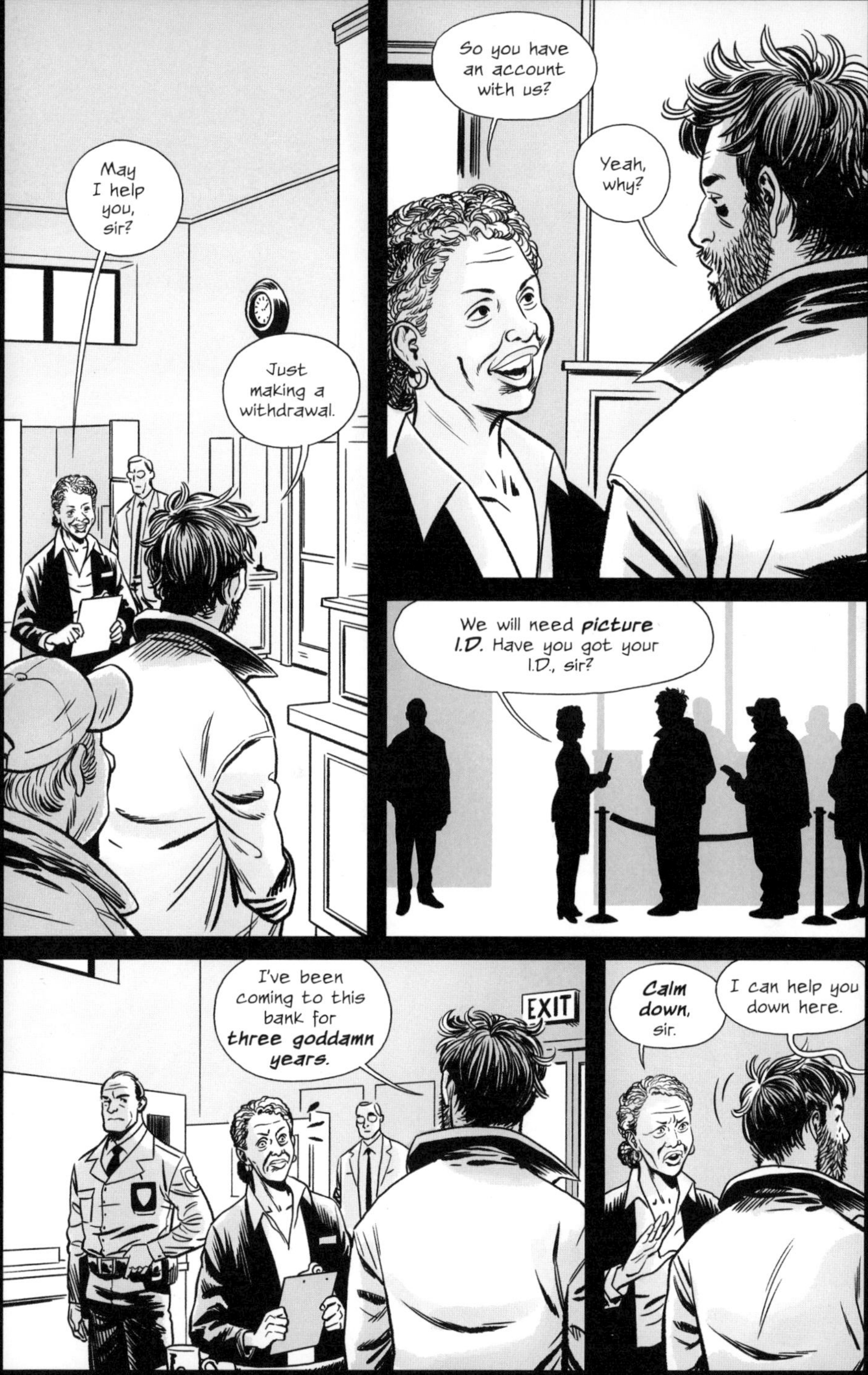
May I help you, sir?
Just making a withdrawal.
So you have an account with us?
Yeah, why?
We will need **picture I.D.** Have you got your I.D., sir?
I've been coming to this bank for **three goddamn years.**
EXIT
Calm down, sir.
I can help you down here.

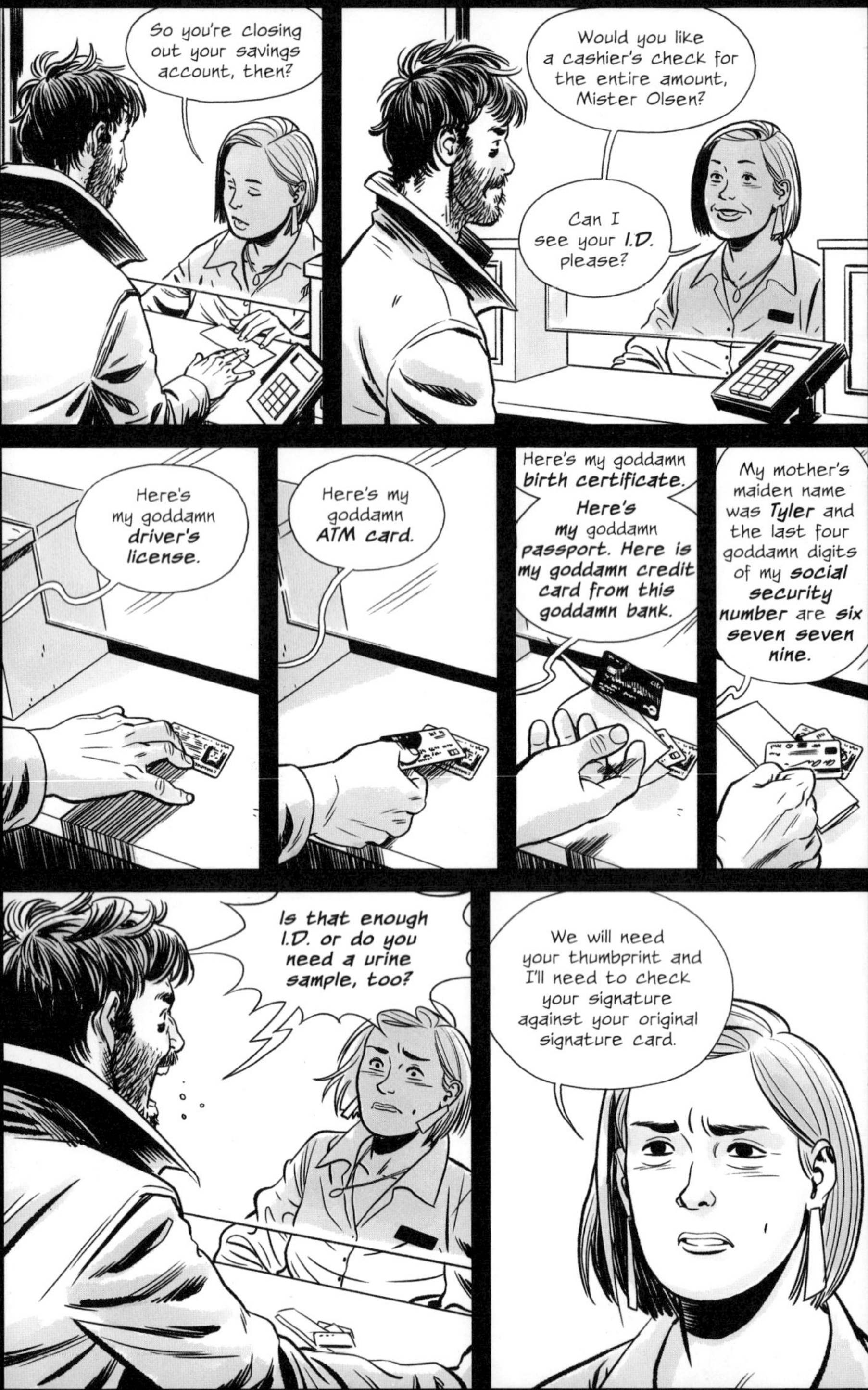

So you're closing out your savings account, then?
Would you like a cashier's check for the entire amount, Mister Olsen?
Can I see your I.D. please?
Here's my goddamn driver's license.
Here's my goddamn ATM card.
Here's my goddamn birth certificate.
Here's my goddamn passport. Here is my goddamn credit card from this goddamn bank.
My mother's maiden name was Tyler and the last four goddamn digits of my social security number are six seven seven nine.
Is that enough I.D. or do you need a urine sample, too?
We will need your thumbprint and I'll need to check your signature against your original signature card.

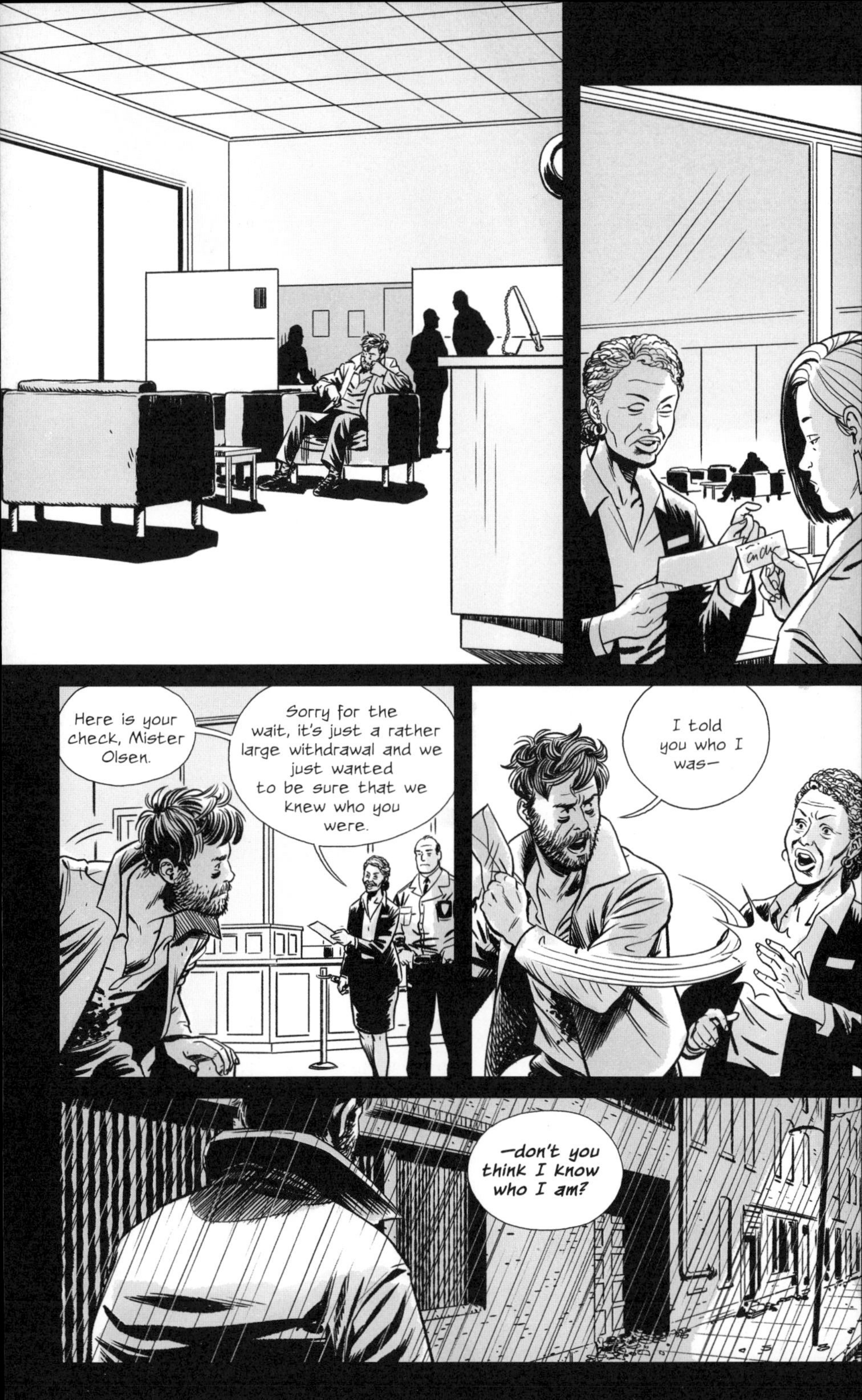

Here is your check, Mister Olsen.
Sorry for the wait, it's just a rather large withdrawal and we just wanted to be sure that we knew who you were.
I told you who I was—
—don't you think I know who I am?

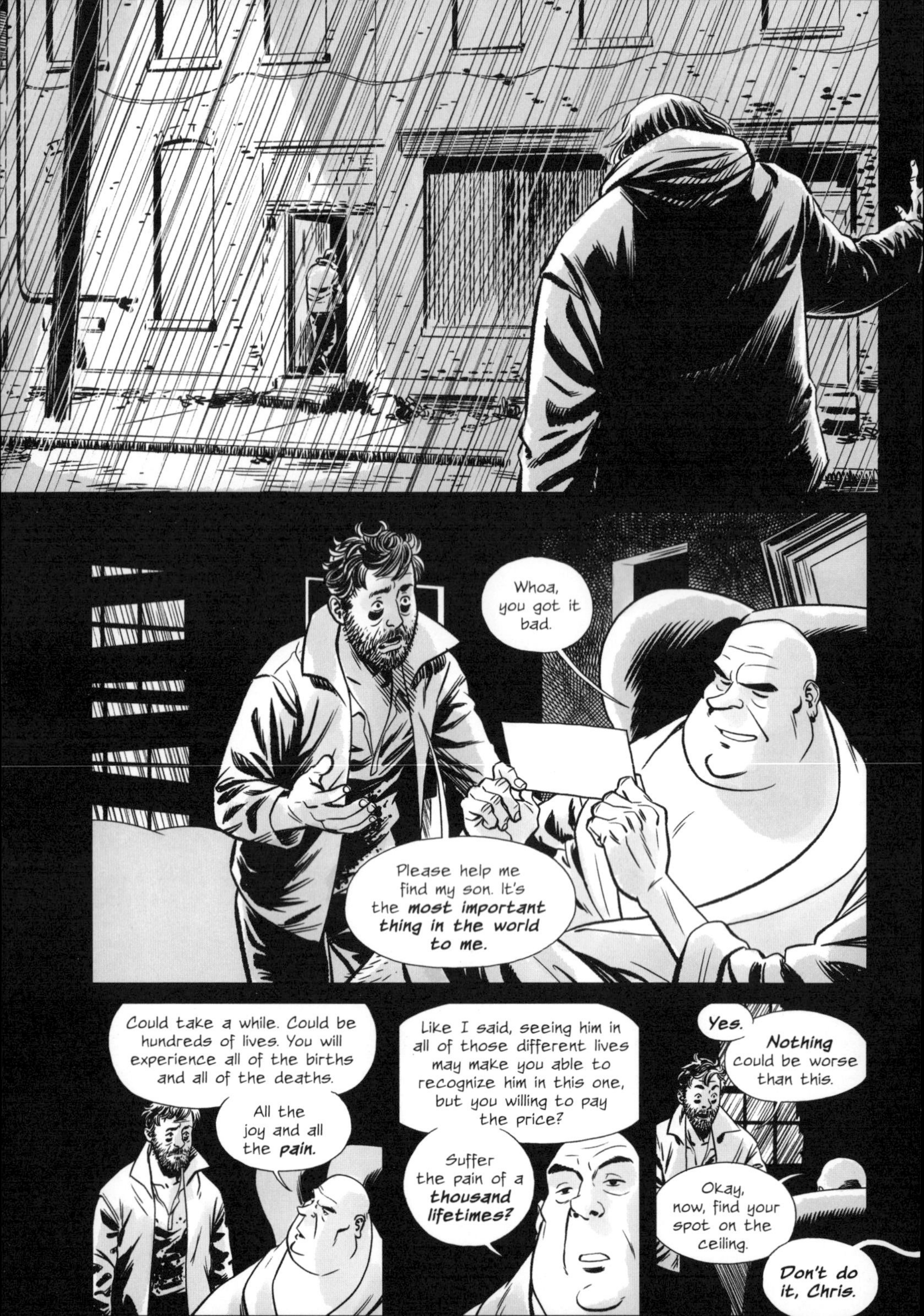

Whoa, you got it bad.
Please help me find my son. It's the **most important thing in the world to me.**
Could take a while. Could be hundreds of lives. You will experience all of the births and all of the deaths.
All the joy and all the **pain.**
Like I said, seeing him in all of those different lives may make you able to recognize him in this one, but you willing to pay the price?
Suffer the pain of a **thousand lifetimes?**
Yes.
Nothing could be worse than this.
Okay, now, find your spot on the ceiling.
Don't do it, Chris.

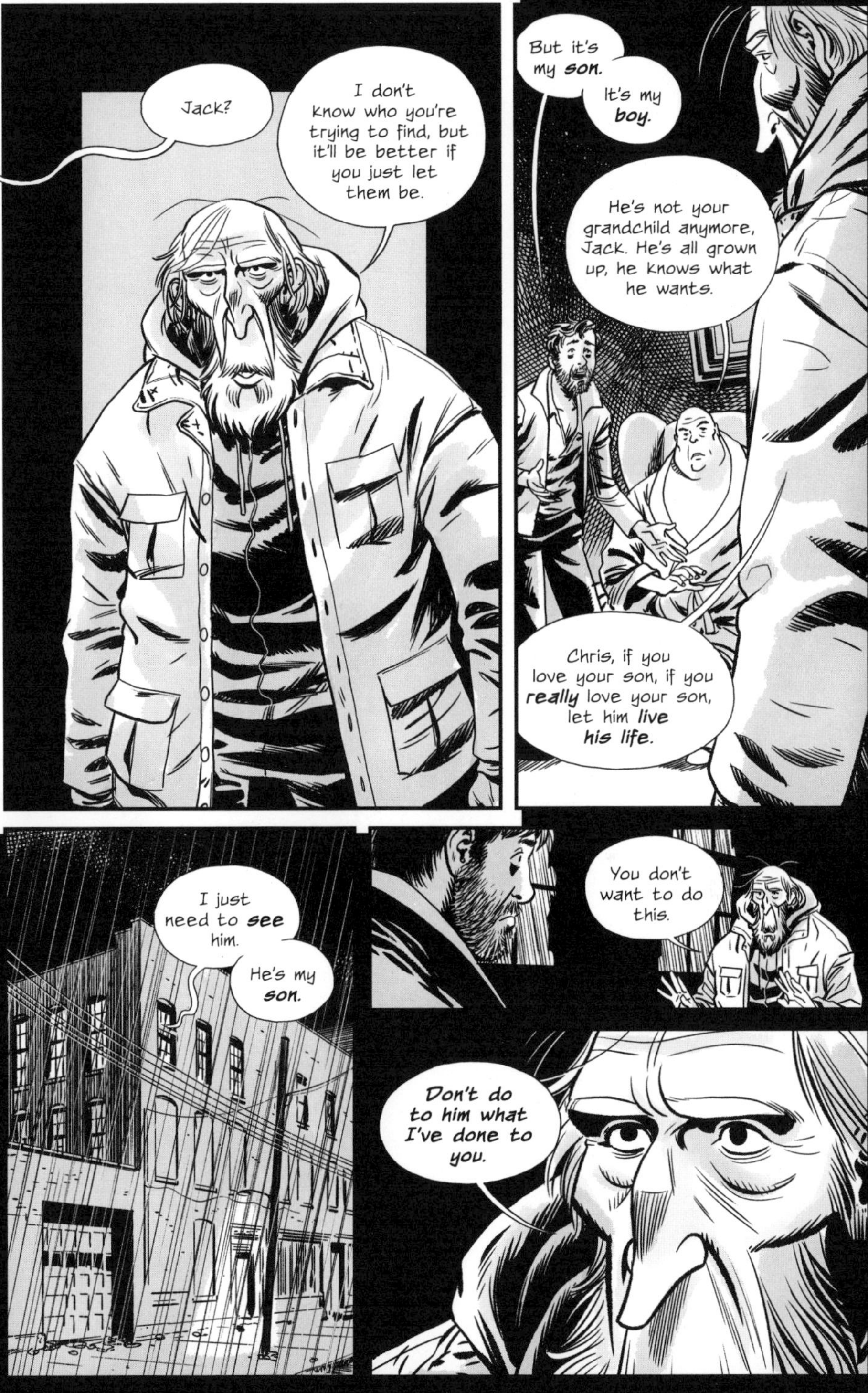
Jack?
I don't know who you're trying to find, but it'll be better if you just let them be.
But it's my **son.**
It's my **boy.**
He's not your grandchild anymore, Jack. He's all grown up, he knows what he wants.
Chris, if you love your son, if you **really** love your son, let him **live his life.**
I just need to **see** him.
He's my **son.**
You don't want to do this.
Don't do to him what I've done to you.

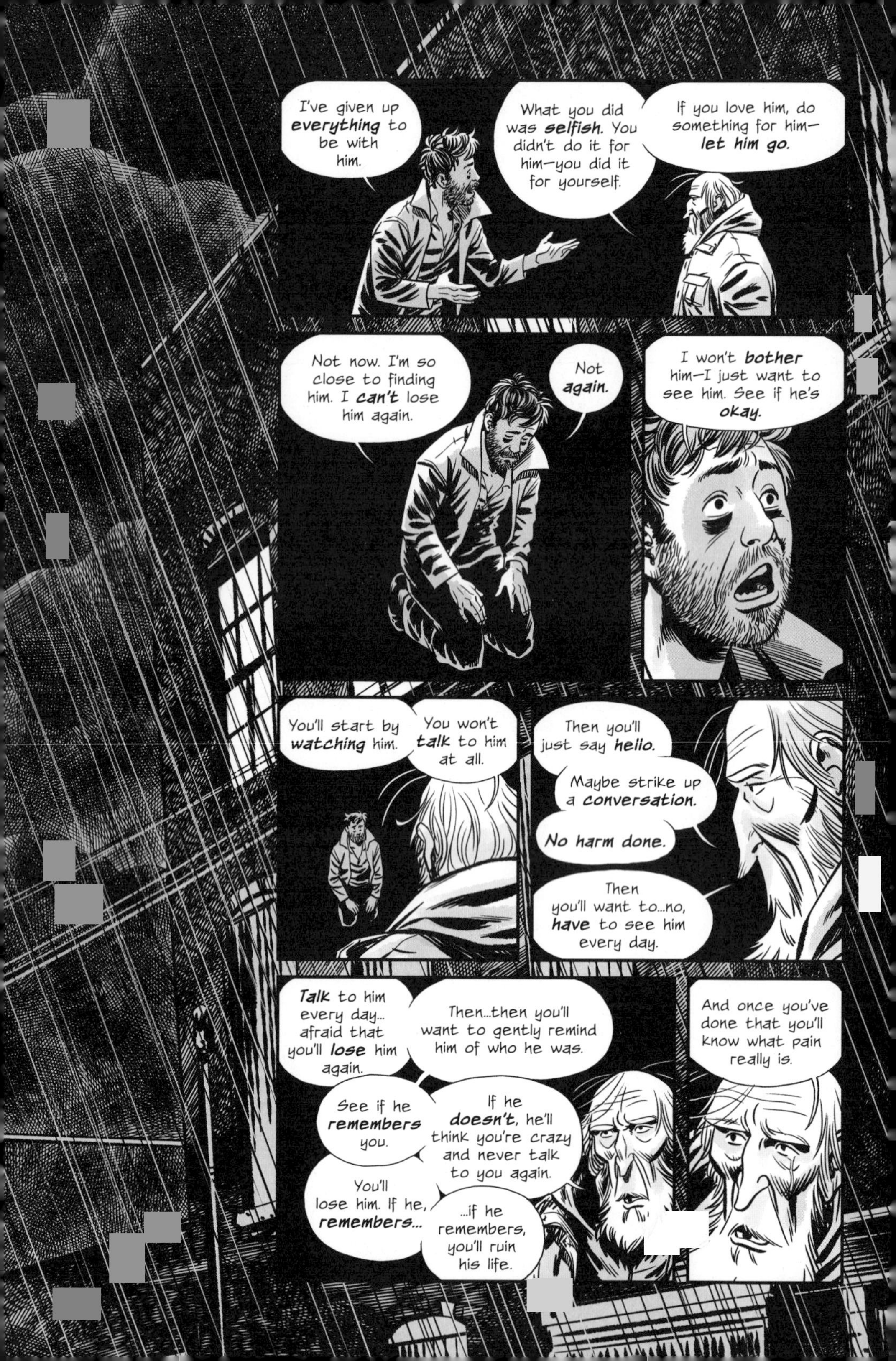
I've given up everything to be with him.
What you did was selfish. You didn't do it for him—you did it for yourself.
If you love him, do something for him—let him go.
Not now. I'm so close to finding him. I can't lose him again.
Not again.
I won't bother him—I just want to see him. See if he's okay.
You'll start by watching him.
You won't talk to him at all.
Then you'll just say hello.
Maybe strike up a conversation.
No harm done.
Then you'll want to...no, have to see him every day.
Talk to him every day... afraid that you'll lose him again.
Then...then you'll want to gently remind him of who he was.
See if he remembers you.
If he doesn't, he'll think you're crazy and never talk to you again.
You'll lose him. If he, remembers...
...if he remembers, you'll ruin his life.
And once you've done that you'll know what pain really is.

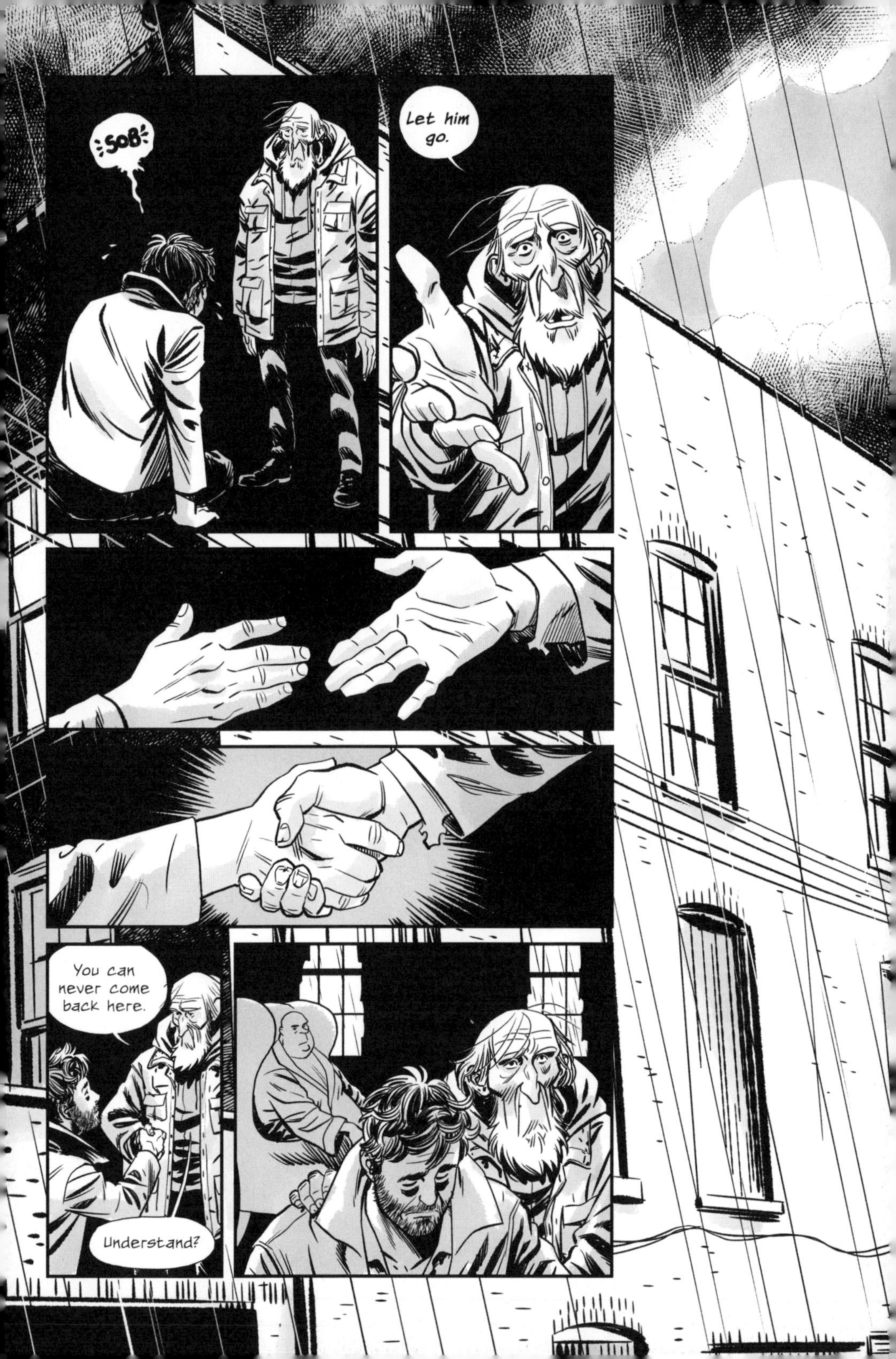
SOB
Let him go.
You can never come back here.
Understand?

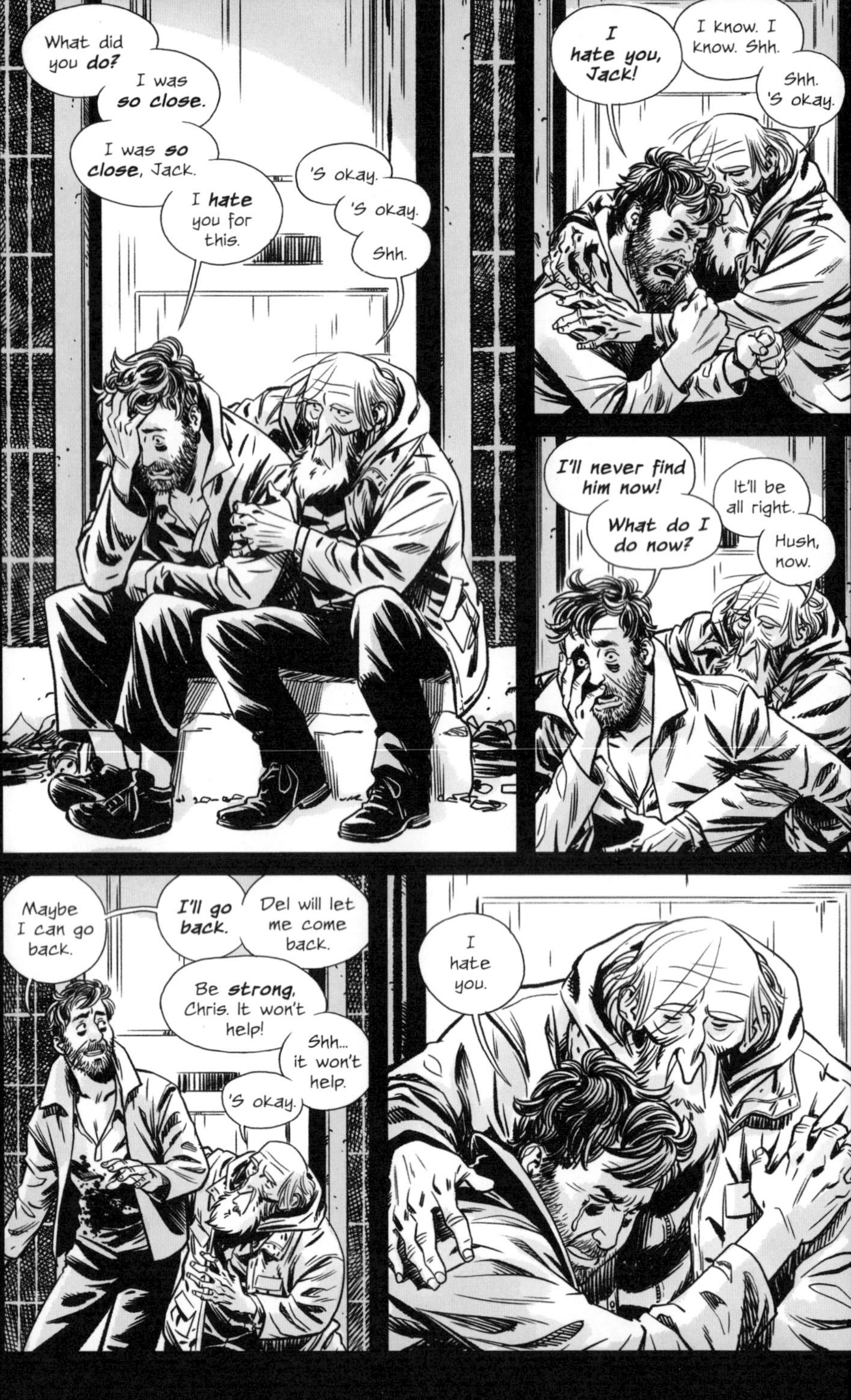
What did you **do?**
I was **so close.**
I was **so close**, Jack.
I **hate** you for this.
'S okay.
'S okay.
Shh.
I hate you, Jack!
I know. I know. Shh.
Shh. 'S okay.
I'll never find him now!
What do I do now?
It'll be all right.
Hush, now.
Maybe I can go back.
I'll go back.
Del will let me come back.
Be **strong**, Chris. It won't help!
Shh... it won't help.
'S okay.
I hate you.

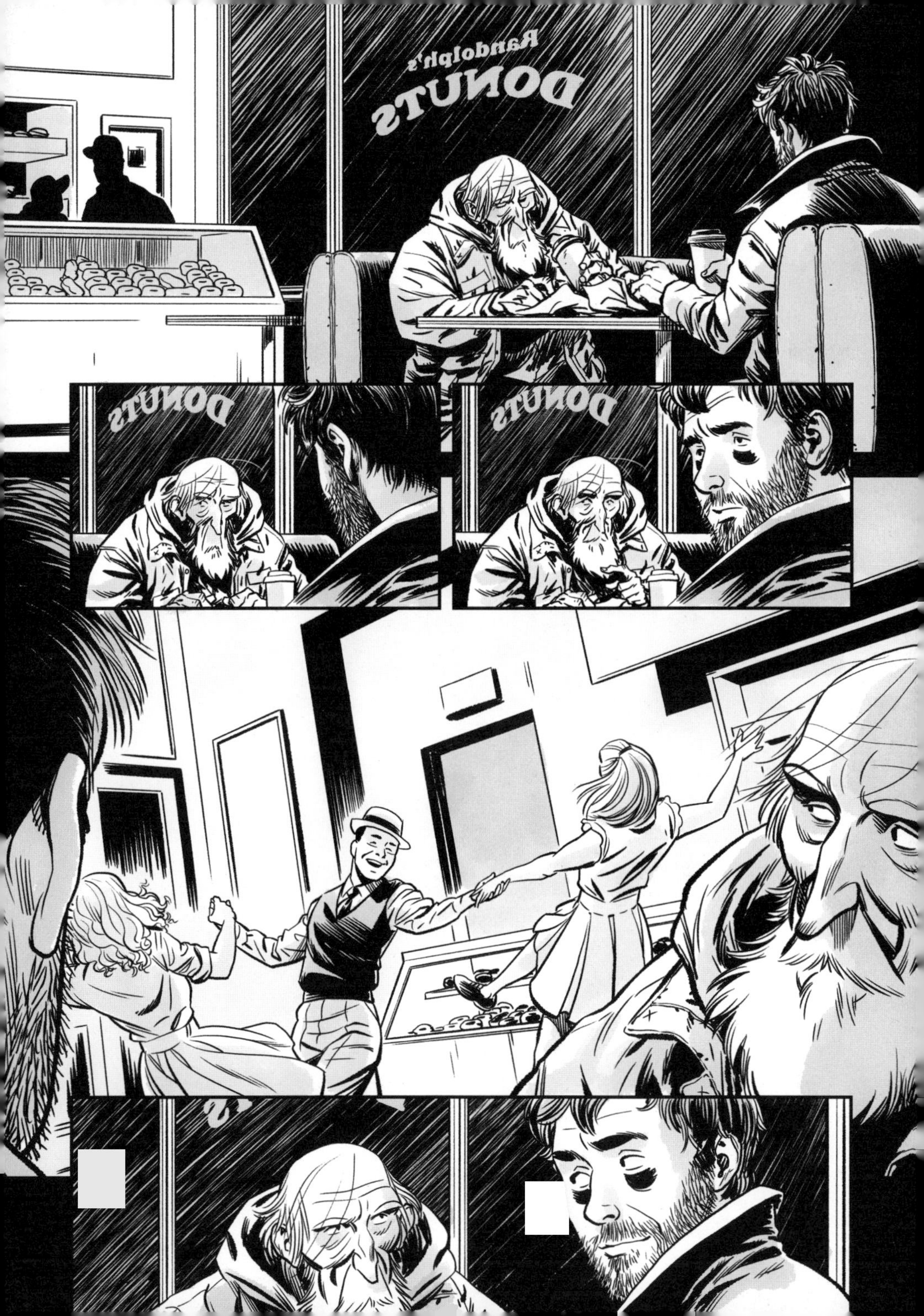
Randolph's
DONUTS

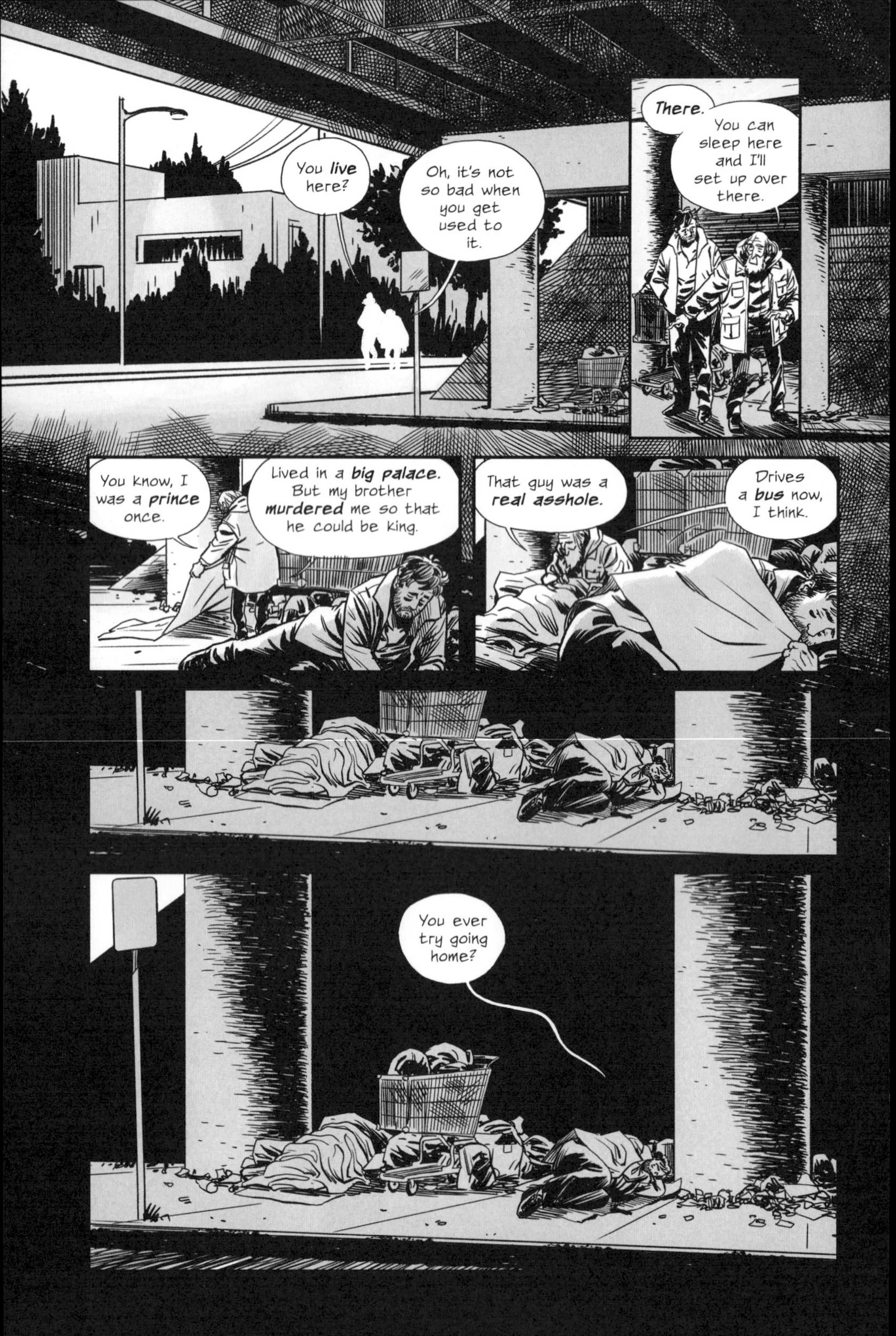
You **live** here?
Oh, it's not so bad when you get used to it.
There.
You can sleep here and I'll set up over there.
You know, I was a **prince** once.
Lived in a **big palace.** But my brother **murdered** me so that he could be king.
That guy was a **real asshole.**
Drives a **bus** now, I think.
You ever try going home?

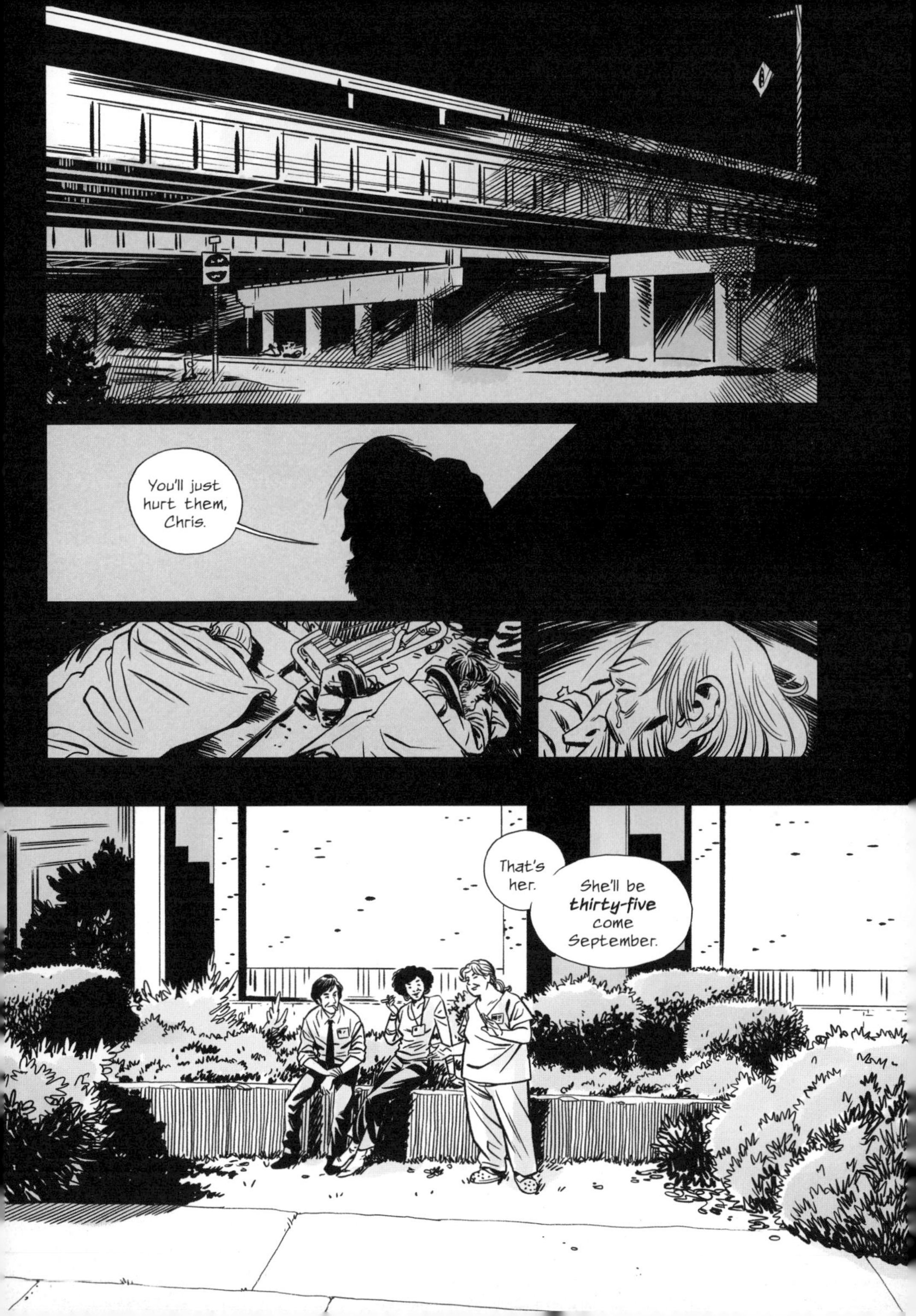
You'll just hurt them, Chris.
That's her.
She'll be thirty-five come September.

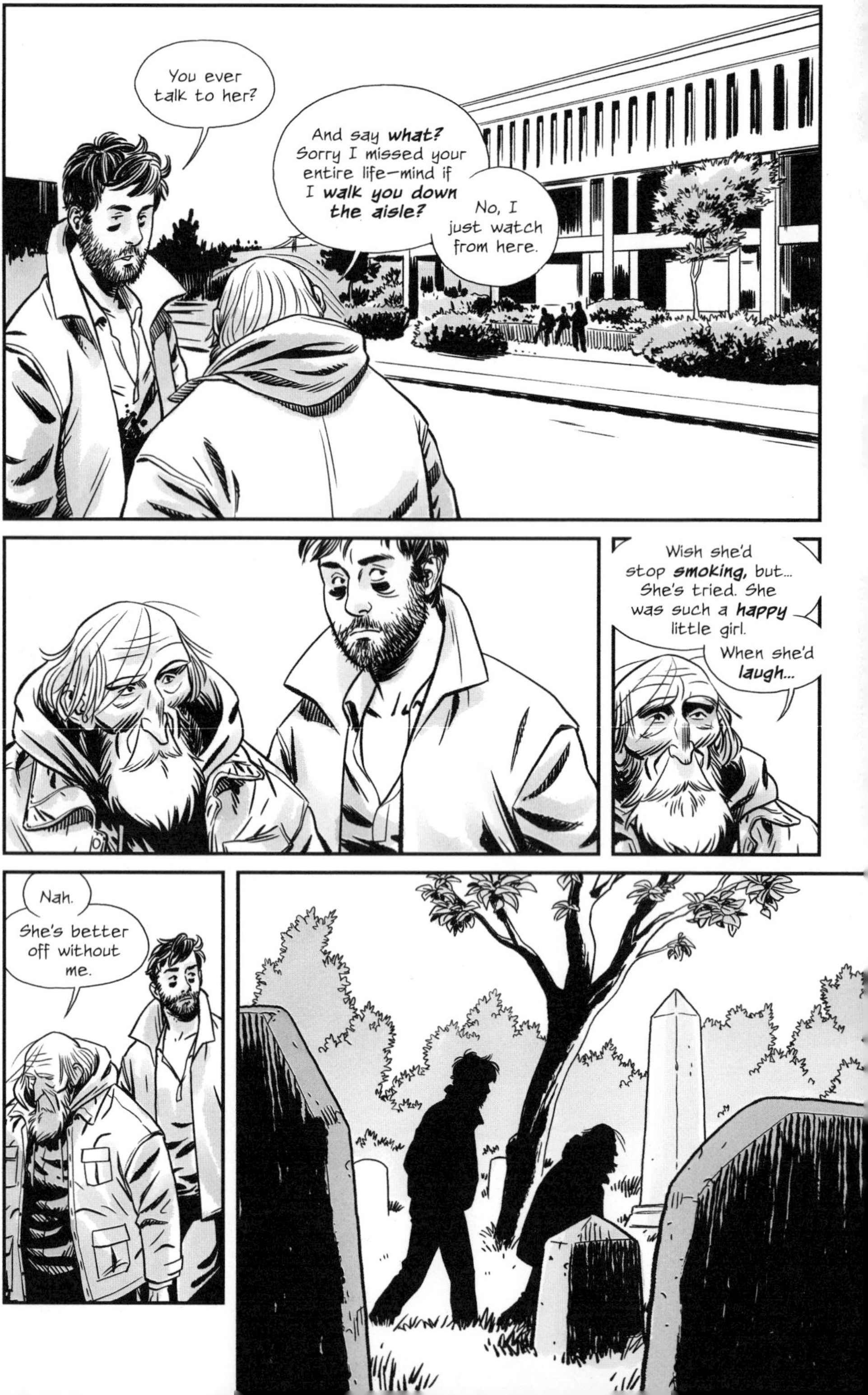
You ever talk to her?
And say **what?** Sorry I missed your entire life—mind if I **walk you down the aisle?**
No, I just watch from here.
Wish she'd stop **smoking,** but... She's tried. She was such a **happy** little girl.
When she'd **laugh...**
Nah.
She's better off without me.

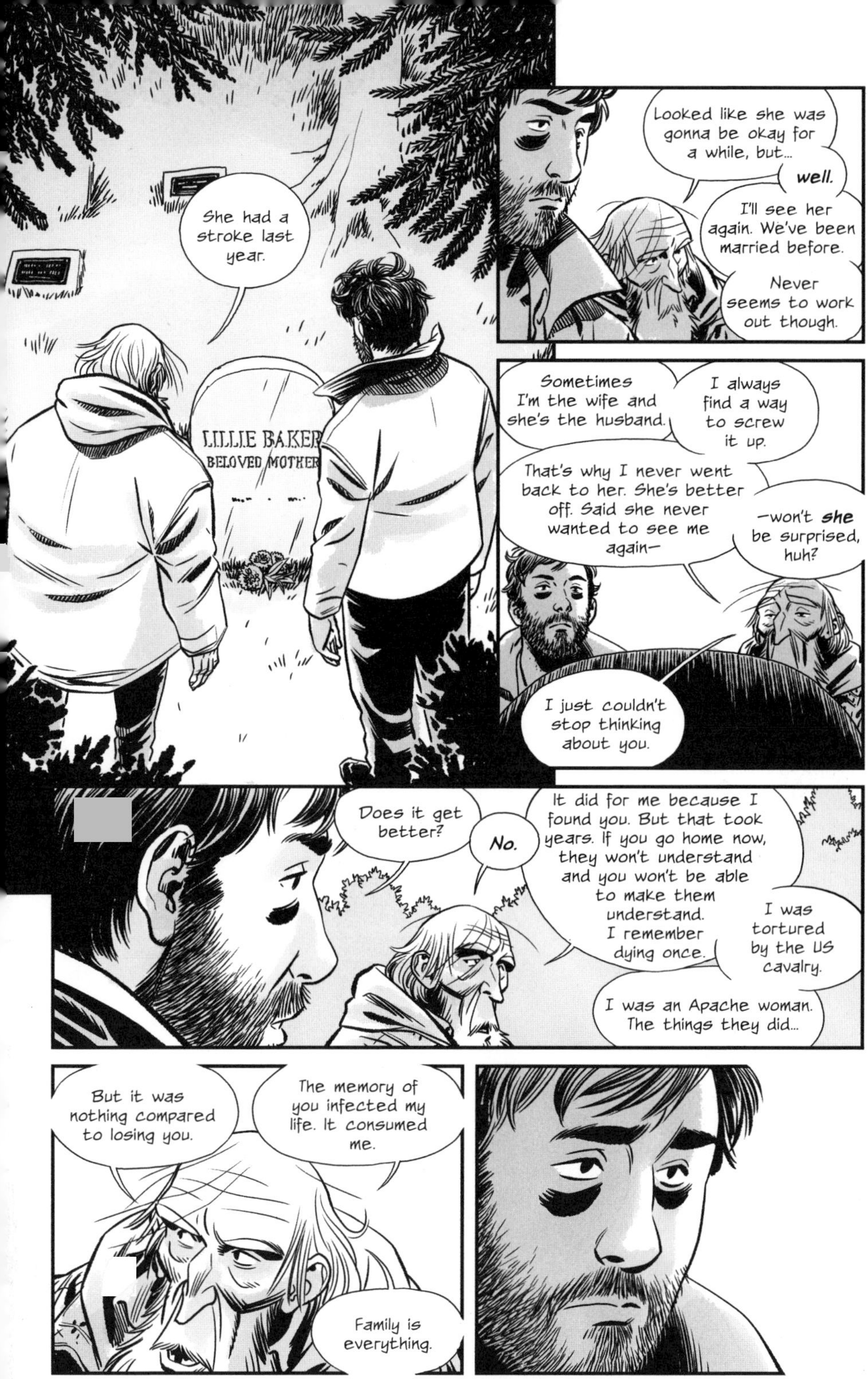
She had a stroke last year.
LILLIE BAKER
BELOVED MOTHER
Looked like she was gonna be okay for a while, but...
well.
I'll see her again. We've been married before.
Never seems to work out though.
Sometimes I'm the wife and she's the husband.
I always find a way to screw it up.
That's why I never went back to her. She's better off. Said she never wanted to see me again—
—won't she be surprised, huh?
I just couldn't stop thinking about you.
Does it get better?
No.
It did for me because I found you. But that took years. If you go home now, they won't understand and you won't be able to make them understand. I remember dying once.
I was tortured by the US cavalry.
I was an Apache woman. The things they did...
But it was nothing compared to losing you.
The memory of you infected my life. It consumed me.
Family is everything.

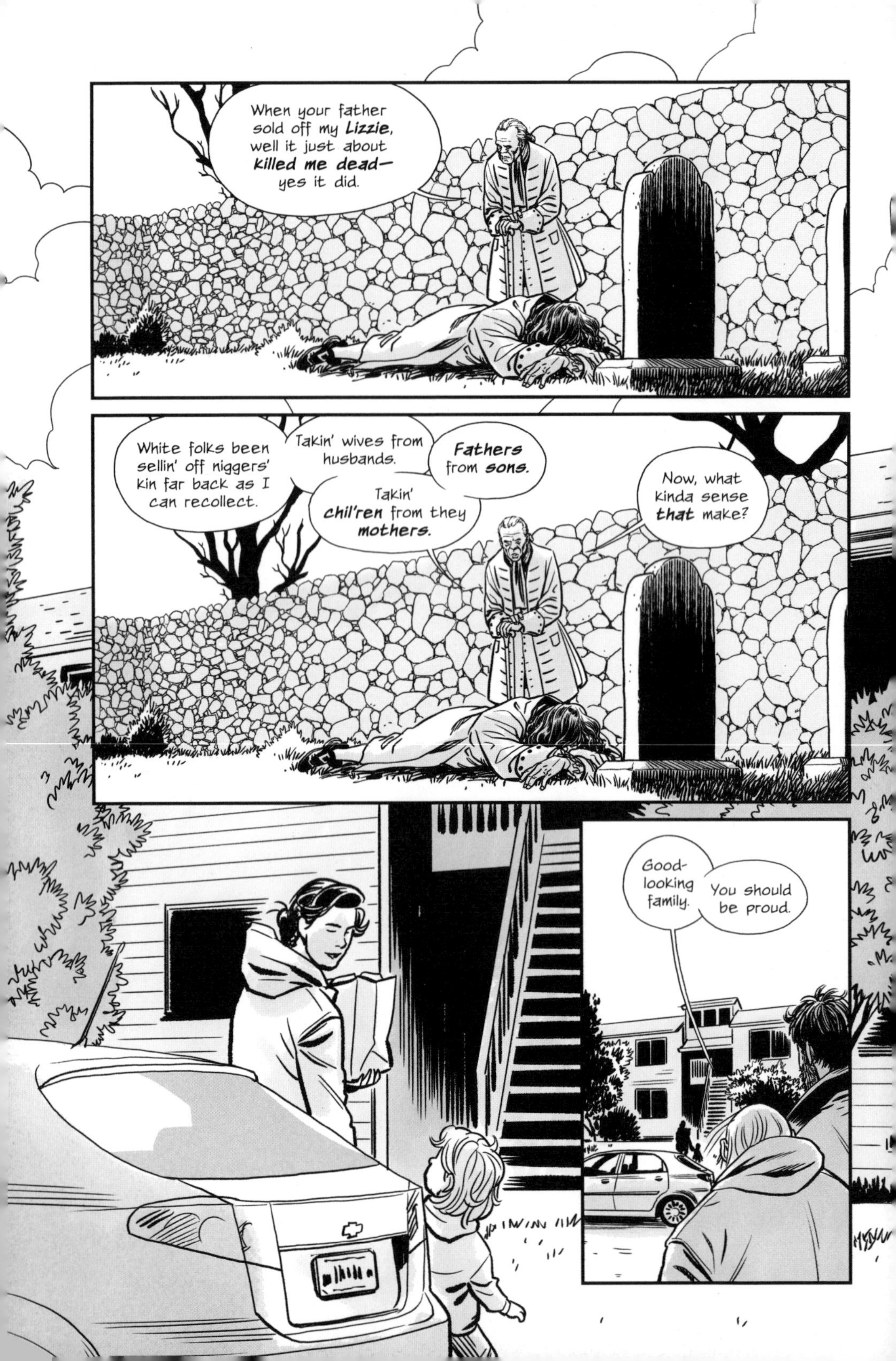
When your father sold off my Lizzie, well it just about killed me dead— yes it did.
White folks been sellin' off niggers' kin far back as I can recollect.
Takin' wives from husbands.
Fathers from sons.
Takin' chil'ren from they mothers.
Now, what kinda sense that make?
Good-looking family.
You should be proud.

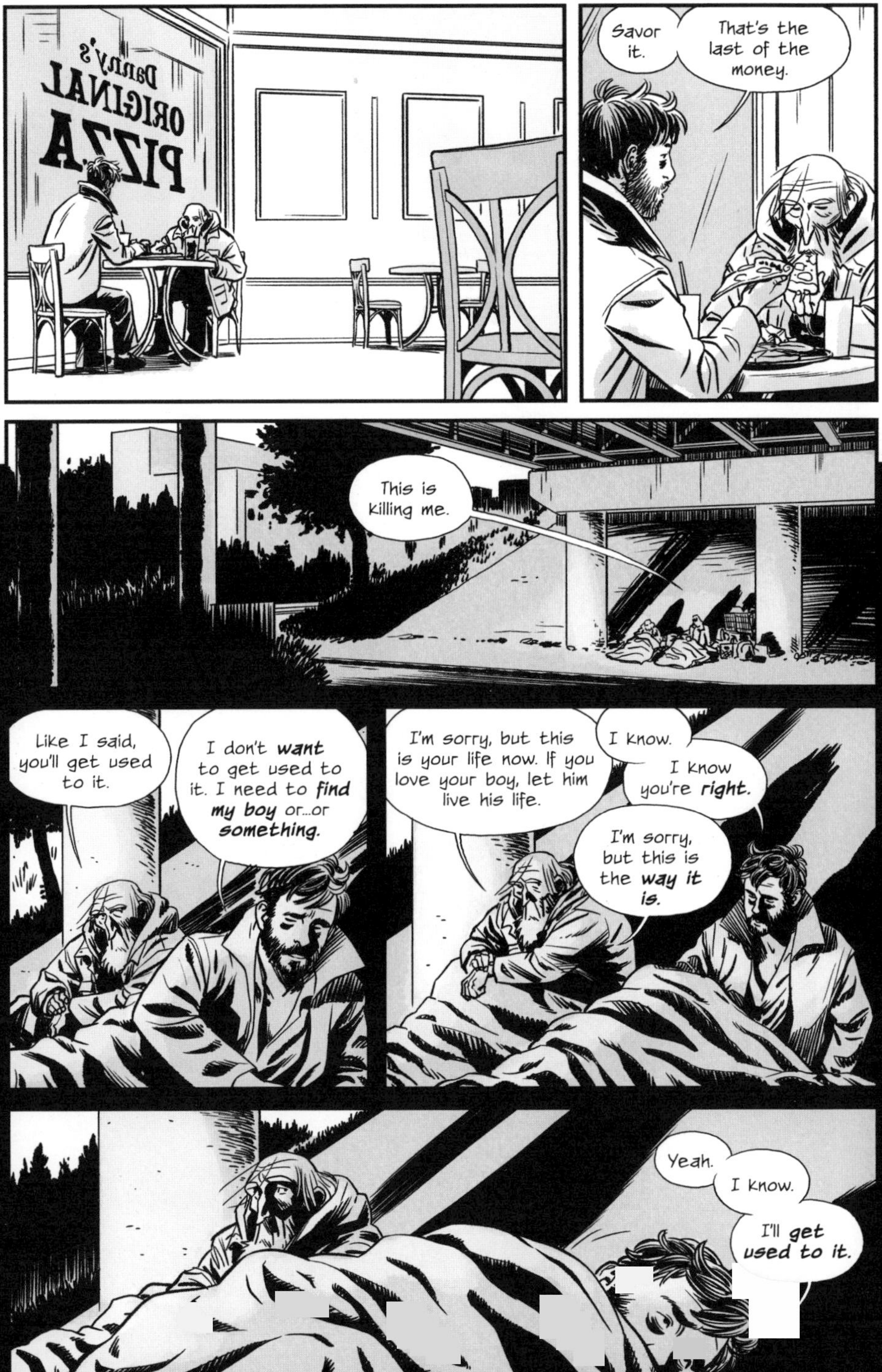
Danny's ORIGINAL PIZZA
Savor it.
That's the last of the money.
This is killing me.
Like I said, you'll get used to it.
I don't **want** to get used to it. I need to **find my boy** or...or **something**.
I'm sorry, but this is your life now. If you love your boy, let him live his life.
I know.
I know you're **right**.
I'm sorry, but this is the **way it is**.
Yeah.
I know.
I'll **get used to it**.

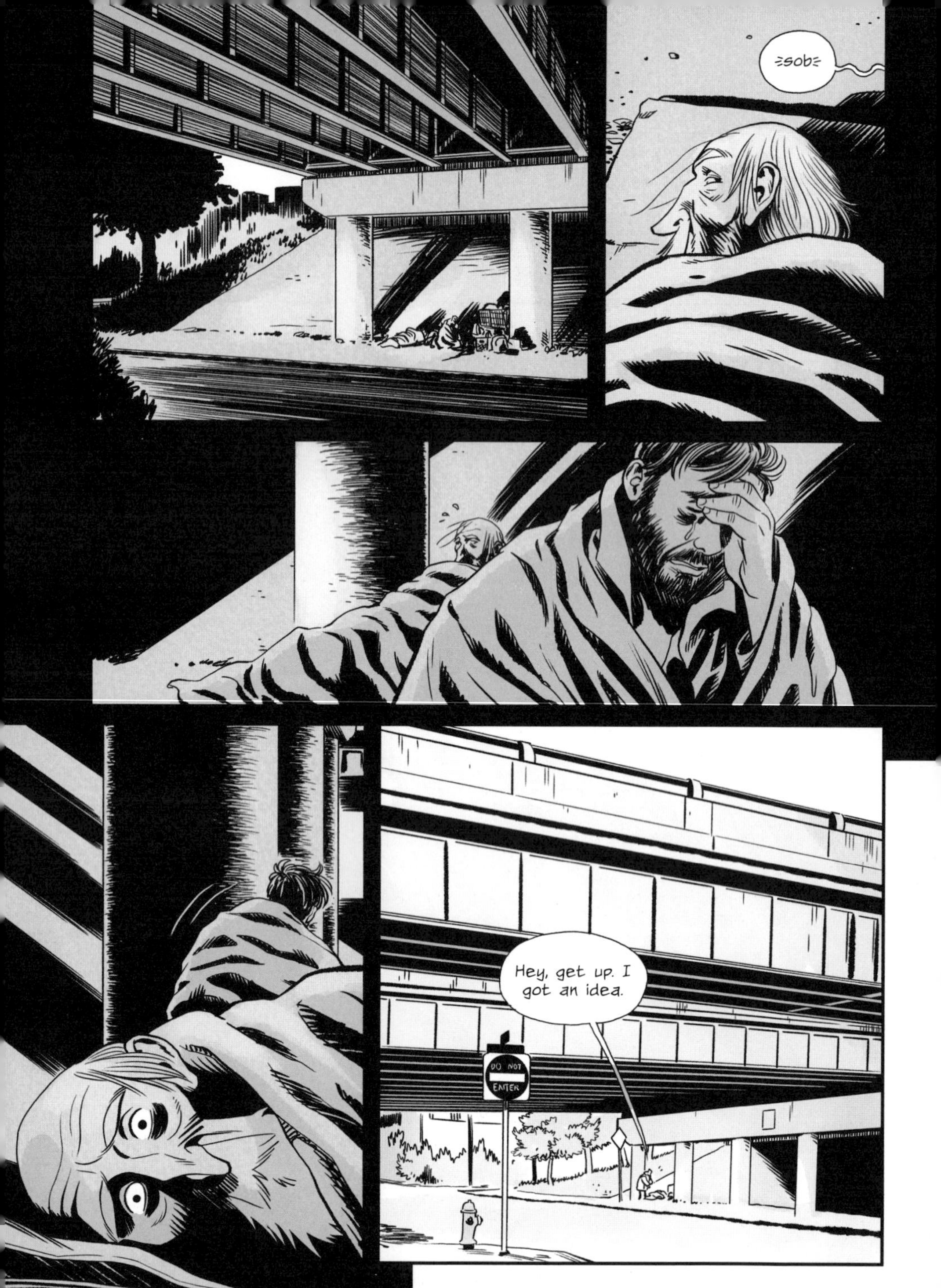
=sob=
DO NOT ENTER
Hey, get up. I got an idea.

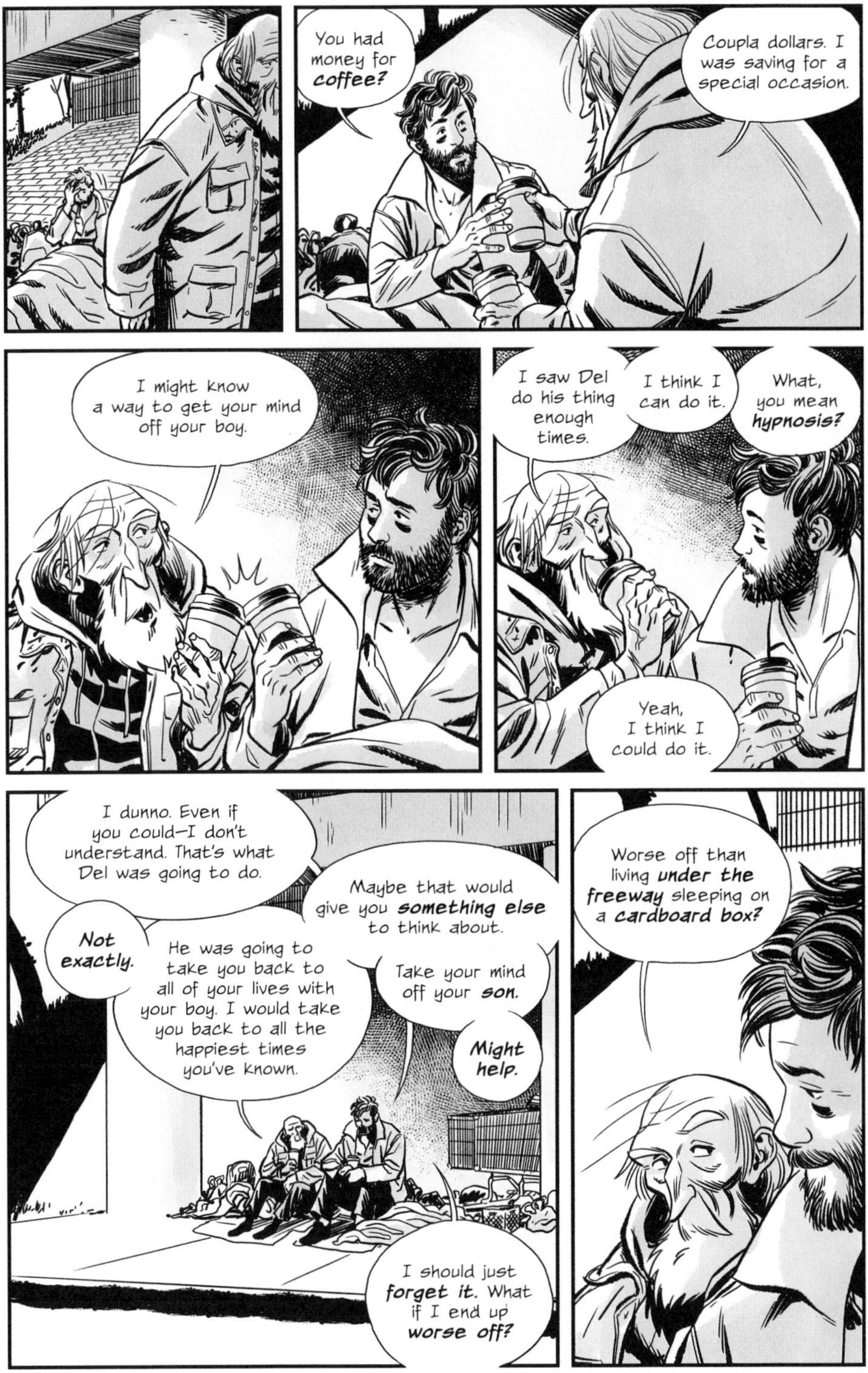
You had money for coffee?
Coupla dollars. I was saving for a special occasion.
I might know a way to get your mind off your boy.
I saw Del do his thing enough times.
I think I can do it.
What, you mean hypnosis?
Yeah, I think I could do it.
I dunno. Even if you could—I don't understand. That's what Del was going to do.
Not exactly.
He was going to take you back to all of your lives with your boy. I would take you back to all the happiest times you've known.
Maybe that would give you something else to think about.
Take your mind off your son.
Might help.
I should just forget it. What if I end up worse off?
Worse off than living under the freeway sleeping on a cardboard box?

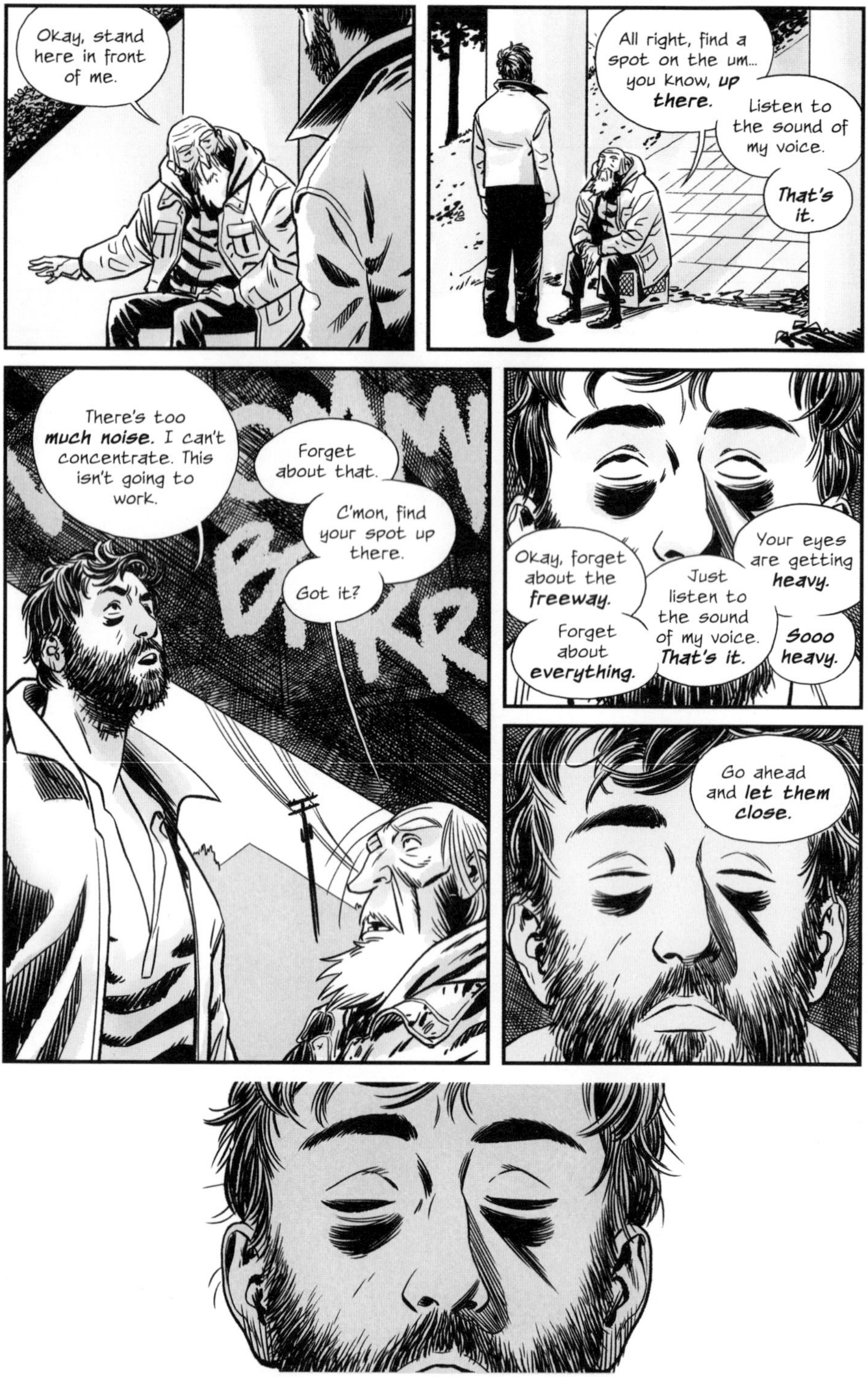
Okay, stand here in front of me.
All right, find a spot on the um... you know, up there.
Listen to the sound of my voice.
That's it.
There's too much noise. I can't concentrate. This isn't going to work.
Forget about that.
C'mon, find your spot up there.
Got it?
Okay, forget about the freeway.
Forget about everything.
Just listen to the sound of my voice. That's it.
Your eyes are getting heavy.
Sooo heavy.
Go ahead and let them close.

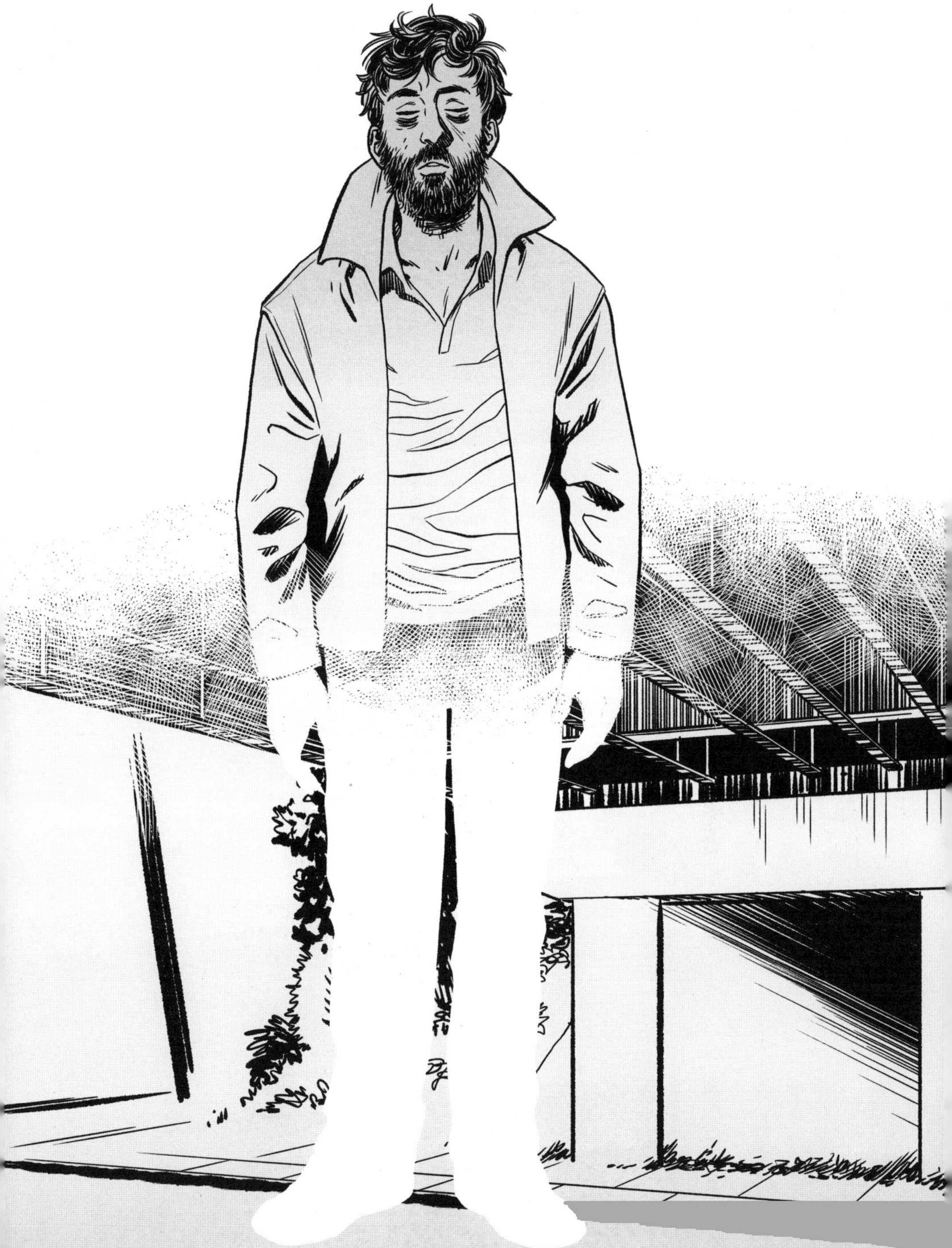

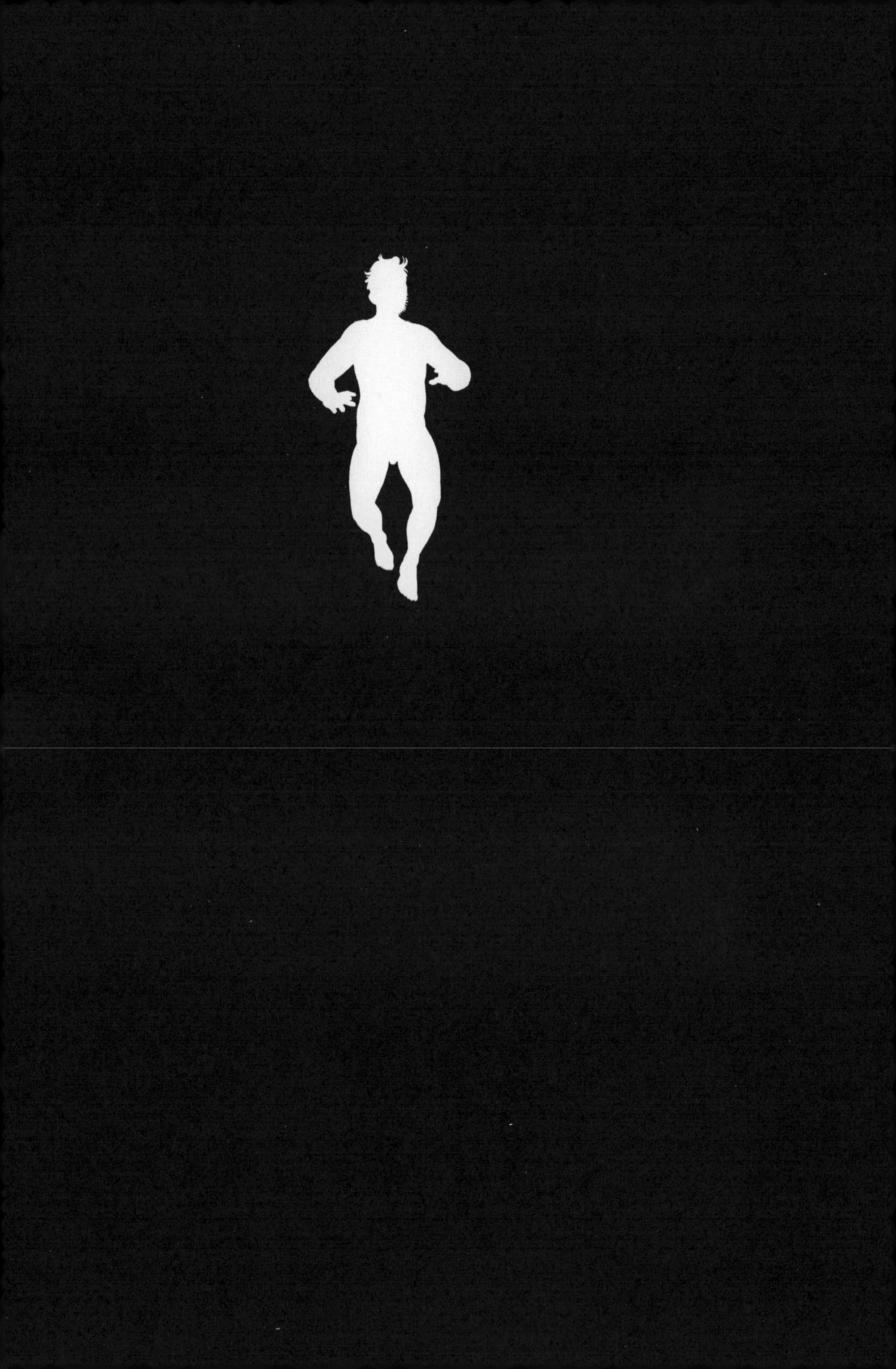

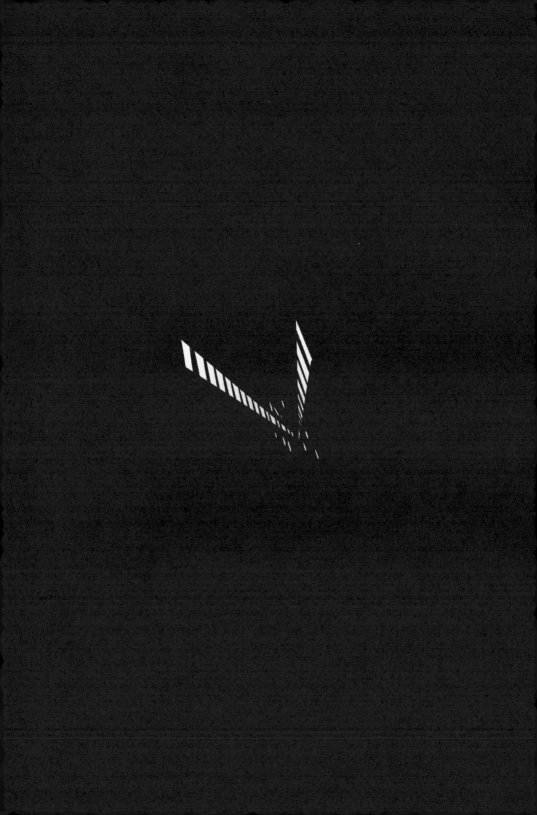

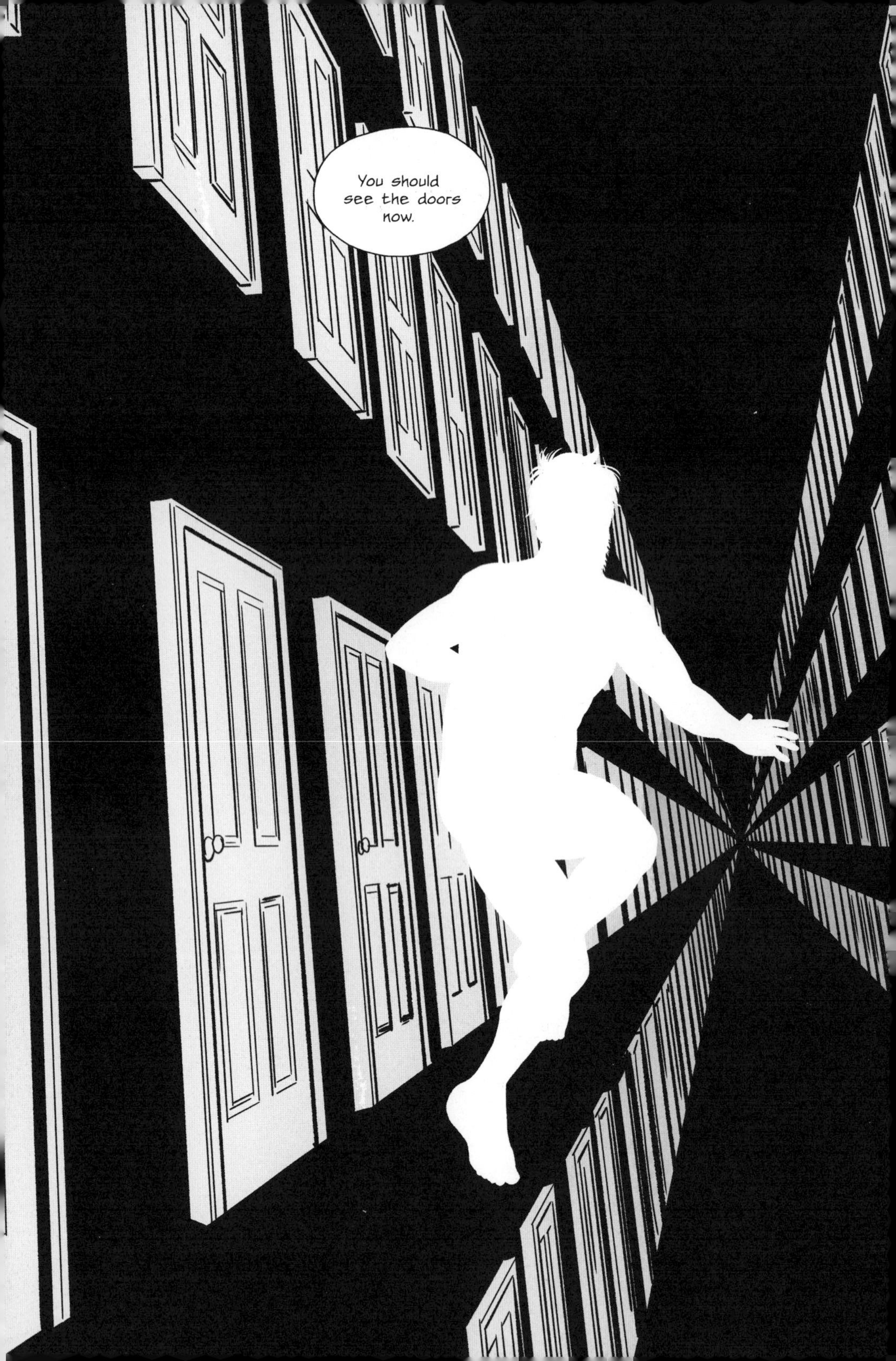
You should see the doors now.

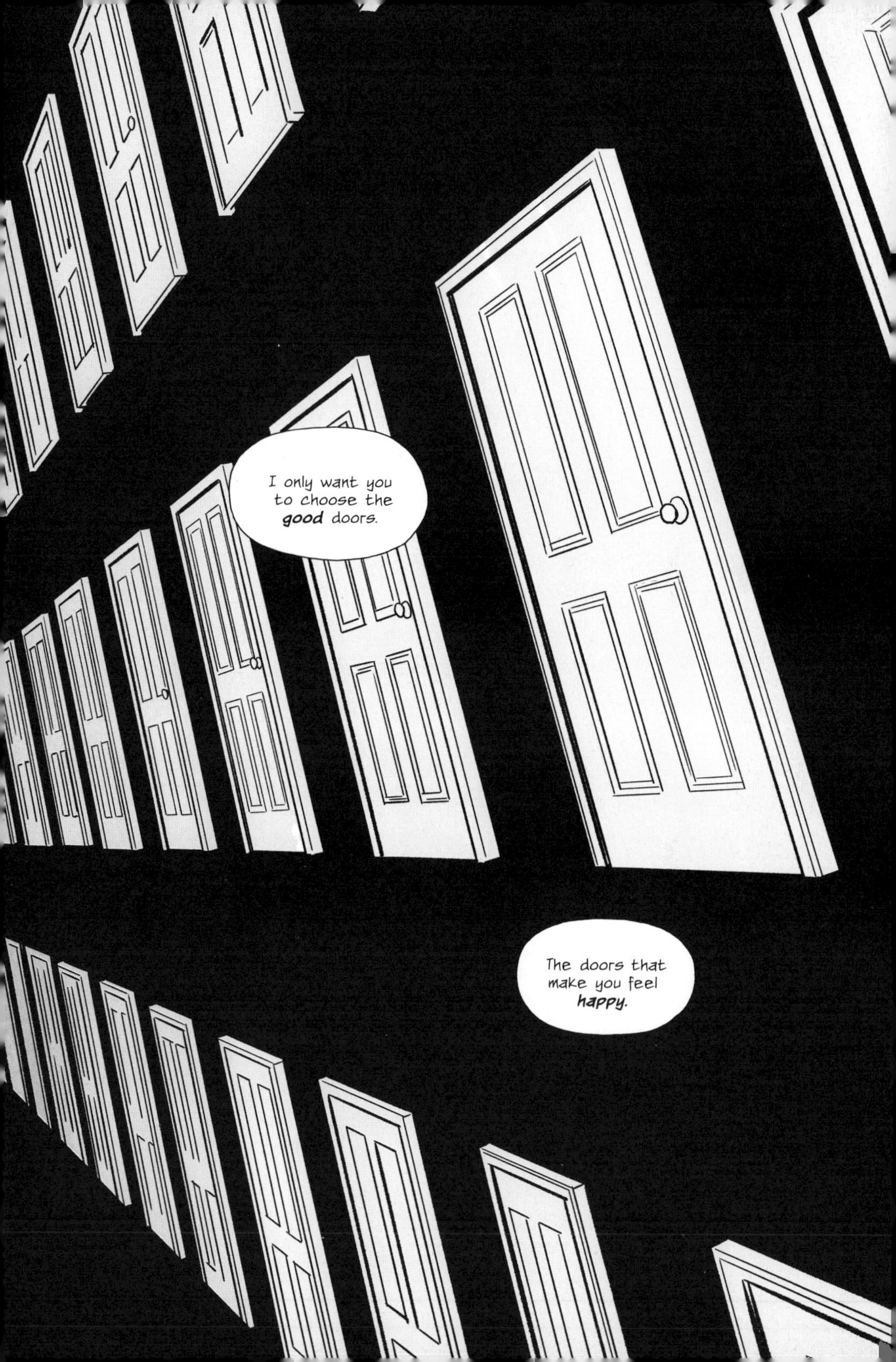
I only want you to choose the **good** doors.
The doors that make you feel **happy.**

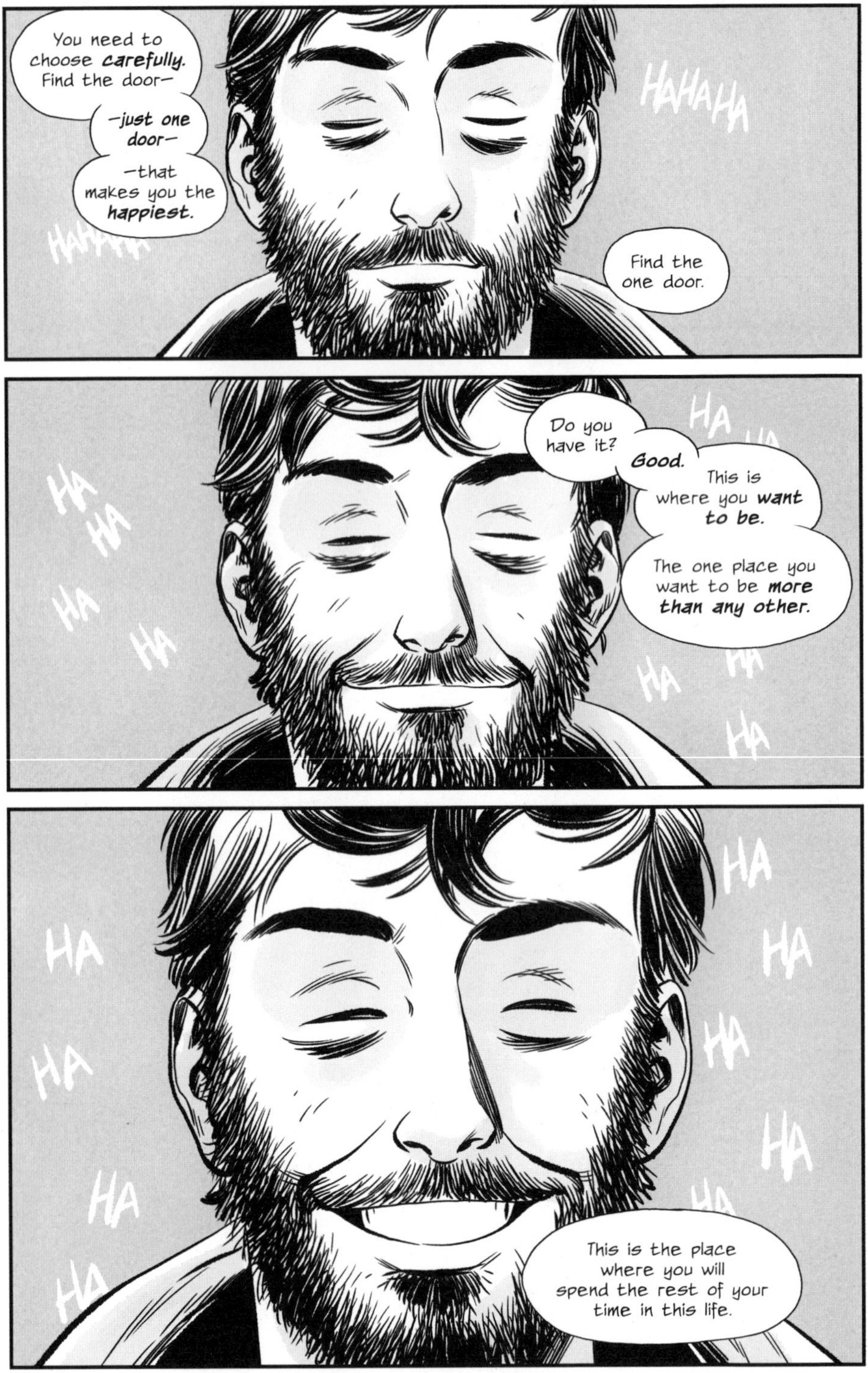
You need to choose **carefully.** Find the door—
—**just one door**—
—that makes you the **happiest.**
HAHAHA
HAHAHA
Find the one door.
HA
HA
HA
HA
Do you have it?
Good.
This is where you **want to be.**
The one place you want to be **more than any other.**
HA
HA
HA
HA
HA
HA
HA
HA
HA
HA
This is the place where you will spend the rest of your time in this life.

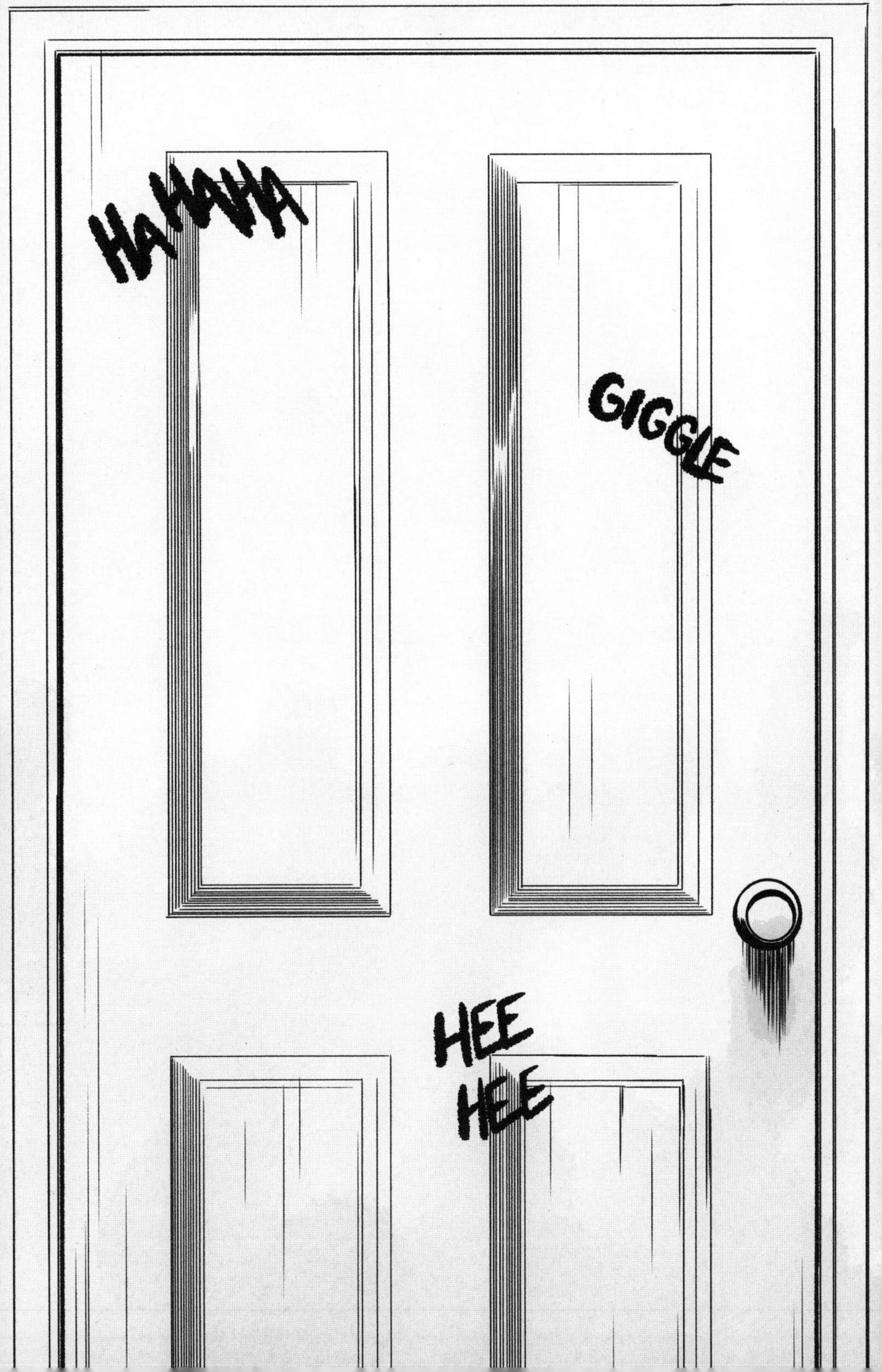
HAHAHA
GIGGLE
HEE HEE

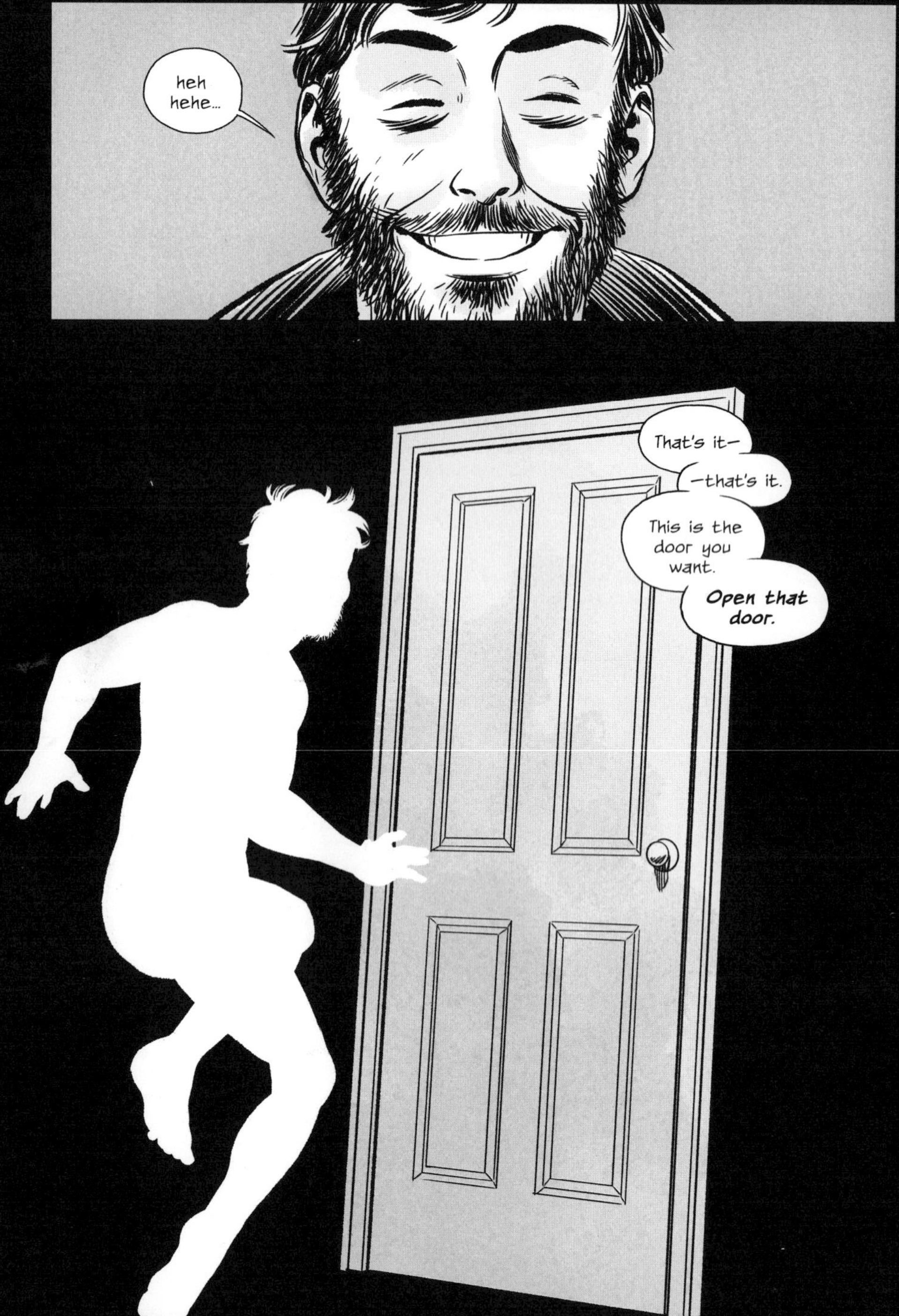
heh hehe...
That's it—
—that's it.
This is the door you want.
Open that door.

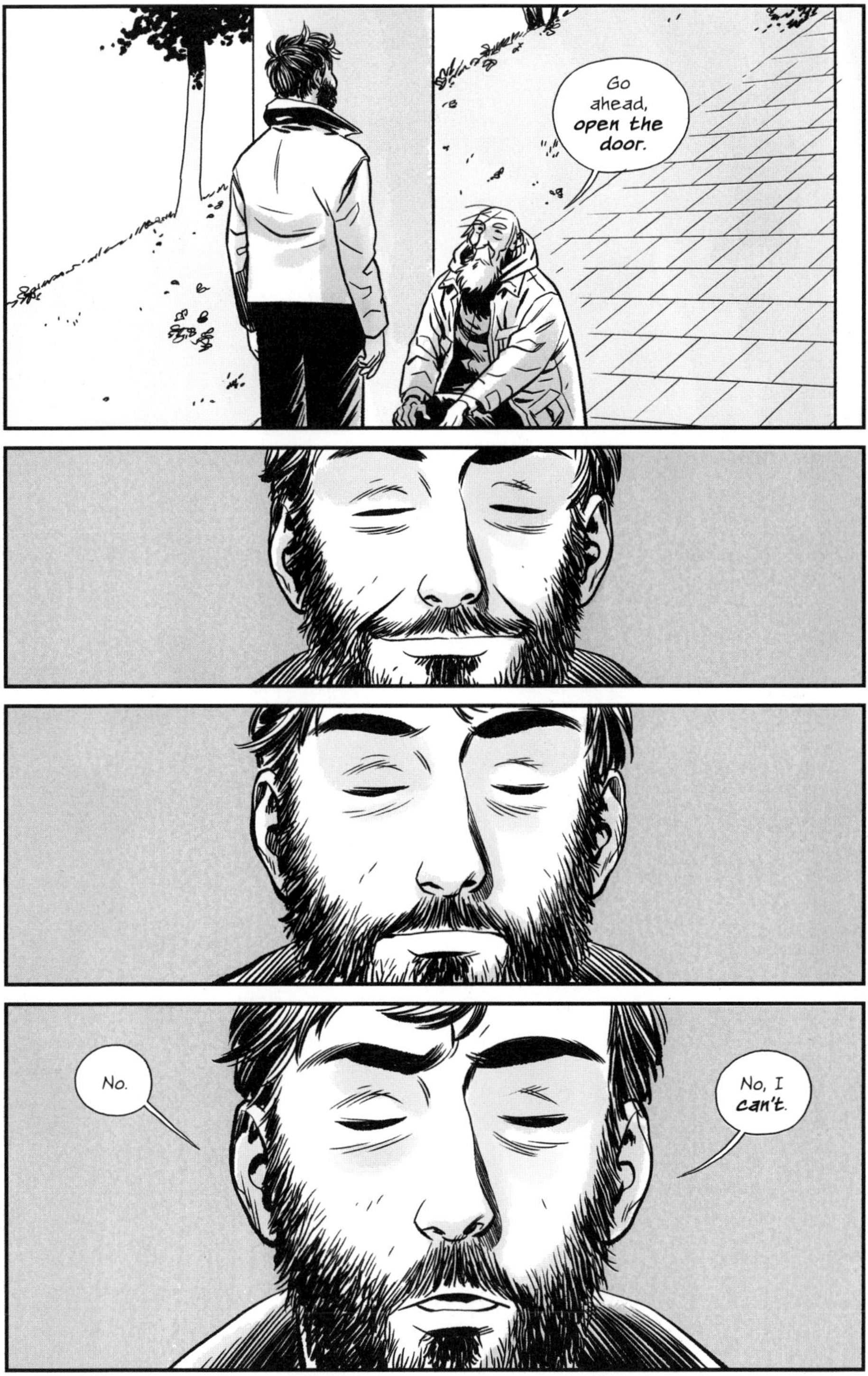
Go ahead, **open the door.**
No.
No, I **can't**.

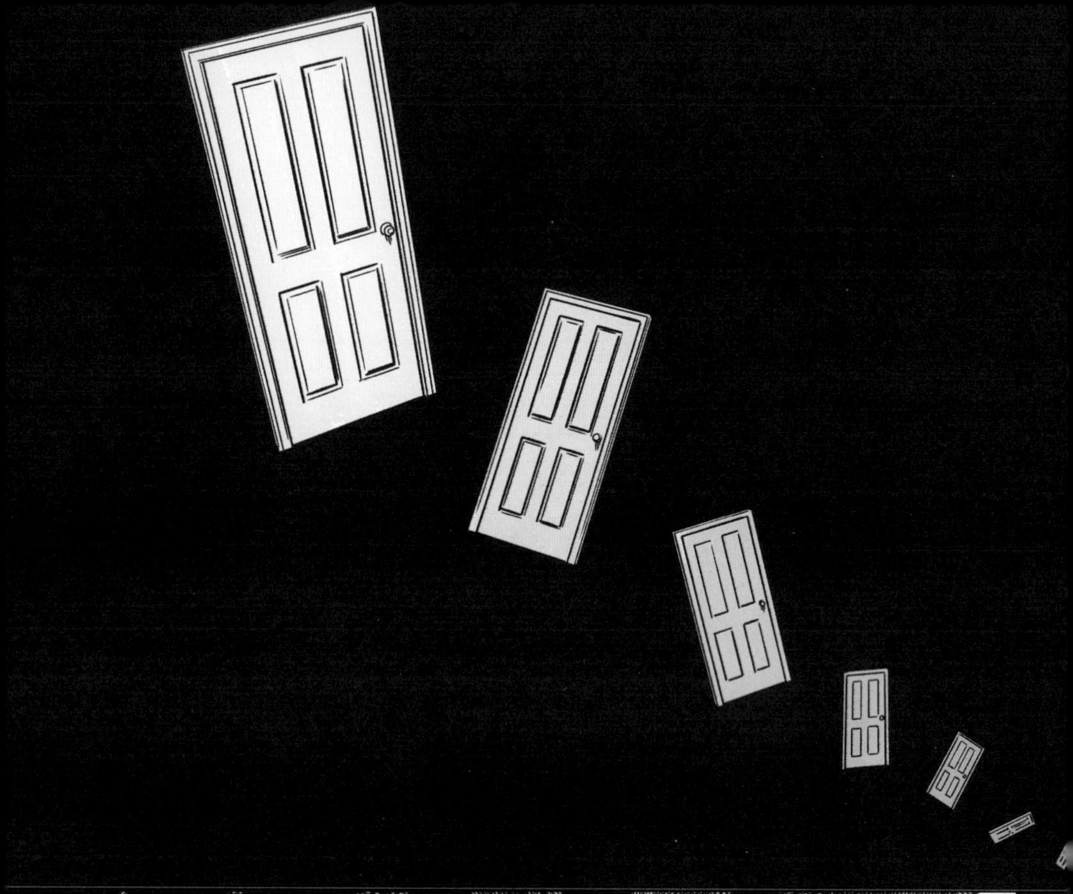

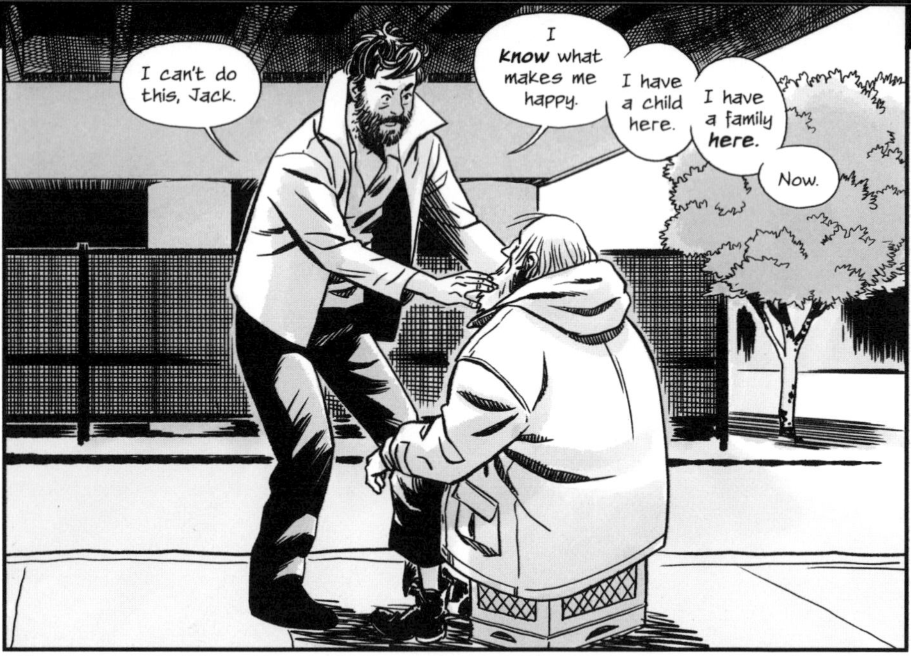

I can't do this, Jack.
I **know** what makes me happy.
I have a child here.
I have a family **here.**
Now.

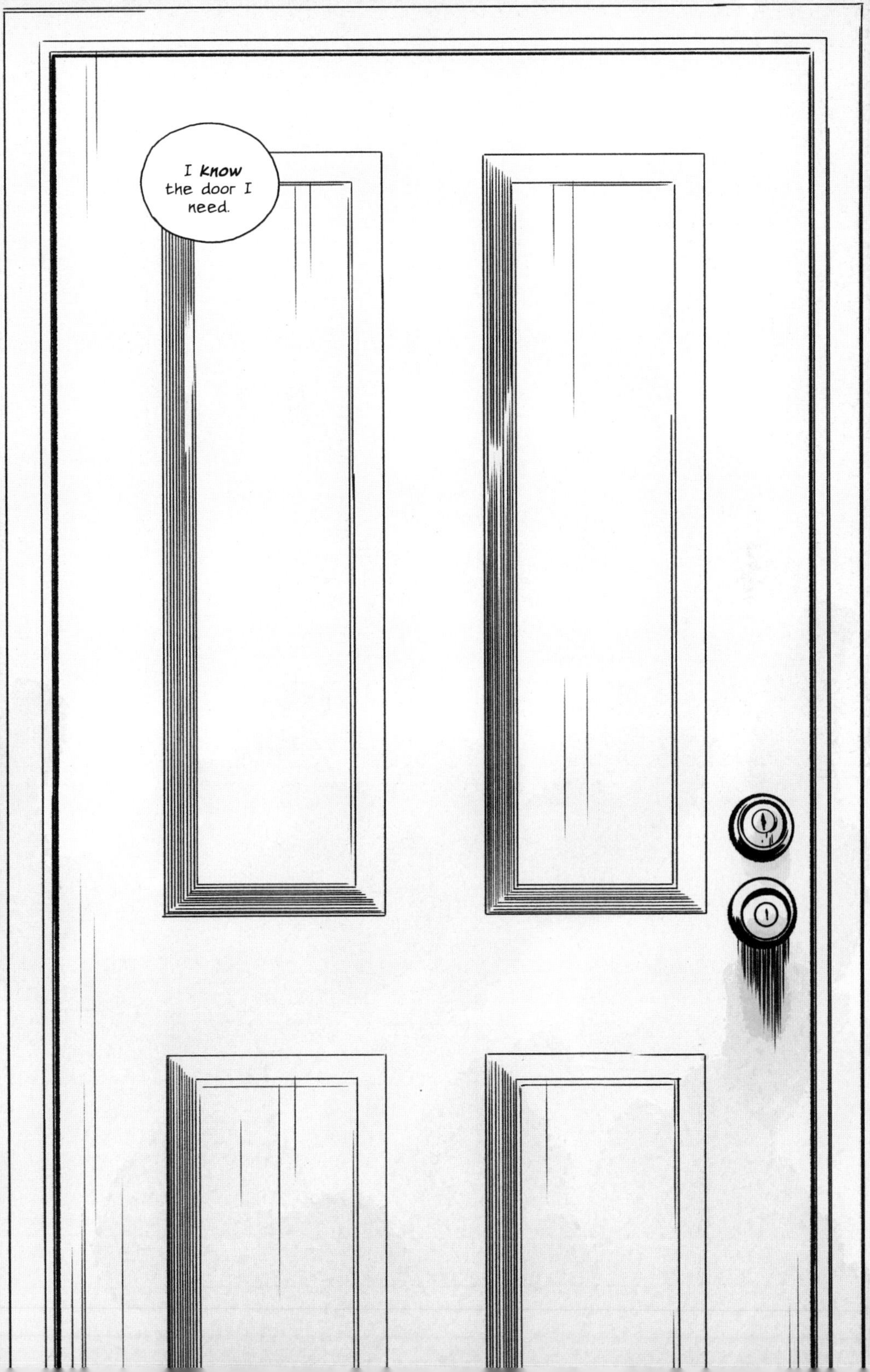
I **know** the door I need.

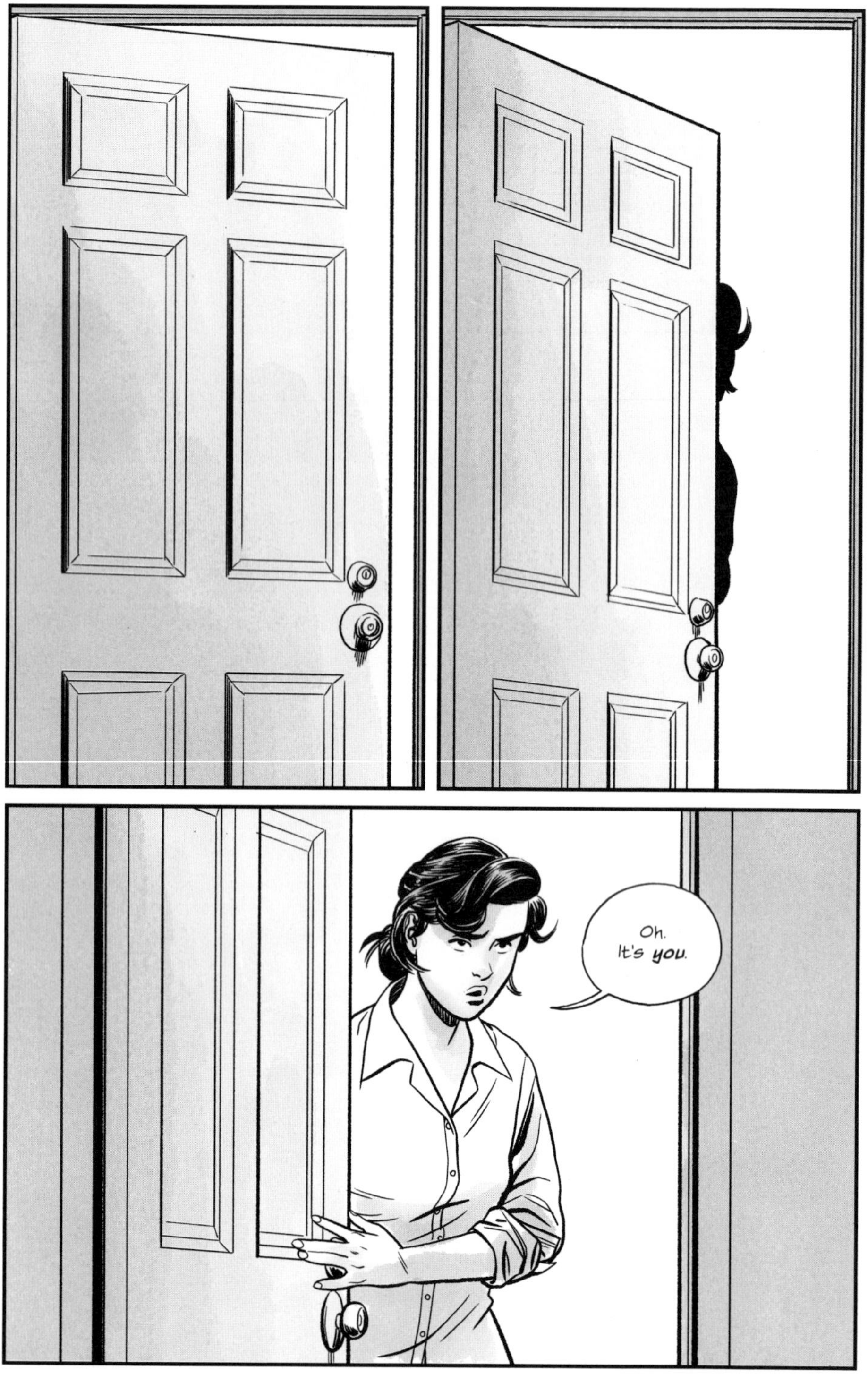
Oh.
It's **you**.

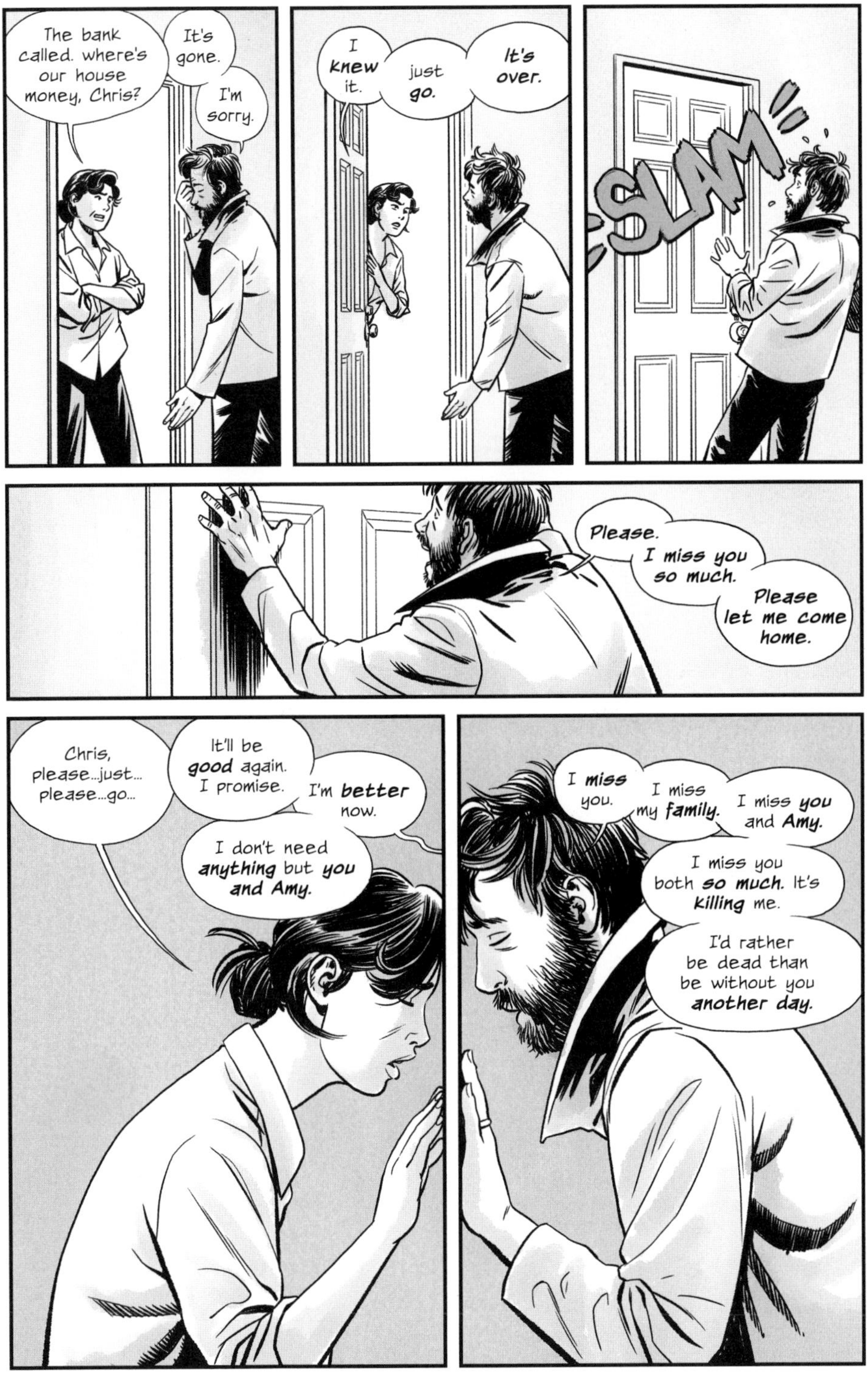
The bank called. where's our house money, Chris?
It's gone.
I'm sorry.
I knew it.
just go.
It's over.
SLAM
Please.
I miss you so much.
Please let me come home.
Chris, please...just... please...go...
It'll be good again. I promise.
I'm better now.
I don't need anything but you and Amy.
I miss you.
I miss my family.
I miss you and Amy.
I miss you both so much. It's killing me.
I'd rather be dead than be without you another day.

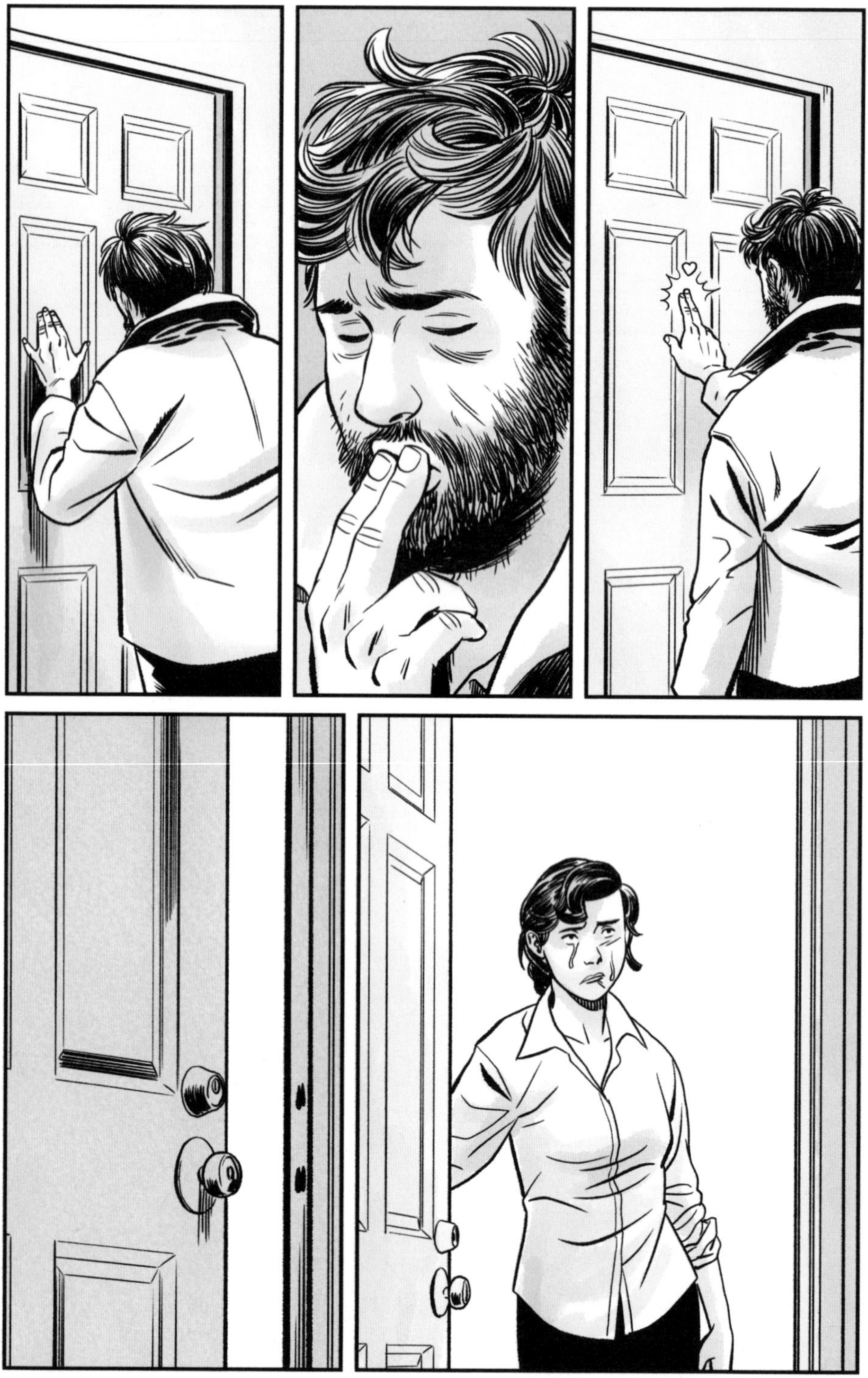

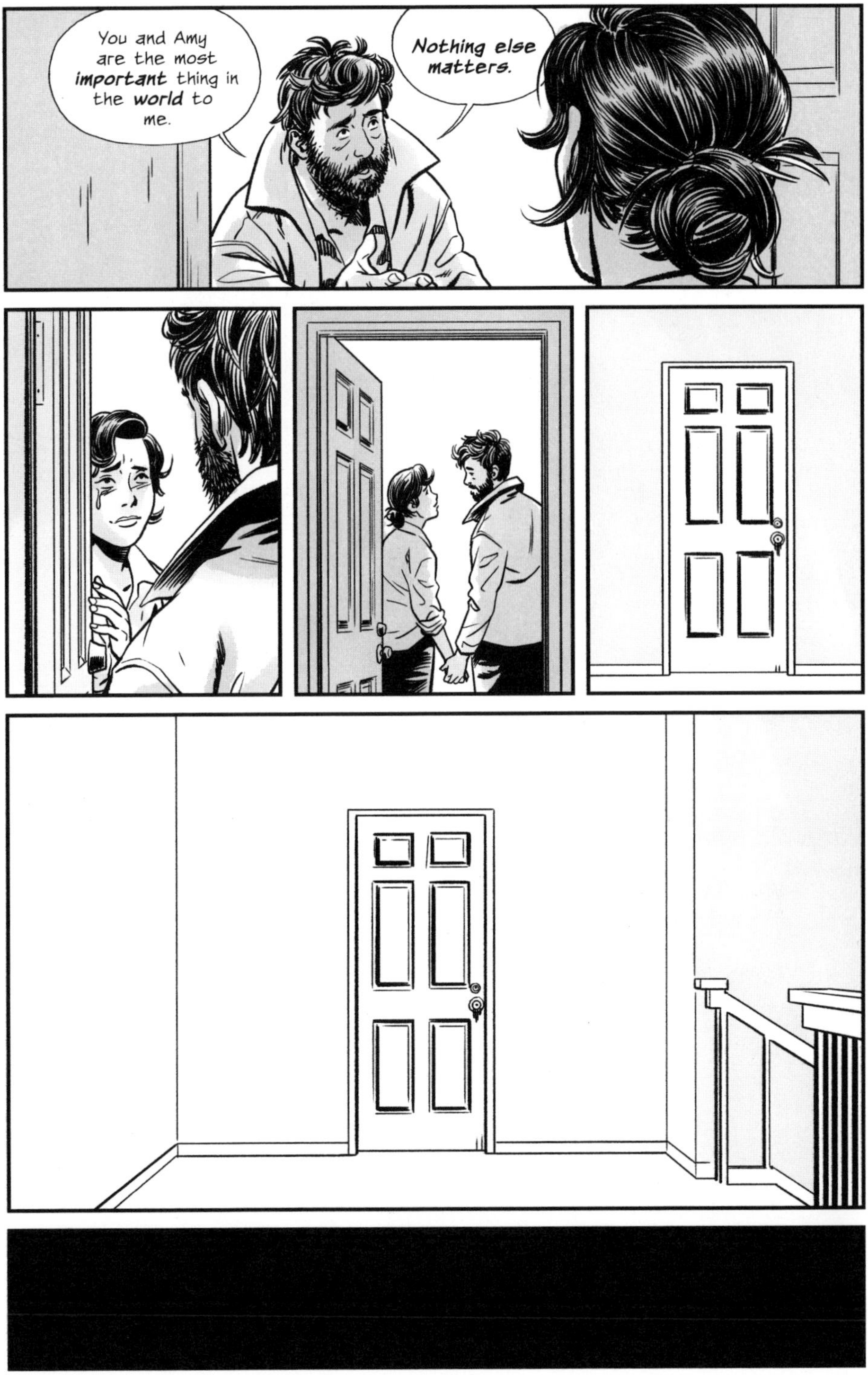
You and Amy are the most important thing in the world to me.
Nothing else matters.

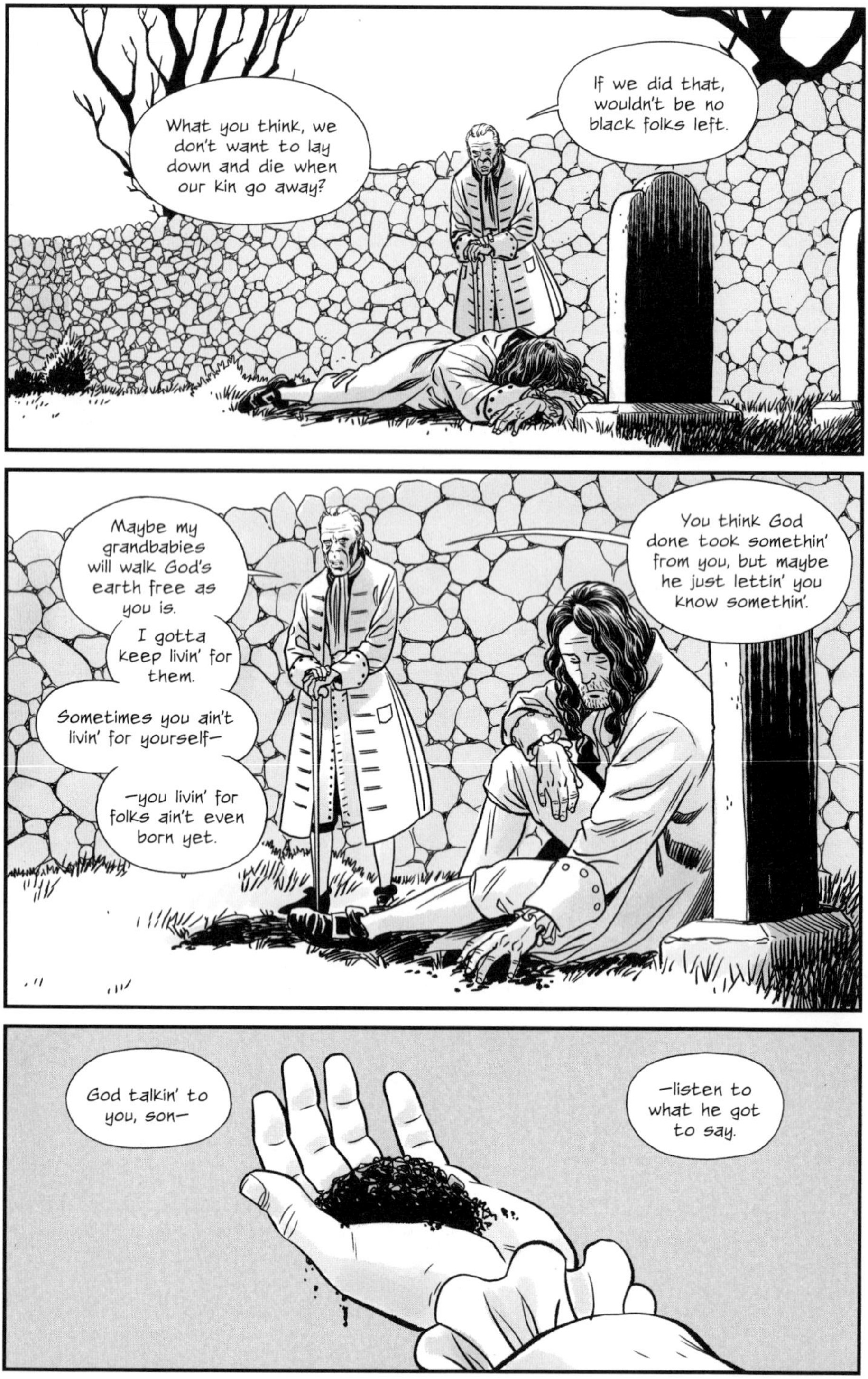
What you think, we don't want to lay down and die when our kin go away?
If we did that, wouldn't be no black folks left.
Maybe my grandbabies will walk God's earth free as you is.
I gotta keep livin' for them.
Sometimes you ain't livin' for yourself—
—you livin' for folks ain't even born yet.
You think God done took somethin' from you, but maybe he just lettin' you know somethin'.
God talkin' to you, son—
—listen to what he got to say.

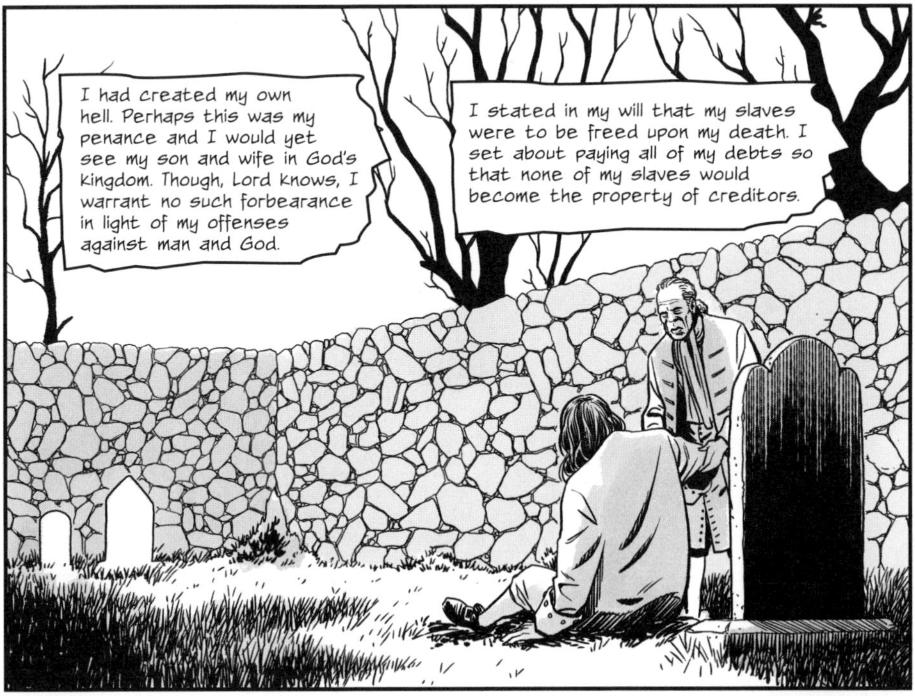
I had created my own hell. Perhaps this was my penance and I would yet see my son and wife in God's kingdom. Though, Lord knows, I warrant no such forbearance in light of my offenses against man and God.
I stated in my will that my slaves were to be freed upon my death. I set about paying all of my debts so that none of my slaves would become the property of creditors.

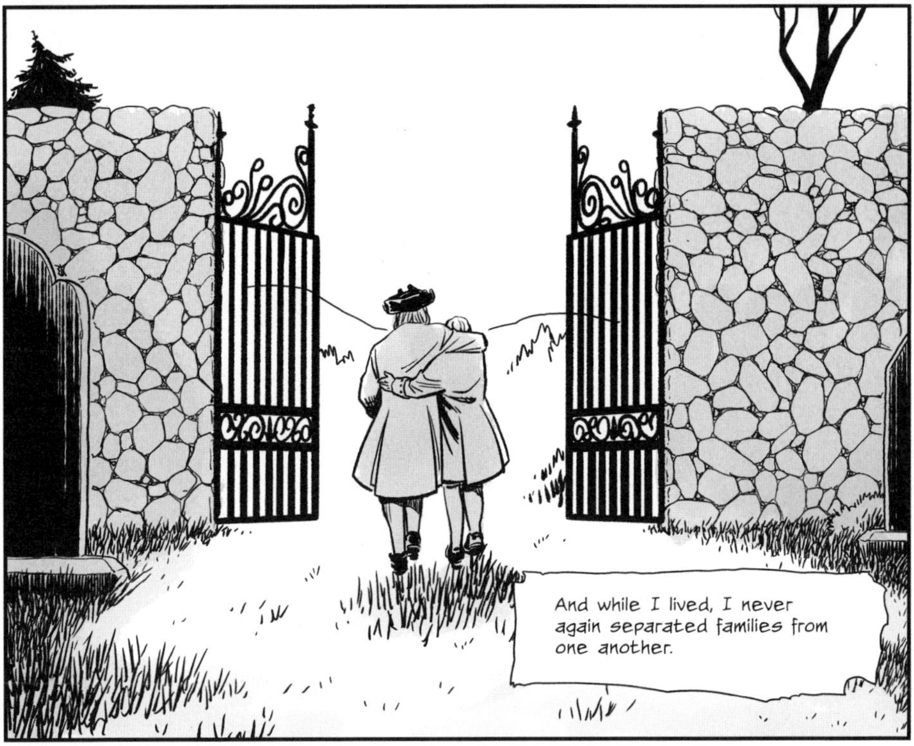
And while I lived, I never again separated families from one another.

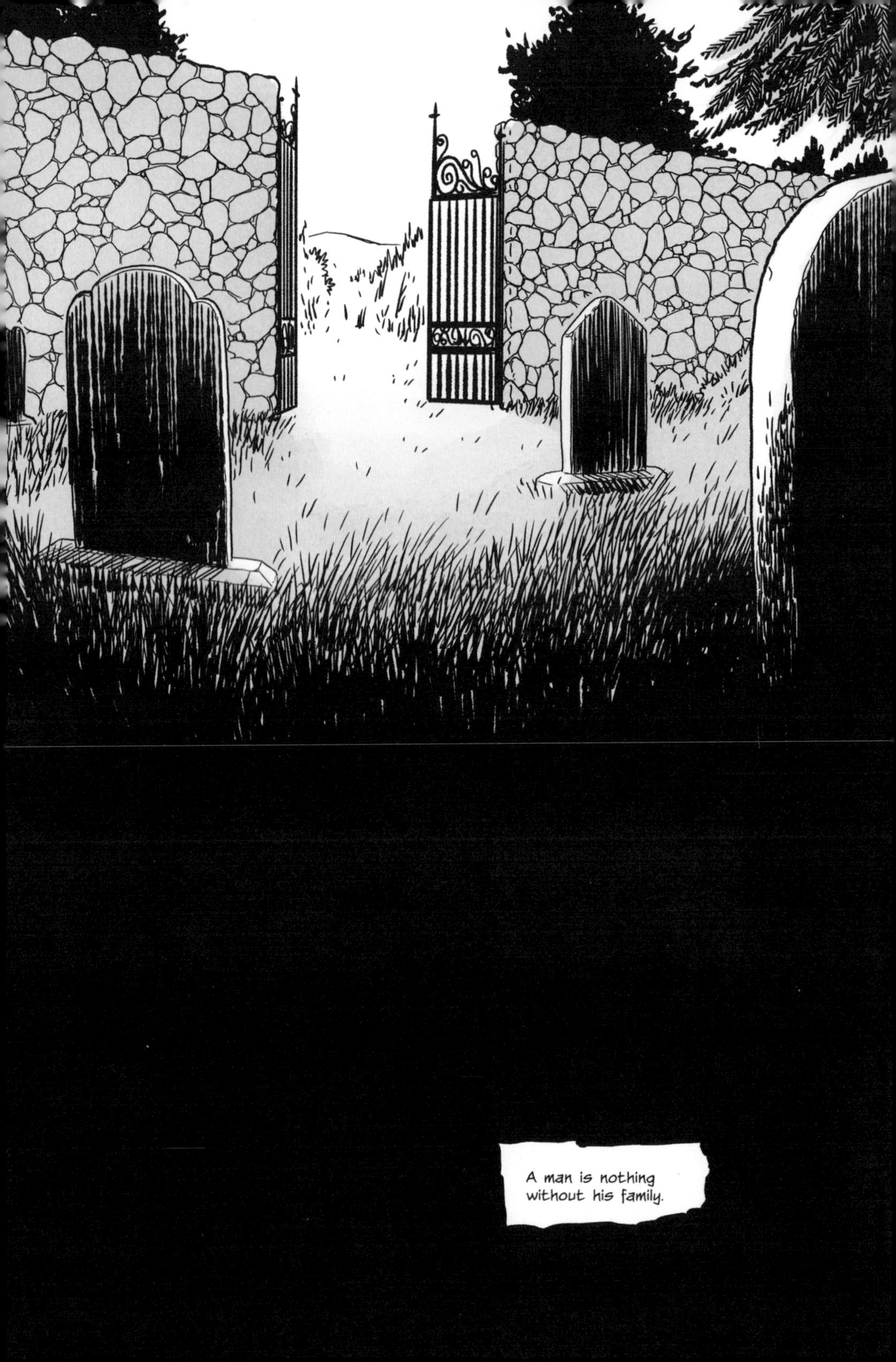
A man is nothing without his family.

Without Gene Luen Yang, this book wouldn't have seen the light of day.
Who knew that a chance meeting at a comic book convention so many years ago
would lead to this? I was impressed with him then, a young kid with a Xeroxed,
homemade comic, and I am impressed with him now.
He's a good dude.

I am grateful to Mark Siegel for his kindness and support. I have
seldom felt so respected and trusted while doing this kind of work.
He allowed me to be myself and tell the story I wanted to tell
the way I wanted to tell it. What a gift.

And I would very much like to thank Pat Hazell for his tireless friendship,
guidance, and support. I am lucky to know him.

—Brian

Brian McDonald, who works for Belief Agency as chief storyteller, has worked in film, television, and comic books for more than thirty years. He is the writer and director of the award-winning short film *White Face*, which aired on HBO. A sought-after lecturer and teacher, McDonald has worked as a speaker and story consultant for clients such as Disney and Cirque du Soleil. His book *Invisible Ink: A Practical Guide to Building Stories That Resonate* is required reading at Pixar Animation Studios, as well as several film studies programs. McDonald teaches for the Film School Seattle and the Red Badge Project, which teaches veterans suffering from PTSD how to tell their stories.

Les McClaine has been drawing comics for more than thirty years and doing it professionally for a little more than half that time. He has worked as a paperboy, a librarian, a record store clerk, and a Santa wrangler. He lives in a little yellow house with his wife and cat and works in a studio at the top of a big building in Portland, Oregon.

GRAPHIC FICTION
AT ITS FINEST

The Sculptor
by Scott McCloud

Demon
by Jason Shiga

PTSD
by Guillaume Singelin

Spill Zone
by Scott Westerfeld
& Alex Puvilland

Idle Days
by Thomas Desaulniers-Brousseau
& Simon Leclerc

Shattered Warrior
by Sharon Shinn
& Molly Knox Ostertag

The Divine
by Boaz Lavie,
Asaf Hanuka & Tomer Hanuka

:01
First Second

TOR

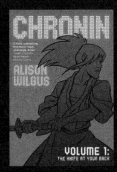

Chronin
by Alison Wilgus

The Furnace
by Prentis Rollins